THE BOOK OF THE KINDRED SAYINGS

(SAṂYUTTA-NIKĀYA)

OR GROUPED SUTTAS

PART V

Pali Text Society
TRANSLATION SERIES, NO. 16

THE BOOK OF THE KINDRED SAYINGS

(SAṂYUTTA-NIKĀYA)

PART II

The Nidāna Book (Nidāna-vagga)

Translated by
C.A.F Rhys Davids, M.A.

Assisted by
F.L. Woodward, M.A.

Published by
The Pali Text Society
Bristol
2015

This reprint was made possible in part by a generous donation to the Pali Text Society from W.Y. Yau and Y.F. Yeong in memory of Mdm. Kui Moy Choong.

First published	1922
Reprinted	1930
Reprinted	1956
Reprinted	1965
Reprinted	1979
Reprinted	1994
Reprinted	2005
Reprinted	2015

ISBN-10 0-86013-012-6

ISBN-13 9780-86013-012-3

Published by the Pali Text Society
c/o CPI Antony Rowe – Melksham
Unit 4 Pegasus Way
Bowerhill Industrial Estate
Melksham, Wilts
SN12 6TR, U.K

www.palitext.com

Printed and bound by CPI Group (UK) Ltd, Croydon, CR0 4YY

INTRODUCTION

HERE we have the last lap of our labours in the translation of the Third Nikāya or Collection of the Sutta Piṭaka, and I with many others heartily congratulate my able colleague, the translator of the major portion,[1] on its completion. The total work has taken intervals of fourteen years, and we (as *aniccā* and, as such, no less *bhavantā* and *bhāventā*) have come to learn much over it, and elsewise, that we had not learnt before. Translation and forewords should testify to this. Woe unto us if they do not! Mr. Woodward is good enough to wish me, as before, to write something of inaugural comment. And I take the opportunity of inviting the reader straightaway to see what an interesting sidelight on the much-buried story of Buddhist evolution he can get from the *series* (apart from the contents) of subjects, according to which, in this volume, the Suttas are grouped.

The main divisions in the whole Nikāya are Five Vaggas. This word, like so many in Pali, is a blend (or a breaking down into one) of two opposed Sanskrit words: it may, as from *varga*, refer to massed contents, or it may, as from *vyagra*, refer to division from other contents. The fifth and last Vagga, filling this volume, of grouped or 'kindred' Sayings, is known, presumably from its bulk, as the Great Vagga.

In this Vagga the first seven subjects are as doctrines very venerable, very important. Together they form a list which *in time* came to be known as the 37 Bodhipakkhiyā Dhammā: the things or states belonging to Enlightenment or Wisdom. I believe that, in the Piṭakas themselves, they occur very rarely *as so-called*, are never numbered as 37, and never refer to the 37 as a whole, but only to this or that section of them,[2]

[1] Vols. III, IV, V.

[2] *Vibhanga*, 249; *cf.* my Preface, *ibid.* xiv-xvi.

or to practices not included in them.[1] Even here it is only the states under 'Books' II and IV which are so called. There is a quasi-historical reference to the 37, which gives some ground for believing that some such sets or categories were compiled during the lifetime of the Founder. In the Book of the Great Decease, before he finally bade farewell to Vesālī, Gotama is said to have charged his church there to practise and teach such a list.[2] It is not called Bodhipakkhiya, and the word Dhammā is freely translated as 'truths.'[3]

The contents of that list are the same as in our 'Books' I-VII, but the *order is very different*. I give both versions:

Dīgha, II, Suttanta XVI.	Saŋyutta, V, Mahā-vagga.
(4) stations of mindfulness.	(8) the Way.
(4) right efforts.	(7) limbs of wisdom.
(4) stages to psychic power.	(4) stations of mindfulness.
(5) powers.	(5) faculties.
(5) faculties.	(4) best efforts.
(7) kinds of wisdom.	(5) powers.
(8) eightfold way.	(4) bases of psychic power.

Can we from this interesting derangement form any worthy hypotheses as to evolution in values which had been going on in the Sangha, not so much between the lifetime of the founders of the Sakya movement and the completion of the Piṭakas:—we are not, alas! justified in going back so far—but between the compilation and authoritative sanction of a certain book in the middle of the First Nikāya (Dīgha) and the compilation and authoritative sanction of a book at the end of the Third Nikāya (Saŋyutta)?

Could we assume that the Four Nikāyas had been compiled in consecutive order, the difference in order would be more markedly significant. It is surmised—we can scarcely do more—that in the 'Long' and the 'Middling' Collections we have records which were at least begun, as records in fixed oral form, before any others.[4] Especially in the Dīgha

[1] *Anguttara*, iii, 70. [2] *Dīgha*, ii, 120. [3] *Dialogues*, ii, 128.

[4] I do not doubt there was a Rājagaha Congress, but I do not believe we must accept the Culla-vagga details as accurate.

Nikāya do we find, as Franke insisted,[1] a plan that amounts to the setting forth of a definite gospel—so to speak—or systematized religious teaching. In the third and fourth Nikāyas we do seem to come up against a number of sweepings-in of miscellaneous memorized Sayings, and a number of pickings-over of such Sayings respectively. Now the orthodox tradition according to the Dīgha Commentary is that, at the first Recital, such of the contents of each of *all four* of the Nikāyas as were then collected were handed over to the school (*nissitakā*) of the predeceased Sāriputta, and to three other Theras respectively, as the stock of sayings each was, not so much to complete (for Commentators, history *in the making* was non-existent), but to keep intact and alive, as brahmans did with their mantras. This tidy piety we must put on one side.

That each Nikāya did form the Smṛti, or formulated tradition of separate groups in the Order:—so much is incidentally and therefore more truthfully revealed by the frequent Commentarial allusions to Dīgha-repeaters, Majjhima- . . . Saŋyutta- and Anguttara-repeaters (*-bhāṇakā*). And for each of these groups the Smṛti in their own Nikāya will have been a teaching differing considerably in subject-matter, in wording, but chiefly in emphasis from those in which the other groups were proficient.

But the question of precedence in time is an obscure and probably a very untidy one. In this way: Whereas it is perhaps probable that the first two Nikāyas, especially the first, were, as definite finished compilations, *begun* before the latter two, both those and these bear fairly clearly marks of being works of accretion—*i. e.*, of having had sayings appended most likely at different dates. In this way there will have been much overlapping in their various stages of progress. Further into this I cannot here go.

But it needs not a great stretch of imagination to picture these accretions as having been largely carried out under the

---

[1] *Dīgha-Nikāya* (a partial translation), xiv: 'das Heilwegschema eines Tathāgata's.'

Pax Maurica of the third century B.C. Not only was travel safer, but the prestige of the Sangha was growing, while the felt need of a corresponding peace and unity in a Sangha much disorganized and demoralized was, if we may so far trust the Commentaries, being widely felt. Revision and standardization may well have been in the air.

The accretions were to a large extent (1) either new materials, or the different versions of already incorporated materials, garnered in by messengers to or from this or that *vihāra* or *āvāsa* in North India; (2) they were also central rewordings and further systematizing of doctrinal matter. Instances of the latter (2) we may see in the last two Suttantas of the Dīgha. Instances of the former (1) we may, I think, find in the present volume. Thus we get here supplementary variants of the sort of parables used in the Anamatagga of Volume II, as well as of the 'Gangā-repetitions'—and the reader can easily find others. In the book on 'Stream-winning' too, among variants of sayings in Volume II, we come upon possible genuine early memories persisting at Kapilavatthu of the Founder's kinsmen, such as Mahānāma, and others of Anāthapiṇḍika (also variants of Majjhima and Anguttara Sayings), and of the independent-minded thinker Kappina, once more pointed out by his brother aristocrat Gotama.[1] The Sayings too here are less concerned with a mysterious short-cut out of the way of life in 'nirvana,' and more with the practically important matter for the Many of the next step, the immediately hereafter, as I conceive the genuine teaching of the First Men to have been, namely, what guarantee had a man against calamity in the next life? The subject is in this part much formalized and edited by the monotonous reference to the later formula: Buddha, Dhamma, Sangha, etc. But the fact that this bunch is not included in the similar bunch in the second volume is for me no weak evidence that it was the result of this later harvest gathered in late in time, during or preceding the long work of revision alleged to have taken place in Asoka's reign. It was my husband who reminded

---

[1] *Cf.* Vol. II, p. 193 *f.*

us that in the Vinaya such garnerings were held as, at least at one time, so urgent that rules of residence were suspended to expedite them.[1]

I suggest that we do get some sort of clue to half tidy, half untidy procedure in the Nikāya compilations, if we bear the foregoing remarks in mind thus: a selection of chief doctrinal teaching-matter as the absolute beginning of fixed wordings in the first two Nikāyas. Next a beginning of a series of collections according to a certain subject, which would allow easily of later incorporating of items and again of new subjects: and finally, when the early limits had become more rigid and traditional, the appending of bunches either relating to subjects already treated of, or relating to subjects which changes of ideas had invested with new importance. A similar process of accretion is to be considered as going on in the first two Nikāyas. And with regard to the Fourth Nikāya, when we welcome Mr. Woodward's translation of that, it will then be time to concentrate on the growth we there find.

I have spoken of ideas as coming to be "invested with a new importance." The arrangement of topics in this volume affords a very suggestive instance of it. Few things in the growth of Sakya are so important. I refer to the strange emergence of a long Collection on the 'four truths' *at the very end of the work*, coupled with the fact of the equally long Collection on the 'Way' *at the beginning* of this, the Great Vagga. What does that mean? Of what is it the now mute indicator?

The inspired message of Gotama the Sakyan was given to men in the figure of the 'Way.' It was so given for reasons I have suggested elsewhere. And I would here thank Mr. Woodward's courtesy and appreciation in consenting to drop the almost classic term 'Path' and use 'Way.' First, Way is more literally correct, corresponding, in its first and second 'intentions,'[2] to 'magga.' Secondly, the way to the use of 'Way' by European readers is familiarized by an often

---

[1] *Buddhist India*, p. 112: *Vinaya*, i, *Mahāvagga*, iii, 5, 9.

[2] An event or phenomenon in space and time, and also a means.

similar noble use of the word in the Christian tradition. 'Path' has a byway sound. Gotama's words: *magga*, *paṭipadā*, refer to the going of each and every man when he has ceased to drift (*saŋsarati*). We who are concerned about the lost implications in this great figure have to salve it from much: from the contraction of it into an 'eightfold' course in ethics, from the much worse suggestion that it was originally only a reference to loose or strict monk-life, and lastly and chiefly from its deposition from the place of honour by Buddhists themselves. During Gotama's day, if only out of respect for him, it was the very central Sakyan gospel; long after his day the word still reverberated on as the chief idea. In Buddhaghosa's phrases it is still an impressive echo. And here we have it put *first*, and not last, in the Bodhipakkhiya series. The old tradition anyway was still going strong.

It is true that in the list, as given in the Book of the Decease, it is deposed and put at the very end, a distortion which persisted and became classical, as may be seen in the manual we have translated as *Compendium of Philosophy* (VII, 6). But this need not baffle us. It is but one more sign of the glaring evidences of editing which so mar the otherwise impressive passages of the Decease-Book of the Dīgha. When it is true to its great theme, it can be moving; when it wavers off into hotchpotch, it is exasperating. The work was probably finished very late, to puff the relic-cult that was springing up (we have seen that phenomenon in other creeds), as an integral part of the Buddha-cult. The book as a whole is a flagrant example of 'gloss.' And when a set sermon for the aged man of genius, tottering on a last tour, was put into his mouth, with no WAY in it at all, and a set list of things, so different from the few live words he said which have been left in, was also put into his mouth as a dying charge, the order in the list had at the time of editing become just a matter of arithmetical progression, as elsewhere: first the fours, then the fives, the sevenfold, the eightfold (*cf.* p. vi *supra*).

But what are we to think of the startling omission from that list, whatever be its order? I am not referring to the fourfold Brahmavihāra category. True, the omission of that is not without significance. But I judge, and have tried to show elsewhere, partly on evidence we get in this present volume (pp. 98 *ff.*), that the Brahmavihāra cult was a rival reformed teaching annexed by the Sakyan Founders.[1] Great play has been made with it since, as Buddhist teaching, in unconscious response to modern religious ideals, but for monastic Buddhism it never was central. No Collection was formed about it in this Nikāya, or elsewhere. It was not Nirvana-cultus. No, it is of course to the omission of the 'Four Truths' that I am referring.

Anyone who is conversant with the procedure in which this category, in scholastic Buddhism, is seen ousting the Way *as the centre* of the teaching, anyone who has noted the consigning the Way to the fourth and last place in them, anyone who knows how this monkish diagnosis of life as Ill, as only to be cured by the suppression of the will or desire, submerged in the 'dog-with-a-bad-name' of 'craving,' leaving no other spring from which betterment can come,—how this is still harped upon as the true centre of Buddhism, cannot but be amazed when he comes to find (when at last he studies the records!), that in the so-called final injunctions of the great Teacher the four truths are not mentioned at all.

There will certainly have been a cause for this silence. And I suggest the Great Vagga is dumbly trying to tell it. Thus: the Way, when the first seven "Books" were made, was still nominally central and chief. (In Indian, or at least in Buddhist method, what is chief comes first. I cannot recollect any instance of leading up to a last as climax.) By the time the Vagga was completed and being closed, the teaching of the Truths had come to loom very large, and either at or before the day of the Patna revisions, it was felt incumbent to remedy the omission by an inclusive treatment in the Nikāya where this might most conveniently be done. And so we find a great sweeping in of allusions to the truths from other records—*i.e.*, that at Koṭigāma from Dīgha and Vinaya—much application of sayings and similes applied differently elsewhere, and

[1] *J.R.A.S.*, 1927: 'The Co-Founders of Buddhism: a Sequel.'

chief of all the First Utterance itself,—the Way-word made into a Four-Truths word,—where I for one[1] see the editorial hand at work rewording and weighting the Founder's reference to life's sorrows into a rigid formula.

It may be said that this is scanty straw wherewith to make the bricks of history. But the alternative is either an acquiescence in historical ignorance, or an acquiescence in taking the Piṭakas at the Buddhists' estimate as history, or the wrong-headed view of a German Neobuddhist lately defunct that Buddhism has no history—a view which is only worth mentioning that it may be dropped as irrational. Ancient documents are not concerned to record developments in the making; they tell us mainly of what has become, of what is made. To a certain extent we can between the lines read the becoming. Very little has yet been attempted in this way of historical criticism; more may yet be done should this literature once more attract intellects now drawn away by the lure of the Further East. Sir Charles Eliot gave us an excellent start in much of his *Hinduism and Buddhism*, reminding us of the snowball gathering accretions as it is propelled. The figure is very apt, and is not left unapplied. But in my judgment, it might have been yet more applied, namely, to accretions which are credited as being original.

As briefly as possible I now touch on a few points also of historical interest. I see on p. 373 one of the references to the claim of Sakya to attain happiness by happiness (*sukhaŋ sukhena adhigantabbaŋ*), which was probably directed against the growing vogue, at its start, in *tapas* or asceticism. The Nigaṇṭhas or Jains were addicted to this, in the belief that by painful methods happiness could more quickly, more surely be won. Gotama went into all that when he left his home, coming to an opposite conclusion. The Saying here has probably suffered in its long transmission; nevertheless

[1] '. . . the form of the first sermon . . . betrays that the four truths have been unorganically appended to a possibly historical first part' (Deussen, *Geschichte der Philosophie*, ii, 156).

the conclusion: 'I would not deem the full comprehension of truth to be won with sorrow and woe but with joy and gladness,' is kindred to such Sayings as *sukhen' anvâgataŋ sukhaŋ*:

... happily
Has happiness been sought after and won,

of the Theragāthā (63 and 220), Anguttara, II, 3; Majjhima, I, 93, etc.

An interesting development of this original concern of the Founders as being more (as I think) with happiness than with multitudinous ill, and which is practically an anticipation of what we were lately calling Couéism, is in the Sutta called Dussīlya (p. 331). Sāriputta treats with efficacy the sick and depressed Anāthapiṇḍika by making him fix his thought not on ill, but on the right wayfaring towards the utterly Well and on his worthy efforts therein. From this to 'day by day in every way I become better and better' is a step more in form than in substance. It seems to me a real survival of the glad message of goodwill given by Gotama and his men, so much of which was submerged in the growing vogue of world-ill and the monastic fleeing from it.

It is again in the Suttas of what I have called the appended Collections (p. 320) that there comes another instance of the way of speaking of the 'man' which is neither good original Sakyan nor good later Buddhism. The man namely is spoken of as if he were just body and mind, as was the case in Volume III (p. 1 *f.*) in the Nakulapitar Saying. Gotama's day was not that of the completed Piṭakas, but 300 years earlier, when the brahman teaching of the man as ātman was paramount. He would have said: 'The body may sink away breaking up like the butterpot, but like the butter "You" will arise to the surface persisting.' This Sutta says 'the mind' will arise. The Buddhism of the Milinda and Buddhaghosa said: 'Neither just You nor just "the mind" will arise.' It is an interesting historical knot which here I pass by. But not before pointing out how we find Sāriputta using the simile (pp. 58, 59) which he is said to have used in the Gosinga Wood (*Majjhima*, i, 215) when commending the man 'who is master of his heart (or mind), not under its mastery.' It seems to me that no teacher, holding that 'the man' was *an-atta*, was not absolutely real, could *possibly* have used such language to his fellow-teachers.

I will not here repeat, lest I be too lengthy, what I have said elsewhere concerning *chanda* in the first of the four 'bases of psychic power,'[1] and concerning *chanda* in the description (p. 243 *f.*) ascribed to Ānanda of the object of the holy life as the putting away of *chanda*.[2] Ānanda was anything but an out-and-out recluse and probably never said anything of the sort, any more than Sāriputta will ever have said that Nirvana was the stopping of becoming (Vol. IV, p. vii, *n.* 2). But it is a frequent disutility in the career of a pioneer to have alien children imputed to him.

The appendix-book No. X, on attention to respiration, in the belief that more than a warding of bodily health could thereby be fostered, does not, I judge, belong to the original Sakya. It is also touched upon in the Dīgha and Majjhima, and must certainly have *come in* as a growing vogue. It does not occur with any mention of the word Yoga, let alone such late terms as Rāja- or Ashta-Yoga, nor is there any allusion to abnormal fakir practices. Nor is there any sign that it was to be cultivated on hygienic grounds. After all, the monk was in a bookless world and only the minority were teachers; he had to fill in his day somehow. The treatment is very mechanical and barren; we are left at the end no further.

I close in raising a point about the subject of Book III which is of etymological interest. The curious and tedious form of early introspection known as the Satipaṭṭhānas is treated with immense respect in the Piṭakas. It is quite possible that, when systematic introspection was in its cradle, when the Sānkhya leaven, slowly spreading, was accustoming the Indian mind to the new fascination of distinguishing between the very man (*ātman*, *puruṣa*) and his mind, the

---

[1] *Gotama the Man*, p. 221.

[2] 'Man as Willer,' *Bulletin Sch. Or. Studies*, iv, 1, 1926.

category appeared less naïf, and more worthy than it does today. The breaking down from the loftier Indian standpoint was going on, and the Sakyan monks were coming to seek to know the man only in body and mind, disregarding the Founder's advice and warning. I am, however, only pausing over it to call attention to the scholastic change in the definition of the compound name. *Sati* is the broken-down Prakrit and Pali form of the old Smṛti—'the Tradition,' literally the remembering. Sakya had to break away from this and create a new Smṛti of its own. *Sati*, with it, came to mean introspection: the finding within one's self the equivalent of what, for the brahman, was already in fixed form and virtually externalized as Veda.

Now the verb for the introspective act is always *upaṭṭhāpeti*, to make present, to call up, and occurs in the Piṭakas in this connexion. *Sati-upaṭṭhāna* is thus the act of introspection. Nevertheless the Commentaries agree in treating the word, never as *satyupaṭṭhāna*, as is the reading in Buddhist Sanskrit texts, but always as *sati plus* "*paṭṭhāna*," a word which has no independent existence, save in that very late appendix to the Abhidhamma Piṭaka: the seventh Book, and for which, in this connexion or in that, a laboured and unhappy definition has had to be sought. We see this, for instance, in the late Ledi Sayadaw's definition of *paṭṭhāna* as cause or *paccaya-par-excellence* (*J.P.T.S.*, 1919). The book *Paṭisambhidā-magga* reads *upaṭṭhāna* (ii, 232), but Buddhaghosa (*Dīgha* and *Majjhima Com.*), though citing this, recognizes only *paṭṭhāna*.

My sincere thanks I here utter to Mr. Woodward for undertaking, with the table of errata, etc., in his own volumes, to make a table of those in mine. I have added a few to the latter, and have supplied one or two omissions to which he referred me.

C. A. F. RHYS DAVIDS.

July, 1929.

NOTE.

Mr. Woodward resides in Tasmania. By some inexplicable miscarriages, postal or extra-postal, he has failed to receive revises of the first eight sheets. To avoid further delays I have revised these myself. For oversights in them he must therefore not be held responsible.

C. A. F. RHYS DAVIDS,
General Editor P.T.S.

PREFACE

THIS volume, concluding the translation of *Saŋyutta-Nikāya*, is aptly called *Mahāvagga* (Great Chapter), for it contains no less than 1,208 Sayings, which, if fully translated, would fill a volume twice the size of this. It is partly due to the numerous repetitions (*peyyālas*), the proper arrangement of which gave much trouble to the editor of the text, M. Léon Feer, as Burmese and Sinhalese MSS. differ in this respect. To put it briefly, a number of similes are selected: then each quality (virtue or vice) to be illustrated is to be expanded accordingly. Here even the original Pali editors are content to abbreviate by *pe* or *la*.

The greater number of Suttas in this collection are labelled '*Sāvatthī*,' and many of these '*Sāvatthī-nidānaŋ*,' which I have translated 'Sāvatthī was the occasion (for the discourse).' As it seems improbable that so many incidents should have happened at one spot, I think it likely, as Mrs. Rhys Davids has conjectured (see *Introd.* to Vol. IV of this series and that to the *Majjhima-Nikāya-Index* volume), that the whole collection was stored and systematized at Sāvatthī. We should thus read *nidhāna* (store-house) for *nidāna* (context or connexion), and picture to ourselves a sort of college or centre for receiving notes of discourses and fitting them into an arbitrary framework, which is about all we have left to-day. For it is obvious, even to the superficial reader, that no teacher would repeat his words so often and use strict formulas to present his message. To the more careful reader many curiosities of editing will present themselves.

For the use of those who would go further into conjecture on this subject I have taken pains to go through the whole of the Four Great Nikāyas searching for Sāvatthī discourses. I tabulate the result very briefly.

Those given at Sāvatthī are thus labelled in the introductory preface to each: 'At Sāvatthī, in Jeta Grove, at Anāthapiṇḍika's Park (or Hermitage).' This is generally given in full at the beginnings of chapters (*vaggas*), but is not always so given. Then it is abbreviated to 'Sāvatthī . . . in the Park': then again to 'Sāvatthī' alone. Other places, at or near Sāvatthī, are also mentioned—*viz.*, East Park, Dark Wood, etc. Other abbreviations are *Sāvatthiyaŋ* (at S.) or *Sāvatthiyaŋ viharati.* It would seem that the repeaters or scribes (later) tired of all this and wrote simply *Sāvatthī-nidānaŋ* (? or *nidhānaŋ*). The Sāvatthī discourses, then, are thus distributed:

		At Jeta Grove.	*At East Park.*	*In Suburbs.*	*Total.*
In Dīgha-N.	..	5	1	—	6
In Majjhima-N.	..	69	6	—	75
In Saŋyutta-N.	..	723	9	4	736
In Anguttara-N.	..	47	7	—	54
Total	..	844	23	4	871

Thus we can see at a glance the preponderance of those at Sāvatthī. Of this total 70 are labelled *S. nidānaŋ*, and these latter again, except two in *Anguttara-N.*, are all in *Saŋyutta-N.* I also noticed that the word *nidāna* is attached to the following places: Rājagaha (once), Benares (thrice), Pāṭaliputta (twice), Kapilavatthu (six times); all of these instances being in *Saŋyutta*-N., mostly in Vols. I and V. Thus I conclude that this particular Nikāya was made up at this centre; that some of the discourses happened there; that the words *nidāna* and *nidhāna* have been confused; that *nidāna* refers to the collection or source, and not to the locality, of events.

Another point of interest to me is the great variety of similes in this volume. There are no less than 70 (for which see Index), some of which occur in other collections. The popularity of this method of teaching by parables is of course widespread, and an interesting comparison might be made with those in the Old and New Testaments. A full list of similes in the Nikāyas will be found in the *J.P.T.S.*, 1906-7-8.

We have also several picturesque tales and incidents of local colour, such as the Jātaka Tale of the Falcon and the Quail; that of the hunter, the monkey and the pitch-trap; the bamboo-acrobat; the wonderful archery of the Licchavī youths; the parable of the blind turtle and the yoke-hole; the tale of the two chamberlains or equerries; Moggallāna's miraculous display; an instance of faith-cure; also the First Sermon at Benares; and the sickness of the Master.

As to the use of terms, I have not felt bound to follow those I have generally used in other volumes. As to this I may quote from the Introduction to *Dialogues of the Buddha*, vol. ii, p. 324:

'We need ourselves to be mindful lest, in interpreting them, we follow too closely European points of view. In trying to avoid this danger, we do not consider that our choice of terms leaves nothing to be desired or to be explained.'

Thus, on further consultation with Mrs. Rhys Davids, I have uniformly adopted 'monks' for *bhikkhū*; 'Way' for *magga*; 'desire' for *chando*, often translated 'will' previously (for it is certain that our word 'will' had no satisfactory equivalent in those days); also 'arisings' for *satipaṭṭhāna*, instead of 'stations' (of mindfulness), though in the earlier pages of this volume I had already printed 'stations.' This word *paṭṭhāna* will be found discussed in the volume of *Dialogues* quoted above.

To conclude: the Pali Text will be found unusually full of misprints, to the chief of which I have referred in the notes. Also, in several passages I have preferred commentarial or other readings, which M. Léon Feer might have done too, had he not been unfortunate in having no copy of the *Commentary*, except for Books I, II (*Sagāthā-* and *Nidāna-Vaggas*). I should further add that several of the points I have discussed here are dealt with in Mrs. Rhys Davids's lately published book *Gotama the Man* (Luzac).

F. L. WOODWARD.

West Tamar, Tasmania,
June, 1929.

CONTENTS

THE BOOK CALLED MAHĀVAGGA (GREAT CHAPTER)

BOOK I

CHAPTER		PAGE
XLV.	KINDRED SAYINGS ON THE WAY:	
	I. IGNORANCE	1
	II. DWELLING	11
	III. PERVERSION	16
	IV. CONDUCT	21
	V. EARNESTNESS	33
	VI. DEEDS REQUIRING STRENGTH	36
	VII. LONGING	43
	VIII. THE FLOOD	47

BOOK II

XLVI.	KINDRED SAYINGS ON THE LIMBS OF WISDOM:	
	I. THE MOUNTAIN	51
	II. THE SICK MAN	65
	III. UDĀYĪ	70
	IV. HINDRANCES	76
	V. ROLLER OF THE WHEEL	81
	VI. PERSEVERANCE IN THE LIMBS OF WISDOM	85
	VII. IN-BREATHING AND OUT-BREATHING	109
	VIII. CESSATION	112
	IX. GANGĀ-REPETITION	114
	X. EARNESTNESS (*rep.*)	115
	XI. DEEDS REQUIRING STRENGTH (*rep.*)	115
	XII. LONGING (*rep.*)	115
	XIII. THE FLOOD (*rep.*)	116
	XIV. GANGĀ-REPETITION (ii)	116

CHAPTER PAGE

XLVI. KINDRED SAYINGS ON THE LIMBS OF WISDOM (*Continued*):

XV. EARNESTNESS (*2nd rep.*) - - 117
XVI. DEEDS REQUIRING STRENGTH (*2nd rep.*) 117
XVII. LONGING (*2nd rep.*) - - - 117
XVIII. THE FLOOD (*2nd rep.*) - - - 117

BOOK III

XLVII. KINDRED SAYINGS ON THE STATIONS (OR ARISINGS) OF MINDFULNESS:

I. AMBAPĀLĪ - - - - 119
II. NĀLANDĀ - - - - 137
III. HABIT AND PERMANENCE - - 151
IV. UNHEARD BEFORE - - - 157
V. THE DEATHLESS - - - 161
VI. GANGĀ-REPETITION (iii) - - - 166
VII. EARNESTNESS (*3rd rep.*) - - - 166
VIII. DEEDS REQUIRING STRENGTH (*3rd rep.*) 167
IX. LONGING (*3rd rep.*) - - - 167
X. THE FLOOD (*3rd rep.*) - - - 167

BOOK IV

XLVIII. KINDRED SAYINGS ON THE FACULTIES:

I. PURITY - - - - - 169
II. IN A LESS DEGREE - - - 175
III. THE SIX FACULTIES - - - 179
IV. THE FACULTY OF EASE - - - 183
V. OLD AGE - - - - 191
VI. [*No title*] - - - - 202
VII. ON THE SIDE OF THE WISDOM - - 211
VIII. GANGĀ-REPETITION (iv) - - - 214
IX. EARNESTNESS (*4th rep.*) - - - 215
X. DEEDS REQUIRING STRENGTH (*4th rep.*) 215
XI. LONGING (*4th rep.*) - - - 215
XII. THE FLOOD (*4th rep.*) - - - 216
XIII. [*The last five reps.*] - - - 216-8

BOOK V

CHAPTER PAGE

XLIX. KINDRED SAYINGS ON THE BEST EFFORTS:

I. GANGĀ-REPETITION (v) - - - 219

II-V. [*As above*] - - - 220-2

BOOK VI

L. KINDRED SAYINGS ON THE POWERS:

I. GANGĀ-REPETITION (vi) - - - 223

II-V. [*As above*] - - - 223-4

BOOK VII

LI. KINDRED SAYINGS ON THE BASES OF PSYCHIC POWER:

I. CĀPĀLA - - - - - 225

II. THE SHAKING OF THE TERRACED HOUSE 235

III. THE WAY - - - - 251

IV. GANGĀ-REPETITION (vii) - - 258

V-VIII. [*As above*] - - - 258-60

BOOK VIII

LII. KINDRED SAYINGS ABOUT ANURUDDHA:

I. IN SOLITUDE - - - - 261

II. THOUSANDFOLD - - - - 269

BOOK IX

LIII. GANGĀ-REPETITION (viii):

I-V. [*As above*] - - - 272-5

BOOK X

LIV. KINDRED SAYINGS ABOUT IN-BREATHING AND OUT-BREATHING:

I. THE ONE CONDITION - - - 275

II. ICCHĀNANGALA - - - 289

BOOK XI

CHAPTER PAGE

LV. KINDRED SAYINGS ON STREAM-WINNING:

I. VELUDVĀRA - - - - 296
II. THOUSANDFOLD, OR ROYAL PARK - 314
III. SARAKĀNI - - - - 320
IV. FLOOD OF MERIT - - - 336
V. THE SAME WITH VERSES - - 342
VI. DISCREET - - - - 346
VII. GREAT INSIGHT - - - - 351

BOOK XII

LVI. KINDRED SAYINGS ABOUT THE TRUTHS:

I. CONCENTRATION - - - 352
II. FOUNDATION OF THE KINGDOM OF THE NORM - - - - 356
III. KOṬIGĀMA - - - - 365
IV. SIṂSAPĀ GROVE - - - - 370
V. THE PRECIPICE - - - - 377
VI. COMPREHENSION - - - 386
VII. CYCLIC REPETITION - - - 390
VIII. FEW ABSTAIN - - - - 393
IX. UNCOOKED-GRAIN REPETITION - - 394
X. MORE NUMEROUS - - - 395
XI. THE FIVE DESTINIES - - - 396

INDEXES:

I. GENERAL - - - - - 401
II. PALI WORDS IN NOTES - - - 408
III. ERRATA AND ADDITIONS - - - 410

THE BOOK OF THE KINDRED SAYINGS

(*SAÑYUTTA NIKĀYA*)

PART V

THE BOOK CALLED *MAHĀVAGGA* OR *GREAT CHAPTER*, CONTAINING KINDRED SAYINGS ON THE WAY AND OTHER METHODS OF PURIFICATION

Honour to him, the Exalted One, Arahant, Buddha Supreme

BOOK I [*CHAPTER* XLV]

KINDRED SAYINGS ON THE WAY

I. On Ignorance.

(i) *Ignorance.*

Thus have I heard: Once the Exalted One was staying near Sāvatthī, at Jeta Grove, in Anāthapiṇḍika's Park. Then the Exalted One addressed the monks, saying: 'Monks.'[1]

'Yes, lord,' replied those monks to the Exalted One. The Exalted One said:

'When ignorance leads the way,[2] by the reaching of states unprofitable, shamelessness and recklessness follow in its train. In one who is swayed by ignorance and is void of sense, wrong view has scope.[3] Wrong view gives scope for wrong aim,

[1] In this volume I revert to the use of the word 'monks' (*bhikkhū*) in preference to 'brethren,' as being less misleading. See Mrs. Rhys Davids's remarks on the subject in the Introduction to Vol. III of this series.

[2] Lit. 'goes before.'

[3] *Pahoti = uppajjati. Comy.*

wrong aim for wrong speech, wrong speech for wrong action, wrong action for wrong living, wrong living for wrong effort, wrong effort for wrong mindfulness, and wrong mindfulness gives scope for wrong concentration.

But, monks, when knowledge leads the way, by the attainment of profitable states, the sense of shame and self-restraint follow in its train. In one who is swayed by knowledge and has good sense, right view has scope. Right view gives scope for right aim, right aim for right speech, right speech for right action, right action for right living, right living for right effort, right effort for right mindfulness, and right mindfulness gives scope for right concentration.'

(ii) *The half.*[1]

Thus have I heard: Once the Exalted One was staying among the Sakyans at Sakkara, a Sakyan township.

Then the venerable Ānanda came to the Exalted One, saluted him and sat down at one side. So seated the venerable Ānanda said this:

'The half of the holy life,[2] lord, it is friendship with what is lovely,[3] association with what is lovely, intimacy with what is lovely!'

'Say not so, Ānanda! Say not so, Ānanda! It is the whole, not the half, of the holy life,—this friendship, this association, this intimacy with what is lovely. Of a monk who is a friend, an associate, an intimate of what is lovely we may expect this,—that he will develop the Ariyaneightfold way, that he will make much of the Ariyan eightfold way.

And how, Ānanda, does such a monk develop and make much of the Ariyan eightfold way?

---

[1] At *S.* i, 87 (*Kosala-saṃyutta*), to which *Comy.* refers here, the Buddha relates this incident to Pasenadi. rājah of Kosala. *Cf. K.S.* i, 112-3 *n.*

[2] *Brahmacariya* = *ariya-magga. Comy.*

[3] *Kalyāṇa.* The word 'lovely' was originally suggested by Mrs. Rhys Davids (*K.S.* i, 112 *n.*) to express 'beauty, physical and moral,' being exactly what is meant by ὅσα προσφιλῆ in the Bible at N.T., Phil iv, 8 ('whatsoever things are lovely').

Herein,[1] Ānanda, he cultivates right view, which is based on detachment, on dispassion, on cessation, which ends in self-surrender. He cultivates right aim, which is so based and concerned: likewise right speech, right action, right living, right effort, right mindfulness and right concentration, which is based on detachment, on dispassion, on cessation, which ends in self-surrender. That, Ānanda, is how a monk who is a friend, an associate, an intimate of what is lovely, cultivates and makes much of the Ariyan eightfold way.

This is the method, Ānanda, by which you are to understand how the whole of this holy life consists in friendship, in association, in intimacy with what is lovely. Indeed, Ānanda, beings liable to rebirth are liberated from rebirth; beings liable to decay, liable to death, liable to grief, woe, lamentation and despair, are liberated therefrom because of my friendship with what is lovely.[2]

It is by this method, Ānanda, that you are to understand how the whole of this holy life consists in friendship, in association, in intimacy with what is lovely.'

(iii) *Sāriputta.*

Sāvatthī (was) the occasion (for this discourse) . . .

Now the venerable Sāriputta came to visit the Exalted One, and on coming to him saluted him and sat down at one side. So seated he said this:

'The whole of the holy life, lord, consists in friendship, in association, in intimacy with what is lovely.'

'Well said! Well said, Sāriputta! It is as you say . . . of a monk who is a friend . . . (*as above*) . . . we may expect that he will make much of the Ariyan eightfold way.

And how, Sāriputta, does a monk who is a friend . . . (*as before to the end*) . . .'

---

[1] *Idha*, 'here,' as usually, *imasmiŋ sāsane* (in this teaching). *Comy.*

[2] *Mamaŋ kalyāṇamittaŋ āgamma* (which last word *Comy.* takes as *ārabbha, sandhāya, paṭicca*, 'beginning with, concerned with, owing to' me). *Comy.* remarks that the above-mentioned statements could not be known as facts by Ānanda, who was *sekha*, learner, only; whereas Sāriputta, an adept (in the next *sutta*), knew them well.

(iv) *The Brahmin.*

Sāvatthī (was) the occasion[1] (for this discourse) . . .

Then the venerable Ānanda, robing himself in the forenoon and taking bowl and outer robe, entered Sāvatthī on his begging round.

Now the venerable Ānanda saw Jānussoṇi,[2] the brahmin, driving out of Sāvatthī in his car, drawn by pure white mares.[3] White were the steeds harnessed thereto and white the trappings, white the car. White were the fittings, white the reins, the goad, the canopy, his turban, his clothes and sandals, and by a white fan was he fanned. And when folk beheld it they cried out: 'Aha! There's the best of cars! There's the best of cars for beauty!'

Now the venerable Ānanda, after going his begging round, came back and ate his meal and went to visit the Exalted One, came to him, saluted him and sat down at one side. So seated he said this to the Exalted One:

'Here, lord, robing myself in the forenoon and taking bowl and outer robe, I entered Sāvatthī on my begging round. Then, lord, I saw Jānusoṇi, the brahmin, driving out . . . (*and he described him as above*). . . . And when folk beheld it they cried out: "Aha! There's the best[4] of cars! There's the best of cars for beauty!" Pray, lord, can one point out the best of cars in this Norm and discipline?'

'One can, Ānanda,' said the Exalted One. "Best of cars," Ānanda, is a term that may be applied to this very Ariyan eightfold way—"best of cars," "Norm-car,"[5] "unsurpassed for its conquest in the fight."[6]

---

[1] *Nidānaṃ*, source? See Mrs. Rhys Davids's remarks in the Introduction to *Kindred Sayings*, Vol. IV, on this subject. I have generally translated 'occasion,' but there are many instances where the word does seem to mean 'source' (*nidhāna*), or at any rate 'centre.'

[2] *Cf. K.S.* ii, *n.*; *A.* i, 36.

[3] Four, according to *Comy.* The fittings were of silver.

[4] *Brahma=seṭṭha. Comy.*

[5] *Cf.* S. i, 33; *K.S.* i, 45; *S.* iv, 291; *K.S.* iv, 199.

[6] 'With the passions.' *Comy.*

Right view, Ānanda, if cultivated and made much of, ends in the restraint of lust, ends in the restraint of hatred, ends in the restraint of illusion. Right aim, Ānanda, . . . right speech . . . right action . . . right living . . . right effort . . . right mindfulness . . . right concentration, Ānanda, if cultivated and made much of, ends in the restraint of lust, ends in the restraint of hatred, ends in the restraint of illusion.

By this method, Ānanda, you are to understand the words "best of cars," "Norm car," "unsurpassed for its conquest in the fight," are terms that may be applied to this same Ariyan eightfold path.'

Thus spake the Exalted One. So saying, the Happy One added this further as Teacher:

> Whoso hath Faith and Wisdom,—these two states
> For ever yoked together lead him on:
> Conscience the pole, and Mind the yoke thereof,
> And Heedfulness his watchful charioteer.
> The car is furnished forth with Righteousness,
> Rapture its axle, Energy its wheels,
> And Calm, yokefellow of the balanced mind,
> Desirelessness[1] the drapery thereof,
> Goodwill and Harmlessness his weapons are,
> Together with Detachment of the mind.
> Endurance is his leathern coat of mail:[2]
> And to attain the Peace this car rolls on.
> 'Tis built by self, by one's own self becometh
> This best of cars, unconquerable (in battle).
> Seated therein the sages leave the world,
> And verily they win the victory.[3]

---

[1] Text *anicchā*; *Comy. aniñja.*

[2] Text *dhamma-sannāho.* *Comys.* vary between *camma* and *vamma* (both meaning armour).

[3] *Cf.* the other chariot-simile, *K.S.* i, 45.

(v) *To what purpose?*[1]

At Sāvatthī was the occasion . . .

Then a number of monks came to visit the Exalted One . . . and sat down at one side. So seated those monks said this to the Exalted One:

'Here, lord, the wanderers holding other views ask us this question: "What is it, friends, for which the holy life is lived under Gotama the recluse?" Thus questioned, lord, we thus reply to those wanderers holding other views: "It is for the full understanding of Ill, friends, that the holy life is lived under Gotama the recluse."

Thus questioned, lord, and thus replying, do we state the views of the Exalted One, without misrepresenting the Exalted One by stating an untruth? Do we answer in accordance with his teaching, so that no one who agrees with his teaching and follows his views could incur reproach?'

'Truly, monks, thus questioned and thus replying, ye do state my views . . . in stating that it is for the full understanding of Ill that the holy life is lived under my rule.[2]

But if, monks, the wanderers holding other views should thus question you: "But, friends, is there any way, is there any practice for the full understanding of this Ill?"—thus questioned, monks, thus should ye reply to those wanderers of other views: "Friends, there is indeed a Way, there is indeed a practice for the full understanding of this Ill."

And what, monks, is that Way, what that practice? It is this very Ariyan eightfold way; to wit, right view, and the rest. . . . This, monks, is the Way. . . . Thus questioned, monks, thus should ye reply to those wanderers holding other views.'

(vi) *A certain monk* (*a*).

Sāvatthī was the occasion . . .

Then a certain monk came to visit the Exalted One. . . Seated at one side that monk said this to the Exalted One:

---

[1] Text *kimattha*. Title *kimatthi*. Uddāna *kimatthiyo*.

[2] As at *K.S.* iv, 27, 87; *Dialog.* i, 192; *Mil. P.*, 49, 101.

'"The holy life! The holy life!" lord, is the saying. Pray, lord, what is the holy life, and what the ending of the holy life?'

'The holy life, monk, is just this Ariyan eightfold way; to wit, right view, and the rest . . . right concentration. Whatsoever destroys lust, destroys hatred, destroys illusion, monk, is this holy life.'

(vii) *A certain monk (b).*

Sāvatthī was the occasion . . .

Then a certain monk . . . said this to the Exalted One:

'"The restraint of lust, the restraint of hatred, the restraint of illusion," lord, is the saying. Pray, lord, what does this restraint imply?'

'It implies, monk, the realm of Nibbāna.[1] By it is meant the destruction of the āsavas.'[2]

At these words that monk said to the Exalted One:

'"The deathless! The deathless!" lord, is the saying. Pray, lord, what is the deathless, and what the way to the deathless?'

'That which is the destruction of lust, the destruction of hatred, the destruction of illusion, monk,—that is called "the deathless." This same Ariyan eightfold way is the way to the deathless; to wit, right view . . . and the rest . . . right concentration.'

(viii) *Analysis.*

Sāvatthī was the occasion . . . (The Exalted One said:)

'I will teach you, monks, the Ariyan eightfold way. I will analyze it for you. Do ye listen. Give careful heed and I will speak.'

'Yes, lord,' said those monks in assent to the Exalted One. The Exalted One then said:

'What, monks, is the Ariyan eightfold way? It is right view, and the rest. And what, monks, is right view? It is the knowledge of Ill, knowledge of the arising of Ill, knowledge

---

[1] *Nibbāna-dhātu.* Nothing spatial is implied.

[2] =*Arahattaŋ. Comy.*

of the ceasing of Ill, and knowledge of the practice leading to the ceasing of Ill. That, monks, is called "right view."

And what, monks, is right aim? It is the aim to renounce, the aim to be free from malice, the aim to be harmless. That, monks, is called right aim.

And what, monks, is right speech? It is the avoiding of lying speech, the avoiding of calumny, of cutting speech, of wanton speech. That, monks, is called "right speech."

And what, monks, is right action? It is the avoiding of taking life, of stealing, of unchastity. That, monks, is called "right action."

And what, monks, is right living? Herein, monks, the Ariyan disciple, by abandoning a wrong way of life, gets his living by a right way of life. That is called "right living."

And what, monks, is right effort? Herein a monk puts forth desire [to do], makes an effort, begins to strive, applies his mind, lays hold of his mind to prevent the arising of ill, unprofitable states not yet arisen. As to ill, unprofitable states that have arisen, he puts forth desire to destroy them. As to profitable states that have not yet arisen, he puts forth desire for their arising. As to profitable states that have already arisen, he puts forth desire, makes an effort, begins to strive, applies his mind, lays hold of his mind for their continuance, for their non-confusion,[1] for their more-becoming, increase, culture and fulfilment. That, monks, is called "right effort."[2]

And what, monks, is right mindfulness?[3] Herein a monk abides contemplating body in body (as transient), ardent, self-possessed, mindful, by restraining the dejection in the world that arises from coveting. He abides contemplating feelings . . . mind . . . mind-states, ardent, self-possessed, mindful, by restraining the dejection arising in the world from coveting. This, monks, is called "right mindfulness."

---

[1] *Asammosāya.*

[2] These are called the 'four right efforts' (*sammappadhānāni*). *Cf. infra*, Book V.

[3] *Cf. K.S.* iv, 160 *ff.*

And what, monks, is right concentration? Herein a monk, aloof from sensuality, aloof from evil states, enters on the first trance, which is accompanied by thought directed and sustained, born of solitude, easeful and zestful, and abides therein. By the calming down of thought directed and sustained, he enters on the inward calm, that one-pointedness of mind, apart from thought directed and sustained, that is born of mental balance, zestful and easeful, that is the second trance.

Then, by the fading out of zest, he abides indifferent, mindful and composed, and experiences ease through the body. Having entered on the third trance, which the Ariyans describe in these terms: "he who is indifferent and mindful dwells happily,"[1] he abides therein.

Then, by the abandoning of ease, by the abandoning of discomfort, by the destruction of the happiness and unhappiness that he had before, having entered on that state which is neither pleasant nor painful, that utter purity of mindfulness reached by indifference, which is the fourth trance, he abides therein. This, monks, is called "right concentration."'

(ix) *Bearded wheat.*[2]

Sāvatthī . . . (The Exalted One said:)

'Suppose, monks, the spike of bearded wheat or bearded barley be wrongly aimed,[3] when pressed by hand or foot will it pierce[4] hand or foot, will it draw blood? It cannot be so. Why not? Because the spike is wrongly aimed. Just so, monks, it cannot be that the monk whose view is wrongly aimed, whose way-culture is wrongly aimed, can pierce through ignorance, draw knowledge and realize Nibbāna. Why not? Because his view is wrongly aimed.

---

[1] Similar phrases are in the *Upānishads* (*e.g.*, *kaṭha-*).

[2] *Sūka* (text *sūka* throughout). *Cf. A.* i, 8; *Dhp.* 311 (*kuso yathā duggahīto*); *KhpA.* 86.

[3] *Micchā-paṇihitaŋ* ('so as not to pierce.' *Comy.*).

[4] Text here and below *bhindissati* (*v.l. chijjati*); but *A.* and *Comys. bhecchati* (fut. of *bhindati*), *chijjati*; *DhpA. checchati.*

But, monks, suppose that the spike of bearded wheat or bearded barley be well aimed. When pressed by hand or foot, it is certain[1] that it will pierce hand or foot and draw blood. Why so? Because, monks, the spike is well aimed.

Just so, monks, it is certain that the monk whose view is well aimed, whose way-culture is well aimed, can pierce through ignorance, draw knowledge, and realize Nibbāna. Why so? Because, monks, of the right aim of his view.

And how does a monk by well aimed view, by well aimed way-culture, so pierce through ignorance, draw knowledge and realize Nibbāna?

Herein, monks, he cultivates right view, which is based on detachment, on dispassion, on cessation, which ends in self-surrender. That is how this monk, by well aimed view, by well aimed path-culture, pierces through ignorance, draws knowledge and realizes Nibbāna.'

(x) *Nandiya.*

Savatthi . . .

Then Nandiya[2] the wanderer came to the Exalted One, and on reaching him greeted him courteously, and after the exchange of greetings and courtesies sat down at one side. So seated, Nandiya the wanderer said this to the Exalted One:

'What conditions are there, master Gotama, which when cultivated and made much of, lead to Nibbāna, have Nibbāna for their goal, end in Nibbāna?'

'There are eight conditions, Nandiya, which when cultivated and made much of . . . end in Nibbāna, to wit, right view . . . and the rest . . . right concentration. These eight conditions, Nandiya, when cultivated and made much of, lead to Nibbāna, have Nibbāna for their goal, end in Nibbāna.'

At these words Nandiya the wanderer said this to the Exalted One:

---

[1] *Ṭhānaŋ vijjati.*

[2] Name of a *bhikkhu* at *M.* i, 205, 462; iii, 155. Here *Comy.* calls him *channa-* (? secret) *paribbājako.*

'Wonderful, master Gotama! Wonderful, master Gotama! May the worthy Gotama accept me as a lay disciple, as one who has gone to him for refuge from this day forth, so long as I have life.'[1]

CHAPTER II.—DWELLING

(i) *Way of dwelling* (*a*).[2]

Sāvatthī was the occasion (for this discourse). . . . The Exalted One said:

'Monks, I desire to dwell in solitude for half a month. I am not to be visited by any save by him alone who brings my food.'[3]

'So be it, lord,' replied those monks to the Exalted One. Thus no one visited the Exalted One save the one who brought his food.

Now at the end of that half-month the Exalted One, leaving his solitude, addressed the monks, saying:

'Monks, I have been dwelling partly[4] in the same manner as I did after I first attained enlghtenment. Thus I came to know what is experienced as a result of wrong view, and what as a result of right view and so on . . . what is experienced as a result of wrong concentration and right concentration: likewise what is experienced as a result of desire,[5] as a result of directed thought,[6] as a result of perception.

When desire is not suppressed, directed thought is not suppressed, perception is not suppressed. Owing to these there is experience.[7] (When desire is suppressed, but directed

---

[1] I omit the translation of the *Uddānas* or summaries at the end of each chapter, as the titles appear as headings to each *sutta*.

[2] I follow *Comy.* in the numbering of *suttas*. Text calls this section § 11.

[3] *Piṇḍa-pāta-nīhāraka*. *Cf. infra* on text 320.

[4] *Padesena*. *Cf. Asl.* 30; *Expos.* i, 38. It seems to mean *partim*, *i.e.* for two weeks he examined certain states, and for three months (as below) certain other states.

[5] The eight kinds of lustful thoughts. *Comy.*

[6] The first trance.

[7] *Vedayitaṃ*.

thought and perception are not suppressed, owing to these there is experience. When desire and directed thought are suppressed, but not perception, then there is experience.)[1] When all three are suppressed, owing to that there is experience.

For one who has not attained there is the effort to do so.[2] When that state is attained, owing to that there is experience.'[3]

(ii) *Way of living* (*b*).

Sāvatthī . . . (The Exalted One said:) . . .

'Monks, I desire to live in solitude for three months. . . .'

Now at the end of those three months the Exalted One, leaving his solitude, addressed the monks, saying:

'I have been dwelling partly[4] in the same manner as I did after I first attained enlightenment.

Thus I came to know what is experienced as a result of wrong view, and what is experienced as a result of suppressing wrong view: what is experienced as a result of right view and what as a result of suppressing right view, and so forth . . . so also as regards concentration, right and wrong, and its suppression. Likewise I came to know what is experienced as a result of desire, what as a result of suppression of desire: what is experienced as a result of directed thought and its suppression: also what is experienced as a result of perception and the suppression thereof.

When desire and directed thought and perception are not suppressed, there is experience as a result . . . (*the rest as in previous section*). . . .

For one who has not attained, there is the effort to do so. When the state is attained, owing to that there is experience.'

---

[1] Text brackets parts not found in Burmese MSS. 1-2.

[2] Text *atthi āyāmaŋ*, but *Comy. vāyāman ti = viriyaŋ*.

[3] *Comy.* 'Super-worldly experiences of the fourth path.'

[4] *Cf. Expos. loc. cit. supra : Padesenā*, as above.

(iii) *Learner.*[1]

Sāvatthī . . .

Then a certain monk came to visit the Exalted One. . . . Seated at one side that monk said this to the Exalted One:

'"A learner, a learner!" lord, is the saying. Pray, lord, how far is one a learner?'

'Herein, monk, a monk is imperfectly[2] possessed of right view, and the rest. He is imperfectly possessed of right concentration. Thus far, monk, he is a learner.'

(iv) *By the uprising* (*a*).[3]

Sāvatthī . . .

'These eight conditions, monks, not having yet arisen, when cultivated and made much of, come into being, but only on the arising of the Tathāgata, an arahant, a fully enlightened one. What eight?

Right view, and the rest, and right concentration. These are the eight conditions, monks, which not having already arisen . . . are so made manifest.'

(v) *By the uprising* (*b*).

Sāvatthī . . .

'These eight conditions, monks, not having yet arisen, when cultivated and made much of, come into being, but only under the rule of the Happy One. What eight? Right view and the rest, right concentration. These, monks, are the eight conditions which, not having yet arisen, come not into being save under the rule of the Happy One.'

(vi) *Utterly pure* (*a*).

Sāvatthī . . . The Exalted One thus addressed the monks: 'These eight conditions, monks, utterly pure, stainless, void of sin, not having yet arisen, come into being only on the

---

[1] *Cf. Nid.* i, 493, etc.; *sikkhati ti sekho.*

[2] *Sekhāya.*

[3] *Cf. K.S.* iii, 34 *n.* 3.

appearance of a Tathāgata, an arahant, a fully enlightened one. What eight? They are these: Right view, and the rest . . . right concentration. These eight conditions . . .'

(vii) *Utterly pure* (*b*).

Sāvatthī . . . The Exalted One thus addressed the monks: 'These eight conditions, monks, utterly pure . . . (*as above*) . . . come not into being save under the rule of the Happy One.'

(viii) *Cock's Pleasaunce* (*a*).

Pāṭaliputta was the occasion (for this incident). . . .

Thus have I heard: Once the venerable Ānanda and the venerable Bhadda[1] were staying at Cock's Pleasaunce at Pāṭaliputta.[2]

Then the venerable Bhadda, rising from his solitude at eventide, came to see the venerable Ānanda, and on coming to him greeted him courteously, and after the exchange of greetings and courtesies sat down at one side. So seated the venerable Bhadda said this to the venerable Ānanda:

'"The unrighteous life! The unrighteous life!" friend Ānanda, is the saying. Pray, friend, what is the unrighteous life?'

'Well said, well said, friend Bhadda![3] Welcome is your penetration,[4] welcome your ready wit, and goodly is your

---

[1] The same couple converse at the same place, *infra* text 171.

[2] Capital of Magadha. *Cf.* Rhys Davids's *Buddhist India*, pp. 203, 262; *UdA.* 416-9.

[3] At *Brethren*, 231 *n.* Mrs. Rhys Davids calls him Faustus ('lucky'). He puns on the name, as below *loc. cit.* and *A.* ii, 177. For *bhaddako cf. Vin.* v, 144, *bhaddako te ummango* (*sic.*), *yoniso paripucchasi.* At *K.S.* iv, 178, the same reply is given to another questioner, not Bhadda. So the fact of the pun is doubtful, or, as seems more probable, the facts are muddled in recording. For in a collection of this size (7,762 *suttas* ?) learned by heart, some confusion is inevitable.

[4] *Ummagga* (lit. a tunnel, an underground way, a boring into). In bad sense, *i.e.* when contrasted as *vāma-maggo* (left-hand path) with *dakkhiṇa-maggo* it means 'wrong path,' as at *Thig.* 94, 1174; *JA.* v, 260, etc. *Comy.* defines as *paññā-ummagga, paññā-vimaŋsatta, paññā-gavesanaŋ.*

question. You ask me the meaning of the unrighteous life, do you not?'

'I do, friend.'

'Well, friend, it is just that wrong eightfold way, to wit: Wrong view, wrong aim, wrong speech, wrong action, wrong living, wrong effort, wrong mindfulness and wrong concentration.'

(ix) *Cock's Pleasaunce* (*b*).

Pāṭaliputta was the occasion . . . So seated the venerable Bhadda said this to the venerable Ānanda:

'"The righteous life, the righteous life!" is the saying, friend Ānanda. Pray, friend, what is the righteous life, and in what does it end?'

'Well said, well said, friend Bhadda . . . (*as above*). . . . Well, friend, it is just that Ariyan eightfold way, to wit: Right view, and the rest . . . right concentration. The destruction of lust, the destruction of hatred, the destruction of illusion, friend,—that is what this righteous life ends in.'

(x) *Cock's Pleasaunce* (*c*).

Pāṭaliputta was the occasion . . . So seated the venerable Bhadda said this to the venerable Ānanda:

'"The righteous life, the righteous life!" is the saying, friend Ānanda. Pray, friend, what is the righteous life, and in what does it end?'

'Well said, well said, friend Bhadda! . . . (*as before*) . . . right concentration. Whoso, friend, is possessed of this Ariyan eightfold way, he is called a "righteous liver."[1] The destruction of lust, the destruction of hatred, the destruction of illusion, friend,—that is what this righteous life ends in.'

---

[1] *Brahmacārin*, often mistranslated and understood (especially in the East) as 'celibate.'

CHAPTER III

PERVERSION

(i) *Perversion.*[1]

Sāvatthī was the occasion . . . The Exalted One said:

'I will teach you, monks, both perversion and perfection.[2] Do ye listen to it.

And what, monks, is perversion? It is as follows: Wrong view, and the rest . . . wrong concentration. This, monks, is perversion.

And what, monks, is perfection? It is as follows: Right view, and the rest . . . right concentration. This, monks, is called "perfection."'

(ii) *Unprofitable states.*

Sāvatthī . . . The Exalted One thus spake:

'I will teach you, monks, both unprofitable states and profitable states. Do ye listen to it. And what, monks, are unprofitable states? They are as follows: Wrong view, and the rest . . . wrong concentration. These, monks, are called "unprofitable states."

And what are profitable states? They are as follows: Right view, and the rest . . . right concentration. These, monks, are called "profitable states."'

(iii) *Practice (a).*[3]

Sāvatthī . . . The Exalted One addressed the monks, saying:

'I will teach you, monks, both wrong practice and right practice. Do ye listen to it. And what, monks, is wrong practice? It is as follows: Wrong view and the rest . . .

---

[1] As before, I follow the enumeration of *Comy.* This section is No. 21 in text.

[2] *Micchattaŋ* and *sammattaŋ*.

[3] *Paṭipadā*, progress, approach, practice, etc.

wrong concentration. This, monks, is called "wrong practice." And what, monks, is right practice? It is as follows: Right view and the rest . . . right concentration. This, monks, is called "right practice."'

(iv) *Practice* (*b*).

Sāvatthī . . . The Exalted One addressed the monks, saying:

'Monks, whether in householder or recluse, I praise no wrong practice. If a householder or recluse practise perversity, then in consequence of and because of his practice of perversity he is no winner[1] of the Method, the Norm and the good.[2] And what, monks, is wrong practice? It is as follows: Wrong view and the rest . . . wrong concentration. This, monks, is called "wrong practice." Whether in householder or recluse, monks, I praise not wrong practice. For if a householder or recluse . . . practise perversity . . .

But, monks, I do praise right practice, whether in householder or recluse. If a householder or recluse be given to right practice, then in consequence of and because of his right practice he is a winner of the Method, the Norm and the good. And what, monks, is right practice? It is as follows: Right view, and the rest . . . right concentration. This, monks, is called "right practice." Whether in householder or recluse, monks, I praise right practice. For, monks, whether a man be householder or recluse, if he be given to right practice, then in consequence of and because of his right practice he is a winner of the Method, the Norm and the good.'

---

[1] *Ārādhako.*

[2] *Ñāyaŋ, dhammaŋ, kusalaŋ. Comy.* defines as *ariya-magga, dhammaŋ.* This passage is quoted by the rājah Milinda to Nāgasena, *M.P.* 243. At *Dialog.* ii, 327 *n.* 'Practical Buddhism is summed up (*M.* i, 181, 197) as exertion in *ñāya, dhamma* and *kusala*, the Method, the Norm and the good. *Ñāya* is defined at *S.* v, 388 as what comes pretty much to our "method" in philosophy.' *Cf.* Mrs. Rhys Davids's *Buddhism* (1912), p. 90.

(v) *The unworthy (a).*[1]

Sāvatthī . . . Then the Exalted One addressed the monks, saying:

'I will teach you, monks, both the unworthy man and the worthy man. Do ye listen to it. And who, monks, is the unworthy man?

Herein, monks, a certain one has wrong view, wrong aim, wrong speech, wrong action, wrong living, wrong effort, wrong mindfulness, and wrong concentration. This one, monks, is called "unworthy." And who, monks, is the worthy?

Herein, monks, a certain one has right view, and the rest . . . right concentration. This one, monks, is called "the worthy."'

(vi) *The unworthy (b).*

Sāvatthī . . . The Exalted One addressed the monks, saying:

'I will teach you, monks, both the unworthy and the still more unworthy than he. I will teach you, monks, both the worthy and the still more worthy than he. And who, monks, is the unworthy? . . . (*As before.*) . . .

And who, monks, is the still more unworthy than he?

Herein, monks, a certain one has wrong view, and the rest . . . wrong concentration: but he has also wrong knowledge and wrong liberation. This one, monks, is called "one who is still more unworthy than the unworthy."

And who, monks, is the worthy and the still more worthy than he?

Herein, monks, a certain one has right view and the rest . . . right concentration; but he has also right knowledge and right liberation. This one, monks, is called "he who is still more worthy than the worthy."'

---

[1] *Asappurisa* (=*asant*+*purisa*).

(vii) *The pot.*

Sāvatthī . . .

'Just as, monks, a pot without support[1] is easily upset,[2] and one with support is hard to upset, even so, monks, the mind that is without support is easily upset, the mind that has support is hard to upset.

And what, monks, is the support of mind? It is just this Ariyan eightfold way, to wit: Right view and the rest . . . right concentration. This is the mind's support.

Just as, monks, a pot that is without support is easily upset, and a pot with support is hard to upset, even so, monks, the mind that is without support is easily upset, the mind that has support is hard to upset.'

(viii) *Concentration.*

Sāvatthī . . . Then the Exalted One thus addressed the monks:

'I will teach you, monks, the Ariyan right concentration, which is associated and equipped.[3] Do ye listen to it.

And what, monks, is the Ariyan right concentration which is associated and equipped? It is (associated with) right view, right aim, right speech, right action, right living, right effort, right mindfulness and right concentration.

Now, monks, the one-pointedness[4] of mind which is equipped with these seven limbs is called "the Ariyan right concentration on which is associated, likewise which is equipped."'

(ix) *Feeling.*

Sāvatthī . . . Then the Exalted One thus addressed the monks:

'There are these three feelings, monks.[5] What three? Feeling that is pleasant, feeling that is painful, feeling

---

[1] *Anādhāro.*

[2] *Suppavattiyo. Comy.* reads *suppavattanīyo,* 'rolls at random.'

[3] *Sa-upanisaŋ sa-parikkhāraŋ. Cf. K.S.* ii, 25 *n. Comy.* paraphrases thus: *sappaccayaŋ saparivāraŋ.*

[4] *Cf. A.* i, 198 (of *puggala*).

[5] *Cf. K.S.* iv, 136, etc.

that is neither pleasant nor painful. These are the three feelings.

By the comprehension, monks, of these three feelings the Ariyan eightfold way must be cultivated. What Ariyan eightfold way? That which is right view and the rest . . . right concentration. By the comprehension of these three feelings . . .'

(x) *Uttiya.*

Sāvatthī . . .

Now the venerable Uttiya[1] came to see the Exalted One. . . . Seated at one side the venerable Uttiya said this to the Exalted One:

'Here, lord, when I was secluded in solitude, this discursive thought came to me: Five sensual elements[2] were spoken of by the Exalted One. I wonder what are those five sensual elements so spoken of by the Exalted One.'

'Well said, well said, Uttiya! Five indeed are the sensual elements spoken of by me. What five?

There are objects cognizable by the eye, objects desirable, pleasant, delightful and dear, passion-fraught, inciting to lust. There are sounds cognizable by the ear, objects desirable . . . there are scents cognizable by the nose . . . savours cognizable by the tongue . . . tangibles cognizable by the body, objects desirable, pleasant, delightful and dear, passion-fraught, inciting to lust. These, Uttiya, are the five sensual elements of which I spoke.

Now, Uttiya, it is by abandoning these five sensual elements that the Ariyan eightfold way is to be cultivated. What Ariyan eightfold way? It is right view and the rest . . . right concentration. By abandoning these five sensual elements, Uttiya, this Ariyan eightfold way must be cultivated.'

---

[1] *Cf. infra*, 166; *A.* v, 193; *Brethren*, 34 *n.* Doubtless the same as there. Text *v.l. Uttika*. *Comy.* does not notice this *sutta* (see note on next section).

[2] *Cf. K.S.* iv, 56 *ff.*, etc.

CHAPTER IV

On Conduct

(i) *Conduct.*[1]

Sāvatthī was the occasion . . . The Exalted One thus addressed the monks:

'Monks, I will teach you wrong conduct and right conduct. Do ye listen to it.

And what, monks, is wrong conduct? It is as follows: Wrong view and the rest . . . wrong concentration. This, monks, is called "wrong conduct."

And what, monks, is right conduct? It is as follows: Right view and the rest . . . right concentration. This, monks, is called "right conduct."'

(ii) *Conducted.*

Sāvatthī . . . The Exalted One thus addressed the monks:

'Monks, I will teach you both the wrongly conducted and the rightly conducted. Do ye listen to it. And who, monks, is the wrongly conducted?

Herein, monks, a certain one has wrong view and the rest . . . wrong concentration. This one is called "wrongly conducted." And who, monks, is rightly conducted?

Herein, monks, a certain one has right view and the rest . . . right concentration. This one is called "rightly conducted."'

(iii) *Neglected and undertaken.*

Sāvatthī . . .

'By whomsoever, monks, the Ariyan eightfold way is neglected,[2] by them is neglected the Ariyan eightfold way that leads to the utter destruction of Ill.

---

[1] *Comy.* does not number the following *suttas* till p. 45 of text, which is unusual. Léon Feerof (Introduction, p. vi vol. v) discusses the matter at length, and concludes that the next two chapters were 'inserted, apparently, as a lengthening of the fourth chapter.' I have therefore numbered them as sub-sections of cap. 4. Text calls them Nos. 31-148.

[2] *Viraddho* (*virajjhati*) as opposed to *āraddho*. *Cf. infra*, pp. 82, 179, 254, 294 of text.

By whomsoever the Ariyan eightfold way is undertaken, by them is undertaken the Ariyan eightfold way that leads to the utter destruction of Ill. And what, monks, is the Ariyan eightfold way?

It is as follows: Right view . . . right concentration. By whomsoever . . .'

(iv) *Crossing over.*[1]

Sāvatthī . . .

'These eight conditions, monks, if cultivated and made much of, conduce to that state in which no further shore and no hither shore exist.[2] What eight? They are as follows: Right view and the rest . . . right concentration. These, monks, are the eight conditions.' Thus spake the Exalted One. So saying the Happy One added this further as Teacher:[3]

Few are they of mortal men
Who have reached the further shore:[4]
But the crowd of other folk
On this side fare up and down.
They who follow in the teaching
Of the Norm expounded well,
They shall reach the shore and pass
The realm of Death so hard to cross.[5]

Giving up the state of darkness[6]
Let the wise pursue the light:[7]
Giving up home for the homeless,
In solitude where joys are rare,[8]

---

[1] *Pārangamo. Cf.* text, pp. 81, 180.

[2] *A-pāra-apāra-Nibbāna.*

[3] *Dhp.* v, 85-9; *A.* v, 232.

[4] *Tīraṃ.* At *A.* v, 233 the Buddha says the two shores are breaking and keeping the precepts. At *A.* v, 232 (as here) it is the right and wrong eightfold way.

[5] *Cf. Itiv.* 57; *S.* iv, 157.

[6] *Kaṇha-dhammaṃ. Cf. Sn.* v, 526. *Comy. akusala-dhammaṃ.*

[7] Read *sukkaṃ* for *kaṇhaṃ* of text.

[8] *Cf. Dhp.* 99, *yathā na ramati jano.* (Fausböll *seclusione difficili delectatu*).

Let him long for bliss unbounded.
Leaving lusts and owning naught
Let the wise man cleanse himself
From the passions of the heart.

They whose mind is rightly cultured
In the wisdom's (seven) limbs,[1]—
Glad to have surrendered clinging,[2]
Glad to be from bondage loosed,[3]
Canker-cured,[4] they, all-resplendent,
E'en in this world are at peace.[5]

(v) *The life of the recluse* (*a*).

Sāvatthī . . .

I will teach you, monks, both the life of the recluse[6] and the fruits thereof. Do ye listen to it. And what, monks, is the life of the recluse?

It is just this Ariyan eightfold way, to wit: Right view and the rest . . . right concentration. This is called 'the life of the recluse.'

And what, monks, are the fruits of the life of the recluse? They are the fruit of stream-winning, the fruit of once returning, the fruit of not returning and the fruit of arahantship. These, monks, are called 'the fruits of the life of the recluse.'

(vi) *The life of the recluse* (*b*).

Sāvatthī . . .

I will teach you, monks, both the life of the recluse and the aim thereof. Do ye listen to it. And what, monks, is the life of the recluse? . . . (*as above*). . . . And what, monks, is the aim of the life of the recluse?

The destruction of lust, the destruction of hatred, the destruction of illusion are called the aim of the life of the recluse.[6]

---

[1] *Satta-bojjhangesu.*
[2] *Cf. S.* i, 236, *anādānā.*
[3] *Anupādāya ratā* (the substrate).
[4] *Khīṇāsavā.*
[5] *Parinibbutā.*
[6] *Cf. Pts. of Controv.*, p. 208.

(vii) *The highest life* (*a*).

Sāvatthī . . .

I will teach you, monks, both the highest life[1] and the fruits thereof. Do ye listen to it. And what, monks, is the highest life?

It is just this Ariyan eightfold way, to wit: Right view and the rest . . . right concentration. This, monks, is called 'the highest life.'

And what, monks, are the fruits of the highest life? They are the fruit of stream-winning, the fruit of once returning, the fruit of not returning and the fruit of arahantship. These, monks, are called 'the fruits of the highest life.'

(viii). *The highest life* (*b*).

Sāvatthī . . .

I will teach you, monks, both the highest life and the aim thereof. Do ye listen to it. And what, monks, is the highest life? It is just this Ariyan eightfold way. . . . And what, monks, is the aim of the highest life? The destruction of lust, of hatred, of illusion is called 'the aim of the highest life.'

(ix) *The best practice* (*a*).

Sāvatthī . . .

I will teach you, monks, both the best practice[2] and the fruits thereof. Do ye listen to it. And what, monks, is the best practice? It is just this Ariyan eightfold way. . . .

And what, monks, are the fruits of the best practice? They are the fruit of stream-winning . . . of arahantship. These, monks, are called 'the fruit of the best practice.'

(x) *The best practice* (*b*).

Sāvatthī . . .

I will teach you, monks, both the best practice and the aim thereof. Do ye listen to it.

And what, monks, is the best practice? . . . (*as above*). . . .

---

[1] *Brahmaññaŋ.*

[2] *Brahmacariya. Cf. n. supra*, and on cap. vi, i, I also translate elsewhere as 'the holy life.'

And what, monks, is the aim of the best practice? The destruction of lust, of hatred, of illusion is called 'the aim of the best practice.'

Of Other Views—Repetition

(i) *Dispassion.*

Sāvatthī was the occasion . . .

Then a great number of monks came to see the Exalted One . . . who said:

'Monks, if the wanderers holding other views should thus question you: "What is it, friends, for which the holy life is lived under (the rule of) Gotama the recluse?"[1] Thus questioned, monks, ye should reply thus to those wanderers of other views: "With dispassion for its aim, friends,[2] the holy life is lived under the rule of Gotama the recluse."

But if, monks, the wanderers of other views should thus question you: "But, friends, is there a way,[3] is there a practice leading to dispassion?"—thus questioned, monks, thus should ye make reply to those wanderers of other views: "Friends, there is indeed a way, there is indeed a practice leading to dispassion."

And what, monks, is the way, what the practice leading to dispassion? It is just this Ariyan eightfold way, to wit: Right view and the rest . . . right concentration. This, monks, is the way, this is the practice leading to dispassion. Thus questioned, monks, thus should ye make reply to those wanderers holding other views.'

(ii) *Fetter.*

'Monks, if the wanderers holding other views should thus question you: "What is it, friends, for which the holy life is lived under the rule of Gotama the recluse?"—thus questioned, monks, thus should ye make reply: "With the aim of destroying the fetters, friends, the holy life is lived under the rule of Gotama the recluse. . . ."

---

[1] *Cf. supra*, I, 1, v (*kimattha*).

[2] *Rāga-virāg' atthaṃ.*

[3] Text omits *maggo.*

(iii) *Tendency.*

" . . . with the uprooting of tendency[1] for its aim, friends, the holy life is lived under the rule of Gotama the recluse. . . ."

(iv) *The way out.*

. . . " with the thorough comprehension of the way out[2] for its aim, friends, the holy life is lived. . . ."

(v) *Destruction of the āsavas.*

" . . . with the destruction of the āsavas for its aim, friends, the holy life is lived. . . ."

(vi) *Release by knowledge.*

" . . . with the realization of the fruits of knowledge for its aim, friends, the holy life is lived. . . ."

(vii) *Knowing.*

" . . . with knowing and seeing[3] for its aim, friends, the holy life is lived. . . ."

(viii) *Without grasping.*

'Monks, if the wanderers holding views should thus question you: " What is it, friends, for which the holy life is lived under the rule of Gotama the recluse ?"—thus questioned, monks, thus should ye make reply: " With final emancipation without grasping,[4] friends, for its aim the holy life is lived under the rule of Gotama the recluse."

But if, monks, the wanderers of other views should ask: " But, friends, is there a way, is there a practice leading to final emancipation without grasping ?"—thus questioned, monks, thus should ye reply to those wanderers of other

---

[1] *Cf. S.* ii, 252; *Compend.* 20, *Anusayaŋ.*

[2] *Addhāna*; text, *infra*, p. 236. *Comy. saŋsār' addhānaŋ* = *nibbānaŋ.*

[3] *Ñāṇa-dassanā.*

[4] *Anupādā-parinibbāna. Cf. K.S.* iv, 25.

views: "There is indeed a way, friends, there is indeed a practice leading to final emancipation without grasping."

And what, monks, is that way, what that practice leading to final emancipation without grasping?

It is just this Ariyan eightfold way, to wit: Right view and the rest . . . right concentration. This, monks, is the way, this the practice so leading. Thus questioned, monks, thus should ye make reply to those wanderers holding other views.'

The Sun—Repetition

All with Sāvatthi as occasion.

I. (Based on Seclusion . . .)

(i) *Friendship with the lovely.*

Just as, monks, the dawn is the forerunner, the harbinger,[1] of the arising of the sun, so friendship with the lovely is the forerunner, the harbinger, of the arising of the Ariyan eightfold way.

Of a monk who is a friend of the lovely, monks, it may be expected that he will cultivate the Ariyan eightfold way, that he will make much of the Ariyan eightfold way. And how, monks, does a monk who is a friend of the lovely cultivate and make much of the Ariyan eightfold way?

Herein a monk cultivates right view, that is based on seclusion, that is based on dispassion, on cessation, that ends in self-surrender,[2] and so on. . . . He cultivates right concentration which is so based. . . . Even so does a monk who is a friend of the lovely cultivate and make much of the Ariyan eightfold way.

(ii) *Virtue.*

Just as, monks, the dawn is the forerunner, the harbinger, of the arising of the sun, even so possession of virtue[3] is the forerunner, the harbinger, of the arising of the Ariyan eightfold way.

Of a monk who is possessed of virtue it may be expected that he will cultivate . . . the Ariyan eightfold way.

---

[1] *Pubba-nimittaŋ.* [2] *Vossagga.* [3] *Sīla-sampadā.*

(iii) *Desire.*

Just as the dawn . . . even so possession of desire[1] is the forerunner. . . .

(iv) *Self-possession.*

Just as the dawn . . . even so self-possession[2] is the forerunner. . . .

(v) *Insight.*

Just as the dawn . . . even so insight[3] is the forerunner. . . .

(vi) *Earnestness.*

Just as the dawn . . . even so possession of earnestness is the forerunner. . . .

(vii) *Systematic.*

Just as the dawn, monks, is the forerunner, the harbinger, of the arising of the sun, even so possession of systematic[4] thought, monks, is the forerunner, the harbinger, of the arising of the Ariyan eightfold way.

Of a monk who is possessed of systematic thought, monks, it may be expected that he will cultivate, that he will make much of the Ariyan eightfold way. And how, monks, does a monk so possessed cultivate and make much of the Ariyan eightfold way?

Herein a monk cultivates right view, that is based on seclusion, that is based on dispassion, on cessation, that ends in self-surrender, and he makes much of it. . . . He cultivates right aim, right speech, right action, right living, right effort, right mindfulness, he cultivates and makes much of right concentration, that is based on seclusion, on dispassion, on cessation, that ends in self-surrender. That is how a monk who is possessed of systematic thought cultivates and makes much of the Ariyan eightfold way.

---

[1] *Chando.* 'Desire to do good' (*kusalaŋ*). *Comy.*

[2] *Atta-sampadā = sampanna-cittatā.* *Comy.*

[3] *Diṭṭhi-sampadā = ñāṇa-sampatti.* *Comy.*

[4] *Yoniso.*

II. Restraint of Passion

(i) *Friendship with the lovely.*

Just as, monks, the dawn is the forerunner, the harbinger, of the arising of the sun . . . even so friendship with the lovely is the forerunner . . . of the arising of the Ariyan eightfold way.

Of a monk who is a friend of the lovely it may be expected that he will cultivate and make much of the Ariyan eightfold way. How does he do so?

Herein, monks, a monk cultivates right view, which ends in the restraint of passion, which ends in the restraint of hatred, which ends in the restraint of illusion . . . so with the rest. . . . He cultivates right concentration, which so ends. Thus, monks, does a monk who is a friend of the lovely cultivate the Ariyan eightfold way . . . and makes much of it.

(ii) *Virtue.*

Just as the dawn . . . even so possession of virtue is the forerunner . . .

(iii) *Desire.*

Just as the dawn . . . even so possession of desire is the forerunner . . .

(iv) *Self-possession.*

Just as the dawn . . . even so self-possession is the forerunner . . .

(v) *Insight.*

Just as the dawn . . . even so possession of insight . . .

(vi) *Earnestness.*

Just as the dawn . . . even so the possession of earnestness is the forerunner . . .

(vii) *Systematic thought.*

Just as the dawn, monks, is the forerunner, the harbinger, of the arising of the sun, even so possession of systematic thought is the forerunner, the harbinger of the arising of the Ariyan eightfold way.

Of a monk who is possessed of systematic thought it may be expected that he will cultivate and make much of the Ariyan eightfold way.

And how, monks, does a monk cultivate and make much of it?

Herein, monks, a monk cultivates right view, and the rest . . . right concentration, which ends in the restraint of passion, of hatred, of illusion. Thus, monks, does a monk who is a friend of what is lovely cultivate and make much of the Ariyan eightfold way.

The-One-Condition-Repetition.—I

Sāvatthī was the occasion of the following . . .

I. Based on Seclusion[1]

(i) *Friendship with the lovely.*

There is one condition, monks, that is most useful for the arising of the Ariyan eightfold way. What is that condition? It is friendship with the lovely.

Of the monk who is a friend of the lovely, monks, it may be expected that he will cultivate and make much of the Ariyan eightfold way.

And how, monks, does a monk who is a friend of the lovely cultivate and make much of it?

Herein, monks, a monk cultivates right view, which is based on seclusion, on dispassion . . .

(*The same for* ii-vii, viz.: *Virtue, Desire, Self-possession, Insight, Earnestness, Systematic thought.*)

II. Restraint of Passion

(*Exactly the same for each of the above seven sections.*)

The-One-Condition-Repetition.—II

Sāvatthī was the occasion . . .

---

[1] No. 77 of text.

I. Based on Seclusion

(i) *Friendship with the lovely.*

I perceive, monks, no other single condition by which the Ariyan eightfold way, if not yet arisen, can arise, or by which, if arisen, the Ariyan eightfold way can reach perfection of culture, save (the condition of) friendship with the lovely.

Of a monk who is a friend of the lovely we may expect that he will cultivate . . . and make much of the Ariyan eightfold way.

And how does a monk cultivate and make much of the Ariyan eightfold way?

Herein a monk cultivates right view which is based on seclusion . . . he cultivates right concentration, which is based on seclusion, on dispassion, on cessation, which ends in self-surrender. Thus, monks, does a monk who is a friend of the lovely cultivate . . . and make much of the Ariyan eightfold way.

(*The same for* ii-vii *as in previous sections.*)

II. Restraint of Passion

(i) *Friendship with the lovely.*

I perceive, monks, no other single condition . . . (*as above*) . . . save that of friendship with the lovely.

Of a monk who is a friend of the lovely we may expect that he will cultivate and make much of the Ariyan eightfold way. And how? . . .

Herein a monk cultivates right view, which ends in the restraint of passion, in the restraint of hatred, which ends in the restraint of illusion . . . and so forth. He cultivates right concentration which so ends. . . . Thus, monks, does a monk who is a friend of the lovely cultivate and make much of the Ariyan eightfold way.

(*The same for* ii-vii.)

Gangā-Repetition

Sāvatthī was the occasion . . .

I. Based on Seclusion

(i) *Eastward* (*a*).

Just as, monks, the river Ganges flows, slides and tends to the East, even so a monk who cultivates and makes much of the Ariyan eightfold way flows, slides, tends to Nibbāna. And how, monks, by cultivating and making much of the Ariyan eightfold way does a monk flow, slide and tend to Nibbāna?

Herein a monk cultivates right view and the rest . . . right concentration which is based on seclusion, on dispassion, on cessation, which ends in self-surrender. Thus cultivating, thus making much of the Ariyan eightfold way a monk flows, slides and tends to Nibbāna.

(ii-v) *Eastward* (*b*).

Just as, monks, the river Yamunā flows, slides and tends to the East, even so a monk who cultivates. . . Just as the river Acīravatī . . . Just as the river Sarabhū . . . Just as the river Mahī flows, slides and tends to the East, even so a monk who cultivates . . .

(vi) *Eastward* (*c*).

Just as, monks, whatsoever great rivers there be, such as the Ganges, Yamunā, Acīravatī, Sarabhū and Mahī, all of them flow, slide and tend to the East, even so, monks, a monk who cultivates and makes much of the Ariyan eightfold way . . . tends to Nibbāna.

(vii-xii) *Ocean.*

(*The same with* Ocean *for* East.)

II. Restraint of Passion

(*In this section* i-vi *are termed* 'Eastward': vii-xii 'Ocean.')

. . . Herein a monk cultivates right view, which ends in the restraint of lust, hatred and illusion.

III. Plunging into the Deathless[1]

(i-vi) *Eastwards.*

(*As before.*)

(vii-xii) *Ocean.*[2]

. . . Herein a monk cultivates right view, and the rest . . . right concentration, which plunges into the deathless, has its goal[3] in the deathless, ends in the deathless.

IV. Flowing to Nibbāna

(i-vi) *Eastwards.*

(*As above.*)

(vii-xii) *Ocean.*

. . . Herein a monk cultivates right view . . . right concentration, which flows, slides and tends to Nibbāna. Thus cultivating and making much of the Ariyan eightfold way a monk flows, slides and tends to Nibbāna.

CHAPTER V.—EARNESTNESS

I. Tathāgata[4]

(i) *Seclusion.*

Sāvatthī was the occasion . . .

Just as, monks, of all creatures, whether footless or having two, four, or many feet; whether having forms or formless; whether conscious or unconscious, or neither conscious nor unconscious,—of these the Tathāgata, the Arahant, the fully Enlightened One, is reckoned chief;—even so, monks, of all profitable conditions which are rooted in earnestness, which join together[5] in earnestness,—of those conditions earnestness is reckoned chief.

Of the earnest monk it may be expected that he will cultivate, that he will make much of the Ariyan eightfold way. And

---

[1] *Amat' ogadha.*
[2] Text, Nos. 115-126.
[3] *Parāyana.*
[4] Text, No. 139.
[5] *Samosaraṇā.* For similar sections see below and *K.S.* iii, 132 *ff.*

how, monks, does a monk who is earnest cultivate and make much of it?

Herein a monk cultivates right view and the rest . . . right concentration, which is based on seclusion, on dispassion, on cessation, which ends in self-surrender. Thus, monks, a monk who is earnest . . .

(*Similarly treated are the other three sections on* dispassion, *etc.*)[1]

II. Ending in Restraint of Passion

. . . Herein, monks, a monk cultivates right view . . . right concentration, which ends in the restraint of passion, of hatred and illusion.

III. Ending in the Deathless

. . . Herein, monks, a monk cultivates right view . . . right concentration, which plunges into the deathless, has its goal in the deathless, ends in the deathless . . .

IV. Ending in Nibbāna (i)

. . . Herein, monks, a monk cultivates right view . . . right concentration, which flows, slides and tends to Nibbāna.

(ii) *The foot.*[2]

Sāvatthī . . .

Just as, monks, of all the foot-characteristics of such creatures as roam about[3] are joined together in the foot of the elephant, and as the elephant's foot in size is reckoned chief, even so, monks, of all profitable conditions which are rooted in earnestness, which join together in earnestness,—of those conditions earnestness is reckoned chief.

Of the earnest monk it may be expected that he will . . .

(*Each section to be developed in four ways, as at* § i *above.*)

---

[1] So text.

[2] No. 140 of text.

[3] *Jangamānaŋ*. *Cf. M.* i, 184; *S.* i, 86; *K.S.* i, 3. In both places *S. Comy.* reads *jangalānaŋ* (as at *S.* v, 231). *P. Dict.* omits; but Childers *s.v. jangamati*.

(iii) *The roof-peak.*[1]

Sāvatthī . . .

Just as, monks, in a peaked house all the rafters whatsoever go together to the roof-peak, slope to the roof-peak, are joined together in the roof-peak, and of them the peak is reckoned chief,—even so, monks, of all profitable conditions . . . (*as above*).

(iv) *Wood.*

Just as, monks, of all scented woods whatsoever the dark sandal-wood is reckoned chief,—even so of all profitable conditions . . .

(v) *Heart-wood.*

Just as, monks, of all scented heart-woods whatsoever the red sandal-wood is reckoned chief,—even so, monks, of all profitable conditions . . .

(vi) *Jasmine.*

Just as, monks, of all scented flowers whatsoever the jasmine[2] is reckoned chief, even so, monks, of all profitable conditions . . .

(vii) *Prince.*

Just as, monks, all petty princes[3] whatsoever follow in the train[4] of the universal monarch, even so, monks, of all profitable conditions . . .

(viii) *Moon.*

Just as, monks, of all starry bodies whatsoever the radiance does not equal one-sixteenth part of the radiance of the moon; just as the moon is reckoned chief of them, even so, monks, of all profitable conditions . .. .

---

[1] *Cf. S.* ii, 262; *K.S.* ii, 175; *S.* iii, 156; *K.S.* iii, 132.

[2] *Comy. sumana-puppha-gandho.*

[3] Text, *kuṭṭa-rājāno*; *Comy. kuḍḍa-*, but refers to a reading *khudda*, which seems preferable. *Cf. JA.* v, 102, where it is taken as equal to *pāpa-rājā.*

[4] *v.l. anuyuttā* ('subject to ').

(ix) *Sun.*[1]

Just as, monks, in the autumn season, when the sky is opened up and cleared of clouds, the sun, leaping up into the firmament, drives away all darkness, and shines and burns and flashes forth, even so, monks, of all profitable conditions . . .

(x) *Cloth.*[2]

Just as, monks, of all woven cloths whatsoever the cloth of Benares[3] is reckoned chief, even so, monks, of all profitable conditions whatsoever which are rooted in earnestness, which join together in earnestness,—of them all earnestness is reckoned chief.

Of the monk who is earnest it may be expected that he will cultivate, that he will make much of the Ariyan eightfold way. And how, monks, does a monk who is earnest cultivate and make much of the Ariyan eightfold way?

Herein a monk cultivates right view and the rest . . . right concentration, which is based on seclusion, on dispassion, on cessation, which ends in self-surrender.

Thus does the monk who is earnest cultivate and make much of the Ariyan eightfold way.

CHAPTER VI

Deeds requiring Strength

(i) *Strength.*[4]

Just as, monks, whatsoever deeds requiring strength are done, all of them are done in dependence on the earth, with the earth for their support, even so a monk, depending on virtue, supported by virtue,[5] cultivates the Ariyan eightfold

---

[1] *Cf. Itv.* 20; *K.S.* i, 89; *K.S.* iii, 133 *n.*

[2] *Cf. J.P.T.S.*, 1906, p. 132.

[3] *Kāsika-vatthaŋ.*

[4] No. 149 of text (repeated at text 135, 246). *Cf. M.* i, 230 for these two sections.

[5] *Cf.* Mrs. Rhys Davids's *Buddhism,* p. 154.

way, makes much of the Ariyan eightfold way. And how does a monk cultivate and make much of the Ariyan eightfold way?

Herein a monk cultivates right view, and the rest . . . right concentration, which is based on seclusion, on dispassion, on cessation, which ends in self-surrender. That is how a monk depending on virtue, supported by virtue, cultivates and makes much of it.

(ii) *Seed.*[1]

Just as, monks, whatsoever species of seed and vegetation come to growth, increase and maturity, all of them depend on the earth, are supported by the earth; even so, monks, a monk who, depending on virtue, supported by virtue, cultivates and makes much of the Ariyan eightfold way, attains growth, increase and maturity of conditions. And how does a monk, so depending, so supported, in cultivating and making much of the Ariyan eightfold way, attain to growth, increase and maturity of conditions?

Herein a monk cultivates right view . . . right concentration . . . That, monks, is how he attains growth, increase and maturity of conditions.

(iii) *The snake.*[2]

Supported, monks, by Himâlaya, lord of mountains, snakes grow a body and get strength. When they have grown a body and got strength there, they go down to the tarns,[3] thence to the lakes, thence to the small rivers, thence to the great rivers, thence they go down to the sea, the mighty ocean. There they get great size and growth of[4] body.

---

[1] *Comy.* 'Here the five sorts of seed are called *bīja-gāmā*. When they have attained greenness they are called *bhūta-gāmā*.'

[2] (Or eel?) *Infra*, Bk. II, i. *Cf. Buddhi. India*, p. 220 *ff.*; *Indian Serpent Lore* (Vogel), 1927. *Comy.* describes the journey of the mothers from the ocean up to the Himālaya, by way of the five great rivers, to bring forth their young, safe from the attacks of boys, the violence of the sea-waves and *garuḍas* or *garuḷas* (? eagles, albatross, or rocs).

[3] *Cf. S.* ii, 30. *Kussubbhe* (*Sn.* 720, *kussobbha*), *ku-s-sobbha*; *ku-n-nadi*; the prefix implies inferiority; hence *kupuriso*, a rogue; *ku-diṭṭhi* = *micchā-diṭṭhi*.

[4] *Comy.* 'A size of a hundred or a thousand fathoms!'

Just so, monks, a monk who, depending on virtue, supported by virtue, cultivates and makes much of the Ariyan eightfold way, attains growth, increase and maturity of conditions. And how, monks, does he, so depending, so supported, so cultivate and so attain?

Herein a monk cultivates right view . . .

That is how he attains growth, increase and maturity of conditions.[1]

(iv) *The tree.*

'Suppose a tree, monks, that inclines to the east, slopes to the east, tends to the east. When cut down at the root, in what direction would it fall?'

'As it slopes, as it inclines, as it tends, lord.'

'Well, monks, even so a monk, cultivating and making much of the Ariyan eightfold way, inclines to Nibbāna, slopes to Nibbāna, tends to Nibbāna. And how does he so incline, slope and tend?

Herein a monk cultivates . . .

That is how . . . he inclines, slopes and tends[2] to Nibbāna.'

(v) *The pot.*

Just as a pot, if overset, empties out its water, and cannot take it in[3] again, even so a monk who cultivates and makes much of the Ariyan eightfold way, empties out ill, unprofitable states and cannot take them in again.[4]

And how, monks, can a monk, by cultivating and making much of the Ariyan eightfold way, empty out ill, unprofitable states and not take them in again?

Herein a monk cultivates right view . . . right concentration, which is based on seclusion, on dispassion, on cessation,

---

[1] *Comy.* interprets thus: 'The Himālaya is the fourfold perfect purity of virtue. The young snakes are the earnest students (*yogâvacarā*). The tarns, etc., are the Ariyan path. The Ocean is Nibbāna. Growth, maturity, etc., are the *abhiññā*.

[2] *Pabbhāro hoti* ('gravitates').

[3] *Nikkujjo vamateva udakaŋ, no paccāvamati.* But *cf. A.* v, 337, where text reads *nikkujjo 'va tam eva [udakaŋ] no vantaŋ pacc.*

[4] *Comy. na antopavesati.*

which ends in self-surrender. Thus cultivating and making much of the Ariyan eightfold way he empties out ill, unprofitable states and cannot take them in again.

(vi) *Bearded wheat.*[1]

Suppose, monks, the spike of bearded wheat or bearded barley be well aimed. When pressed by hand or foot, it is possible that it will pierce hand or foot and draw blood. Why so? Because, monks, the spike is well aimed.

Even so, monks, owing to the right aim of way-culture it is possible that a monk will pierce ignorance, will draw knowledge, will realize Nibbāna. Why so? Because, monks, his view is well aimed. And how, monks, does a monk by view well aimed, by well aimed way-culture so pierce[2] ignorance, draw knowledge and realize Nibbāna?

Herein a monk cultivates . . . (*as above*). Thus by well aimed view, by well aimed way-culture . . . he realizes Nibbāna.

(vii) *The sky.*[3]

Just as, monks, divers winds blow in the sky,—some winds blow from the east, some from the west, some from the north, some from the south: winds dusty, winds dustless, cool winds and hot winds, winds soft and boisterous, even so, monks, when a monk cultivates the Ariyan eightfold way, makes much of the Ariyan eightfold way, then in him the four stations of mindfulness[4] by culture reach fulfilment, the four best efforts, the four bases of psychic power, the five faculties, the five powers and the seven limbs of wisdom by culture reach fulfilment.

And how, monks, when a monk cultivates the Ariyan eightfold way . . . do the four stations of mindfulness, and the rest, by culture reach fufilment?

Herein a monk cultivates right view . . . and the rest . . . right concentration.

Thus cultivating . . . the four stations of mindfulness, and the rest, by culture reach fulfilment in him.

---

[1] *Cf. supra*, I, 9.

[2] Text *bhindati* here.

[3] As at *S.* iv, 218; *K.S.* iv, 146

[4] *Cf. K.S.* iv, 259 *ff.*

(viii) *The rain-cloud* (*a*).

Just as, monks, in the last month of the hot season[1] the dust and dirt fly up,[2] and then out of due season a great rain-cloud in a moment[3] lays and makes them vanish,—even so does a monk who cultivates and makes much of the Ariyan eightfold way lay and cause to vanish the ill unprofitable states that rise from time to time. And how does he do so?

Herein a monk cultivates . . . So cultivating, so making much of the Ariyan eightfold way, he lays and causes to vanish the ill, unprofitable states that rise and rise again.[4]

(ix) *The rain-cloud* (*b*).

Just as, monks, from time to time a strong wind scatters and causes to vanish a great mass of clouds that has arisen, even so a monk who cultivates and makes much of the Ariyan eightfold way from time to time scatters and causes to vanish the ill, unprofitable states that rise and rise again. And how does he do so?

Herein a monk cultivates right view, and the rest . . . right concentration, that is based on seclusion, on dispassion, on cessation, that ends in self-surrender. Thus cultivating, thus making much of the Ariyan eightfold way does a monk from time to time scatter and cause to vanish the ill, unprofitable states that rise and rise again.

(x) *The ship.*[5]

Just as, monks, in the case of a sea-faring vessel rigged with masts and stays and stranded on the bank, for six months it is worn by the water,[6] while in the dry season its rigging is

---

[1] *Cf.* text 321 (*gimhānaŋ pacchime māse*)=*Āsāḷhi-māse* (our June-July). *Comy.*

[2] Text *uggataŋ*. *Comy. ūhataŋ*, explained as *uddhaŋ gataŋ*.

[3] *Ṭhānaso* (lit. there and then, on the spot); *VM.* i, 268, *khaṇen' eva.*

[4] *Cf. Expos.*, p. 90.

[5] *Cf. S.* iii, 155; *K.S.* iii, 131, where I would correct as here; *A.* iv, 127.

[6] Text *pariyenāya* (? *pariyāyena*, whirling round and round); *v.l. pariyādāya* (*S.* iii; *A.* iv). *Comy.* refers to previous comment on *S.* iii, where it has *mahāsamudde pariyādānaŋ* (the wasting away in the ocean) and *mahāsamudd' odakena khajjamānānaŋ khandhānaŋ* (the timbers being eaten away by the water).

spoiled by wind and sun: then, overstrung[1] by a shower in the rainy season, it is easily weakened and rots away,—just so, in a monk who cultivates and makes much of the Ariyan eightfold way right easily the fetters are weakened and rot away. And how, monks, in one so cultivating and making much of the Ariyan eightfold way are the fetters weakened and rot away?

Herein a monk cultivates right view . . . right concentration, that is based on seclusion, on dispassion, on cessation, that ends in self-surrender. That, monks, is how . . . the fetters rot away.

(xi) *For all comers.*[2]

Suppose, monks, a guest-house. Thither come folk from the eastern quarter, who take up residence therein. From the western, northern and southern quarters they come and dwell therein, noblemen and brahmins, commoners and serfs.[3] Even so, monks, a monk who cultivates the Ariyan eightfold way, who makes much of the Ariyan eightfold way, by full comprehension realizes those states which are by full comprehension to be fully understood.[4] Those states that are to be abandoned by full comprehension he so abandons: those states that are to be realized by full comprehension he so realizes: those states that are to be cultivated by full comprehension, by full comprehension he cultivates.

What, monks, are the states to be realized by full comprehension?

To that question you must reply: 'It is the five factors that have to do with grasping.'[5] What five? They are these: The body-factor that has to do with grasping, the factor of feeling that has to do with grasping, the perception-factor . . . the activities-factor . . . the consciousness-factor that has to do with grasping.

And what, monks, are the states that are to be abandoned

---

[1] Text *abhipavuṭṭhāni*; at *A.* and *S.* iii, *-pavaṭṭāni*.

[2] *Āgantukā*. *Cf. S.* iv, 219; *K.S.* iv, 147 (where it represents the body). *Comy.* 'built in the midst of a merit-desiring town.'

[3] *Vessā, suddā.*

[4] *Cf. S.* iv, 29. *Abhiññā-pariññeyyā.*

[5] *K.S.* iii, 41; *Compend.*, p. 185.

by full comprehension? They are ignorance, and lust of becoming. These are the states to be abandoned by full comprehension

And what, monks, are the states that are to be realized by full comprehension? They are knowledge and release. These are the states to be realized by full comprehension.

And what, monks, are the states that are to be cultivated by full comprehension? They are calm and insight. These are the state to be cultivated by full comprehension.

And how does a monk, cultivating and making much of the Ariyan eightfold way, realize, abandon, fully comprehend and cultivate (these states)?

Herein a monk cultivates right view, and the rest . . . right concentration. Thus does he realize . . . abandon, fully comprehend and cultivate those states . . . that are to be cultivated by full comprehension.

(xii) *The river.*[1]

'Suppose, monks, the river Ganges, that flows, slides and tends towards the east, and there comes a great crowd of folk, armed with pick and basket, saying: "We will make this river Ganges flow, slide and tend towards the west." What think ye, monks? Would that great crowd of folk make the river Ganges flow, slide and tend towards the west?'

'Surely not, lord.'

'And why not?'

'Because, lord, the river Ganges flows, slides and tends towards the east, it were no easy thing to make it flow, slide and tend towards the west; insomuch that fatigue and vexation would be the lot of that great crowd of folk.'

'Just so, monks, if the rājah's royal ministers or his friends or boon companions or kinsmen or blood relatives were to come to a monk who is cultivating and making much of the Ariyan eightfold way, and were to seek to entice him with wealth, saying: "Come, good man! Why should these yellow robes torment you? Why parade about with shaven crown

---

[1] *Cf. S.* iv, 191; v, 300; *K.S.* iv, 124.

and bowl? Come! Return to the lower life and enjoy possessions and do deeds of merit,"—for that monk so cultivating and making much of the Ariyan eightfold way return to the life is impossible. Why so? Because, monks, that monk's heart has for many a long day been bent on detachment, inclined to detachment, turned towards detachment, so that there is no possibility for him to return to the lower life.

And how, monks, does a monk cultivate and make much of the Ariyan eightfold way?

Herein a monk cultivates right view, and the rest . . . right concentration, that is based on seclusion, on dispassion, on cessation, that ends in self-surrender. That is how a monk cultivates and makes much of the Ariyan eightfold way.'

CHAPTER VII.—ON LONGING

Sāvatthī was the occasion [for the following] . . .

(i) *Longing.*[1]

(*a*) Full Comprehension

Monks, there are these three longings. What three? The longing for sensual delights, the longing for becoming, the longing for the holy life.[2] These, monks, are the three longings. It is for the full comprehension of these three longings, monks, that the Ariyan eightfold way must be cultivated. What Ariyan eightfold way?

---

[1] *Esanā*; § 161 of text.

[2] *Comy.* takes this to mean 'holy life with wrong views'; but even to long for the 'holy life' is a subtle fault, according to the Master's teaching. The word *brahmacariya* (best practice) had degenerated, by the time of Buddhaghosa (*cf. VibhA.* 504) to mean only 'celibacy' or 'chastity' (*methuna-virati*); but see above, I, 4, vii. At *Vibh.* 366 it is defined as holding contrary views (*vipariyesa-gāho*) such as 'the world is eternal,' etc.! Or should we translate 'longings of (incidental to) the holy life'?

Herein a monk cultivates right view, which is based on seclusion. . . . It is for the full comprehension of these three longings that the Ariyan eightfold way . . .

Herein a monk cultivates right concentration, which ends in the destruction of lust, of hatred, of illusion.

He cultivates . . . right concentration, which plunges into the deathless,[1] which has the deathless for its aim, which has the deathless for its end.

He cultivates . . . right concentration, which flows to Nibbāna, which slides to Nibbāna, which tends to Nibbāna.

(*b*) Realization

Monks, there are these three longings. What three? The longing for sensual delights, the longing for becoming, the longing for the holy life. It is for the realization of (the meaning of) these three longings that the Ariyan eightfold way is to be cultivated. . . .

(*All to the end of* § 11 *to be expanded as above*).[2]

(*c*) Wearing Out

Monks, there are these three longings. What three? . . . It is for the wearing out of these three longings that the Ariyan eightfold way . . .

(*d*) Abandoning

Monks, there are these three longings. . . . It is for the abandoning of these three longings that the Ariyan eightfold way . . .

(ii) *Conceits* (*a-d*).

Monks, there are these three conceits.[3] What three? The 'better than I' conceit, the 'equal am I' conceit, the 'worse am I' conceit. These are the three conceits. It is

---

[1] *Cf. Pts. of Contr.*, 363.

[2] So text of Burmese MSS. Sinhalese omit.

[3] *Vidhā* (modes or forms of false opinion and strife springing from *māno*). *Cf. K.S.* iii, 42 *n.*; *Vibh.* 367; *Budd. Psych. Eth.*, 298.

for the full comprehension of these three conceits, monks, that the Ariyan eightfold way is to be cultivated. What Ariyan eightfold way?

Herein a monk cultivates and makes much of right view. . . .

(iii) *Āsava* (*a-d*).

Monks, there are three āsavas.[1] What three? The āsava of sensual delight, the āsava of becoming, the āsava of nescience. These are the three. It is for the full comprehension of these three āsavas that the Ariyan eightfold way is to be cultivated. . . .

(iv) *Becoming* (*a-d*).

Monks there are three becomings. What three? Becoming in the sensuous world, becoming in the world of form, becoming in the formless world. These are the three. It is for the full comprehension of these three becomings that the Ariyan eightfold way is to be cultivated. . . .

(v) *Suffering* (*a-d*).

Monks, there are these three forms of suffering.[2] What three? The sort of suffering caused by pain, the sort caused by the activities, the sort of suffering caused by the changeable nature of things. These are the three. It is for the full comprehension of these three forms of suffering that the Ariyan eightfold way is to be cultivated. . . .

(vi) *Obstructions* (*a-d*).

Monks, there are these three (mental) obstructions.[3] What three? The obstruction of lust, the obstruction of hatred,

---

[1] For this word, translated 'cankers' by Lord Chalmers in his *Further Dialogues*, see Introduction to *K.S.* iii. With the addition of *diṭṭhi* there are sometimes four.

[2] *Dukkhatā*. *Cf. S.* iv, 259; *K.S.* iv, 175; *Pts. of Contr.*, 316.

[3] *Khilā*, fallow or unploughed land. At *Vibh.* 377 five *ceto-khilā*, viz.: Doubt and wavering in the Teacher, Norm, Order and training; peevishness, etc., to co-disciples. Not to be confused with *khīlā* (bar or post).

the obstruction of illusion. These are the three. It is for the full comprehension of these three obstructions that the Ariyan eightfold way is to be cultivated. . . .

(vii) *Stain* (*a-d*).

Monks, there are these three stains. What three? The stain of lust, the stain of hatred, the stain of illusion. These are the three. It is for the full comprehension of these three stains that the Ariyan eightfold way must be cultivated. . . .

(viii) *Pains* (*a-d*).

Monks, there are these three pains.[1] What three? The pain of lust, the pain of hatred, the pain of illusion. These are the three. It is for the full comprehension of these three pains that the Ariyan eightfold way must be cultivated. . . .

(ix) *Feelings* (*a-d*).

Sāvatthī . . .

Monks, there are these three feelings. What three? Feeling that is pleasant, feeling that is painful, feeling that is neither pleasant nor painful. These are the three. It is for the full comprehension of these three feelings that the Ariyan eightfold way must be cultivated. . . .

(x) *Craving* (*a-d*).

Sāvatthī . . .

Monks, there are these three cravings. What three? The craving for sensual delights, the craving for becoming, the craving for ceasing to become.[2] These are the three. It is for the full comprehension of these three cravings, for their realization, for their wearing down, for their abandoning that the Ariyan eightfold way must be cultivated. What Ariyan eightfold way?

---

[1] *Nighā.* *Comy.* explains thus: 'A term for pains which destroy, in whomsoever they arise' (*taŋ purisaŋ nihanti*).

[2] *Vibhava* (sometimes 'excessive wealth' = 'accentuated existence'). *Cf. Dialog.* iii, 208 and compare with § 1, where its parallel is *brahmacariya.* Thus it would here mean an annihilationist in view.

Herein a monk cultivates right view, which is based on seclusion, on dispassion, on cessation, which ends in self-surrender. . . . He cultivates right concentration which is based . . .

It is for the full comprehension, realization, wearing down and abandoning of these three cravings that the Ariyan eightfold way must be cultivated

(xi) *Thirst* (*b-d*).

Monks, there are these three thirsts.[1] What three? (*as above*). It is for the full comprehension, realization, wearing down and abandoning of these three thirsts that the Ariyan eightfold way must be cultivated. What Ariyan eightfold way?

Herein a monk cultivates right view . . . right concentration, which is based on seclusion . . . which ends in the destruction of lust, of hatred, of illusion . . . which plunges into the deathless, which has the deathless for its goal, which ends in the deathless . . . which flows to Nibbāna, which slides to Nibbāna, which tends to Nibbāna. It is for the full comprehension . . . that the Ariyan eightfold way must be cultivated.

CHAPTER VIII.—THE FLOOD

Sāvatthī was the occasion (for the following). . . .

(i) *The flood.*[2]

Monks, there are these four floods. What four? The flood of sensual desire,[3] the flood of becoming, the flood of view,[4] the flood of nescience.[5] These are the four. It is for the full

---

[1] *Tasinā* (=*taṇhā*), *cf. Dhp.* 342. This is not in Sinh. MSS.

[2] *Ogha; cf. S.* iv, 175; *K.S.* iv, 110. *Five* at *S.* i, 126. *Cf. Buddh. Psych. Eth.*, p. 308 *n.*

[3] *Comy. chanda-rāga.*

[4] *Comy.* The sixty-two heretical views.

[5] *Comy.* 'Of the four truths.'

comprehension, realization, wearing down and abandoning of these four floods that the Ariyan eightfold way must be cultivated.

(ii) *Bond.*

Monks, there are these four bonds. What four ? The bond of sensual desire, the bond of becoming, the bond of view, the bond of nescience. These are the four. It is for the full comprehension . . .

(iii) *Grasping.*[1]

Monks, there are these four graspings. What four ? The grasping of[2] sensual desire, the grasping of view, the grasping of rite and ritual, the grasping of the self-heresy. These are the four. It is for the full comprehension . . .

(iv) *(Bodily) ties.*

Monks, there are these four (bodily) ties.[3] What four ? The bodily tie of covetousness, the bodily tie of malevolence, the bodily tie of contagion of rite and ritual, the bodily tie of tendency to dogmatic view.[4] These are the four bodily ties. It is for the full comprehension . . .

(v) *Tendency.*

Monks, there are these seven tendencies. What seven ? The tendency to sensual lust, the tendency to resentment, the tendency to view, the tendency to doubt and wavering, the tendency to conceit, the tendency to nescience. These are the seven. It is for the full comprehension of . . .

(vi) *The sense-pleasures.*

Monks, there are these five pleasures of sense.[5] What five ? There are objects cognizable by the eye, objects desirable, desirable, pleasant, delightful and dear, passion-fraught, inciting to lust. There are sounds cognizable by the ear . . .

---

[1] *Yoga.* [2] *I.e.* arising from.
[3] *Ganthā.* *Cf. Buddh. Psych. Eth.*, § 1139; *Asl.* 377.
[4] *Saccâbhiniveso.* To say '*this* is the truth.' *Comy.*
[5] *K.S.* iv, 56.

scents cognizable by the nose . . . savours cognizable by the tongue . . . contacts cognizable by the body, desirable, pleasant, delightful and dear, passion-fraught, inciting to lust. These, monks, are the five pleasures of sense. It is for the full comprehension . . .

(vii) *Hindrances.*

Monks, there are these five hindrances.[1] What five? The hindrance of sensual desire, the hindrance of malevolence, the hindrance of sloth and torpor, the hindrance of excitement and flurry,[2] the hindrance of doubt and wavering.[3] These are the five hindrances. It is for the full comprehension of these five . . .

(viii) *Factors.*

Monks, there are these five factors of grasping.[4] What five? The factor of grasping of[5] body, the factor of grasping of feeling, the factor of grasping of perception, the factor of grasping of the activities, the factor of grasping of consciousness. These are the five. It is for the full comprehension . . .

(ix) *The lower set (of fetters).*

Monks, there is this set of five lower fetters.[6] What five? The individual-group-view,[7] doubt and wavering, contagion of rite and ritual, desire and lust, malevolence. These are the five. It is for the full comprehension . . .

(x) *The higher set (of fetters).*

Monks, there is this set of five higher fetters.[8] What five? Lust of form, lust of the formless, conceit, excitement, nescience. These are the five. It is for the full comprehension, the

---

[1] *Nīvaraṇāni.* *D.* iii, 49; *Buddh. Psych. Eth.*, 310.

[2] *Do.* 119-20, lit. 'fidgeting and nerves.'

[3] *Do.* 121.

[4] *Cf. K.S.* iii, 16-18, 41-42.

[5] *I.e.* dealing with.

[6] *Orambhāgiya*, those concerned with the lower stages of life.

[7] *Cf. K.S.* iii, 86 *n.*

[8] *Uddhambhāgiya*, the second five, by abandoning which the goal is reached.

realization, the wearing out and abandoning of these five fetters of the higher sort that the Ariyan eightfold way must be cultivated. What Ariyan eightfold way?

Herein a monk cultivates right view, that is based on seclusion, on dispassion, on cessation, that ends in self-surrender. It is for the full comprehension, monks, of these five fetters of the higher sort that this Ariyan eightfold way must be cultivated.

Just as, monks, the river Ganges flows to the east, slides to the east, tends to the east . . .[1]

There are these five fetters of the higher sort . . . (*as above*). . . . And how does a monk cultivate the Ariyan eightfold way?

Herein a monk cultivates right view . . . right concentration, that ends in the restraint of lust, of hatred, of illusion; that plunges into the deathless, that has the deathless for its goal, that ends in the deathless; that flows to Nibbāna, that slides to Nibbāna, that tends to Nibbāna.

It is for the full comprehension, for the realization, for the wearing out and abandoning of these five fetters of the higher sort, monks, that this Ariyan eightfold way must be cultivated.

---

[1] Text abbreviates.

BOOK II [*CHAPTER XLVI*]

KINDRED SAYINGS ON THE LIMBS OF WISDOM[1]

CHAPTER I

THE MOUNTAIN

(i) *Himâlaya.*[2]

SUPPORTED, monks, by Himâlaya, lord of mountains, snakes grow a body and get strength. When they have grown a body and got strength there, they go down to the tarns, thence to the lakes, thence to the small rivers, thence to the great rivers, thence they go down to the sea, they go down to the mighty ocean, and there they win to greatness and growth of body.

Just so, monks, a monk supported by virtue, fixed in virtue, cultivating the seven limbs of wisdom and making much of them, wins to greatness and growth in conditions.[3] And how does a monk, so supported, so fixed in virtue, cultivating the seven limbs of wisdom, and making much of them, win to greatness and growth in conditions?

Herein a monk cultivates the limb of wisdom that is mindfulness, which is based on seclusion, on dispassion, on cessation, which ends in self-surrender.

He cultivates investigation of the Norm, the limb of wisdom that is so based. He cultivates the limb of wisdom that is energy and is so based. He cultivates the limb of wisdom that is tranquillity that is so based. He cultivates the limb of wisdom that is concentration that is so based. He cultivates the limb of wisdom that is equanimity, that is based on seclusion, on dispassion, on cessation, that ends in self-surrender.

That is how a monk, supported by virtue, fixed in virtue, by

---

[1] Text, pp. 63-140. [2] *Cf. supra*, I, 6, iii. Are *nāgā* here eels?
[3] *Comy.* refers to *Kosala-Saŋyutta*; *S.* i, 68-102; *K.S.* i, 93 *ff.*

cultivating the seven limbs of wisdom, by making much of the seven limbs of wisdom, wins to greatness and growth in conditions.

(ii) *Body.*

I

Sāvatthī . . .

Just as this[1] body, monks, is supported by material food and stands in dependence on it, stands not without it,—even so, monks, the five hindrances are supported by (their own) material food, stand in dependence on it, stand not without it.

And what, monks, is food for the arising of sensual lust not yet arisen, or for the increase and growth of sensual lust that has arisen? It is the alluring feature[2] of things. Unsystematic attention to that is the food for the arising of sensual lust not yet arisen, and for the increase and growth of sensual lust that has already arisen.

And what, monks, is food for the arising of malevolence not yet arisen, or food for the increase and growth of malevolence that has already arisen? It is the repulsive feature[3] of things. Unsystematic attention to that is this food for the arising of malevolence not yet arisen. . . .

And what, monks, is food for the arising of sloth and torpor not yet arisen, or for the increase and growth of sloth and torpor that has already arisen? It is regret, drowsiness, languor, surfeit after meals, torpidity of mind.[4] Unsystematic attention to that is this food for the arising of sloth and torpor. . . .

And what, monks, is food for the arising of excitement and flurry not yet arisen, or for the increase and growth of excitement and flurry that have already arisen? It is non-tran-

---

[1] *Cf. Expos.*, 204.

[2] *Subha-nimittaŋ*; *infra*, text 103. *Cf. Pts. of Contr., App.* 387, 'The alluring feature (which to one who does not practise systematic thought (*ayoniso manasikarontassa*) is a snare and danger)'; *K.S.* i, 239. The threefold sign is the deceptive appearance of permanence, happiness and soul, to be abolished by the cultivation of the signless (*animittaŋ*).

[3] *Paṭigha-nimittaŋ* (at *A.* i, 3, *asubha-nimittaŋ*).

[4] *Arati, tandī, vijambhitā, bhatta-sammado, cetaso līnattaŋ.* See *Vibh.* 352; *Vibh.* 272, 478; *SA.* on *S.* i, 7; *JA.* vi, 57, etc.

quillity of mind. Unsystematic attention to that is this food for the arising of excitement and flurry. . . .

And what, monks, is food for the arising of doubt and wavering not yet arisen, or for the increase and growth of doubt and wavering that have already arisen? It is things which are based on[1] doubt and wavering. Unsystematic attention to that, monks, is this food for the arising of doubt and wavering that have not yet arisen, and for the increase and growth of doubt and wavering that have already arisen.

Just as this body, monks, is supported by material food and stands in dependence of it, stands not without it,—even so, monks, the five hindrances are supported by (their own) material food, stand in dependence on food, stand not without food.

II

Just as this body, monks, is supported by material food, and stands in dependence on it, stands not without it,—even so, monks, the seven limbs of wisdom are supported by (their own) material food, stand in dependence on it, stand not without food.

And what, monks, is food for the arising of the limb of wisdom that is mindfulness not yet arisen, or for the cultivation and fulfilment of the limb of wisdom which is mindfulness that has already arisen? There are, monks, things that are based on the limb of wisdom which is mindfulness. Systematic attention thereto, if made much of, is this food for the arising of . . .

And what, monks, is food for the arising of the limb of wisdom which is searching of the Norm not yet arisen, or for the cultivation and fulfilment of it if already arisen? There are, monks, things good and bad, things blameworthy and things not blameworthy, things mean and things exalted, things resembling darkness and things resembling light.[2] Systematic attention thereto, if made much of, is this food for the arising . . .

And what, monks, is food for the arising of the limb of

---

[1] *Ṭhāniyā.*

[2] *Cf. Dialog.* i, 225; *D.* ii, 215. *Comy. sadisa-vipāka-koṭṭhāsā.*

wisdom which is energy not yet arisen, or for the cultivation and fulfilment thereof if already arisen? There is, monks, the element of putting forth effort,[1] the element of exertion,[2] the element of striving.[3] Systematic attention thereto, if made much of, is this food for the arising . . .

And what, monks, is food for the arising of the limb of wisdom which is zest if not yet arisen, or for the cultivation and fulfilment thereof if already arisen? There are, monks, things based on the limb of wisdom that is zest. Systematic attention thereto, if made much of, is this food for the arising . . .

And what, monks, is food for the arising of the limb of wisdom which is tranquillity if not yet arisen, or for its cultivation and fulfilment if already arisen? There are, monks, tranquillity of body and tranquillity of mind. Systematic attention thereto, if made much of, is this food for the arising . . .

And what, monks, is food for the arising of the limb of wisdom which is concentration if not yet arisen, or for its cultivation and fulfilment if already arisen? There are, monks, sights that calm, that bewilder not.[4] Systematic attention thereto, if made much of, is this food for the arising . . .

And what, monks, is food for the arising of the limb of wisdom which is equanimity if not yet arisen, or for its cultivation and fulfilment if already arisen? There are, monks, things based on the limb of wisdom[5] that is equanimity. Systematic attention thereto, if made much of, is this food

---

[1] *Ārambha-dhātu*. *Cf. Expos.*, 192. *Comy. paṭhama-viriya* (*dhātu* = source, seed).

[2] *Nikkama*. *Cf. S.* i, 194; *VM.* i, 132 + *Comy. kosajjato nikkhantattā tato balavataraŋ*.

[3] *Parakkama*. *VM.* + *Comy. paraŋ ṭhānaŋ akkamanato pi balavataraŋ*.

[4] *Samatha-* and *avyagga-nimittaŋ* (lit. the mark of calm and non-distraction). *Cf. S.* i, 96, *abyagga-manaso naro*. The latter, according to *Comy.*, a synonym of the former. For details *cf. VM.* i, 134.

[5] *Comy.* 'Things of middle state, indifference.'

for the arising of the limb of wisdom which is equanimity if not yet arisen, or for the cultivation and fulfilment thereof if it has already arisen.

(iii) *Virtue.*[1]

Monks, whatsoever monks are possessed of virtue, possessed of concentration, possessed of insight, of release, of release by knowledge and insight—the very sight of such brings much profit, I declare.

The very hearing about[2] such monks brings much profit, I declare. To visit such, to sit beside[3] them, to remember such,[4] to follow such in giving up the world[5] brings great profit, I declare.

What is the cause of that? On hearing the teaching of such monks one dwells aloof in two forms of aloofness, to wit: of body and of mind. Such an one, so dwelling aloof, remembers that Norm-teaching and turns it over in his mind.

When a monk, so dwelling aloof, remembers and turns over in his mind the teaching of the Norm, it is then that the limb of wisdom which is mindfulness is established[6] in that monk. When he cultivates the limb of wisdom which is mindfulness, then it is that the monk's culture of it comes to perfection. Thus he, dwelling mindful, with full recognition[7] investigates and applies insight[8] to that teaching of the Norm and comes to close scrutiny of it.

Now, monks, at such time as a monk, dwelling thus mindful, with full recognition investigates and applies insight to that

---

[1] For this section see *Vibh.* 227; *VibhA.* 310.

[2] According to *Comy.* 'not listening to, but having good report of such and such.'

[3] *Comy.* 'questioning them about the Norm.'

[4] *Cf. Pugg.* iii, 13, iv, 23; *Itiv.*, p. 106, *anussaraṇaŋ.*

[5] *Anupabbajjaŋ. Comy.* mentions the Elders Mahākassapa, Chanda-gutta, Suriyagutta, Assagutta, Yonakadhammarakkhita, Tissa (younger brother of Dharmasoka) and Mahinda.

[6] *Āraddho.*

[7] *Paññāya* is to be taken as gerund, not as a noun.

[8] *Pavicarati. Comy. tattha ñāṇaŋ carāpeti.*

teaching of the Norm, then it is that the limb of wisdom which is Norm-investigation is established in that monk. It is when he cultivates the limb of wisdom which is Norm-investigation that, as he comes to close scrutiny of it, by his culture of it, it comes to perfection. As with full recognition he investigates and applies insight to that Norm-teaching, then unshaken energy[1] is established in him.

Now, monks, at such time as unshaken energy is established in a monk who with full recognition is investigating, applying insight and coming to close scrutiny of that Norm-teaching, then it is that the limb of wisdom which is energy is established in him. When he cultivates this limb of wisdom, at such time, by culture of it, does it come to perfection in that monk. In him who has energy established there arises zest, which is free from carnal taint.[2]

Now, monks, when zest free from carnal taint arises in a monk who has energy established, then it is that the limb of wisdom which is zest is established in him. When he cultivates this limb of wisdom, at such time, by culture of it, does it come to perfection in him. Of one who is zestful body is tranquil and mind is tranquil.

Now, monks, when a monk who is zestful has body and mind tranquillized, then it is that the limb of wisdom which is tranquillity is established in him. When he cultivates this, at such time, by his culture of it, it comes to perfection in him. Happy is he whose body is tranquillized. Of him that is happy the mind is concentrated.

Now, monks, when the mind is concentrated in a monk whose body is tranquillized, at such time the limb of wisdom which is concentration is established in that monk. When he cultivates this limb of wisdom, by his culture of it does it come to perfection. He is now thorough overseer of his mind thus calmed.

Now, monks, when he becomes a careful looker-on of his mind thus calmed, then it is that the limb of wisdom which is

---

1 *Asallīnaṃ*. *Cf. D.* ii, 157; *S.* iv, 125.

2 *Cf. S.* iv, 219; *K.S.* iv, 147. *Nirāmisā pīti.*

equanimity is established in a monk. When he cultivates it, at such time by his culture of it does it come to perfection.

Now, monks, when the seven limbs of wisdom are thus cultivated, thus made much of, seven fruits, seven advantages[1] may be looked for. What seven?

In this very life, beforehand, he establishes realization[2]: and if he do not so beforehand,[3] in this very life, at any rate he establishes realization at the time of his death.

And if in this very life, beforehand, he do not establish realization, nor do so at the time of death, then, through having worn down the five fetters of the lower sort, he wins release midway.[4]

But if he do not establish perfect insight, beforehand, in this very life, nor yet at the time of death, and if he, by wearing down the five fetters of the lower sort, win not release midway, —then at any rate, after having worn down the five fetters of the lower sort, he wins release by reduction of his (allotted) time.[5]

But if he (do none of these) . . . at any rate, by having worn down the five fetters of the lower sort, he wins release without much trouble.[6]

Again, if he (do none of these) . . . at any rate, by having

---

[1] Text *infra*, 237.

[2] *Aññaŋ* = gnosis, realization of arahantship.

[3] Text *paṭihacca*; probably influenced by *upahacca* following. This should be (as *v.ll.*) *paṭikacca* (see *Pāli Dict.* and *K.S.* i, 319), which is equal to *pubbe yeva* or *paṭhamaŋ yeva*. *Cf. UdA.* 347. *Comy.* reads *paṭigacca*, explaining 'before his time of death has reached him' he knows for certain. Again at text 204-5. (*Paṭihacca* would mean 'knocking against' [?]).

[4] *Antarā-parinibbāyī* (*infra*, text 201). He is a non-returner and completes his course of existence in Brahma-loka, where time is beyond our conception or computation, before half his life there is finished.

[5] *Upahacca-parinibbāyī*. *Cf. Pts. of Contr.*, p. 158. *Comy.* 'He spends another five hundred *kalpas*(!) and so attains arahantship.'

[6] *Cf. PuggA.* (p. 199 of *J.P.T.S.*, 1914); *Expos.* 207. *Asankhāra*, lit. without *sankhārā*, activities or aggregates (? without a residue of karma); but according to *Comy. appayogena*, without effort (*cf. Dialog.* iii, 227); but it would seem to be more like *an-upādi-sesa-nibbāna*. So also with regard to the following term.

worn down the five fetters of the lower sort, then he wins release with some trouble.[1]

Again, if he (do none of these) . . . at any rate, by having worn down the five fetters of the lower sort, then he is 'one who goes upstream,'[2] and he goes to the Pure Abodes.[3]

Thus, monks, when the seven limbs of wisdom are thus cultivated, these seven fruits, these seven advantages may be looked for.

(iv) *Practice.*

On a certain occasion the venerable Sāriputta was staying near Sāvatthī, at Jeta Grove, in Anāthapiṇḍika's Park.

Then the venerable Sāriputta addressed the monks, saying: 'Brother monks!'

'Yes, friend,' replied those monks to the venerable Sāriputta.

The venerable Sāriputta said this:

'Friends, there are these seven limbs of wisdom. What seven? The limb of wisdom that is mindfulness, that which is Norm-investigation, that which is energy . . . zest . . . tranquillity . . . concentration, and the limb of wisdom which is equanimity. These are the seven. Of these seven limbs of wisdom, friends, in whichsoever I desire to abide during the early part of the day, in that limb of wisdom I abide. In whichsoever limb of wisdom I desire to abide in the middle of the day, in that I abide. In whichsoever limb of wisdom I desire to abide in the evening, in that I abide.

If, friends, it is the limb of wisdom that is mindfulness, in such case I fully know that it is boundless in me, or that it is well begun in me, or, when it is established in me, I fully know that it is so.

Again, if it fails me, I fully know that it is owing to this or

---

1 *Sa-sankhāra* (where *Comy.* takes it to be *sappayogena*).

2 *Uddhaŋ-soto.*

3 *Akaniṭṭha-(brahmalokaŋ)gāmī.* *Cf.* *Pts. of Contr.*, p. 78, *n.* 2. 'Stream' is 'natural desire' or 'the round of rebirth' or 'path-stream.'

that cause. So also with regard to the other limbs of wisdom, (*down to*) the limb of wisdom that is equanimity. If it fails me I fully know that it is owing to this or that cause.

It is just like the wardrobe of a rājah or great nobleman, full of garments of various hues. Whatsoever suit he desires to don in the forenoon, that he dons in the forenoon. Whatsoever suit he desires to don at midday, that he dons at midday. Whatsoever suit he desires to don at eventide, that he dons at eventide. Even so, friends, in whichsoever of these seven limbs of wisdom I desire to abide in the forenoon, or at midday, or in the evening, in such do I abide . . . (*as above, down to*) . . . owing to this or that cause.'[1]

(v) *The monk.*

Then a certain monk came to visit the Exalted One, saluted him and sat down at one side. So seated that monk said this to the Exalted One: '"Wisdom limb! Wisdom limb!" is the saying, lord. Pray, lord, how far is this name applicable?'

'They conduce to wisdom, monk, That is why they are so called.

Herein a monk cultivates the limb of wisdom that is mindfulness, which is based on seclusion, on dispassion, on cessation, which ends in self-surrender . . . He cultivates the limb of wisdom that is equanimity, that is so based and so ends. As he cultivates these seven limbs of wisdom he frees his heart from the āsava of sensuality, from the āsava of becoming, from the āsava of nescience. The knowledge comes to him: "Freed am I by being freed": so that he fully knows: "Cut off is rebirth, lived is the holy life, done is the task, there is no more of being here for me."

They conduce to wisdom, monk. That is why they are so called.'

---

[1] *Cf. M.* i, 215 (of Sāriputta), where the passage aims at showing that a monk rules his own mind, is not ruled by it. *Cf. Mln.* 254.

(vi) *Kuṇḍalī.*[1]

Once the Exalted One was staying at Sāketa,[2] in Anjana Grove, in Antelope Park.

Now on that occasion Kuṇḍaliya the wanderer came to visit the Exalted One, and on coming to him he greeted him courteously and, after the exchange of the compliments of friendship and courtesy, sat down at one side. So seated, Kuṇḍaliya the wanderer said this to the Exalted One:

'Master Gotama, I live near the Park and am a frequenter of companies.[3] Well, Master Gotama, this is my practice when I have had my morning meal. I roam and wander from park to park, from garden to garden. There I behold certain recluses and brahmins debating on the profit of freedom from controversy[4] and the profit of wrangling. But what profit is there in the worthy Gotama's way of living?'

'A Tathāgata, Kuṇḍaliya, lives enjoying the profits of the fruit of release by knowledge.'

'Pray, Master Gotama, what are the conditions which, when cultivated and made much of, complete the release by knowledge?'

'There are seven limbs of wisdom, Kuṇḍaliya, which, when cultivated and made much of, complete the release by knowledge.'

'What conditions, Master Gotama, are these which, cultivated and made much of, complete the seven limbs of wisdom?'

'Four stations of mindfulness, Kuṇḍaliya, if cultivated and made much of, complete the seven limbs of wisdom.'

'But, Master Gotama, what conditions, if cultivated and made much of, complete the four stations of mindfulness?'

---

1 One who wears ear-rings.

2 In Oudh, once the capital of Kosala. *Cf. infra*, text 219; *K.S.* i, 77 *n.*; *Buddh. India*, 39, 103.

3 *Parisāvacaro* (*A.* v, 10). 'One who attended gatherings where views are aired ("debating societies").' *Comy.*

4 The 'thus-talk' of views. *Iti-vāda-pamokkha.* *Cf. M.* i, 133; *A.* ii, 26; *Dial.* i, 13 *n.*

'The three virtuous habits,[1] Kuṇḍaliya . . . complete the four stations of mindfulness.'

'But, Master Gotama, what are the conditions which, if cultivated and made much of, complete the three virtuous habits?'

'Control of the sense faculties, Kuṇḍaliya, if cultivated and made much of, completes the three virtuous habits. But how cultivated and how made much of, Kuṇḍaliya, do they complete the three virtuous habits?

Herein, Kuṇḍaliya, a monk, seeing a delightful object with the eye, does not hanker for it, does not thrill[2] thereat, does not develop lust for it. His body is unmoved, his mind is unmoved, inwardly well established and released. If with the eye he behold an object repulsive, he is not shocked[3] thereat, his mind is not unsettled[4] or depressed[5] or resentful because of that, but his body is unmoved, his mind is unmoved, inwardly well established and released.

Again, Kuṇḍaliya, a monk, hearing a delightful sound with the ear[6] . . . smelling a delightful scent with the nose . . . tasting a delightful savour with the tongue . . . contracting with body a delightful touch . . . with mind cognizing a delightful state, does not hanker for it, does not thrill thereat, does not develop lust for it. His body is unmoved, his mind is unmoved, inwardly well established, well released. If with the mind he be conscious of a repulsive state, he is not shocked thereat, his mind is not unsettled or depressed or resentful because of that, but his body is unmoved, his mind is unmoved, inwardly well established and released.

Now, Kuṇḍaliya, since on seeing an object with the eye, whether objects are delightful or repulsive, his body is unmoved, his mind is unmoved, but inwardly well established

---

[1] *A.* i, 49: *Kāya-*, *vacī-*, *mano-caritāni*.

[2] Text *abhihaṃsati* (? to bristle or tingle with delight), but *Comy. abhihasati*.

[3] *Maṅku*=*désolé*. [4] *Apatiṭṭhita-citto* (*Comy. atiṭṭha-*).

[5] *Adīna-mīnaso. Comy. Domanassa vasena ādīna-citto* (*ādīna*=not depressed).

[6] *Cf. K.S.* iv, 63, 69, 71, 105, etc.

and released; since on hearing a sound with the ear . . . smelling a scent with the nose . . . tasting a savour with the tongue . . . with body contacting a tangible . . . since with mind cognizing a mental state, whether mental states be delightful or repulsive, his body is unmoved, his mind is unmoved, but inwardly well established and released,—restraint of faculties thus cultivated, thus made much of, completes the three virtuous habits (of body, speech and mind).

And how cultivated, Kuṇḍaliya, how made much of, do the three virtuous habits complete the four stations of mindfulness?

Herein, Kuṇḍaliya, a monk, by abandoning vicious habit of body, cultivates virtuous habit of body. Abandoning vicious habit of speech, he cultivates virtuous habit of speech. Abandoning vicious habit of mind, he cultivates virtuous habit of mind. Thus cultivated, Kuṇḍaliya, thus made much of, the three virtuous habits complete the four stations of mindfulness.

And how cultivated, Kuṇḍaliya, how made much of, do the four stations of mindfulness complete the seven limbs of wisdom?

Herein, Kuṇḍaliya, a monk abides in body contemplating body[1] (as transient), ardent, self-possessed and mindful, by restraining the dejection in the world that arises from coveting. He abides in feelings contemplating feelings (as transient), ardent . . . He abides in mind-states contemplating mind-states (as transient), ardent, self-possessed and mindful, by restraining in the world the dejection that arises from coveting. Thus cultivated, Kuṇḍaliya, thus made much of, the four stations of mindfulness complete the seven limbs of wisdom.

And how cultivated, Kuṇḍaliya, how made much of, do the seven limbs of wisdom complete the release by knowledge?

Herein, Kuṇḍaliya, a monk cultivates the limb of wisdom that is mindfulness, that is based on seclusion, on dispassion,

---

[1] *K.S.* iv, 259.

on cessation, that ends in self-surrender . . . and the rest. He cultivates the limb of wisdom that is equanimity . . . that ends in self-surrender. Thus cultivated, Kuṇḍaliya, thus made much of, do the seven limbs of wisdom complete the release by knowledge.'

At these words the wanderer Kuṇḍaliya exclaimed:

'Excellent, lord! Excellent, lord! Just as if one should lift up the fallen, discover the hidden, point out the way to the bewildered, show a light in the gloom, saying: "Now they that have eyes to see can see objects,"—even so in divers ways has the Exalted One expounded the truth. I, even I, lord, do go for refuge to the Exalted One, to the Norm and to the Order of monks. May the Exalted One accept me as his follower, as one who from this time forth even to life's end hath gone to refuge in him.'[1]

(vii) *Peak.*[2]

Just as, monks, in a peaked house all rafters whatsoever go together to the peak, slope to the peak, join in the peak, and of them all the peak is reckoned chief, even so, monks, the monk who cultivates and makes much of the seven limbs of wisdom, slopes to Nibbāna, inclines to Nibbāna, tends to Nibbāna.

And how, monks, does a monk who cultivates and makes much of the seven limbs of wisdom so slope, incline and tend?

Herein a monk cultivates the limb of wisdom that is mindfulness . . .

(viii) *Upavāṇa.*

On a certain occasion the venerable Upavāṇa[3] and the venerable Sāriputta were staying near Kosambī in Ghosita Park.[4]

On that occasion the venerable Sāriputta, rising at eventide from his solitude, went to visit the venerable Upavāṇa, and

[1] Text abbreviates the usual formula.

[2] *Cf. supra*, text 43; *K.S.* iii, 132.

[3] *K.S.* i, 220, ii, 32, iv, 21. He was personal attendant on the Buddha before Ānanda.

[4] *Cf. K.S.* iv, 62, 102.

on coming to him greeted him courteously, and after the exchange of greetings and courtesies, sat down at one side. So seated the venerable Sāriputta said this to the venerable Upavāṇa:

'Pray, friend Upavāṇa, could a monk thus know of himself:[1] "The seven limbs of wisdom, by systematic attention to them,[2] being well established in me, conduce to pleasant living?" '

'He could thus know of himself, friend Sāriputta. By striving to start[3] the limb of wisdom that is mindfulness he knows: "My heart is well released. Sloth and torpor in me are well abolished. Excitement and flurry are well restrained. Resolute energy is mine. By making it my object,[4] I give it my attention. It is not slack[5] in me." And so of the other limbs of wisdom. . . . By striving to start the limb of wisdom that is equanimity he knows: "My heart is well released. . . . Resolute energy is mine. . . . It is not slack in me."

Thus, friend Sāriputta, a monk could know of himself: "By systematic attention to them, thus well established in me, the seven limbs of wisdom conduce to pleasant living." '

(ix) *Arisen (or Arising) (a).*

Monks, these seven limbs of wisdom, not having yet arisen, if cultivated and made much of, do arise, but not without the manifestation of a Tathāgata, an Arahant, a fully enlightened one. What seven? The limb of wisdom that is mindfulness . . . the limb of wisdom that is equanimity. These seven limbs of wisdom, monks, . . . arise not without the manifestation of a Tathāgata, an Arahant, a fully enlightened one.

(x) *Arisen (or Arising) (b).*

Monks, these seven limbs of wisdom, if not yet arisen, when cultivated and made much of, do arise, but not without

---

[1] *Paccattaŋ.*

[2] Text *manasikārā*, but MSS. and *Comy.* *-kāro.*

[3] Text *ārambhamāno.* *Comy.* *ārabbhamāno=kurumāno.*

[4] *Cf.* *S.* ii, 120; *K.S.* ii, 149 (*aṭṭhikatvā, manasikatvā*); *infra*, text 95.

[5] *Līnaŋ.* *Cf.* text 64 (*līnatta*); *infra*, text 112 (*līnaŋ cittaŋ hoti*); lit. 'stuck fast.'

the rule of the Happy One. What seven? The limb of wisdom that is mindfulness . . . that which is equanimity. These seven lims of wisdom. . . .

CHAPTER II.—THE SICK MAN

(i) *Creatures.*[1]

Just as, monks, whatsoever creatures adopt the four postures, now going, now standing still, now sitting, now lying, all do so in dependence on the earth; even so, monks, dependent on virtue, supported by virtue, does a monk cultivate the seven limbs of wisdom, make much of the seven limbs of wisdom.

And how does a monk, dependent on virtue, supported by virtue, cultivate and make much of the seven limbs of wisdom?

Herein a monk cultivates the limb of wisdom that is mindfulness, which is based on seclusion, on dispassion, on cessation, which ends in self-surrender . . . he cultivates the limb of wisdom that is equanimity, so based and so ending. That, monks, is how a monk, dependent on virtue, supported by virtue, cultivates and makes much of the seven limbs of wisdom.

(ii) *The simile of the sun* (*a*).

Just as, monks, the dawn is the forerunner, the harbinger, of the sun's arising, even so friendship with what is lovely is the forerunner, the harbinger of the arising of the seven limbs of wisdom in a monk. Of a monk who is a friend of what is lovely this may be expected: that he will cultivate the seven limbs of wisdom, that he will make much of the seven limbs of wisdom. And how does a monk who is a friend of what is lovely cultivate and make much of the seven limbs of wisdom?

Herein a monk cultivates the limb of wisdom that is mindfulness . . . and the rest. That is how a monk who is a friend . . . cultivates and makes much of . . .

---

[1] No. 11 of text. I follow *Comy.* in enumeration.

(iii) *The simile of the sun* (*b*).

Just as, monks, the dawn . . . even so systematic attention is the forerunner, the harbinger of the arising of the seven limbs of wisdom in a monk. And how does a monk who is possessed of systematic attention cultivate and make much of the seven limbs of wisdom ?

Herein a monk cultivates the limb of wisdom that is mindfulness. . . . That is how . . .

(iv) *Sick* (*a*).

Thus have I heard: Once the Exalted One was staying near Rājagaha in Bamboo Grove at the Squirrels' Feeding-ground.

Now at that time the venerable Kassapa the Great was staying in Pepper Tree Grotto,[1] and was sick, afflicted, stricken with a sore disease.

Then the Exalted One, rising from his solitude at eventide, went to visit the venerable Kassapa the Great, and on coming to him sat down on a seat made ready. So the Exalted One as he sat said to the venerable Kassapa the Great:

'Well, Kassapa, I hope you are bearing up. I hope you are enduring. Do your pains abate and not increase ? Are there signs of their abating and not increasing ?'[2]

'No, lord. I am not bearing up. I am not enduring. Strong pains come upon me. There is no sign of their abating, but of their increasing.'[3]

---

[1] *Cf. Ud.* i, 4; *UdA.* 59; *DhpA.* 427.

[2] *K.S.* iii, 102 *n.* (*sānaŋ=etesaŋ. Comy.*).

[3] A good example of the reduction to formulæ. *Cf. S.* iii, 119; iv, 46=*K.S.* iv ,23, 30. It seems unlikely that on such an occasion the Master would thus expound to this old follower teachings which he must have known by heart. In this Collection the sick man is generally introduced to serve as an occasion for emphasizing a fresh doctrine. *Comy.* adds: 'He had (it is said) carefully listened to this teaching about the seven limbs of wisdom, and seven days from his taking the robes he penetrated the truth about them, and they were manifested to him. Now, as he pondered on the profit of the Master's teaching, his blood was calmed, his system purified, and the sickness fell away like a drop of water from a lotus leaf.'

'Kassapa, these seven limbs of wisdom fully expounded by myself, when cultivated and made much of, conduce to full comprehension, to the wisdom, to Nibbāna. What seven? The limb of wisdom, Kassapa, that is mindfulness, fully expounded by myself, if cultivated . . . The limb of wisdom that is investigation of the Norm, fully expounded by myself . . . The limb of wisdom that is energy, fully expounded by myself . . . The limb of wisdom that is tranquillity, fully expounded by myself . . . The limb of wisdom that is concentration, fully expounded by myself . . . The limb of wisdom that is equanimity, fully expounded by myself, if cultivated and made much of, conduces to full comprehension, to the wisdom, to Nibbāna. These seven limbs of wisdom, Kassapa, fully expounded by myself, if cultivated, and made much of, conduce to full comprehension, to the wisdom, to Nibbāna.'

'Verily, lord, they are limbs of wisdom! Verily, O Happy One, they are limbs of wisdom!'

Thus spake the Exalted One, and the venerable Kassapa the Great was delighted thereat, and took pleasure in what was said by the Exalted One. And the venerable Kassapa the Great rose up from that sickness. There and then that sickness of the venerable Kassapa the Great was abandoned.

(v) *Sick* (*b*).

Once the Exalted One was staying near Rājagaha, in Bamboo Grove, at the Squirrels' Feeding-ground.

Now on that occasion the venerable Moggallāna the Great was staying on the hill Vulture's Peak, and was sick, afflicted, stricken with a sore disease.

Then the Exalted One, rising from his solitude at eventide, went to visit the venerable Moggallāna the Great, and on coming to him sat down on a seat made ready . . . (*exactly the same as before. Comy. abbreviates thus*). There and then that sickness of the venerable Moggallāna the Great was abandoned.

(vi) *Sick* (*c*).

Once the Exalted One was staying near Rājagaha, in Bamboo Grove, at the Squirrels' Feeding-ground.

Now on that occasion the Exalted One was sick, afflicted, stricken with a sore disease.

Then the venerable Cunda the Great[1] came to visit the Exalted One, and on coming to him saluted him and sat down at one side. As he thus sat the Exalted One said to the venerable Cunda the Great:

'Cunda, call to mind[2] the limbs of wisdom.'

'These seven limbs of wisdom, lord, fully expounded by the Exalted One, if cultivated and made much of, conduce to full comprehension, to the wisdom, to Nibbāna. What are the seven? The limb of wisdom, lord, that is mindfulness, fully expounded by the Exalted One . . . and the rest . . . the limb of wisdom that is equanimity. These seven limbs of wisdom, lord, fully expounded by the Exalted One, if cultivated and made much of, so conduce . . .

'Verily, Cunda, they are limbs of wisdom! Verily, Cunda, they are limbs of wisdom!'

Thus spake the venerable Cunda the Great, and the Master was approving of it. Then the Exalted One rose up from that sickness. There and then that sickness of the Exalted One was abandoned.

(vii) *Crossing over* or *No more*.

'These seven limbs of wisdom, monks, if cultivated and made much of, conduce to no more going to the hither or the further shore.[3] What seven? . . . (*as before*).' Thus spake the Exalted One. So saying, the Happy One added this further as Teacher:

---

[1] Younger brother of Sāriputta, and one of the chief Elders. *Cf. Brethren*, 119; *K.S.* iv, 30.

[2] *Paṭibhantu taŋ*, lit. 'let them occur to you' (*cf.* vol., i., 241, 243, 245; *Ud.*, p. 39: *paṭibhati maŋ = upaṭṭhāti maŋ. Comy.*).

[3] *Suvra*, text 24 (*Nibbāna*).

Few are they of mortal men
Who have reached the further shore:
But the crowd of other folk
On this side fare up and down. . . .

They whose mind is rightly cultured
In the seven wisdom limbs,
Glad to have surrendered clinging,
Glad to be from bondage loosed,
Canker-cured, they all-resplendent,
E'en in this world are at peace.[1]

(viii) *Neglected and undertaken.*

By whomsoever, monks, the seven limbs of wisdom are neglected, by them is neglected this Ariyan eightfold way for the utter destruction of Ill.

By whomsoever, monks, the seven limbs of wisdom are undertaken, by them is undertaken this Ariyan eightfold way for the utter destruction of Ill. What are the seven? They are the limb of wisdom that is mindfulness and the rest . . . the limb of wisdom that is equanimity.

By whomsoever, monks, the seven limbs of wisdom are neglected or undertaken, by them is neglected or undertaken this Ariyan eightfold way for the utter destruction of Ill.

(ix) *Ariyan.*

These seven limbs of wisdom, monks, if cultivated and made much of, are the Ariyan profitable things.[2] For him that acts in accordance therewith they conduce to the utter destruction of Ill. What seven? The limb of wisdom that is mindfulness . . .

(x) *Revulsion.*

These seven limbs of wisdom . . . conduce to downright revulsion, to dispassion, to cessation, to calm, to full comprehension, to the wisdom, to Nibbāna. What seven? The limb of wisdom that is mindfulness . . . and the rest.

---

[1] The verses are in full, *supra*, text 24.

[2] *Niyyānikā* (leading to salvation); *cf. infra*, text 255 (of the Four Bases of Psychic Power).

CHAPTER III.—UDĀYI

(i) *Knowing.*[1]

Now a certain monk came to see the Exalted One, and on coming to him saluted him and sat down at one side. So seated that monk said this to the Exalted One:

'They say "Limb of wisdom! Limb of wisdom," lord. Pray, lord, how far is this name applicable?'[2]

'They conduce to the wisdom, monk. That is why they are called "limbs of wisdom." Herein a monk cultivates the limb of wisdom that is mindfulness . . . the limb of wisdom that is equanimity, that is based on seclusion, on dispassion, on cessation, that ends in self-surrender. They conduce to the wisdom, monk. That is why they are so called.'

(ii) *Instruction.*

I will teach you, monks, the seven limbs of wisdom. Do ye listen to it. And what, monks, are the seven limbs of wisdom? They are . . . (*as before*).

(iii) *Conditions.*

Sensual desire,[3] monks, that has not yet arisen, arises owing to much attention being given to conditions based upon lust and passion: and, when it has already arisen, sensual desire conduces to the still more-becoming and growth thereof.

Malevolence, monks, that has not yet arisen, arises owing to much attention being given to conditions based upon malevolence: and, when it has already arisen, malevolence conduces to the still more-becoming and growth thereof.

Sloth and torpor, monks, (in like manner) . . .

Excitement and flurry, monks, . . .

Doubt and wavering, monks, . . .

---

[1] *Bodhanā.* [2] As at I, § 5 of this part.

[3] *Kāma-cchando.* *Cf. Buddh. Psychology*, p. 123.

The limb of wisdom that is mindfulness, monks, which has not yet arisen, arises owing to much attention being given to conditions based upon mindfulness: and, when it has already arisen, the limb of wisdom that is mindfulness, by the cultivation thereof, goes to fulfilment.

So also with regard to the other limbs of wisdom . . . the limb of wisdom that is equanimity, by the cultivation thereof, goes to fulfilment.

(iv) *Unsystematic.*[1]

In one who gives unsystematic attention, monks, sensual desire which has not yet arisen, arises; and, when arisen, sensual desire conduces to the still more-becoming and growth thereof.

Likewise, monks, malevolence which has not yet arisen . . .

Likewise sloth and torpor . . . excitement and flurry . . . doubt and wavering, which have not yet arisen, arise; and, having arisen, conduce to the still more-becoming and growth thereof.

So also, monks, the limb of wisdom that is mindfulness, not having arisen, does not arise; and, if it has already arisen, it fades away.

So with the other limbs of wisdom . . . and that which is equanimity . . . it fades away.

But, monks, in one who gives systematic attention, sensual desire which has not arisen does not arise, and, if it has arisen, it is abandoned.

So with malevolence . . . sloth and torpor . . . excitement and flurry . . . doubt and wavering,—they arise not: and, if they have arisen, they are abandoned.

But, monks, the limb of wisdom that is mindfulness, not having yet arisen, does arise, and having done so, by cultivation thereof, it goes to fulfilment. So it is with the other limbs of wisdom . . . and that which is equanimity . . . by cultivation thereof it goes to fulfilment.

---

[1] *Ayoniso* (a slack thinker); *cf. Dialog.* iii, 251 *n.*: 'disorderly thinking.' Also *supra* 52, *n.* 2.

(v) *Undeclining.*[1]

I will teach you, monks, seven conditions that decline not. Do ye listen to it. And what, monks, are those seven conditions that decline not?

They are the seven limbs of wisdom. Which seven? The limb of wisdom that is mindfulness, that which is investigation of the Norm, that which is energy, that which is tranquillity, that which is concentration, and the limb of wisdom that is equanimity. These, monks, are the seven conditions that decline not.

(vi) *Destruction.*

'The way, monks, and the practice leading thereto which conduces to the destruction of craving,—do ye cultivate that way and practice.

And what is the way, monks, what the practice that so conduces? It is the seven limbs of wisdom. What seven? That which is mindfulness and the rest, and the limb of wisdom that is equanimity.'

At these words the venerable Udāyi[2] said to the Exalted One:

'Pray, lord, how are the seven limbs of wisdom cultivated? How, if made much of, do they conduce to the destruction of craving?'

'Herein, Udāyi, a monk cultivates the limb of wisdom that is mindfulness, which is based on seclusion, on dispassion, on cessation, which ends in self-surrender: which is far-spreading, lofty, boundless, free of malevolence. As he cultivates the limb of wisdom that is mindfulness, which is based on seclusion . . . craving is abandoned. By the abandoning of craving action (that is rooted in craving) is abandoned. By the abandoning of action (rooted in craving) Ill is abandoned.

So it is with regard to the other limbs of wisdom.

He cultivates the limb of wisdom that is equanimity, which is based on seclusion, on dispassion, on cessation, which ends

---

[1] *Aparihāni*; *cf. K.S.* ii, 139.

[2] *Cf. K.S.* iv, 77 *ff.* and *n.* *Comy.* imagines the Buddha to think: This Udāyi is good at drawing conclusions (*anusandhi-kusalo*).

in self-surrender; which is far-spreading, lofty, boundless, free of malevolence. As he does so, craving is abandoned. By the abandoning of craving, action (rooted in craving) is abandoned. By the abandoning of action (rooted in craving) Ill is abandoned. Thus, Udāyi, by the destruction of craving (comes) destruction of action (rooted in craving).[1] By destruction of action comes destruction of Ill.'

(vii) *Cessation.*

The way, monks, and the practice leading thereto, which conduce to the cessation of craving,—do ye cultivate that way and practice.

And what is the way, monks, what the practice that so conduces?

It is the seven limbs of wisdom. What seven? That which is mindfulness and the rest, and the limb of wisdom that is equanimity.

And how cultivated, monks, how made much of, do the seven limbs of wisdom conduce to the destruction of craving?

Herein a monk cultivates the limb of wisdom that is mindfulness . . . that ends in self-surrender . . . So of the others, and the limb of wisdom that is equanimity . . . that ends in self-surrender. Thus cultivated, monks, the seven limbs of wisdom conduce to the destruction of craving.

(viii) *Penetration.*

'I will teach you, monks, the way concerned with penetration.[2] Do ye listen to it. And what, monks, is that way? It is the seven limbs of wisdom, mindfulness and the rest and equanimity.'

At these words the venerable Udāyi said this to the Exalted One:

'Pray, lord, how cultivated, how made much of, do these seven limbs of wisdom conduce to penetration?'

'Herein, Udāyi, a monk cultivates the limb of wisdom that

---

[1] Words in brackets express *Comy.*'s def. of *kamma*. To say that action as such should be abandoned would be contrary to the Buddha's 'doctrine of the deed.'

[2] *Nibbedha-bhāgiyaŋ*=*nibbijjana-koṭṭhāsikaŋ*; *cf. VM.* 15.

is mindfulness, that is based on seclusion, on dispassion, on cessation, that ends in self-surrender: that is far-spreading, lofty, boundless, free of malevolence. He, with mind that has cultivated the limb of wisdom which is mindfulness, pierces through, breaks down the great mass of lust that hitherto had not been pierced through or broken down.[1] In like manner he pierces through, breaks down, the great mass of hatred . . . the great mass of illusion that hitherto had not been pierced through or broken down. (And so he does in the case of the other limbs of wisdom.)

Thus cultivated, Udāyi, thus made much of, the seven limbs of wisdom do conduce to penetration.'

(ix) *The one condition.*

I behold not, monks, any other single condition which, thus cultivated and made much of, is so conducive to abandonment of the conditions that bind as the seven limbs of wisdom. What seven? That of mindfulness and the rest, and the limb of wisdom that is equanimity.

And how cultivated, monks, how made much of do the seven limbs of wisdom conduce to the abandonment of conditions that bind?

Herein a monk cultivates the limb of wisdom that is mindfulness . . .

And what, monks, are the conditions that bind?

The eye, monks, is a condition that binds. Herein spring up attachments that bind and cleave to one. The tongue is a condition that binds. Herein spring up . . . The mind is a condition that binds. Herein spring up attachments that bind and cleave to one. These, monks, are called 'conditions that bind.'[2]

(x) *Udāyi.*

On a certain occasion the Exalted One was staying among the Sumbhā, at Desaka,[3] a district of the Sumbhā.

---

[1] *Cf. Pts.* ii, 201.

[2] *Cf. K.S.* iv, *passim.*

[3] At *JA.* i, 393 (the only place where I find it mentioned) Desaka (text here *Setaka? v.l. Sedaka*) is a district of Sumbha-raṭṭha, the scene of §§ *infra,* (text), 168-70.

Now the venerable Udāyi came to visit the Exalted One, and on coming to him saluted him and sat down at one side. So seated the venerable Udāyi said this to the Exalted One :

'Strange it is, lord ! A wonder it is, lord ! how strongly the affection and respect for the Exalted One, the modesty and delicacy of feeling for him, have worked[1] in me.

Formerly, lord, when I was living the life of a householder, I was not much concerned about the Norm, not much concerned about[2] the Order. But, lord, when I beheld the affection, the respect, the modesty and delicacy of feeling for the Exalted One, I went forth from home to the homeless. To me it was that the Exalted One taught the Norm, to wit: "Thus is body, thus the arising of body, thus the perishing of body. Thus is feeling, thus the arising of feeling, thus the perishing of feeling. Thus is perception, thus the arising of perception, thus the perishing of perception. Thus are the activities . . . thus is consciousness, thus its arising and its perishing."

Now, lord, when I had gone into solitude, while pondering over the rise and fall[3] of these five factors of existence, I fully realized, as in truth it is, the meaning of "This is Ill: this is the arising of Ill: this is the ceasing of Ill." I fully realized, as in truth it is, the meaning of "This is the practice that leads to the ceasing of Ill."

Then, lord, I fully grasped the Norm. I laid hold of[4] the way, which, cultivated and made much of, will lead me, thus and thus abiding, to the attainment of being such : so that I shall come to know: "Cut off is rebirth: lived is the holy life: done is the task: there is no more of being here for me."

Then, lord, I laid hold of the limb of wisdom that is mindfulness, which, cultivated and made much of, will lead me on, thus and thus abiding, to the state of being such: so that I shall come to know: "Cut off is rebirth."

---

[1] *Bahukato.* [2] *Abahukato=akata-bahumāno. Comy.*

[3] *Ukkujj' āvakujjaŋ,* lit. 'topsy-turvy.' *Comy. udayo* and *vayo* (*udayabbaya*).

[4] Text *Abhisamito.* Perhaps the *v.l. abhisameto* of text, which *Comy.* follows, is the better reading. *Comy.=vipassanā dhammo abhisamāgato.* Thus he was now *sotâpanno* according to *Comy.*

I laid hold of the other limbs of wisdom and that which is equanimity, which, culitivated and made much of, will lead me on to such knowledge. Indeed, lord, I have laid hold of this path, which, cultivated and made much of, will lead me on, thus and thus abiding, to the state of being such[1]: so that I shall come to know . . . "there is no more life in these conditions."'

'Well said! Well said, Udāyi! Indeed you have laid hold of this way, which, cultivated and made much of by you, will lead you, thus and thus abiding, to the state of being such: so that you will come to know: "Cut off is rebirth: lived is the holy life: done is the task: there is no more of being here for me."'

CHAPTER IV.—ON HINDRANCES

(i) *The good* (*a*).

Whatsoever conditions, monks, are the constituent parts of good and bad,[2] but are on the side of[3] goodness, all of them have their root in earnestness, converge in earnestness; earnestness is reckoned the chief of those conditions.

Of the monk who is earnest we may expect that he will cultivate the seven limbs of wisdom, that he will make much of the seven limbs of wisdom. And how does the earnest monk cultivate and make much of the seven limbs of wisdom?

Herein a monk cultivates the limb of wisdom that is mindfulness, which is based on seclusion, on dispassion, on cessation, which ends in self-surrender. . . . He cultivates the limb of wisdom that is equanimity, which is so based and so ends. That, monks, is how a monk who is earnest cultivates the seven limbs of wisdom, makes much of the seven limbs of wisdom.

---

[1] *Tathattāya = tathābhāvāya*. *Comy*. *Cf*. *infra*, text 213; *K.S.* iv, 202; *M.* i, 301. A term for *Nibbāna* commonly used in Sanskrit Buddhism, 'thusness.' *Cf*. *itthattaŋ*, 'hereness,' the present state, this world or life, of the next phrase.

[2] For the *kusalâkusalā cf*. *M.* i, 489.

[3] *Pakkhikā* or *pakkhiyā* (*infra*, text 97); lit. 'the wings or sides.' *Cf*. *Compendium*, 179 *n.*; *Dialog*. iii, 93.

(ii) *The good* (*b*).

Whatsoever conditions, monks, are the constituent parts of good and bad, but are on the side of goodness, all of them have their root in systematic attention, converge in systematic attention. Of those conditions systematic attention is reckoned chief.

Of a monk who possesses systematic attention we may expect that he will cultivate the seven limbs of wisdom, that he will make much of the seven limbs of wisdom.

And how, monks, does a monk who is possessed of systematic attention cultivate and make much of the seven limbs of wisdom?

Herein a monk cultivates the limb of wisdom that is mindfulness . . . and the rest. He cultivates the limb of wisdom, that is equanimity. That is how a monk . . .

(iii) *Corruptions* (*a*).[1]

Monks, there are these five corruptions of gold,[2] tainted by which corruptions gold is neither soft, nor pliable, nor gleaming. nor easily broken up, nor fit for perfect workmanship. What are the five?

Iron, monks, is a corruption of gold, tainted by which corruption gold is neither soft nor . . .

Copper[3] . . . tin . . . lead . . . silver,[4] monks, is a corruption of gold, tainted by which corruption gold is neither soft, nor pliable, nor gleaming, nor easily broken up, nor fit for perfect workmanship. These, monks, are the five corruptions of gold. . . .

In like manner, monks, there are these five corruptions of the heart,[5] tainted by which corruptions the heart is neither

---

[1] *Cf. Buddh. Psych. Eth.*, 251, 281. We may call them 'depravities.' *Upakkilesā* here means the other metals which are mixed with gold as alloy. See the talk to Visākhā, *A.* i., 205-15, esp. 210.

[2] *Jātarūpa* is unworked gold, as opposed to *suvaṇṇa*.

[3] Lit. 'red metal,' iron being *kāla-loha*.

[4] *Sajjhu*=*rajataŋ*.

[5] *Citta*; *cf. Expos.* ii, 488. The word *khilā* (*supra*, text 57) expresses the hard crust of individuality which has to be broken through.

soft, nor pliable, nor gleaming, nor easily broken up, nor perfectly composed for the destruction of the āsavas. What are the five ?

Sensual desire, monks, is a corruption of the heart, tainted by which the heart is neither soft, nor pliable, nor gleaming, nor easily broken up, nor perfectly composed for the destruction of the āsavas.

Malevolence . . . sloth and torpor . . . excitement and flurry . . . doubt and wavering, monks, are corruptions of the heart, tainted by which . . . of the āsavas.

(iv) *Corruptions* (*b*).

Monks, these seven limbs of wisdom, which are without check and hindrance, if cultivated and made much of with uncorrupted heart, conduce to realizing the fruits of liberation by knowledge. What are the seven ?

The limb of wisdom which is mindfulness, if unrestrained by check and hindrance . . . the limb of wisdom which is equanimity. . . . These are the seven.

(v) *Systematic* (*a*).

Monks, in him who practises unsystematic attention,[1] sensual desire, if not already risen, arises: and, if already arisen, sensual desire conduces to the more-becoming and growth thereof.

So also malevolence, sloth and torpor, excitement and flurry, doubt and wavering, if not yet arisen, do arise: and, if arisen, conduce to the more-becoming and growth thereof.

(vi) *Systematic* (*b*).

But, monks, in him who gives systematic attention, the limb of wisdom which is mindfulness, if not yet arisen, arises: and, if already arisen, by cultivation it goes to fulfilment. So also with the other limbs of wisdom.

[1] *Cf. Expos.* ii, 490; *supra*, 71, *n.*

(vii) *Increase* or *Not decrease.*

These seven limbs of wisdom, monks, if cultivated and made much of, conduce to increase and not to decrease. What seven?

The limb of wisdom which is mindfulness, and the rest. . . . These seven . . .

(viii) *Restraint and hindrance.*

Monks, there are these five checks, hindrances and corruptions of the heart, which weaken insight.[1] What five?

Sensual desire, monks, is a check and hindrance, a corruption of the heart, that weakens insight. Malevolence . . . sloth and torpor . . . excitement and flurry . . . doubt and wavering . . . These five . . . weaken insight.

The seven limbs of wisdom, monks, if unrestrained, unhindered, if cultivated and made much of with uncorrupted heart, conduce to realizing the fruits of liberation by knowledge. What seven? (*as before*) . . .

Now, monks, at the time when the Ariyan disciple makes the Norm his object,[2] gives attention to it, with all his mind considers it, with ready ear listens to the Norm,—at such time these five hindrances exist not in him: at such time the seven limbs of wisdom by cultivation go to fulfilment. What five hindrances at such time exist not?

The hindrance that is sensual desire at such time exists not. The hindrance which is malevolence . . . sloth and torpor . . . excitement and flurry . . . that which is doubt and wavering at such time exists not. In that man the five hindrances at such time exist not.

And what seven limbs of wisdom by cultivation at such time go to fulfilment?

---

[1] *Cf. infra*, text 160; *Buddh. Psych. Eth.*, p. 310 *n.*

[2] *Aṭṭhikatvā* (*supra*, text 76); quoted *KhpA.* 148. *Cf. S.* i, 112, ii, 220; *J.P.T.S.*, 1886, p. 107; *A.* iii, 162, 402 (where the context implies 'giving close attention to') reads *sabbaŋ cetasā* for *sabbacetaso* of our text. (Read *samann-* for *sammannāharitvā*.)

At the time, monks, when the Ariyan disciple makes the Norm his object, gives attention to it, with all his mind considers it, with ready ear listens to the Norm,—at such time the five hindrances exist not in him, at such time these seven limbs of wisdom by cultivation go to fulfilment.

(ix) *The tree.*

There are mighty trees, monks, grown from tiny seeds, of mighty bulk, which overspread[1] (other) trees. The trees thus overspread[2] break up, break down, fall to the ground and so lie.

What mighty trees, monks, are they that do so? Trees such as the bo-tree, the banyan, the wave-leafed fig, the bunched fig, the cedar,[3] the wood-apple tree.[4] These are the mighty trees, monks, grown from tiny seeds, of mighty bulk, which overspread other trees: by which being overspread, these trees break up, break down, fall to the ground and so lie.

Just in the same way, monks, here maybe is such and such a clansman, who, whatsoever lusts he abandons and goes forth from home to the homeless, just by such lusts, or by lusts still worse than these, is broken up, broken down: down he falls and so lies.

Monks, there are these five checks, hindrances which overspread the heart, which weaken insight. What five? Sensual desire, monks, is a check, a hindrance which overspreads the heart and weakens insight. Malevolence . . . sloth and torpor . . . excitement and flurry . . . doubt and wavering: each of these, monks, is a check, a hindrance which overspreads the heart and weakens insight.

---

1 *Ajjhārūhā* or *-rūḷhā*. *Comy.* =*abhirūhakā* (parasitic growths).

2 *Ye hi* of text should read *yehi*.

3 *Kacchako* (*Comy.* =*aṭṭhi-gacchako*; ? 'of bone-like growth.') ? Cedar. These trees appear in several lists, *e.g.* at *Vin.* iv, 35.

4 Text *kapitthako*. *Comy. kapitthano; Vin. kapiṭhano; DA.* i, 81 *kapitthano; VM.* 183, *kapitthako* (*v.l.-no*), given as examples of *khandhabījā*. But whether it is of the fig-tree family or a wood-apple I cannot say. *Comy.* says it produces *pilakkhā*. Dictionaries call it *Feronia elephantum*. *Cf. Brethren,* p. 333 *n.*; *Mil.* 189 (*kapittho*)=*Trans.*, vol. i. 262; also *JA.* v, 132, *v.l. kaviṭṭhaṃ*.

These seven limbs of wisdom, monks, which are without check and hindrance, which overspread not the heart, if cultivated and made much of, conduce to realizing the fruits of liberation by knowledge. What are the five? They are the limb of wisdom which is mindfulness, and the rest; the limb of wisdom which is equanimity, which is without check and hindrance, which overspreads not the heart, which, if cultivated and made much of, conduces to the realization of the fruits of liberation by knowledge.

(x) *Hindrance.*

Monks, there are these five hindrances which cause blindness, loss of sight and ignorance; which obstruct insight, consort with pain[1] and conduce not to Nibbāna. Which five?

The hindrance of sensual desire, monks, causes blindness. . . . Malevolence . . . sloth and torpor . . . excitement and flurry . . . doubt and wavering, monks, these are the five hindrances which cause blindness, loss of sight and ignorance; which obstruct insight, consort with pain and conduce not to Nibbāna.

These seven limbs of wisdom, monks, cause sight, knowledge, growth of insight: they consort not with pain, and conduce to Nibbāna. What are the seven? They are the limb of wisdom that is mindfulness, which causes sight, knowledge, growth of insight . . . and the other limbs of wisdom. These are the seven limbs of wisdom, monks, which cause sight . . . which conduce to Nibbāna.

CHAPTER V.—ROLLER OF THE WHEEL

(i) *Conceits.*

Sāvatthī was the occasion (for the following). . . . The Exalted One said: 'Monks, whatsoever recluses or brahmins in past times have abandoned the three conceits,[2] all of them

---

[1] *M.* i, 115, *vighāta-pakkhikā* (*cf. supra*, text iv, 1); *Itiv.* 81. *Comy.* = *dukkha-pakkhikā*.

[2] *Tisso vidhā. Cf. supra*, text 56. *Comy. Tāyo māna-koṭṭhāsā.*

did so by the fact of cultivating and making much of the seven limbs of wisdom. Whatsoever recluses or brahmins in future times shall abandon the three conceits, all of them will do so by the fact of cultivating and making much of the seven limbs of wisdom. Whatsoever recluses or brahmins, monks, do now abandon the three conceits, all of them do so by the fact of cultivating and making much of the seven limbs of wisdom. What seven limbs of wisdom? The limb of wisdom that is mindfulness, and the rest . . . the limb of wisdom that is equanimity. Whatsoever recluses or brahmins have abandoned, shall abandon, or do now abandon the three conceits, monks, all of them do so by the fact of cultivating and making much of the seven limbs of wisdom.'

(ii) *Roller of the wheel.*

Monks, together with the appearance of a monarch who rolls the wheel[1] there is the appearance of the seven treasures. What seven treasures? The treasure of the Wheel, the Elephant, the Horse, the Jewel, the Woman, the Housefather, and the treasure of the Heir Apparent. These, monks, are the seven treasures that appear along with the appearance of a monarch who rolls the wheel.

Likewise, monks, together with the appearance of a Tathāgata who is Arahant, a fully Enlightened One, there is the appearance of these seven treasures. What seven?

There is the appearance of the seven treasures of wisdom; the treasure of wisdom that is mindfulness, that which is searching the Norm, that which is energy, zest, tranquillity, concentration, and the treasure of wisdom that is equanimity.

Monks, together with the appearance of a Tathāgata . . . there is the appearance of these seven treasures of wisdom.

---

[1] *Cakka-vatti*, a term for the ideal monarch. *Cf. Dialog.* ii, 327; *M.* i, 55; *Pts. of Contr.*, 107. *Comy.* refers to *Mahāsudassana Sutta*, *D.* ii, 169.

(iii) *Māra.*

I will teach you, monks, a way for crushing Māra's host. Do ye listen to it. And what, monks, is that way ?

It is the seven limbs of wisdom. What seven ? The limb of wisdom that is mindfulness, and the rest. This, monks, is the way for crushing Māra's host.

(iv) *Witless.*

Now a certain monk came to visit the Exalted One. . . . As he sat at one side that monk said this to the Exalted One:

' " A witless imbecile ![1] A witless imbecile !" is the saying, lord. Pray, lord, how far is this name applicable ?'

' By the fact, monk, of not cultivating, not making much of the seven limbs of wisdom, one is called " a witless imbecile." What seven ? . . . (*as before*). . . . It is for this reason that one is so called, monk.'

(v) *Intelligent.*[2]

(A certain monk said to the Exalted One):

' " Intelligent, no imbecile ! Intelligent, no imbecile !" is the saying, lord. Pray, lord, how far is this term applicable ?'

' By the fact, monk, of cultivating and making much of the seven limbs of wisdom one is so called. What seven ? The limb of wisdom that is mindfulness, and the rest, and that which is equanimity. It is by cultivating . . .'

(vi) *Wretched.*

(A certain monk said to the Exalted One):

' " A poor wretch ! A poor wretch !" is the saying, lord. Pray, lord, how far is this term applicable ?'

---

[1] *Eḷa-mūga* (often with *dupañño*), generally translated 'deaf and dumb,' but, as Rhys Davids shows at *Milinda* ii, 71 *n.*, there is no authority for this. *Cf. M.* i, 20: 'dummies,' or *eḷamukhā*; *M.* i, 527 (*App. n.*); *A.* ii, 252 ('dribbling at the mouth '). *Comys.* give the literal interpretation (? the meaning of 'drivelling idiot '). *Comy. asampanna-vacano* (*DA.* i, 282), of indistinct speech.

[2] *Paññavā.*

'By the fact, monk, of not cultivating and making much of the seven limbs of wisdom one is so called. What seven? The limb of wisdom that is mindfulness, and the rest. . . .'

(vii) *Well-to-do.*

(A certain monk said to the Exalted One):

'"Well-to-do! Well-to-do!" is the saying, lord. Pray, lord, how far is this term applicable?'

'By the fact of cultivating, by making much of the seven limbs of wisdom, monk, one is so called. What seven? The limb of wisdom that is mindfulness, and the rest. . . .'

(viii) *The sun.*[1]

Just as, monks, the dawn is the forerunner, the harbinger of the arising of the sun, even so friendship with what is lovely is the forerunner, the harbinger of the arising of the seven limbs of wisdom in a monk.

Of a monk who is a friend of what is lovely we may expect that he will cultivate, that he will make much of the seven limbs of wisdom. And how does a monk, who is a friend of what is lovely, cultivate and make much of them?

Herein a monk cultivates the limb of wisdom that is mindfulness, which is based on seclusion . . . the limb of wisdom which is equanimity, that is based on seclusion, on dispassion, on cessation, that ends in self-surrender. That, monks, is how a monk, who is a friend of what is lovely, cultivates and makes much of the seven limbs of wisdom.

(ix) *Factor* (*a*).

As a matter concerning one's own self,[2] monks, I see no other single factor so potent for the arising of the seven limbs of wisdom as systematic attention.

---

[1] *Supra*, text 29.

[2] *Ajjhattikaŋ angan ti karitvā* (the personal factor), as opposed to *bāhiraŋ angaŋ* of next §. B. does not comment here, but at *A*. i, 16 he says: *Idaŋ vuttaŋ hoti: Bhikkhave, ajjhattaŋ paccattaŋ attano santāne samuṭṭhitaŋk āraṇan ti katvā na aññaŋ ekaŋ kāraṇan pi passāmī ti*. *Cf. infra*, text 110.

Of a monk who is possessed of systematic attention we may expect that he will cultivate, that he will make much of the seven limbs of wisdom. And how does a monk so possessed cultivate . . . ?

Herein a monk cultivates the limb of wisdom that is mindfulness . . .

(x) *Factor* (*b*).

As a matter concerning the outside,[1] monks, I see no other single factor so potent for the arising of the seven limbs of wisdom as friendship with what is lovely.

Of a monk who is possessed of systematic attention we may expect that he will cultivate the seven limbs of wisdom, that he will make much of the seven limbs of wisdom. And how does a monk who is a friend of what is lovely cultivate . . . ? (*as before*) . . .

CHAPTER VI.—PERSEVERANCE IN THE LIMBS OF WISDOM[2]

(i) *Food.*

I will teach you, monks, what is food and what is no food for the five hindrances and for the seven limbs of wisdom. Do ye listen to it.

I. The Food of the Hindrances

And what, monks, is food for the arising of sensual lust that has not yet arisen, or for the more-becoming and growth of sensual lust already arisen? It is, monks, the alluring feature of things.[3] Unsystematic attention to that is this

---

[1] *Comy.* seems to regard the difference thus: Your own person, hair, nails, or cleanliness is *ajjhattikaŋ*; your robe, lodging, etc., is *bahiraŋ*.

[2] Text has for chapter-heading and tailpiece *Bojjhanga-sākaccaŋ*. ? for *sakkaccaŋ* = *sādhukaŋ* or *sātaccaŋ*, perseverance in. *Comy.* does not help here.

[3] *Cf.* II, 1, i, for a similar section on Food.

food for the arising of sensual lust that has not yet arisen, or for the more-becoming and growth thereof, if arisen.

And what, monks, is food for the arising of malevolence not yet arisen, or for the more-becoming and growth thereof, if already arisen? It is, monks, the repulsive feature of things. Unsystematic attention to that is this food for the arising of malevolence that has not yet arisen . . .

And what, monks, is food for the arising of sloth and torpor not yet arisen, or for the more-becoming and growth thereof, if already arisen? It is, monks, regret, drowsiness, languor, surfeit after meals, torpidity of mind.[1] Unsystematic attention to that, monks, is this food for the arising of sloth and torpor . . .

And what, monks, is food for the arising of excitement and flurry not yet arisen, or for the more-becoming and growth thereof if already arisen? It is non-tranquillity of mind. Unsystematic attention to that, monks, is this food for the arising of excitement and flurry not yet arisen . . .

And what, monks, is food for the arising of doubt and wavering not yet arisen, or for the more-becoming and growth thereof, if already arisen? It is things which are based on doubt and wavering. Unsystematic attention to that, monks, is this food for the arising of doubt and wavering not yet arisen, or for the more-becoming and growth of doubt and wavering that have already arisen.

II. The Food of the Limbs of Wisdom

And what, monks, is food for the arising of the limb of wisdom that is mindfulness not yet arisen, or for the cultivation and fulfilment thereof, if already arisen?

There are, monks, things based on the limb of wisdom that is mindfulness. Systematic attention thereto, if made much of, is this food for the arising of mindfulness.

And what, monks, is food for the arising of Norm-investigation which has not yet arisen, or for the cultivation and fulfilment thereof if already arisen?

---

[1] *Cf. A.* i, 3; *supra*, text 64 *n.*

There are, monks, things good and bad, things blameworthy and things not blameworthy, things mean and things exalted, things that are constituent parts of darkness and light. Systematic attention thereto, if made much of, is this food for the arising of the limb of wisdom which is Norm-investigation, if not yet arisen (or for the more-becoming and growth thereof), for its cultivation and fulfilment, if already arisen.[1]

And what, monks, is food for the arising of the limb of wisdom that is energy not yet arisen, or for the cultivation and fulfilment thereof, if already arisen ?

There is, monks, the element of putting forth effort, the element of exertion, the element of striving.[2] Systematic attention thereto, if made much of, is this food . . .

And what, monks, is food for the arising of the limb of wisdom that is zest which has not yet arisen, or for the cultivation and fulfilment thereof, if already arisen ?

There are, monks, things based on the limb of wisdom that is zest. Systematic attention thereto, if made much of, is this food for the arising . . .

And what, monks, is food for the arising of the limb of wisdom that is tranquillity which has not yet arisen, or for the cultivation and fulfilment thereof, if already arisen ?

There is, monks, tranquillity of body and there is tranquillity of mind. Systematic attention thereto, if made much of, is this food for the arising of the limb of wisdom that is tranquillity which has not yet arisen, (or for the more-becoming and growth thereof), for its cultivation and fulfilment, if already arisen.[3]

And what, monks, is food for the arising of the limb of wisdom that is concentration which has not yet arisen, or for . . .

---

[1] Quoted *VM.* i, 131, where the words in brackets are added.

[2] *Ārambha-dhātu.* *Cf. Expos.* i, 192. The initial effort of striving. *Cf. MA.* 284. *Nikkama-dhātu*, the same, grown stronger by casting off sloth. *Parakkama-dhātu*, the same, still stronger as it draws nearer and nearer to the goal.

[3] *VM.* i, 133, brackets as above.

There are, monks, sights that calm, that bewilder not. Systematic attention thereto is this food for the arising of concentration . . . or for its cultivation and fulfilment, if already arisen.

And what, monks, is food for the arising of the limb of wisdom, that is equanimity not yet arisen, or for its cultivation and fulfilment, if it has already arisen?

There are, monks, things based on the limb of wisdom that is equanimity. Systematic attention thereto, if made much of, is this food for the arising of the limb of wisdom that is equanimity not yet arisen, or for its cultivation and fulfilment, if it has already arisen.

III. No Food for the Hindrances

And what, monks, is no food for the arising of sensual lust not yet arisen, or for the more-becoming and growth thereof, if already arisen?

There is, monks, the repulsive feature of things. Systematic attention thereto, if made much of, is no food for the arising of sensual lust, if not yet arisen, or for its more-becoming and growth if already arisen.

And what, monks, is no food for the arising of malevolence not yet arisen, or for the more-becoming and growth thereof, if already arisen?

It is a heart released by goodwill.[1] Systematic attention thereto, if made much of, is no food for the arising of malevolence, if not yet arisen, or for its more-becoming, if already arisen.

And what, monks, is no food for the arising of sloth and torpor not yet arisen, or for the more-becoming and growth thereof, if already arisen?

It is the element of putting forth effort, the element of exertion, the element of striving. Systematic attention thereto if made much of, is no food for the arising of sloth and torpor not yet arisen . . .

[1] *Mettā-ceto-vimutti.*

And what, monks, is no food for the arising of excitement and flurry not yet arisen, or for the more-becoming and growth thereof, if already arisen ?

It is tranquillity of mind. Systematic attention thereto, if made much of, is no food for the arising of excitement and flurry not yet arisen or for the more-becoming thereof, if already arisen.

And what, monks, is no food for doubt and wavering not yet arisen, or for the more-becoming and growth thereof, if already arisen ?

There are, monks, things good and things bad, things blameworthy and things not blameworthy, things mean and things exalted, things that are constituent parts of darkness and light. Systematic attention thereto, if made much of, is no food for the arising of doubt and wavering not yet arisen, or for the more-becoming and growth thereof, if already arisen.

IV. No Food for the Limbs of Wisdom

And what, monks, is no food for the arising of the limb of wisdom that is mindfulness, if not yet arisen, or for the cultivation and fulfilment of mindfulness that is already arisen ?

There are, monks, things based on the limb of wisdom that is mindfulness. Unsystematic attention thereto, if made much of, is no food for the arising of the limb of wisdom that is mindfulness not yet arisen, or for the cultivation and fulfilment thereof, if already arisen.

And what, monks, is no food for the arising of the limb of wisdom that is Norm-investigation, if not yet arisen, or for the cultivation and fulfilment thereof, if already arisen ?

There are, monks, things good and things bad, things blameworthy and things not blameworthy, things mean and things exalted, things that are constituent parts of darkness and light. Unsystematic attention thereto, if made much of, is no food for the arising of the limb of wisdom that is Norm-investigation, or for the cultivation and fulfilment thereof, if already arisen.

And what, monks, is no food for the arising of the limb of wisdom that is energy not yet arisen . . . ?

There is, monks, the element of putting forth effort, the element of exertion, the element of striving. Unsystematic attention thereto, if made much of,—this is no food for the arising of the limb of wisdom that is energy . . .

And what, monks, is no food for the arising of the limb of wisdom that is zest not yet arisen, or for the cultivation and fulfilment thereof if arisen. There are, monks, things based on the limb of wisdom that is zest. Unsystematic attention thereto, if made much of,—this is no food for the arising of the limb of wisdom that is zest. . . .

And what, monks, is no food for the arising of the limb of wisdom that is tranquillity not yet arisen, or for the cultivation and fulfilment thereof, if already arisen ?

There is, monks, a tranquillity of body and a tranquillity of mind. Unsystematic attention thereto, if made much of,—this is no food for the arising of the limb of wisdom that is tranquillity not yet arisen.

And what, monks, is no food for the arising of the limb of wisdom that is equanimity not yet arisen, or for the cultivation and fulfilment thereof if already arisen ?

There are, monks, things based on the limb of wisdom that is tranquillity. Unsystematic attention thereto, if made much of,—this is no food for the arising of the limb of wisdom that is tranquillity not yet arisen, or for the cultivation and fulfilment thereof, if already arisen.

(ii) *The method.*

Now a number[1] of monks, robing themselves in the forenoon, and taking bowl and outer robe, set off for Sāvatthī to beg for food.

And it occurred to those monks: 'It is full early to go to Sāvatthī to beg. Suppose we pay a visit to the Park of the Wanderers[2] who hold other views.'

---

[1] *Sambahulā. Comy.* as at *VinA.* i, 1 says: According to the *Vinaya* method three folk are called 'a number'; more than that is a company. According to the *Suttanta* method three is just 'three': above that, 'a number.' Here we are to understand it according to the latter.

[2] Not far from Jeta Grove. *Comy.*

So those monks went there and on coming to them courteously greeted the Wanderers of other views, and after the exchange of greetings and civilities, sat down at one side. As they thus sat the Wanderers of other views said this to those monks:

'Friends, Gotama the recluse teaches his disciples doctrine thus:

"Come ye, monks, Abandoning the five hindrances, the corruptions of the heart, which cause weakening of insight, do ye cultivate the seven limbs of wisdom." Now, friends, we also thus teach doctrine to our disciples, saying: "Come ye, friends! Abandoning the five hindrances, the corruptions of the heart which cause weakening of insight, do ye cultivate the seven limbs of wisdom."[1] Now herein, friends, what is the distinction,[2] what the peculiarity[3] of, what is the difference between Gotama the recluse's teaching of doctrine and our teaching, between his instruction and our instruction?'

Thereupon those monks made no reply, either of approval or of disapproval to those Wanderers holding other views; but, without expressing either approval or disapproval, they rose up and went away, saying: 'We will learn the meaning of this saying from the Exalted One.'

So those monks, after wandering through Sāvatthī for alms, on returning from their alms-round and eating their meal, went to visit the Exalted One, and on coming to him saluted him and sat down at one side. So seated those monks said this to the Exalted One:

'Lord, here in the forenoon we robed, and taking bowl and

---

[1] *Comy.* thinks these Wanderers hung about gatherings when the Buddha was teaching and, while pretending to be otherwise engaged, picked up these doctrines and put them into practice in their own teachings. I am of opinion, however, that similar doctrines prevailed among other teachers than the Buddha. For this subject see Mrs. Rhys Davids's article in *J.R.A.S.*, April, 1927, entitled *The Unknown Co-founders of Buddhism*, and *Indian Hist. Quarterly*, December, 1927, *Dhyāna in Early Buddhism.*

[2] *Cf. K.S.* ii, 19, iii, 58, iv, 141. *Viseso*=moreness.

[3] *Adhippāyo*=extra practice.

outer robe we set off for Sāvatthī to gather alms. Then, lord, it occurred to us thus: " It is full early . . . (*and they described in detail what had happened*). So, lord, we made no reply to those Wanderers holding other views, either of approval or of disapproval, but without expressing approval or disapproval, we rose up and came away, saying: " We will learn the meaning of this saying from the Exalted One." '

'Monks, when the Wanderers of other views say this, they should be answered thus: " But there is a method, friends, following which the five hindrances are ten in number, and the seven limbs of wisdom fourteen." When questioned as to this, monks, the Wanderers of other views will be unable to explain themselves, and further will come to an ill pass.[1] Why so ? Because, monks, it is beyond their scope. For I behold not, monks, anyone in the world, with its devas and its Māras, its Brahmās, with its host of recluses and brahmins, with its devas and mankind, who could satisfy the mind[2] with an answer to these questions, save only a Tathāgata or a Tathāgata's disciples, or at any rate after hearing it of them.[3]

I. The Five are Ten

'And what, monks, is the method of explanation according to which the five hindrances are ten ?

Sensual lust of the personal,[4] monks,—that is a hindrance. Sensual lust of the external, monks,—that is a hindrance. So when we speak of the hindrance of personal lust, that is what is meant.[5] Therefore, according to this method it is twofold.

---

[1] They would fail miserably. *Cf. K.S.* iv, 8, 39. *Comy.* as at *DA.* i, 117, *sampādetvā kathetuŋ na sakkhissanti . . . asampāyanato uttarim pi dukkhaŋ āpajjanti. DA.* adds (of *vighātaŋ*) 'trouble of dryness of lip, palate, tongue and throat.'

[2] *Cf. D.* i, 118, *veyyākaraṇena cittam ārādheyya.* (*Comy.*=*paritoseyya*).

[3] *Ito vā pana sutvā.*

[4] As usual, *Comy.* explains 'personal' as one's own *pañca-kkhandhā*; 'external' as that of others.

[5] *Cf. Asl.* 145; *Expos.* i, 192, *uddesaŋ* (=*gaṇanaŋ*) *āgacchati.*

One's own personal malevolence, monks,—that is a hindrance. The malevolence of others,—that is a hindrance. When we speak of the hindrance of malevolence, that is what is meant. Therefore, according to this method it is twofold.

Sloth, monks, is a hindrance. Torpor is a hindrance. So when we speak of the hindrance of sloth and torpor, that is what is meant. By this method it is twofold.

Excitement,[1] monks, is a hindrance. Flurry is a hindrance, So when we speak of the hindrance of excitement and flurry that is what is meant. By this method it is twofold.

Doubt and wavering in one's own conditions,[2] monks, is a hindrance. Doubt and wavering as to externals[3] is a hindrance. Thus when we speak of the hindrance of doubt and wavering, that is what is meant. By this method it is twofold.

This, monks, is the method of explanation according to which the five hindrances are ten.

II. The Seven are Fourteen

'And what, monks, is the method of explanation according to which the seven limbs of wisdom are fourteen?

Mindfulness, monks, as to one's own personal conditions—that is the limb of wisdom that is mindfulness. Mindfulness, monks, as to external conditions,—that is the limb of wisdom that is mindfulness. So in speaking of the limb of wisdom which is mindfulness, that is what is meant. So by this method it is twofold.

The limb of wisdom that is Norm-investigation,[4] in the sense of searching, investigation, scrutinizing, for insight into one's own personal conditions, is so called. And it is the same as regards externals. So when we speak of the limb of wisdom that is Norm-investigation, that is what is meant. Thus by this method it is twofold.

---

[1] *Cf. Buddh. Psych. Eth.*, 120 *n.*

[2] *Ajjhatta-dhammesu vicikicchā=attano khandhesu vimati. Comy.*

[3] *Bahiddhā dhammesu vicikicchā=bahiddhā aṭṭhasu ṭhānesu mahāv. Cf. V.M.* ii, 431 (*aṭṭhasu ārammanesu*); *Expos.* ii, 457.

[4] *Cf. Expos.* 195; *vicaya*=search; *pavicaya*=research.

Now, monks, that which is bodily[1] energy, is energy as a limb of wisdom. That which is mental[2] energy, that also is energy as a limb of wisdom. So when we speak of the limb of wisdom which is energy, that is what is meant. So by this method it is twofold.[3]

Now, monks, zest that is accompanied by thought directed and sustained,[4]—that is zest as a limb of wisdom. Zest unaccompanied by thought directed and sustained,—that also is zest as a limb of wisdom. So when we speak of the limb of wisdom that is zest, that is what is meant. Thus by this method it is twofold.

Now, monks, tranquillity of body,—that is a limb of wisdom that is tranquillity. Tranquillity of mind,—that also is a limb of wisdom that is tranquillity. So when we speak of the limb of wisdom that is tranquillity, that is what is meant. Thus by this method it is twofold.[5]

Again, monks, concentration accompanied by thought directed and sustained,—that is concentration as a limb of wisdom. Concentration unaccompanied by thought directed and sustained,—that also is a limb of wisdom that is concentration. Thus when we speak of the limb of wisdom that is concentration, that is what is meant. Thus by this method it is twofold.

Now, monks, equanimity as to one's own personal conditions,—that is equanimity as a limb of wisdom. Equanimity as to external conditions,—that also is equanimity as a limb of wisdom. So when we speak of the limb of wisdom that is equanimity, that is what is meant. Thus by this method it is twofold.

So, monks, this is the method of explanation according to which the seven limbs of wisdom are fourteen.'

---

[1] *Comy. kāyikaŋ* = bodily energy which comes to one who practises walking up and down. Tranquillity of the *kāya* (the three aggregates of feeling, perception and activities) is the calming of the three groups of mental factors.

[2] *Cetasikaŋ. Comy.* 'I will not abandon this sitting posture till my mind be absolved from the āsavas without grasping.' Tranquillity of consciousness (*citta*) is the calming of mind.

[3] *Expos.* 192. [4] *Savitakka-savicārā pīti.* [5] *Expos.* 171-2.

(iii) *Fire.*

Now a number of monks, robing themselves in the forenoon and taking bowl and outer robe set off to Sāvatthī for alms.

. . . (*As in the previous section.*[1] *They go to the Exalted One, who said*):

'When the Wanderers of other views thus speak, monks, thus should they be answered: "Whenever, friends, the mind is sluggish,[2] at such time which of the limbs of wisdom is it unreasonable to cultivate? To cultivate which limb of wisdom is it reasonable?

Again, friends, when the mind is elated,[3] at such time which of the limbs of wisdom is it unreasonable to cultivate? To cultivate which is reasonable?"

Thus questioned, monks, the Wanderers of other views will be unable to explain themselves, and further will come to an ill pass. Why so?

Because, monks, it is beyond their scope. For I behold not, monks, anyone in the world, with its devas and Māras, its Brahmās, with its host of recluses and brahmins, with its devas and mankind, who could satisfy the mind with an answer to these questions, save only a Tathāgata or a Tathāgata's disciples, or at any rate only after hearing it of them.'

I. Wrong Season

'At such time, monks, as the mind is sluggish,[4] then is the wrong season for cultivating the limb of wisdom that is tranquillity, then is the wrong season for cultivating the limb of wisdom that is concentration, or for cultivating that which is equanimity. Why so? When the mind is sluggish, monks, it is hard to raise it up[5] by these conditions.

---

[1] Text abbreviates.

[2] *Līna*, 'stuck fast,' adhering. *Cf. infra*, text 263.

[3] *Uddhata*, 'puffed up, inflated.'

[4] *I.e. atisithila-viriyâdīhi līnaŋ.*

[5] *Dussamutthāpayaŋ.*

Suppose, monks, a man wants to make a little fire blaze up. If he heap thereon wet grass, wet cowdung and wet sticks; if he expose it to rain and wind and[1] sprinkle it with dust,[2] pray would that man be able to make a little fire blaze up ?'

'Surely not, lord.'

'Just so, monks, at such time as the mind is sluggish, that is the wrong season for cultivating the limb of wisdom that is tranquillity, that which is concentration, or that which is equanimity. Why so ? Because, monks, when the mind is sluggish it is hard to raise it up by these conditions.

II. Season

But at such time, monks, as the mind is sluggish, then is the season for cultivating the limb of wisdom that is Norm-investigation, the season for cultivating the limb of wisdom that is energy, the season for cultivating the limb of wisdom that is zest. Why so ? Because, monks, the sluggish mind is easily raised by up such conditions.

Suppose, monks, a man wants to make a little fire blaze up. If he heap thereon dry grass, dry cowdung and dry sticks; if he blow it up with his mouth,[3] if he sprinkle it not with dust, pray, would that man be able to make a little fire blaze up ?'

'Surely, lord.'

'Just so, monks, at such time as the mind is sluggish, then is the season for cultivating the limb of wisdom that is Norm-investigation, the season for cultivating the limb of wisdom that is energy, for cultivating the limb of wisdom that is zest. Why so ? Because, monks, the sluggish mind is easily raised up by such conditions.

---

[1] *Udaḳa-vātaŋ* (? read *uḍaka-cāṭiŋ*); ? wet wind as opposed to *sukkha-vāta*. *Cf. infra*; *VM.* i, 130, 248.

[2] Text *pɔŋsukāna* (?). *VM. paŋsukena*; but correct in next §.

[3] *Mukha-vāta* ('mouth wind'). *VM.* has *v.l. sukka-v.* (a bright, clear, not rainy wind), or should it be *sukkha*, dry? The balance of the two phrases suggests that one of these two is the right reading.

III. Wrong Season

At such time, monks, as the mind is elated, then is the wrong season for cultivating the limb of wisdom that is Norm-investigation, the wrong season for cultivating the limb of wisdom that is energy, or the limb of wisdom that is zest. Why so? Because, monks, the elated mind is hard to be calmed by such conditions.

Suppose, monks, a man should want to quench a great fire. If he heap thereon dry grass, dry cowdung, dry sticks; if he blow it with his mouth, if he sprinkle no dust thereon, would that man be able to quench a great fire?'

'Surely not, lord.'

'Just so, monks, at such time as the mind is elated, then is the wrong season for cultivating the limb of wisdom that is Norm-investigation, the limb of wisdom that is energy, or the limb of wisdom that is zest. Why so? Because, monks, the elated mind is hard to be calmed by such conditions.

IV. Season

At such time, monks, as the mind is elated, then is the season for cultivating the limb of wisdom that is tranquillity, for cultivating that which is concentration and that which is equanimity. Why so? Because, monks, the elated mind is easily raised up by such conditions.

Suppose, monks, a man should want to quench a great fire. If he heap on it wet grass, wet cowdung, wet sticks, and expose it to rain and wind; if he sprinkle dust thereon, would that man be able to quench a great fire?'

'Surely, lord.'

'Just so, monks, at such time as the mind is elated, then is the season for cultivating the limb of wisdom that is tranquillity, for cultivating that which is concentration, that whicn is equanimity. Why so? Because, monks, the elated mind is easily calmed[1] by such conditions.

---

[1] Correct text's *surūpasamayaŋ* to *suv-*, and *bhikkhavi* of next line.

But as to mindfulness, monks, that is profitable on all occasions,[1] I declare.'

(iv) *Goodwill.*[2]

On a certain occasion the Exalted One was staying among the Koliyans,[3] at Haliddavasana,[4] a township of the Koliyans.

Now a great number of monks, robing themselves in the forenoon and taking bowl and outer robe, entered Halidda-vasana for alms.

And it occurred to those monks thus: It is yet full early to quest for alms in Haliddavasana. How if we paid a visit to the Park of the Wanderers of other views?

So those monks did so, and on reaching them courteously greeted those Wanderers of other views, and after the exchange of greetings and courtesies they sat down at one side. So seated the Wanderers of other views said this to those monks:

'Friends, Gotama the recluse thus teaches doctrine to his disciples:

"Come ye, monks, abandoning the hindrances that are corruptions of the heart, that weaken insight, do ye abide suffusing one quarter of the world with a heart possessed of goodwill: so also as to the second, third and fourth quarters: and in like manner above, below, across, everywhere, for all sorts and conditions,—do ye abide suffusing the whole world with a heart possessed of goodwill that is widespread, grown great and boundless, free from enmity and untroubled.[5] . . .

---

[1] *Sabbatthikaŋ. Comy.* 'like salt seasoning, is desirable on all occasions, just as an "all-round" royal minister can also fight or counsel or do special service equally well.'

[2] *Cf. Buddh. Psych.* 104; *VM.* i, 293, 308 (to which *Comy.* here refers).

[3] *Cf. K.S.* iv, 244.

[4] This name does not occur elsewhere, so far as I know. It would mean 'turmeric-clothing,' or 'turmeric-place,' and may refer to the occupation of the inhabitants as dyers, for the similes here given are those of dyeing (*infra*).

[5] The *brahma-vihāras* or 'best modes of life,' or ? 'dwelling with Brahma.' *Cf. K.S.* iv, 204 *n.*; Mrs. Rhys Davids's article in *J.R.A.S.*, Part II, 1928, entitled *The Unknown Co-founders of Buddhism: a Sequel*, where she discusses this passage and similar ones in the Canon,

So do ye also . . . with heart possessed of compassion . . . possessed of sympathy . . . possessed of equanimity, that is widespread, grown great and boundless, free from enmity and untroubled. . . ."

Now, friends, we also thus teach doctrine to our disciples, Herein, friends, what is the distinction, what is the peculiarity of, what is the difference between Gotama the recluse's teaching of doctrine and this of ours, between his instruction and our instruction ?'

Thereupon those monks could make no reply, either of approval or of disapproval, but without expressing either approval or disapproval they rose up and went away, saying: 'We will learn the meaning of this saying from the Exalted One.'

So those monks, after going their begging-round in Haliddavasana and returning and eating their meal, went to visit the Exalted One, and on coming to him, saluted him and sat down at one side. So seated those monks said this to the Exalted One:

'Here, lord, robing ourselves in the forenoon we took bowl and outer robe and set out for Haliddavasana to beg for alms . . . (*and they related what had happened, as above*).' . . . The Exalted One replied:

'Monks, when the Wanderers of other views say this they should be answered thus: "But, friends, how is the heart's release by goodwill cultivated ? What is its goal,[1] wherein is its excellence ? What is its fruit and its ending ? Likewise how is the heart's release by compassion cultivated. . . . How is the heart's release by sympathy cultivated . . . by equanimity ? What is its fruit and what its ending ?" Thus questioned, monks, the Wanderers of other views will be unable to explain themselves, and further will come to an ill pass. Why so ?

---

and thinks, as I do, that we have here an example of a doctrine added to his own by the Buddha. *Cf. supra, n.* on text 109. This passage seems worked up and put into the mouths of the Wanderers to fit this particular section. Maybe some of the Wanderers were ex-bhikkhus.

[1] Text misprints *kingātikā*. *Comy.* = *kiŋ nibbatti hoti.*

Because, monks, it is beyond their scope. For I behold not anyone in the world, with its devas, its Māras, its Brahmās, with its host of recluses and brahmins, with its devas and mankind, who could satisfy the mind with an answer to those questions, save only a Tathāgata or a Tathāgata's disciples, or at any rate after hearing it of them.

And how, monks, does one cultivate the heart's release by goodwill? What is its goal, wherein its excellence, what is its fruit and its ending?[1]

Herein, monks, a monk cultivates the limb of wisdom that is mindfulness, accompanied by goodwill . . . and the other limbs of wisdom in like manner. He cultivates the limb of wisdom that is equanimity, accompanied by goodwill, which is based on seclusion, on dispassion, on cessation, which ends in self-surrender. If he desires: Let me abide conscious of repugnance[2] in what is not repugnant; he so abides conscious of repugnance. If he desires: Let me abide unconscious of repugnance in what is repugnant; he so abides. . . . If he desires: Let me abide conscious of repugnance both in what is repugnant and in what is not repugnant; he so abides. . . . If he desires: Let me abide unconscious of repugnance both in what is repugnant and in what is not repugnant; he so abides. . . . If he desires: Avoiding[3] both the repugnant and the non-repugnant, let me abide indifferent, mindful and self-possessed; he so abides indifferent, mindful and self-possessed. Or, attaining the release called "beautiful" he abides therein.

Monks, the heart's release by goodwill has the beautiful for its excellence, I declare. Herein comes insight for the monk who has not penetrated to a still higher release.[4]

And how, monks, does one cultivate the heart's release by compassion? What is its goal, wherein its excellence, what is its fruit and ending?

Herein a monk cultivates the limb of wisdom that is mind-

---

[1] *Cf. K.S.* ii, 176.

[2] *Paṭikkūla-saññī.* *Cf. Pṭs.* ii, 212 (ref. to by *Comy.*).

[3] *Abhinivajjetvā.* *Cf. J.P.T.S.*, 1886, p. 137; *A.* iii, 1, 2; *Itiv.* 81.

[4] *VM.* i, 324. It is still *lokiya* (mundane). Transcendental is *lokuttara.*

fulness accompanied by compassion . . . he cultivates the limb of wisdom that is equanimity accompanied by compassion, that is based on seclusion, on dispassion, on cessation, that ends in self-surrender. If he desires: Let me abide conscious of repugnance in what is not repugnant; conscious of repugnance he abides . . . (*as above*) . . . indifferent, mindful and self-possessed. Or, by passing utterly beyond all consciousness of object, by putting an end to consciousness of reaction,[1] by disregarding consciousness of diversity, thinking " Infinite is space " he attains and abides in the sphere of infinite space. Monks, the heart's release by compassion has the infinity of space for its excellence, I declare. Herein comes insight to a monk who has not penetrated to a higher release.

And how, monks, does one cultivate the heart's release by sympathy ? What is its goal, wherein its excellence, what is its fruit and ending ?

Herein a monk cultivates the limb of wisdom that is mindfulness, accompanied by sympathy . . . the limb of wisdom that is equanimity, accompanied by sympathy, that is based on seclusion, on dispassion, on cessation, which ends in self-surrender. If he desires: Let me abide conscious of repugnance in what is not repugnant; he so abides . . . (*as above*). If he desires: Avoiding both the repugnant and the non-repugnant, let me abide indifferent, mindful and self-possessed; indifferent he abides. Or, by passing utterly beyond the sphere of infinite space, with the idea of " consciousness is infinite," he attains and abides in the sphere of infinite consciousness. Monks, the heart's release by sympathy has the sphere of infinite consciousness for its excellence, I declare.

And how, monks, does one cultivate the heart's release by equanimity ? What is its goal, wherein its excellence, what is its fruit and its ending ?

Herein a monk cultivates the limb of wisdom that is mindfulness, accompanied by equanimity, and the other limbs of wisdom so accompanied; he cultivates the limb of wisdom that is equanimity, accompanied by equanimity, which is based on

---

[1] *Cf. M.* ii, 13; *Dialog.* ii, 119, *Paṭigha.*

seclusion, on dispassion, on cessation, which ends in self-surrender. If he desires: Let me abide conscious of repugnance in what is repugnant; he so abides. If he desires: Let me abide unconscious of repugnance in what is repugnant; he so abides. If he desires: Let me abide conscious of repugnance both in what is non-repugnant and what is repugnant; he so abides. If he desires: Avoiding both the repugnant and the non-repugnant, let me abide indifferent, mindful and self-possessed; he does so.

Or, passing utterly beyond the sphere of infinite consciousness, he attains and abides in the sphere wherein he is conscious of the existence of nothing.

Monks, the heart's release by equanimity has for its excellence the sphere wherein nought exists. Herein there is insight for the monk who has not penetrated to a further release.'[1]

(v) *Sangārava.*

Sāvatthī . . .

Now the brahmin Sangārava[2] came to visit the Exalted One, and on coming to him greeted him courteously, and after the exchange of civil courtesies, sat down at one side. So seated the brahmin Sangārava said this to the Exalted One:

'What is the reason, Master Gotama, what is the cause why the chants which I once learned by heart for many days do not recur to me, not to speak of those I have not learned by heart. And again, Master Gotama, what is the reason, what is the cause why the chants I once did not learn by heart, do recur to me, not to speak of those I did learn by heart?'

I

'Well, brahmin, when one dwells with heart possessed by sensual lust, overwhelmed by sensual lust, and knows not in very truth any refuge from sensual lust that has arisen,—at such time he neither knows nor sees in very truth his own

[1] There are still two more stages before Nibbāna.

[2] *Cf. S.* i, 182; *K.S.* i, 231. He was a 'Purity-by-water' man, had a large following, and was converted by the Master at *S.* i *loc. cit.*

profit; he neither knows nor sees in very truth the profit of others: at such time he knows not, he sees not in very truth the profit both of himself and of others. Then it is that chants learned by heart even for a time long recur not, not to speak of those not so learned.

Suppose, brahmin, a bowl of water[1] mixed with lac or turmeric or blue or yellow dye, and suppose a man with good sight should look closely therein for the reflection of his own face. He would not know or see it as it really is. Just so, brahmin, when one dwells with his heart possessed by sensual lust, overwhelmed by sensual lust, and knows not in very truth any refuge[2] from sensual lust that has arisen,—at such time he neither knows nor sees in very truth his own profit. . . .

Then again, brahmin, when one dwells with heart possessed by malevolence, overwhelmed by malevolence . . . at such time he knows not, he sees not in very truth his own profit.[3] He knows not, he sees not in very truth the profit of others: he knows not, he sees not in very truth the profit both of self and others. Then it is, brahmin, that chants learned by heart even for a long time recur not, not to speak of those not so learned.

Suppose, brahmin, a bowl of water heated on the fire, boiling up and bubbling over: and suppose a man with good eyesight should look closely therein for the reflection of his own face. He would not know or see it as it really is. Just so, brahmin, when one dwells with heart possessed by malevolence . . . at that time he sees not, he knows not in very truth the profit both of self and of others. Then it is, brahmin, that chants even long learned by heart do not recur, not to speak of those not so learned.

Then again, brahmin, when one dwells with heart possessed by sloth and torpor, overwhelmed by sloth and torpor . . . chants even long learned by heart do not recur. . . .

Suppose, brahmin, a bowl of water overspread with mossy

---

[1] The same occurs at *A.* iii, 230 *ff.*

[2] *Nissaraṇaŋ*, *i.e.* 'shaking up and rooting out.' *Comy.*

[3] *Attatthaŋ*. For parables of a mirror *cf. D.* i, 80; *M.* i, 100; *A.* v, 92, etc.

water-plants,[1] and suppose a man with good eyesight should look closely therein for the reflection of his own face. He would not know or see it as it really is. Just so, brahmin, when one dwells with heart possessed by sloth and torpor, overwhelmed by sloth and torpor, . . . at such time chants even long learned by heart recur not. . . .

Again, brahmin, when one dwells with heart possessed by excitement and flurry, overwhelmed by excitement and flurry . . . chants even long learned by heart recur not. . . .

Suppose, brahmin, a bowl of water ruffled by the wind, stirred up, whirling round and rippling with waves: and suppose a man with good eyesight should look closely therein for the reflection of his own face. He would not know or see it as it really is. . . . At such time chants even long learned by heart recur not. . . .

Once more, brahmin, when one dwells with heart possessed by doubt and wavering, overwhelmed with doubt and wavering, and knows not in very truth any refuge from doubt and wavering that has arisen,—at such time he neither knows nor sees in very truth his own profit: he neither knows nor sees in very truth the profit of others: he neither knows nor sees in very truth the profit both of self and of others. Then it is that chants even long learned by heart recur not, not to speak of those not so learned.

Suppose, brahmin, a bowl of water stirred up, troubled and muddied, set in the dark: and suppose a man with good eyesight should look closely therein for the reflection of his own face. He would not know it, would not see it as it really is. Even so, brahmin, when one dwells with heart possessed by doubt and wavering, overwhelmed by doubt and wavering, and knows not in very truth any refuge therefrom,—at such time he knows not, sees not in very truth his own profit; he knows not, he sees not the profit of others; he knows not, he sees not in very truth the profit both of self and of others. Then it is, brahmin, that chants even long learned by heart recur not, not to speak of chants not so learned.

---

[1] *Cf. VM.* i, 261.

This, brahmin, is the reason, this is the cause why chants even learned by heart for many a day do not recur, not to speak of chants not so learned.

II[1]

But, brahmin, when one dwells with heart not possessed by sensual lust . . . (*the negative of the passage at* § I) . . . then even chants not long learned by heart do recur, not to speak of those learned by heart.

Suppose, brahmin, a bowl of water unmixed with lac or turmeric or blue or yellow dye, and suppose a man with good eyesight should look closely therein for the reflection of his own face,—he would know, he would see it as it really is. Just so, brahmin, when one dwells with heart not possessed by sensual lust, not overwhelmed by sensual lust, then indeed he knows in very truth the refuge from sensual lust that has arisen.

Again, brahmin, when one dwells with heart not possessed by malevolence . . . then even chants not long learned by heart do recur, not to speak of those learned by heart.

Suppose, brahmin, a bowl of water not heated on the fire, not boiling up, not bubbling over. Then a man with good eyesight looks therein for the reflection of his own face: he would know, he would see it as it really is. Just so, brahmin, when one dwells with heart not possessed by malevolence . . . then even chants not long learned by heart do recur, not to speak of those learned by heart.

Again, brahmin, when one dwells with heart not possessed by sloth and torpor, not overwhelmed by sloth and torpor . . . then even chants not long learned by heart do recur. . . .

Suppose, brahmin, a bowl of water not overspread with mossy water-plants, and a man with good eyesight should look closely therein for the reflection of his own face. He would know, he would see it as it really is. Just so, brahmin, when one dwells with heart not possessed by sloth and torpor

---

[1] The editor of text, Leon Feer, remarks that this section occurs in full only in Burmese MSS.

. . . even chants not long learned by heart do recur, not to speak of those so learned.

Again, brahmin, when one dwells with heart not possessed by excitement and flurry, not overwhelmed by excitement and flurry . . . then even chants not long learned by heart do recur. . . .

Suppose, brahmin, a bowl of water not ruffled by the wind, not stirred up, not whirling round or rippling with waves: and suppose a man with good eyesight should look closely therein for the reflection of his own face. He would know it, he would see it as it really is. Just so, brahmin, when one dwells with heart not possessed by excitement and flurry . . . then even chants not long learned by heart do recur. . . .

Once more, brahmin, when one dwells with heart not possessed by doubt and wavering, not overwhelmed by doubt and wavering, and knows in very truth the refuge from doubt and wavering that have arisen: at such time he knows, he sees in very truth the profit of himself: he knows, he sees in very truth the profit of others: he knows, he sees in very truth the profit both of self and of others. At such time even chants not long learned by heart do recur to him, not to speak of chants he has long learned by heart.

Suppose, brahmin, a bowl of water, translucent and untroubled, not muddied, but set forth in the light. Then a man with good eyesight looks closely therein for the reflection of his own face. He would see it, he would know it as it really is.[1] Just so, brahmin, when one dwells with heart not possessed by doubt and wavering, not overwhelmed by doubt and wavering, and knows in very truth the refuge from doubt and wavering,—at such time he knows, he sees his own profit in very truth: he knows, he sees in very truth the profit of others: he knows, he sees in very truth the profit both of himself and of others. Then it is that even chants not long learned by heart do recur, not to speak of those long learned by heart.

This, brahmin, is the reason, this is the cause why even

---

[1] At *Milinda* 35 *saddhā* is called 'the water-clearing gem.'

chants not long learned by heart do recur, not to speak of those long learned by heart.

Brahmin, there are these seven limbs of wisdom, which are without let or hindrance, without corruption of the heart, which, if cultivated and made much of, conduce to realizing the fruits of release by knowledge. What seven? They are, brahmin, the limb of wisdom that is mindfulness, and the rest . . . the limb of wisdom that is equanimity. . . . These seven limbs of wisdom, which are without let and hindrance . . . conduce to the realization of the fruits of release by knowledge.'

At these words Sangārava the brahmin said to the Exalted One:

'Wonderful, Master Gotama! Marvellous, Master Gotama! . . . Let the worthy Gotama accept me as a disciple, as one who from this day forth, so long as life shall last, has gone to him for refuge.'

(vi) *Abhaya.*

Thus have I heard: Once the Exalted One was staying near Rājagaha, on the hill Vulture's Peak. Then Prince Abhaya[1] came to visit the Exalted One, and on coming to him saluted him and sat down at one side. So seated, Prince Abhaya said this to the Exalted One:

'Lord, Pūraṇa Kassapa[2] says this: "There is no condition, there is no cause of not knowing and not seeing. Not knowing and not seeing are without condition, without cause. There is no condition, there is no cause of knowing and seeing. Knowing and seeing are without condition, without cause." Herein what says the Exalted One?'

'There is condition, prince, there is cause of not knowing, of not seeing. Not knowing and not seeing have a condition, have a cause. There is indeed a condition, prince, there is indeed a cause of knowing and seeing, Knowing and seeing have a condition, have a cause.'

---

[1] *A.* i, 220, ii, 200. One of the Licchavi. At *M.* i, 392 he is sent by Nāta's son, the Unclothed, to confute the Buddha.

[2] He taught that deeds have no result. *Cf. K.S.* i, 90 *n.*, iii, 61 *n.*, iv, 279. He is *ahetu-vādo.*

I

'But, lord, what is the condition, what the cause of not knowing and not seeing? How do not knowing and not seeing have a condition and cause?'

'At such time, prince, as one dwells with heart possessed and overwhelmed by sensual lust, and knows not, sees not in very truth any refuge from sensual lust that has arisen,—this, prince, is the cause of not knowing, of not seeing. Thus not knowing, not seeing have a condition, a cause.

Then again, prince, at such time as one dwells with heart possessed and overwhelmed by malevolence . . . by sloth and torpor . . . by excitement and flurry . . . by doubt and wavering, and knows not, sees not in very truth any refuge therefrom,—this, prince, is the condition, this is the cause of not knowing, of not seeing. Thus, prince, not knowing and not seeing have a condition, have a cause.'

'What, lord, is this method of teaching called?'

'These, prince, are called "the hindrances."'

'Verily are they hindrances, Exalted One! Verily are they hindrances, O Happy One! Why, lord, if overpowered even by one single hindrance, one could not know, one could not see in very truth,—not to speak of being overpowered by five hindrances.

II

But, lord, what is the condition, what the cause of knowing and seeing? How do knowing and seeing have condition and cause?'

'Herein, prince, a monk cultivates the limb of wisdom that is mindfulness, that is based on seclusion, on dispassion, on cessation, that ends in self-surrender. With mind that is cultivated he knows, he sees as it really is the limb of wisdom that is mindfulness. This, prince, is the condition, this is the cause of knowing and seeing. Thus, knowing and seeing have a condition, have a cause. So with regard to the other limbs of wisdom, and that which is equanimity, which is based on seclusion, on dispassion, on cessation, which ends in self-surrender. With mind that is cultivated he knows, he sees as it really is the limb of wisdom that is equanimity. This, prince, is the condition, this is the cause of knowing and seeing. Thus knowing and seeing have condition, have cause.'

'What, lord, is this method of teaching called?'

'These, prince, are called "the limbs of wisdom."'

'Verily, lord, they are limbs of wisdom! Verily are they limbs of wisdom, O Happy One? Why, lord, possessed only of one limb of wisdom, one might both know and see,—not to speak of being possessed of all seven limbs of wisdom. Lord, the fatigue of body and mind that I had in climbing up the hill Vulture's Peak is all allayed, and I have fully grasped the Norm.'[1]

CHAPTER VII.—IN-BREATHING AND OUT-BREATHING

(i) *The skeleton.*[2]

I. Great the Fruit and Great the Profit

Sāvatthī (was the occasion for the following). . . .

Monks, the idea of the skeleton, if cultivated and made much of, is of great fruit and great profit. And how cultivated and made much of is the idea of the skeleton of great fruit and great profit?

Herein a monk cultivates the limb of wisdom that is mindfulness, accompanied by the idea of the skeleton, that is based

---

[1] *Dhammo ca me abhisameto.*

[2] For these methods of concentration see *Manual of a Mystic*, p. 70, etc.; *A.* i, 42; *VM.* i, 112; Warren, *Buddhism in Translations*, 353; *Buddh. Psych. Eth.*, 69-70 (*the jhāna of foul things*). This procedure was 'prescribed for such as were proved to be passionately affected by the beauty of the body' . . . 'the essential procedure lay in getting a clear and courageous grasp of the transience of any living organism.' *Comy.* refers to *Vis. Magg.*, *loc. cit.*, quoted at *Expos.* i, 92. 'Here *sahagata* should be understood as "dependence." The meaning is: "depending on the notion of the skeleton and developing the idea of mindfulness as a factor of wisdom has been obtained."'

on seclusion, on dispassion, on cessation, that ends in self-surrender. . . . So of the other limbs of wisdom. . . . He cultivates the limb of wisdom that is equanimity, that is so based and so ends.

Thus cultivated, monks, thus made much of, the idea of the skeleton is of great fruit and great profit.

II. Realization or No Return

Monks, from the cultivation and making much of the idea of the skeleton, of two fruits one may be looked for even in this very life, to wit: realization,[1] or, if there be any substrate left, the state of non-return.

How should it be cultivated, monks, how should it be made much of that one may expect these fruits?

Herein a monk cultivates the limb of wisdom that is mindfulness, accompanied by the idea of the skeleton . . . the limb of wisdom that is equanimity, so accompanied, that is based on seclusion, on dispassion, on cessation, that ends in self-surrender.

If the idea of the skeleton be thus cultivated, thus made much of, one may look for one of two fruits even in this very life, to wit: realization, or, if there be any substrate left, at any rate the state of non-return.

III. Great Benefit

Monks, the idea of the skeleton, if cultivated and made much of, conduces to great benefit. . . . How should it be cultivated? . . . Herein . . . non-return.

IV. Great Peace from Bondage

Monks, the idea of the skeleton, if cultivated . . . conduces to great peace from bondage.[2] . . .

---

[1] *Aññā, sati vā upādisese anāgāmitā* (*aññā*=arahantship).

[2] *Yoga-kkhema.*

V. A Great Thrill.

Monks, the idea of the skeleton . . . conduces to a great thrill.[1] How should it be cultivated . . .? Herein . . . non-return.

VI. Great Pleasantness of Living

Monks, the idea of the skeleton . . . conduces to great pleasantness of living.[2]

(ii) *Worm-eaten.*

(*The following are developed as above*, i-vi, *in each case.*)

Monks, the idea of the worm-eaten corpse, if cultivated and made much of, is of great fruit and great profit . . .

(iii) *Discoloured.*

Monks, the idea of the discoloured[3] corpse, if cultivated and made much of . . .

(iv) *The fissured.*

Monks, the idea of the fissured[4] corpse, if cultivated and made much of . . .

(v) *The Inflated.*

Monks, the idea of the inflated[5] corpse, if cultivated and made much of . . .

---

[1] *Saŋvegan*; lit. 'agitation, stirring up'; generally used with *ātāpin*, *e.g. Dhp.* 144 (*cf. K.S.* i, 13, § 8):

Asso yathā bhadro kasāniviṭṭho
Ātāpino saŋvegino bhavatha.

The particular emotion aroused by this process would seem to be horror of instability and keenness to get out of it.

[2] *Phāsu-vihāra.*

[3] *Vinīlaka*, 'turned bluish.'

[4] *Vicchiddaka.*

[5] *Uddhumātaka. Cf. uddhumāyiko, M.* i, 23 (like 'a bladder'). The usual number of these *asubhas*, 'foul things,' contemplated is ten.

(vi) *Goodwill.*

Monks, the idea of goodwill, if cultivated and made much of, is of great fruit and great profit . . .

(vii) *Compassion.*

Monks, the idea of compassion, if cultivated and made much of . . .

(viii) *Sympathy.*

Monks, the idea of sympathy, if cultivated and made much of . . .

(ix) *Equanimity.*

Monks, the idea of equanimity, if cultivated and made much of . . .

(x) *Inbreathing and outbreathing.*

Monks, the idea of inbreathing and outbreathing, if cultivated and made much of, is of great fruit and great profit . . .

CHAPTER VIII.—CESSATION[1]

(*Each of the following to be developed as above.*)

(i) *The foul.*

Monks, the idea of the foul, if cultivated and made much of, conduces to great fruit and great profit . . .

(ii) *Death.*

Monks, the idea of death[2] . . .

(iii) *The repulsive.*

Monks, the idea of the repulsiveness of food[3] . . .

---

[1] Lit., stopping, making to cease (*nirodha*).

[2] *Comy.* 'By thinking: Surely my life must ĕnd, my life is bound to death.'

[3] *Comy.* 'the absorption of rice and gruel, etc.'

(iv) *Distaste* or *All the world.*

Monks, the idea of distaste for all the world[1] . . .

(v) *Impermanent.*

Monks, the idea of impermanence . . .

(vi) *Ill.*

Monks, the idea of Ill . . .

(vii) *Not self.*

Monks, the idea of not self . . .

(viii) *Abandoning.*

Monks, the idea of abandoning . . .

(ix) *Dispassion.*

Monks, the idea of dispassion . . .

(x) *Cessation.*

I. Of Great Fruit and Great Profit

Monks, the idea of cessation,[2] if cultivated and made much of, is of great fruit and great profit.

And how cultivated, monks, is . . . ?

Herein a monk cultivates the idea of mindfulness accompanied by the idea of cessation . . . (*as above*). . . . Thus cultivated . . .

II. Realization or No Return

Monks, from the cultivating and making much of the idea of cessation, of two fruits one may be looked for even in this very life, to wit: realization, or, if there be any substrate left, the state of non-return.

---

[1] *Comy.* 'The idea that arises in one who conceives distaste for all the world.'

[2] In the sense of 'stopping, making to cease.'

And how cultivated . . . ?

Herein a monk cultivates the limb of wisdom that is mindfulness, accompanied by the idea of cessation. . . . . Thus cultivated . . .

III-VI. Great Benefit, Peace from Bondage, Thrill, Great Pleasantness of Living

Monks, the idea of cessation, if cultivated and made much of, conduces to great benefit, great peace from bondage, a great thrill and great pleasantness of living.

And how cultivated, monks, how made much of, does the idea of cessation so conduce ?

Herein a monk cultivates the limb of wisdom that is mindfulness, accompanied by the idea of cessation . . . and so with the other limbs of wisdom. He cultivates the limb of wisdom that is equanimity, accompanied by the idea of cessation, that is based on seclusion, on dispassion, on cessation, that ends in self-surrender.

Thus cultivated, monks, the idea of cessation conduces to great benefit, to great peace from bondage, to a great thrill, to great pleasantness of living.

CHAPTER IX.—GANGĀ-REPETITION[1]

(i) *Eastward.*

Just as, monks, the river Ganges flows, slides and tends to the east, even so a monk who cultivates and makes much of the seven limbs of wisdom flows, slides and tends towards Nibbāna. And how . . . ?

Herein a monk cultivates the limb of wisdom that is mindfulness . . . the limb of wisdom that is equanimity, that is based on seclusion, on dispassion, on cessation, that

[1] *Cf.* text, p. 38.

ends in self-surrender. Thus cultivating . . . a monk flows, slides and tends to Nibbāna.

(ii-xii) (*Longings.*)

(*To be similarly developed.*)

CHAPTER X.—EARNESTNESS[1]

(i-x) (*Seclusion.*)

Just as, monks, all creatures whether footless or having two, four or many feet . . .

(*The whole as before, by way of the Seven Limbs of Wisdom.*)

CHAPTER XI.—DEEDS REQUIRING STRENGTH[2]

(i-xii) (*Seclusion.*)

Just as, monks, whatsoever deeds requiring strength are done, all of them are done in dependence on the earth. . . .

(*The whole as before, by way of the Seven Limbs of Wisdom.*)

CHAPTER XII.—LONGING[3]

(i-xii) (*Seclusion.*)

There are these three longings, monks. What three? The longing for sensual delights, the longing for becoming, the longing for the holy life. . . .

(*The whole as before, by way of the Seven Limbs of Wisdom.*)

---

[1] Text, p. 41. [2] Text, p. 45. [3] Text, p. 54.

CHAPTER XIII.—THE FLOOD[1]

(i-ix) (*Seclusion.*)

Sāvatthī was the occasion . . .

There are these four floods, monks. What four? The flood of sensuality, the flood of becoming, the flood of view, the flood of nescience.

(*The whole as before, by way of the Seven Limbs of Wisdom.*)

(x) *The higher (sort of) fetters.*

There are these five fetters of the higher sort, monks. What five? The lust of form, the lust of the formless, conceit, excitement, nescience. These, monks, are the five fetters of the higher sort. It is by the full comprehension, realization, wearing out and abandoning of these five fetters of the higher sort that these seven limbs of wisdom must be cultivated. Of what five?

Herein a monk cultivates the limb of wisdom that is mindfulness . . . which ends in self-surrender. . . .

CHAPTER XIV.—GANGĀ-REPETITION[2]

(i) (*Restraint of lust.*)

Just as, monks, the river Ganges flows to the east . . . even so a monk tends to Nibbāna. And how?

By cultivating the seven limbs of wisdom. What seven?

Herein a monk cultivates the limb of wisdom that is mindfulness, which ends in the restraint of lust, the restraint of hatred, the restraint of illusion. . . .

(ii-xii).

(*In the same way for the Longings.*)

---

[1] Text, p. 59.

[2] 121 of text. As stated above, I follow the enumeration of *Comy.*, which disregards these higher numbers.

CHAPTER XV.—EARNESTNESS

(i-x) (*Restraint of lust.*)

(*So also for* The Foot, Peak, Wood, Heartwood, Jasmine, Prince, Moon, Sun and Cloth, *of* Pt. I, *to be developed under the title of* Restraint of Lust.)

CHAPTER XVI.—DEEDS REQUIRING STRENGTH

(i-xii) (*Restraint of lust.*)

(*So also for* Strength, Seed, Snake, Tree, Pot, Bearded Wheat, Sky, Raincloud (2), Ship, For All Comers *and* The River, *all to be developed under the title* Restraint of Lust.)

CHAPTER XVII.—LONGINGS

(i-x) (*Restraint of lust.*)

(*So also for* Longings, Conceits, Āsava, Becoming, Suffering, Obstacles, Stain, Pains, Feelings, Craving, Thirst, *as above.*)

CHAPTER XVIII.—THE FLOOD

(i-ix) (*Restraint of lust.*)

Sāvatthī was the occasion (for the following). . . .

Monks, there are these four floods. What four? The flood of sensuality, the flood of becoming, the flood of view, the flood of nescience. . . .

(x) *The higher sort* (*of fetters*).

There are these five fetters, monks, of the higher sort. What five? The fetter of sensual lust, lust for the formless, pride, excitement, nescience. These are the five. The seven limbs of wisdom, monks, are to be cultivated for the full comprehension, realization, wearing out and abandoning of these five fetters of the higher sort. What seven?

Herein a monk cultivates the limb of wisdom that is mindfulness . . . the limb of wisdom that is equanimity, for the restraint of lust, hatred and illusion, (the limb of wisdom) which plunges into the Deathless, has its goal in the Deathless, ends in the Deathless, which flows to Nibbāna, slides to Nibbāna, tends to Nibbāna.

It is for the full comprehension, realization, wearing out and abandoning of these five fetters of the higher sort, monks, that these seven limbs of wisdom are to be cultivated.

BOOK III

KINDRED SAYINGS ON THE STATIONS OF MINDFULNESS

CHAPTER I.—AMBAPĀLĪ

(i) *Ambapāli.*

THUS have I heard: On a certain occasion the Exalted One was staying at Vesālī, in Ambapālī's Grove.[1]

Then the Exalted One addressed the monks, saying, 'Monks.'

'Lord,' replied those monks to the Exalted One. The Exalted One said:

'This, monks, is the sole way[2] that leads to the purification of beings, to the utter passing beyond sorrow and grief, to the destruction of woe and lamentation, to the winning of the Method,[3] to realizing Nibbāna, to wit: The four stations of mindfulness. What are the four?

Herein a monk dwells, as regards body, contemplating body[4] (as transient), by having restrained[5] the dejection in the world[6]

---

[1] *Ambapāli-vana; D.* ii, 94. For *Ambapālī* (mango-guard), a courtezan, who presented this grove to the Buddha, see *D.* ii, 95-8; *Dialog.* ii, 102 *ff.*: *Sisters*, 120 *ff.*

[2] *Ekâyano* (text misprints twice as *ekāya no*). *Comy.* reads *ekâyanâyaŋ*; below there is a *vl. ekâyanvâyaŋ. Cf. M.* i, 55, *ekâyano ayaŋ maggo;* i, 74; *D.* iii, 221; *Pts. of Contr.* 105, 107, 'the sole conveying path'; *Mahānidd.* i, 455. *Comy. ekâyano=eka maggo; maggassa hi maggo pantho patho pajjo añjasaŋ vatumâyanaŋ,* etc. . . . *na dvedhā-patha-bhūto* (not diverging).

[3] *Ñāya=ariyo aṭṭhangiko maggo. Comy.*

[4] *Cf. K.S.* iv, 142 *n.*

[5] *Vineyya. Comy. tadanga-vinayena vā vikkhambhana-vinayena vā vinayitvā.*

[6] *Loke=kāye. Comy.* which refers to *Vibhanga s.v.*

arising from coveting. He dwells, as regards feelings . . . He dwells, as regards mind, contemplating mind (as transient), ardent, composed and mindful. . . . He dwells, as regards mind-states,[1] contemplating mind-states (as transient), ardent, composed and mindful, by having restrained the dejection in the world arising from coveting.

This, monks, is the sole way that leads to the purification of beings, to the utter passing beyond sorrow and grief, to the destruction of woe and lamentation, to the winning of the Method, to realizing Nibbāna, to wit: The four stations of mindfulness.'

(ii) *Mindful.*

Once the Exalted One was staying at Vesālī, in Ambapālī's Grove. Then the Exalted One addressed the monks, saying; 'Monks' . . . (The Exalted One said): 'A monk should dwell mindful and composed. This is our instruction to you. And how does a monk dwell mindful?

Herein a monk dwells, as regards body, contemplating body (as transient), ardent, composed and mindful, by having restrained the dejection in the world arising from coveting. He so dwells as regards feelings . . . as regards mind . . . as regards mind-states. . . . Thus is a monk mindful.

And how is a monk composed?[2]

Herein a monk, in his going forth and in his returning, acts composedly. In looking in front and looking behind he acts composedly. In bending or relaxing (his limbs) he acts composedly. In wearing his robe and in bearing bowl and outer robe he acts composedly. In eating, drinking, chewing and tasting he acts composedly. In easing himself, in going, standing, sitting, in sleeping, waking, in speaking and keeping silence he acts composedly. Thus is a monk composed.

A monk should dwell mindful and composed, monks. This is our instruction to you.'[3]

---

[1] *Dhammesu.* [2] *Cf. Dialog.* i, 81.

[3] *Comy.* discusses this section at great length and repeats *DA.* i, 196, etc.

(iii) *Monk.*

Once the Exalted One was staying near Sāvatthī, at Jeta Grove, in Anāthapiṇḍika's Park.

Then a certain monk[1] came to visit the Exalted One, and on coming to him saluted him and sat down at one side. So seated, that monk said this to the Exalted One:

'Well for me, lord, if the Exalted One would teach me a doctrine in brief, such that, on hearing it, I might dwell remote, earnest, ardent and aspiring. And thus maybe some silly fellows[2] here may inquire of me, and when I preach them doctrine they may think it worth their while to follow after me. Let my lord the Exalted One teach me doctrine in brief! Let the Happy One teach me doctrine in brief! Surely I could understand the meaning of the Exalted One's words! Surely I should become an heir[3] to the Exalted One's words!'

'Well then, monk, you must purify the rudiments in good states.[4] And what are the rudiments in good states? They are virtue that is truly pure, and straight view.

Now, monk, when your virtue shall be truly pure and your view straight, thenceforward, monk, leaning on virtue, established in virtue,[5] you can cultivate the four stations of mindfulness in a threefold way. What four?

Herein, monk, as regards your own self, in body contemplating body (as transient) do you abide ardent, composed and mindful, having restrained the dejection in the world that arises from coveting. Or, as regards externals, in body contemplating body (as transient) do you abide ardent, composed and mindful, having restrained . . . or, both as regards your own self and as regards externals, in body contemplating body. . . . Next,

---

[1] *Comy.* This monk had neglected his concentration-lesson (*kammaṭṭhāna*) and had failed to attain.

[2] *Mogha-purisā.*

[3] *Dāyādo.* *Cf.* *K.S.* iv, 42.

[4] Quoted at *VM.* i, 4: 'virtue is the beginning of the religion.' *Cf.* *Dhp.* 183, *Sabbapāpassa*, etc., and *infra*, text 165; *Brethren*, p. 35, 'virtue (habit = *sīla*) is habitual good conduct.'

[5] *S.* i, 13 (the text with which *Visuddhi Magga* or *Path of Purity* begins) *sīla-patiṭṭhāya naro sappañño*, etc.

as regards your own self, in feelings, and as regards externals in feelings. . . . Or as regards both your own self and externals, in feelings contemplating feelings (as transient) do you abide ardent, composed and mindful. . . . Then as regards mind in your own self, or as regards mind in externals. . . . Or as regards both your own self and externals, in mind contemplating mind (as transient) do you abide ardent, composed and mindful. . . . Then as regards your own self, in mind-states contemplating mind-states (as transient) do you abide ardent . . . or as regards externals, in mind-states . . . or as regards both your own self and externals, in mind-states contemplating mind-states (as transient) do you abide ardent, composed and mindful, having restrained the dejection that arises in the world owing to coveting.

Now, monk, when you, leaning on virtue, established in virtue, shall have cultivated these four stations of mindfulness in this threefold manner, then, monk, you may look for that growth in good states which shall come to you, whether by night or by day, and not for falling away in good states.'

Thereupon that monk was delighted with the words of the Exalted One, and was glad of them. And he rose up, saluted the Exalted One by the right and went away.

And that monk, dwelling solitary, remote, earnest, ardent and aspiring, in no long time attained that goal for which the clansmen rightly leave home for the homeless, even that unrivalled goal of right living,—attained it even in this very life, and knowing it for himself, realizing it for himself, abode therein, so that he came to know: Destroyed is rebirth, lived is the holy life, done is the task, for me there is no more of being here.

And that monk was yet another of the Arahants.

(iv) *Sālā*.[1]

Thus have I heard. Once the Exalted One was staying among the Kosalans at Sālā, a brahmin village.

[1] Text gives as title *Sallaŋ* (? barb) and *infra*, text 227, *Sālaŋ*. So also *Uddāna ad fin.*; but *B. v.ll. Kosalāyaŋ*, *Kosālāyaŋ*, *Kosallāyaŋ*. *Cf. M.* i, 285. We must read *Sālā*.

Then the Exalted One addressed the monks, saying: 'Monks' . . . and said this:

'Monks, those who are novices, not long gone forth (from home), late-comers into this Norm and Discipline,[1]—such monks should be roused[2] and admonished for, and established in, the cultivation of the four stations of mindfulness. Of what four and how? (Ye should say this:)

"Come ye, friends, do ye abide in body contemplating body (as transient), ardent, composed and one-pointed,[3] of tranquil mind, calmed down, of concentrated mind,[4] for insight into body as it really is.

In feelings do ye abide contemplating feelings (as transient), ardent, . . . for insight into feelings as they really are.

In mind do ye abide contemplating mind (as transient), ardent, . . . for insight into mind as it really is.

In mind-states do ye abide contemplating mind-states (as transient), ardent, composed, one-pointed, of tranquil mind, calmed down, of concentrated mind, for insight into mind-states as they really are."

Monks, those monks who are imperfect,[5] who have not attained their goal, who abide aspiring for the peace from bondage unsurpassed,[6]—they also abide in body contemplating body (as transient), ardent, composed, one-pointed, of tranquil mind, calmed down, of concentrated mind, for the comprehension of body. . . . So also do they abide . . . for the comprehension of feelings, of mind and of mind-states.

Monks, those monks who are Arahants,[7] destroyers of the āsavas, who have lived the life, done what was to be done,

---

[1] *Cf. K.S.* iii, 77.

[2] *Sampādetabbā* = *gaṇhāpetabbā*. *Comy.* *Cf. DA.* 300; *UdA.* 242; *infra*, text, 155.

[3] *Ekodi-bhūtā. Khaṇika-samādhinā ekagga-bhūtā samāhitā*, 'by a momentary concentration become one-pointed and tranquillized.' *Comy. Cf. VM.* 144; *Manual of a Mystic* (*passim*).

[4] *Ekagga-cittā* means much the same. *Comy. upacār' appanā-vasena*, 'by way of the preliminary processes.'

[5] *Sekhā. Cf. M.* i, 4; *S.* i, 121, and below, text 326 *n.*: *A* i, 231 *ff.*

[6] *Anuttaraŋ yoga-kkhemaŋ.*

[7] *M.* i, 4; *K.S.* iv, 80.

who have removed the burden, who have won their highest good,[1] who have utterly destroyed the fetters of becoming, who by perfect knowledge have become free,[2]—they also abide in body contemplating body (as transient), ardent, composed, one-pointed, of tranquil mind, calmed down, of concentrated mind, with respect to body being released.

So also in feelings, they are released from feelings . . . and in mind, they are released.

In mind-states they abide contemplating mind-states (as transient), ardent, composed, one-pointed, of tranquil mind, calmed down, of concentrated mind, in respect of mind-states they are released.

(For such reasons), monks, those who are novices, not long gone forth, late-comers into this Norm and Discipline,—such monks should be roused, admonished for, and established in, the cultivation of these stations of mindfulness.'

(v) *A heap of merit.*

Sāvatthī . . . Then the Exalted One said this:

'"A heap of demerit," monks. If any one should thus name the five hindrances, rightly would he do so: for indeed one entire mass of demerit are the five hindrances. What five?

The hindrance of sensual desire, the hindrance of malevolence, the hindrance of sloth and torpor, that of excitement and flurry, and the hindrance of doubt and wavering. "A heap of demerit," monks. If any one should thus name them, rightly would he do so.

"A heap of merit," monks. If any one should thus name the four stations of mindfulness, rightly would he do so: for indeed one entire mass of merit are the four stations of mindfulness. What four?

Herein a monk abides in body contemplating body (as transient), ardent, composed and mindful, having restrained the dejection in the world that arises from covetousness. So also with regard to feelings and mind and mind-states. In-

---

[1] *Anuppatta-sadatthā.*

[2] *Samma-d-aññā vimuttā.*

deed, monks, if one named the four stations of mindfulness "a heap of merit," rightly would he so name them: for one entire mass of merit are these four stations of mindfulness.'

(vi) *The falcon.*[1]

Once upon a time, monks, a she-falcon suddenly swooped down upon and seized a quail. Then, monks, the quail, upon being seized by the falcon, thus lamented: 'Just my bad luck, and lack of merit! (It serves me right) for trespassing outside my own pastures into others' property. If I had kept my own native beat today, this she-falcon would have been no match for me, if it came to a fight.'

'Why, quail,' said the falcon, 'what is your own native beat?'

''Tis a field turned up by the ploughshare,[2] a place all covered with clods.'

Well, monks, the she-falcon relaxed her efforts,[3] did not increase her grip,[4] and let the quail go free.

So, monks, the quail went off to a ploughed field, to a place all covered with clods, perched on a great clod, and stood challenging the falcon thus: 'Now come on, you falcon! Now come on, you falcon!'[5]

Well, monks, the she-falcon, putting forth her effort,[6] not

---

[1] *Cf. JA.* ii, p. 58, No. 8. Editor of text remarks (p. 192) that reference to this Sutta occurs frequently. See *Milinda* (*Pāli*, p. 365); Julien's *Avadānas*, N. 9; Lane's *Arabian Nights*, ii, 58. *Dialog.* iii, 60 *n.* The Pāli here is much corrupted, as in an oft-told tale, and I have had to emend the text by copying *JA.* and *Comy.*

[2] Text, *nangalena-kaṭṭha-karaṇaŋ*. *Comy. nangalena-kasika-karaṇaŋ.*

[3] Text *apatthaddhā* (lit. 'not persisting in her strength'); *v.l. apath-*; *JA. atthaddhā* (same *v.l.*) as opposed to *thaddhā* below of *JA. Comy.* does not notice it.

[4] Text *asaŋvadamānā* (for *B. avadamānā*, evidently by confusion with *vadamāno* in next §. *JA.* omits phrase. But *Comy.* has *avacamānā-vadamānā*, *attano balassa suṭṭhu-vaṇṇa-vadamānā ti* (*i.e.*, cajoled or flattered about her strength). I should read here *avaḍḍhamānā*. Apparently both text and *Comy.* are wrong, the passage being already corrupt, for the repetition below lacks point.

[5] Text adds *me*, omitted by *JA.*

[6] Reading with *JA. thaddhā* for text's *apatthaddhā* (which has no sense).

relaxing her effort and folding[1] both her wings, swooped swiftly down upon the quail.

As soon as the quail saw this he thought: Here comes the falcon full tilt upon me; and slipped inside the clod. But the falcon, monks, shattered her breast thereon.

So it is, monks, with one who goes roaming out of his own range in others' property. Wherefore roam ye not outside your range in others' property. To those, monks, who so roam Māra gets access, Māra gets opportunity.

And what, monks, is not one's own range, but belongs to others? It is the five sensual elements. What five?

There are, monks, objects cognizable by the eye, objects desirable, pleasant, delightful and dear, passion-fraught, inciting to lust. There are sounds cognizable by the ear . . . scents cognizable by the nose . . . savours cognizable by the tongue . . . tangibles cognizable by the body, objects desirable, pleasant, delightful and dear, passion-fraught, inciting to lust. This, monks, is not one's own range but belongs to others.

Do ye range your own pasture-ground. Keep to your own native beat.[2] To those who range their own pasture-ground, who keep their own native beat, Māra gets no access, Māra gets no opportunity of them.

And what is a monk's own pasture-ground? What is his own native beat?[3] It is the four stations of mindfulness. What four?

Herein a monk abides in body contemplating body (as transient), ardent, composed and mindful. . . . So with regard to feelings, mind and mind-states, contemplating mind-states (as transient), ardent, composed and mindful, having restrained the dejection in the world that arises from coveting. This, monks, is a monk's own pasture-ground, this is his native beat.

---

[1] Text *sannāyha, v.l. JA.* and *Comy. Sandhāya* = *sandhahitvā, suṭṭhu ṭhapetvā.*

[2] *Pettiko visayo,* 'one's ancestral range.'

[3] Quoted *VM.* i, 19.

(vii) *The monkey.*[1]

In Himâlaya, king of mountains, monks, there is a tract of land that is rough and hard to cross, where neither monkeys nor humans do resort. Likewise there is a tract of land where monkeys do resort, but not humans.

There are tracts, monks, in Himâlaya, tracts of level country, delightful spots, where both monkeys and humans do resort.

In those spots, monks, a hunter[2] sets a trap of pitch[3] in the monkeys' tracks to catch the monkeys. Now those monkeys who are free from folly and greed, on seeing that pitch-trap keep far away from it. But a greedy, foolish monkey comes up to the pitch and handles it with one paw, and his paw sticks fast in it. Then, thinking: I'll free my paw, he seizes it with the other paw: but that too sticks fast. To free both paws he seizes them with one foot, and that too sticks fast. To free both paws and the one foot, he lays hold of them with the other foot: but that too sticks fast. To free both paws and both feet he lays hold of them with his muzzle: but that too sticks fast.

So that monkey thus trapped in five ways[4] lies down and howls,[5] thus fallen on misfortune, fallen on ruin, a prey for the hunter, to work his will upon him. So the hunter spits him and prepares him (for eating) there and then over a charcoal fire,[6] and goes off at his pleasure.

Just so it is, monks, with one who roams in wrong pastures that belong to others. Wherefore do not ye so roam. For to

---

[1] Translated *Buddh. Psych.* p. 35, where the resemblance to Brer Rabbit and the Tar Baby is pointed out.

[2] Here text and Sinh. MSS. have plural. *Comy.* and Burmese MSS. singular.

[3] *Lepa*, apparently a sort of bird-lime or plaster. *Comy.* says it is made from *vaṭa-khīra-rukkhā* (fig-and-sap-tree), etc. So it may include pitch and tar.

[4] *Pañc' oḍḍito* (*Comy. uḍḍito*), strung up for carrying on a pole or pingo.

[5] Text *thunaŋ seti*. *Comy. thanaŋ* = *thananto.*

[6] Text is doubtful here. Sinh. MSS. would seem to mean 'trussing him up and carrying him off on a stick.' *Comy.* has no remark.

those who so roam Māra gets access, of them Māra gets opportunity.

And what, monks, is not one's own range, but belongs to others? It is the five sensual elements. What five?

There are, monks, objects cognizable by the eye, objects desirable, pleasant, delightful and dear, passion-fraught, inciting to lust. . . . There are sounds cognizable by the ear . . . scents cognizable by the nose . . . savours cognizable by the tongue . . . tangibles cognizable by the body, objects desirable, pleasant, delightful and dear, passion-fraught, inciting to lust. This, monks, is the range that is not yours, but belongs to others. Do ye range your own pasture-ground, keep to your own native beat, monks. To those who so range Māra gets no access, of them Māra gets no opportunity.

And what is a monk's own pasture-ground? What is his own native beat? It is the four stations of mindfulness. What four?

Herein a monk abides in body contemplating body . . . (*as above*). . . . This is a monk's own pasture-ground, this is his own native beat.

(viii) *The cook.*[1]

I

Suppose, monks, a foolish, inexperienced, unskilful cook of rājahs or royal ministers, put in charge of the various sorts of soup,[2] to wit: soups to be classified as sour,[3] bitter, pungent, sweet, alkaline, non-alkaline, salt or otherwise.

Now, monks, that foolish, inexperienced, unskilful cook does not take proper note[4] of his master's[5] taste, thus: 'Today my

---

[1] Comm. at *VM.* i, 150.

[2] *Nānā-ccayehi* (not *accayehi*)=*nānā-sayehi, nānā-vidhehi. Comy.*

[3] *Ambil' aggehi*, etc.=*ambila-koṭṭhāsehi. Comy.*

[4] For *nimitta-gāhī*, *cf. Dialog.* i, 80 *n.*; *Buddh. Psych. Eth.*, p. 351.

[5] Text *bhattassa* throughout, but Sinh. MSS. *bhattussa. VM. Bhattu-* (gen. of *bhattar*, 'supporter, employer,' not 'husband' as generally translated. Thus in the same sentence we should read *bhattu sūpeyyaŋ* for *bhatta-s*).

master likes this soup,' or 'he reaches out for that,' or 'he takes a good helping of this,' or 'he praises this one'; or 'today master likes sour soup,' or 'today he reaches out[1] for sour soup,' or 'today he takes a good helping of sour soup,' or 'today he praises sour soup.' And so on with regard to the other sorts of soup, whether bitter, pungent or sweet, or alkaline, non-alkaline, salt or otherwise,—in each case he does not take note of his master's likes and dislikes.

Therefore, monks, that foolish, inexperienced, unskilful cook gets no perquisites of clothing or gratuities or offerings.[2] Why so? Because, monks, that foolish . . . cook does not take note of his master's tastes.

Just in the same way, monks, here some foolish, inexperienced, unskilful monk abides in body contemplating body (as transient), ardent, composed, and mindful, by restraining the dejection in the world arising from coveting; but, though he abides in body contemplating body, his mind is not concentrated, the corruptions[3] of mind are not abandoned, he takes no proper note of that. So as regards feelings . . . mind and mind-states . . . though he abides in mind-states contemplating mind-states, yet his mind is not concentrated, the corruptions of mind are not abandoned, he takes no proper note[4] of that matter.

Thus that foolish, inexperienced, unskilful monk gets no perquisites of pleasant living in this very life, he has no perquisites of mindfulness and composure. Why so? Because that foolish, inexperienced, unskilful monk takes no note of his own mind.

II

But suppose, monks, that there is a wise, experienced, skilful cook of rājahs or royal ministers, put in charge of the various sorts of soup, to wit: soups that are classed as sour, bitter, pungent, sweet, alkaline or non-alkaline, soups salt or otherwise.

---

[1] *Abhiharati* = *gahaṇ' atthāya hatthaŋ pasāreti*. *Comy.*

[2] *Abhihārānaŋ* = *dāyānaŋ*. *Comy.*

[3] The five hindrances. *Comy.*

[4] As above on *nimitta*. He takes no note of the progress or stages of his lesson (*kammaṭṭhānaŋ*). *Comy.*

Thus, monks, that wise, experienced, skilful cook takes proper note of his master's tastes, thus: 'Today master likes this soup,' or 'he reaches out for that,' or 'he takes a good helping of this,' or 'he praises this soup,' or again 'today master likes sour soup' and so on.

Well, monks, that wise, experienced, skilful cook has perquisites of clothing, gratuities and offerings. Why so? Because the wise fellow studies his master's tastes.

Just in the same way, monks, here we may have some wise, experienced, skilful monk. He abides in body contemplating body (as transient), ardent, composed and mindful, by restraining the dejection in the world that arises from coveting. As he thus abides, his mind is concentrated, the corruptions are abandoned, he takes proper note of that matter. So also with regard to feelings . . . mind and mind-states, in contemplating mind-states his mind is concentrated, the corruptions are abandoned, he takes proper note of that matter.

Thus, monks, this wise, experienced, skilful monk gets the perquisites of pleasant living even in this very life, he has the perquisites of mindfulness and composure. What is the cause of that? It is because this wise, experienced, skilful monk takes proper note of his own mind.

(ix) *Sick.*

Thus have I heard: Once the Exalted One was staying near Vesālī at Beluva village.[1] Then the Exalted One addressed the monks, saying:

'Come ye, monks! Go ye and spend the rainy season round about Vesālī, where are your friends, acquaintances and bosom friends.[2] I myself will spend the rainy season just here.'[3]

---

[1] *Cf. D.* ii, 98. 'A village on a slope at the foot of a hill near Vesālī.' *Comy. Cf. Dialog.* ii, 106; *Buddhist Suttas*, p. 34. *Beluva* is the *vilva* tree.

[2] Texts, both here and at *D.*, read *mittaŋ*, etc., but *Comy.* MSS. *mittā, sandiṭṭhā, sambhattā.*

[3] *Comy.* says there was poor accommodation at Beluva, and the Master said this for their comfort; also that they might be at hand when he was to pass away, ten months later.

'Very well, lord,' replied those monks to the Exalted One, and went to spend the rainy season round about Vesālī, where dwelt their friends, acquaintances and bosom friends. But the Exalted One passed the rainy season at Beluva village.

Now when the Exalted One had begun to spend the rainy season, there arose in him a sore sickness. Strong pains came upon him, like to end in death. Thereupon the Exalted One endured them, mindful and composed, without complaint.

Now it occurred thus to the Exalted One: It is not fitting that, without addressing my supporters, without taking leave of the Order of monks, I pass finally away. What if I should by effort bend down this sickness and remain holding fast to my sum of life?[1]

So the Exalted One bent down that sickness, and remained holding fast to the sum of his life.

And the Exalted One rose up from that sickness; and not long after he had arisen therefrom he went forth from his lodging, and sat down in the shade behind the lodging on a seat made ready.

Then the venerable Ānanda came to the Exalted One, and on reaching him saluted and sat down at one side. So seated, the venerable Ānanda said this to the Exalted One:

'I saw,[2] lord, what the Exalted One had to endure. I saw how he bore up. Indeed, lord, my body became as if drugged.[3] Indeed my bearings were confused. Indeed the doctrines[4] were no longer clear to me because of the sickness of the Exalted One. Yet, lord, I had thus much of comfort in thinking: Surely the Exalted One will not pass utterly away

---

[1] *Jīvita-*, like *āyu-saṅkhārā*.

[2] Here *D.* has a different reading *diṭṭhā me phāsu, . . . khamanīyaŋ . . . yāpanīyaŋ Bhagavato.*

[3] *Madhuraka-jāto; Cf. K.S.* iii, 90 *n.* (where I have discussed the word). *Comy. sanjāta-sarubhāvo, sanjāta-thaddha-bhāvo, sūle uttāsita-sadiso viya* (he became heavy and lumpish, like one impaled on a stake); and below on text 162; Ānanda was all of a tremble like a cock escaping from the mouth of a cat.

[4] *Dhammā = satipaṭṭhāna-dhammā mayhaŋ pākaṭā na honti; tanti-dhammā pana therassa suppaguṇā.* At *S.* iii, *loc. cit. Comy.* says *pariyatti-dhammā. Cf. Thag.* 1034 = *Brethren*, 356, and *infra* II, iii (Cunda).

until[1] he has made some pronouncement concerning the Order of monks.'

'What is it, Ānanda, that the Order of monks expects of me now? I have taught the Norm, Ānanda, making no inner and no outer.[2] There is no "teacher's" fist, Ānanda, in the Tathāgata's teachings.[3]

If, Ānanda, anyone thinks: *I* will carry on[4] the Order of monks, or: The Order of monks is under *my* direction,[5]—let such an one make some pronouncement concerning the Order of monks. It never occurs thus to the Tathāgata, Ānanda: *I* will carry on the Order of monks, or: The Order of monks is under *my* direction. What,[6] Ānanda? Shall the Tathāgata make any pronouncement concerning the Order of monks?

As for me, Ānanda, I am now a broken-down old man, aged, far gone in years. I have reached the journey's end. I am come to life's limit. My age is now turning eighty years. Just as, Ānanda, a worn-out cart is kept going by being tied together with helps,[7] even so, Ānanda, the Tathāgata's body is kept going by helps.

---

[1] Text *tāva*, but *D. yāva*.

[2] *Anantaraŋ abāhiraŋ katvā*. It is worth while quoting *Comy.* on the much disputed question of exoteric and esoteric in Buddhism. *Comy.* (reading *anantara-sa-bāhiraŋ*) '*It refers either to the teaching or the person taught.* With the thought: I will not teach thus much to another, one makes doctrine inner (*antaraŋ*). With the thought: I will teach thus much to another, one makes doctrine outer (*bāhiraŋ*). With the thought: I will teach this particular person, he admits another person (*abbhantaraŋ karoti*). With the thought: I will not teach this particular person, he bars out a person (*bāhiraŋ karoti*). Here the meaning is that he did neither of these.' *Cf. JA.* ii, 221, *Bodhisattā nāma sippaŋ vācentā ācariya-muṭṭhiŋ na karonti; Mil. P.* 144.

[3] *Comy.* 'Teachers on their deathbed confide to a favourite private disciple things they had kept back in youth, untold to any. Not so the Tathāgata.'

[4] *Cf. DhpA.* i, 139 (of Devadatta).

[5] *Mam-uddesiko*, 'indicating me as giving directions what to do and what not to do.' *Comy.*

[6] Text has *sakim*, but *D. kim?*

[7] Text *vedha-missakena*. *Comy. vega-m. Cf. UdA.* 330 *n.* The *v.ll.* are numerous. *Buddhist Suttas*, 37, 'with much additional care'

Only at times when the Tathāgata, by not attending to any features (of things), by the cessation of feelings one and all, attains and abides in that mental concentration which is featureless, only at such times, Ānanda, is the Tathāgata more at ease.[1]

Wherefore, Ānanda, do ye abide grounded on self, self-refuged, taking refuge in none other. Do ye abide with the Norm for your ground,[2] taking refuge in the Norm, having none other refuge.

Whoso, Ānanda, either now or when I have passed away, shall abide with self for their ground, self-refuged, taking refuge in none other; with the Norm for their ground, taking refuge in the Norm, having none other refuge,—they, Ānanda, shall be my monks, they shall be atop of the gloom[3] [that is, they who are anxious to learn].'[4]

(where see note, quoting *DA. Comy. arahatta-phala-veghanena* (?); our *Comy.* has *-vaḍḍhanena*); *Dialog.* ii, 107, 'with the help of thongs, by bandaging up,' where see note. Our *Comy. bāḷha*[*v.l. bāhā*]*-bandha-* (? *baddha*)*-cakka-bandhanādi-paṭisaṅkhārena vega-missakena*, and adds that the Buddha was supported by the fruits of Arahantship (as at *DA.*).

[1] Text *phāsutaraŋ*, but *D. phāsukato . . . kāyo.*

[2] *Dīpa*='lamp' and 'solid ground' (island). This latter meaning seems preferable. *Comy.* 'by Norm, the ninefold transcendental Norm is meant (*i.e.*, the four paths, four fruits and *Nibbāna*).'

[3] *Tamatagge.* This somewhat obscure phrase is thus explained by *Comy.: tam' agge. Majjhe* ta kāro *padasandhi-vasena vutto* (the *t* in the middle is euphonic). . . . *Ime agga-tamā, evaŋ sabbaŋ tama-sotaŋ* (*DA. yogaŋ*) *chinditvā, ativiya agge uttama-bhāve . . . sabbe te catuvīsati satipaṭṭhāna-gocarā va bhikkhū agge bhavissanti.* 'On the peak of darkness . . . these are on top of the darkness; thus having cut off every stream of darkness they shall be "on the summit (of it)." Our *Comy.* is nearly the same as *DA.*, quoted by Professor Rhys Davids *ad loc.* I quote these parts of it as all may not have access to *Buddhist Suttas*, the note to which is later condemned in *Dialog. loc. cit.* Following *Comy.* (*uttama-bhāve*) he translated: 'They shall reach the topmost height,' but as is evident, and as *Pāli Dict. s.v.* has shown, the word refers to darkness. *Agge*=arahantship. *Comy.*

[4] This phrase in brackets, Professor Rhys Davids remarks, seems to have been added afterwards. *Comy.*, however, has it in the paraphrase.

(x) *The Nuns' Lodging.*[1]

Sāvatthī (was the occasion for these events). . . .

Now the venerable Ānanda, robing himself in the forenoon and taking bowl and outer robe, went to visit a certain settlement of nuns, and on reaching them sat down on a seat made ready.

Then a number of nuns came to see the venerable Ānanda, and on reaching him, saluted the venerable Ānanda and sat down at one side. So seated, those nuns said this to the venerable Ānanda:

'There are here dwelling, lord Ānanda, a number of nuns with their minds well established in the four stations of mindfulness, and they have attained to greater excellence of comprehension than before.'[2]

'So it is, sisters. So it is, sisters. Whosoever, be it monk or nun, dwells with mind well established in the four stations of mindfulness, such may be expected to attain to greater excellence of comprehension than before.'

So the venerable Ānanda, after instructing those nuns with a talk about doctrine, having roused, incited and gladdened them,[3] rose up and went away.

Now the venerable Ānanda, after going his begging round in Sāvatthī and having returned and eaten his meal, went to visit the Exalted One, and on coming to him saluted him and sat down at one side. So seated, the venerable Ānanda said this to the Exalted One:

'Lord, here (in Sāvatthī) robing myself in the forenoon . . . I paid a visit to a certain settlement of nuns, and on getting there I sat down on a seat made ready. Then, lord, a number

---

[1] *Bhikkhuni-vāsako*. *Cf. K.S.* ii, 145, as here (*bhikkhun' upassayo*). *Comy.* 'As the nuns were practising concentration exercises the venerable Ānanda went there to encourage them.' In fact, Ānanda seems to have been fond of the company of women. *Cf. loc. cit. supra.*

[2] *Pubbenâparaṃ visesaṃ* (in gradual succession, more and more) *sampajānanti*. *Cf. Dialog.* i, 296 *n.* *Comy.* *pubba-visesato aparaṃ uḷāra-visesaṃ*. *A.* iv. 47.

[3] For these terms *cf. DA.* i, 300; *UdA.* 242; *SnA.* 446.

of nuns came to see me, saluted me and sat down at one side. So seated, lord, those nuns said this to me: " There are here dwelling, lord Ānanda, a number of nuns with their minds well established in the four stations of mindfulness, and they have attained to greater excellence of comprehension than before." At these words, lord, I said to those nuns: " So it is, sisters. So it is, sisters. Whosoever, be it monk or nun, dwells with mind well established in the four stations of mindfulness, such may be expected to attain to greater excellence of comprehension than before." '

'So it is, Ānanda. So it is, Ānanda. Whosoever, be it monk or nun, dwells with mind well established in the four stations of mindfulness shall so attain.[1] In what four stations?

Herein, Ānanda, a monk dwells in body contemplating body (as transient), ardent, composed and mindful, by restraining the dejection in the world that arises from coveting. As he thus abides in body contemplating body, either some bodily object arises, or bodily discomfort or drowsiness of mind scatters his thoughts abroad to externals. Thereupon, Ānanda, his attention should be directed to some pleasurable object of thought.[2] As he thus directs it to some pleasurable object of thought, delight springs up in him. In him, thus delighted, arises zest. Full of zest his body is calmed down. With body so calmed he experiences ease. The mind of one at ease is concentrated.[3] He thus reflects: The aim on which I set my mind I have attained. Come, let me withdraw my mind (from the pleasurable object of thought). So he withdraws his mind therefrom, and neither starts nor carries on thought-process.[4] Thus he is fully conscious: I am without thought initial or sustained. I am inwardly mindful. I am at ease.

Again, Ānanda, a monk abides contemplating feelings . . . mind . . . he abides contemplating mind-states in mind-

---

[1] Text *sañjānissati* for *sampajān.* of previous section.

[2] 'Such as the Buddha.' *Comy.*

[3] *Cf. K.S.* iv, 253.

[4] *Paṭisaŋharāmi. Comy.* He withdraws attention and fixes it on the asic exercise (*mūla-kammaṭṭhānaŋ*).

states, ardent, composed and mindful. . . . As he so abides contemplating mind-states, either some mental object arises, or bodily discomfort or drowsiness of mind scatters his thoughts abroad to externals. Thereupon, Ānanda, his attention should be directed to some pleasurable object of thought. As he so directs it, delight springs up in him. In him thus delighted arises zest. Full of zest as he is, his body is calmed down. With body calmed he experiences ease. In one at ease the mind is concentrated. He thus reflects: That aim on which I set my mind I have attained. Come, let me withdraw my mind therefrom. So he withdraws his mind therefrom, and neither starts nor carries on thought-process. Thus he is fully conscious: I am without thought initial or sustained. I am inwardly mindful. I am at ease.

Such, Ānanda, is the practice for the direction of mind.

And what, Ānanda, is the practice for the non-direction of mind?

A monk, by not directing his mind[1] to externals, is fully aware: My mind is not directed to externals. Then he is fully aware: My mind is not concentrated either on what is before or on what is behind,[2] but it is set free, it is undirected. Then he is fully aware: In body contemplating body I abide, ardent, composed and mindful. I am at ease.

And he does the same with regard to feelings . . . to mind . . . and mind-states. Thus he is fully aware: In mind-states contemplating mind-states I abide, ardent, composed and mindful. I am at ease.

This, Ānanda, is the practice for the non-direction of mind.

Thus have I shown you these two practices,—that for the direction of mind, and that for the non-direction of mind. Whatsoever, Ānanda, should be done by a teacher who seeks the welfare of his disciples, in compassion, feeling compassion have I done that for you.[3]

Here, Ānanda, are the roots of trees. Here are empty places.

---

[1] *Comy.* 'He now abandons the mind-exercise (*kammaṭṭhānaṃ*).'

[2] The inclining to the exercise is *pure*; arahantship is *pacchā*. He now attends neither to practice nor to goal, so is indifferent.

[3] *Cf. K.S.* iv, 261, etc.

Do ye meditate. Be not remiss. Be not remorseful hereafter. This is our instruction to you.'[1]

Thus spake the Exalted One, and the venerable Ānanda delighted in what was said by the Exalted One.

CHAPTER II.—NĀLANDĀ

(i) *The Superman.*[2]

Sāvatthī was the occasion . . .

Now the venerable Sāriputta came to visit the Exalted One, and on coming to him saluted him and sat down at one side. So seated the venerable Sāriputta said this to the Exalted One:

'"A superman, a superman," is the saying, lord. Pray, lord, how far is one a superman?'

'It is by emancipation of mind, Sāriputta, that I call a man "superman." Without emancipation of mind there is no superman, I declare. And how, Sāriputta, is one's mind emancipated?

Herein, Sāriputta, a monk abides in body contemplating body (as transient), ardent, composed and mindful, by restraining that dejection in the world that arises from coveting. As he so abides in body contemplating body, his mind is purified, emancipated, by freedom from the āsavas. So also with regard to feelings . . . mind . . . mind-states . . . his mind is purified, emancipated by freedom from the āsavas.

Thus, Sāriputta, is one's mind emancipated. Indeed,

---

[1] The verbs, etc., are plural, as in the usual frame-work of the formula.

[2] I borrow this term from *Dialog.* iii, 134, *q.v.* *Cf. A.* ii, 35; *Dhp.* 352. *Comy.* has no remarks on this *sutta*. At *D. loc. cit.* the editors remark: 'These are the only passages in the sixteen volumes of the *Four Nikāyas* in which the word has so far been traced. This is sufficient to show that the word (*mahāpuriso*) is not in use as a technical term in the Buddhist doctrine. It occurs only when the brahmin use of the term is referred to (Sāriputta was a brahmin), and is there used to show the startling contrast between the brahmin and the Buddhist conceptions of what a superman must be.' *Cf.* also *Sn.* 1040.

Sāriputta, it is by emancipation of mind that I call a man "superman." Without this emancipation of mind there is no superman, I declare.'

(ii) *Nālandā.*

On a certain occasion the Exalted One was staying at Nālandā,[1] in Clothseller's Mango Grove.[2]

Now the venerable Sāriputta came to visit the Exalted One. . . . As he sat at one side the venerable Sāriputta said this to the Exalted One:

'Lord, I have such faith in the Exalted One! There never was, methinks, nor shall be, nor is there now existing anyone, whether recluse or brahmin, who is greater or more accomplished;[3] that is, in the higher wisdom!'[4]

'Splendid,[5] indeed, Sāriputta, is your bull-like utterance![6] You have laid hold of certainty.[7] You have uttered a lion's roar, in saying as you do, "Lord I have such faith in the Exalted One! There never was, methinks, nor shall be, nor is there now existing anyone, whether recluse or brahmin, who is greater or more accomplished; that is, in the higher wisdom!"

Come now, Sāriputta. Those who in past time were Arahants, fully Enlightened Ones,—pray, have you seen mind to mind[8] with all those Exalted Ones (so as to say of them): "Such was the virtue of those Exalted Ones, such the teachings of those Exalted Ones, such their wisdom. Thus they dwelt and thus those Exalted Ones were released"?'

'Surely not, lord.'

---

[1] In Magadha, once the seat of the famous university.

[2] *Cf. K.S.* iv, 67, etc. *Comy.* says the garden belonged to a rich seller of cloth (*dussa-pāvārika-seṭṭhi*). On hearing the Master teach he was delighted and, after fitting up the garden with hut-shelters and a pavilion, presented it. Like Jīvaka's Mango Grove it was thus called. This Sutta repeats that at *D.* ii, 81 = *Dialog.* ii, 87, iii, 95.

[3] *Bhiyyo 'bhiññataro.*

[4] *Sambodhi = arahatta-ñāṇaŋ. Comy.*

[5] *Uḷāraŋ = paṇītaŋ, seṭṭhaŋ, mahantaŋ. Cf. VvA.* 10, 11.

[6] Here *āsabhī = usabhavācāya sadisā, acalā, asampavedhi. Comy.*

[7] *Ekaŋso gahito.*

[8] *Ceto-pariyāya-ñāṇaŋ.*

'Then again, Sāriputta, those who shall be Arahants, fully Enlightened Ones in future times,—pray, have you seen mind to mind with all those Exalted Ones, so as to say of them: "Such shall be the virtue of those Exalted Ones, such the teaching of those Exalted Ones, such their wisdom. Thus shall they dwell and thus those Exalted Ones shall be released"?'

'Surely not, lord.'

'Again, Sāriputta, he who is now Arahant, a fully Enlightened One,—pray, is he seen mind to mind by you (so that you can say of him): "Such is the virtue of the Exalted One, such his teaching, such his wisdom. Thus and thus he dwells, thus is that Exalted One released"?'

'Surely not, lord.'

'So then, Sāriputta, in this matter you have no power of seeing mind to mind with these Arahants, these fully Enlightened Ones, whether in past or future or present time. What then, Sāriputta, is the meaning of your splendid bull-like utterance, your laying hold of certainty, your uttering of the lion's roar, in saying: "Lord, I have such faith in the Exalted One! There never was, methinks, nor shall be, nor is there now existing anyone, whether recluse or brahmin, who is greater or more accomplished; that is, in the higher wisdom"?'

'True it is, lord, as to those Arahants, those fully Enlightened Ones, whether in time past or future or present, I have no power of seeing mind to mind with them. I only infer from my knowledge which is in accordance with the Norm.[1]

Suppose, lord, there is a border town[2] with strong foundations, strong walls and towers, but a single gate, and over that is set a warden, wise, shrewd and watchful, who keeps out strangers and welcomes friends. As he patrols all round that town in order due he might not mark a crevice in the

---

[1] *Dhammanvayo vidito. Comy.* 'inferential knowledge (*anumāna-ñāṇaŋ*) proceeding in accordance with Norm-knowledge = *naya-ggāho*.'

[2] *Cf. D.* ii, 83.

wall or a hole just big enough for a cat to slip through, but he would think: Whatsoever creatures of any size enter this town or go out therefrom, all of them must enter or go out by this same gate. Just so, lord, is my inference from knowledge in accordance with the Norm.

Those, lord, who in time past were Arahants, fully Enlightened Ones,—all of those Exalted Ones, by abandoning the five hindrances, those corruptions of the heart that weaken insight, being well established in the four stations of mindfulness, by cultivating in very truth the seven limbs of wisdom, did attain enlightenment in the unsurpassed perfect wisdom.

They, lord, who in future time shall be Arahants, fully Enlightened Ones . . . shall do likewise.

The Exalted One, lord, who even now is Arahant, a fully Enlightened One, by abandoning the five hindrances, those corruptions of the heart which weaken insight, he, well established in the four stations of mindfulness, by cultivating in very truth the seven limbs of wisdom, is enlightened with the unsurpassed perfect wisdom.'[1]

'Well said, Sāriputta! Well said, Sāriputta! Wherefore, Sāriputta, you should repeat this Norm-teaching again and again to monks and nuns, to disciples, both men and women; and whatsoever silly fellows have any doubt or perplexity about the Tathāgata, when they hear my method of Norm-teaching, all such doubt and perplexity shall be abandoned.'

(iii) *Cunda.*[2]

On a certain occasion the Exalted One was staying near Sāvatthī, at Jeta Grove, in Anāthapiṇḍika's Park.

On that occasion the venerable Sāriputta was staying

---

[1] The passage at *D.* is much longer and embraces the whole method of Norm-teaching.

[2] *Cf. Dialog.* iii, 112 *n.*; *K.S.* iv, 30; *Brethren,* 119. According to *Comy.* the younger brother of Sāriputta. *Comy.* on *S.* i, 174 says he was one of the series of the Buddha's personal attendants before Ānanda was appointed, the others being Nāgasamāla, Upavāṇa, Sunakkhatta, Sāgato, Bodhi and Meghiya (for whom see *Udāna*).

among the Magadhese at Nālagāmaka,[1] being sick, afflicted, stricken with a sore disease. Now Cunda the novice was in attendance on the venerable Sāriputta. And it was owing to this sickness that the venerable Sāriputta passed away.

So Cunda the novice, taking the venerable Sāriputta's bowl and outer robe, went to Sāvatthī, to Jeta Grove, and so to Anāthapiṇḍika's Park, where he went to visit the venerable Ānanda,[2] and on coming to him saluted him and sat down at one side. So seated, Cunda the novice said this to the venerable Ānanda:

'Sir, the venerable Sāriputta has passed away: Here are his bowl and outer robe. [This water-strainer holds his relics.]'[3]

'Friend Cunda, this piece of news[4] will be an excuse for seeing the Exalted One. Let us go, friend Cunda, to visit the Exalted One, and when we get there we will tell him about this matter.'

'Very good, sir,' said Cunda the novice in reply to the venerable Ānanda.

So the venerable Ānanda and Cunda the novice went to see the Exalted One, and on coming to him saluted him and sat down at one side.

As they thus sat the venerable Ānanda said this to the Exalted One:

'Lord, this Cunda the novice said to me: "Sir, the venerable Sāriputta has passed away. Here are his bowl and outer robe. This water-strainer holds his relics." Indeed, lord, thereat my body was as if drugged. My bearings were confused.[5]

---

[1] *Comy.* on *S.* iv, 251, 'not far from Rājagaha, on his family property.'

[2] *Comy.* thinks he did not like to break the news to the Master himself.

[3] Burmese MSS. of text add *dhātuparibhāvanam* (?). *Comy.* adds: *idaŋ dhātu-parissāvanan* ti ('this water-strainer holds his relics'), but says 'he said this to each person'; so I add it in brackets.

[4] *Kathā-pābhataŋ* = *kathā-mūlaŋ* (lit. 'topic of conversation'). *Comy.*

[5] *Cf. supra*, i, § 9. Here, says *Comy.*, Ānanda was 'all of a tremble, like a cock escaping from the mouth of a cat.'

The teachings[1] were not clear to me when I heard the words "the venerable Sāriputta has passed away."'[2]

'But tell me, Ānanda, when the venerable Sāriputta passed away, did he take with him the constituents of virtue? When he passed away did he take with him the constituents of concentration or those of wisdom? Did he take with him, when he passed away, the constituents of release, the constituents of release by knowing and seeing?'[3]

'Nay, lord, when the venerable Sāriputta passed away he did not take with him the constituents of virtue . . . the constituents of release by knowing and seeing, But he was to me an adviser, one who was well grounded.[4] He was an instructor, one who could arouse, incite and gladden. He was unwearied in teaching the Norm. He was the patron[5] of those who lived the righteous life along with him. We bear in mind that essence of the Norm, that patronage of the Norm possessed by the venerable Sāriputta, lord.'

'Have I not aforetime[6] declared to you this, Ānanda,—

---

[1] *Dhammā. Thag. Comy.* says: *pariyatti-dhammā* (the doctrines to be learned by heart). Our *Comy. uddesa-paripucchā-dhammā* (advice and questioning).

[2] *Cf. Thag.* v, 1034; *Brethren,* p. 356 (on Ānanda): 'The following verse the thera uttered on hearing of the passing away of the General of the Norm:

> The firmament on every hand
> Grows dim, yea, all confusèd stand
> The truths I seemed to understand.'

[3] *Sīla-samādhi-paññā-vimutti-vimuttiñāṇadassanā-kkhandhaṃ* (the constituents of the Path to Nibbāna).

[4] *Otiṇṇo.* See *Pāli Dict. s.v.* (recommending its deletion from the text); but *Comy.* has it, and thus comments: *Tiṇṇesu vatthusu nānappakārena ovadana-sīlo. Cf. UdA.* 23, *otiṇṇa-vatthuka-puggale* (? one who has reached solid ground). For the words following, *cf. It.* 107.

[5] *Anuggāhako. Cf. K.S.* iii, 6; to the comment on which *Comy.* here refers.

[6] *Paṭigacc' eva. Cf. Trenckner, Milinda, App.* and *Pāli Miscellany. Comy. paṭikacc' eva* (not from *paṭigacchati,* but *paṭikaroti,* 'to provide for the future,' so 'provisionally, previously'). *Cf. Buddhist Suttas,* 119; *Dialog.* ii, 184.

how in all things that are dear and delightful there is the nature of diversity, the nature of separation, the nature of otherness? How is it possible, Ānanda, in the case of what is born, what is become, what is compounded, what is transitory,—how is it possible to have one's wish fulfilled: Oh! may it not perish? Nay, such a thing cannot be.

Just as, Ānanda, from some mighty tree, standing firm and full of vigour,[1] one of the greater limbs rots off,—even so, Ānanda, from the mighty Order of monks, standing firm and full of vigour, Sāriputta has passed away. How is it possible, Ānanda, I say, in the case of what is born, what is become, what is compounded, what is transitory,—how is it possible that one's wish can be fulfilled: Oh! may it not perish? Nay, such a thing cannot be.

Wherefore, Ānanda, do ye abide grounded on self, self-refuged, taking refuge in none other. Do ye abide grounded on the Norm, taking refuge in the Norm, having none other refuge. And how, Ānanda, does a monk so abide?

Herein, Ānanda, a monk abides in body contemplating body (as transient), ardent, composed and mindful, restraining the dejection in the world that arises from coveting. So also with regard to feelings . . . mind . . . and mind-states. . . . That, Ānanda, is how a monk abides grounded on self, self-refuged, taking refuge in none other.

Whoso, Ānanda, either now or when I have passed away, shall abide grounded on self, self-refuged, taking refuge in none other; grounded on the Norm, with the Norm for refuge, taking refuge in none other,—they, Ananda, shall be my monks, they shall be atop of the gloom; that is, they who are anxious to learn.'[2]

(iv) *Ukkāvela.*[3]

Once the Exalted One was staying among the Vajjians at Ukkāvela on the river Ganges together with a great company

---

[1] *Sāravant*, in the case of a tree 'heartwood, pith, timber.'

[2] *Cf. supra*, § 9.

[3] Text-title is *Celam*, and below *Ukkācelāyaŋ*, for which I read *Ukkāvela*, as at *K.S.* iv, 177 *n.*, and *UdA.* 322.

of monks, not long after the passing away of Sāriputta and Moggallāna the Great.[1]

Now at that time the Exalted One was seated in the open air, surrounded by the Order of monks. Then the Exalted One, observing that the Order of monks was become silent, thus addressed the monks:

'Monks, truly this company seems empty. Now that Sāriputta and Moggallāna have passed away my company is empty of them. It is indifferent as to that quarter in which Sāriputta and Moggallāna are dwelling.

Monks, whosoever in past times have been Arahants, fully Enlightened Ones,—each one of those Exalted Ones had such a noble pair of disciples as were Sāriputta and Moggallāna to me. Monks, whosoever in future times shall be Arahants, fully Enlightened Ones, each of them shall have such a noble pair of disciples as were Sāriputta and Moggallāna to me.[2]

A wonder of disciples it is, monks! A marvel of disciples it is, monks! To think how they carry out the Master's teachings, how they give advice accordantly, how dear to the fourfold company, how delightful, how revered and sought after they must be.

A wonder it is, monks! A marvel it is, monks, in the Tathāgata! For though such a pair of disciples has passed away, there is in the Tathāgata no sorrow or lamenting. How is it possible, monks, in the case of what is born, what is become, what is compounded, what is transitory,—how is it possible to have one's wish fulfilled: Oh! may it not perish? Nay, such a thing cannot be.

Just as if, monks, from some mighty tree, standing firm and full of vigour, the greater limbs should rot away: even so monks, from the mighty Order of monks, standing firm and full of vigour, Sāriputta and Moggallāna have passed away. How is it possible, I say, in the case if what is born, what is become, what is compounded, what is transitory,—how is it

---

[1] *Comy.* Sāriputta died on the full-moon day of the month Kattika (October to November); Moggallāna a fortnight later. *Cf. Dialog.* ii, 193.

[2] *D.* ii, 5.

possible to have one's wish fulfilled: Oh! may it not perish? Nay, such a thing cannot be.

Wherefore, monks, do ye abide grounded on self . . . taking refuge in none other. And how does a monk so abide?

Herein a monk abides in body contemplating body . . .

Whosoever, monks, either now or when I am gone, shall abide grounded on self, self-refuged, taking refuge in none other; grounded on the Norm, with the Norm for refuge, taking refuge in none other,—they shall be my monks, they shall be atop of the gloom: that is, they who are anxious to learn.'

(v) *Bāhiya* (or *Bāhika*).[1]

Sāvatthī was the occasion . . .

Now the venerable Bāhiya came to see the Exalted One, and on coming to him saluted him and sat down at one side. So seated the venerable Bāhiya said this to the Exalted One:

'Well for me, lord, if the Exalted One would teach me a teaching in brief, hearing which teaching from the Exalted One I might dwell solitary, remote, earnest, ardent and aspiring.'

'In such case, Bāhiya, you must purify the rudiments in good states.[2] And what are the rudiments in good states? It is virtue that is truly pure and straight view. Now, Bāhiya, when your virtue shall be truly pure and your view straight, thenceforward, leaning on virtue, established in virtue, you can cultivate the four stations of mindfulness. What four?

Herein, Bāhiya, do you abide in body contemplating body (as transient), ardent, composed and mindful, by restraining the dejection in the world that arises from coveting. Do so likewise in feelings . . . in mind . . . in mind-states. . . . Indeed, Bāhiya, when you, leaning on virtue, established in virtue, shall have thus cultivated the four stations of mindfulness, thenceforward, Bāhiya, you may look for that growth

---

[1] *Cf. K.S.* iv, 37; *Ud.* i, 10. He was called *Dāru-cīriya*, because he wore a dress of bark or fibre. There also he asks for teaching, and is given instruction on the organs of sense.

[2] *Cf. Brethren*, p. 35; *supra*, text 143.

in good states which shall come to you,[1] whether by night or by day, and not for falling away.'

Thereupon the venerable Bāhiya was delighted with the words of the Exalted One and was glad of them. And he rose up, saluted the Exalted One by the right and went away.

And the venerable Bāhiya, dwelling solitary and remote, earnest, ardent and aspiring, in no long time attained that goal for which the clansmen rightly leave home for the homeless, even that unrivalled goal of righteous living, attained in even this very life: and, knowing it for himself, realizing it for himself, abode therein, so that he came to know: 'Destroyed is rebirth. Lived is the righteous life. Done is what I had to do. Indeed there is no more of being here for me.'

And the venerable Bāhiya was yet another of the Arahants.

(vi) *Uttiya*.[2]

Sāvatthī was the occasion . . .

Then the venerable Uttiya came to visit the Exalted One . . . (*the whole is abridged in text, as in the previous* sutta, *except*) . . . Thenceforward, Uttiya, you shall pass beyond the realm of death. . . .[3]

And the venerable Uttiya was yet another of the Arahants.

(vii) *Ariyan*.

Sāvatthī . . . The Exalted One said:

'These four stations of mindfulness, monks, if cultivated and made much of, these Ariyan straight paths lead on, for one who acts accordingly with them, to the utter destruction of Ill. What four?[4]

Herein a monk dwells in body contemplating body (as

---

[1] Text misprints *āgamissasi* for *āgamissati*.

[2] *Cf. Brethren*, 34 *n.*; *A.* v, 193. Perhaps it is the same one in all these cases. In the former he is given the same lesson in 'rudiments' as here. In the second case he is a Wanderer, and probably it is an incident of his earlier life.

[3] *Maccudheyyassa pāraŋ*.

[4] *Cf. Dialog.* i, 302, etc., *ariyā, niyyānikā niyyanti takkarassa*.

transient), ardent, composed and mindful, by restraining the dejection in the world that arises from coveting. . . . So with regard to feelings . . . mind, and mind-states, he so dwells. . . .

These four stations of mindfulness, monks . . . these Ariyan straight paths lead on, for one who acts accordantly with them, to the utter destruction of Ill.'

(viii) *Brahmā.*

On a certain occasion the Exalted One was staying near Uruvelā, on the bank of the river Nerañjarā, under the Goatherds' Banyan,[1] after he had just attained enlightenment.

Then, as the Exalted One meditated in solitude, there arose in his mind this train of thought: This is the one sole way[2] that leads to the purification of beings, to the utter passing beyond sorrow and grief, to the destruction of woe and lamentation, to the winning of the Method, to the realizing of Nibbāna, to wit: the four stations of mindfulness. What four?

A monk[3] should dwell in body contemplating body (as transient), ardent, composed and mindful, by restraining the dejection in the world that arises from coveting. So with regard to feelings . . . to mind . . . to mind-states. This is the one sole way that leads to the purification of beings . . . to the realizing of Nibbāna, to wit: the four stations of mindfulness.

Now Brahmā Sahampati,[4] reading with his mind the mind of the Exalted One, just as a strong man might stretch out

---

[1] *Ajapāla-nigrodhe. Cf. Vin.* i, 2, 3; *UdA.* 51; *K.S.* i, 128 *n.*; and *infra*, text p. 185.

[2] *Supra*, Bk. III, 1, i, *ekâyano.* Here as before it is *ekamaggo. Comy.*

[3] *Comy.* 'At that time there were no *bhikkhus.* This being so, he intended to show that whosoever cultivates the stations of mindfulness, by the fact of breaking up (*bhindanena*) the corruptions is thereby a *bhikkhu.*' This is a doubtful explanation, but in accordance with the defs. at *Vibhanga*, 245 (where sixteen explanations are given): *e.g.*, 'one is a *bhikkhu* by name, by the vows, by begging, by mendicancy, by living the life of an almsman, by breaking ill states, etc.' At any rate, the name already existed in Sanskrit, solely in the meaning of 'almsman, mendicant.'

[4] *Cf. K.S.* i, 172 *n.*

his bent arm, or draw in his arm stretched out,—even so did Brahmā Sahampati vanish from the Brahma World and appear before the Exalted One. Then drawing his outer robe over one shoulder, joining his hands he raised them to the Exalted One and said:

'Thus it is, Exalted One! Thus it is, O Happy One! This is the one sole way that leads to the purification of beings . . . (*and he repeated all that the Exalted One had thought*) . . . to wit: the four stations of mindfulness.' Thus spake Brahmā Sahampati. Having so said Brahmā Sahampati added this further:

> Beholding this one way for ending birth,[1]
> This way the All-compassionate doth know:
> By this way men ere now have crossed the flood,
> Shall cross and do cross now.

(ix) *Desakā* (or *Sole ending*).[2]

On a certain occasion the Exalted One was staying among the Sumbhā, at Desakā, a district of the Sumbhā.

On that occasion the Exalted One addressed the monks, saying:

'Once upon a time, monks, a bamboo acrobat[3] set up his pole and called to his pupil, Medakathālika,[4] saying:

---

[1] *Jāti-khay' anta-dassī*. *Cf. Sn.* v, 209, 476; *SnA*. ii, 410 (*infra*, text 186); quoted *M. Nidd.* 456.

[2] Text title is *Sedaka* or (?) *Ekantaka*. These titles are from the *Uddāna*, generally corrupt. As above at text 89, I read *Desakā* of *JA*. i, 393.

[3] *Caṇḍāla-vaŋsika*, not as *Pāli Dict.* (*s.v. vaŋsika*) 'a *caṇḍāla* (of scavenger caste) by descent,' but 'bamboo acrobat' (*vaŋsa* is primarily 'bamboo'; secondarily 'family'). For castes see *Dialog* i, 95 *ff*. *Caṇḍāla* according to *Comy.* at *DA*. i, 84 (*cf. Dialog.* i, 9), is a game with an iron ball (*caṇḍa-gula-kīla*). The name means 'ball-and-bamboo-acrobat.' The man balances a bamboo on forehead, chin, shoulder, or breast (as may be often seen in Ceylon or India). The pupil climbs up and balances himself, standing, sitting, or lying, on the point of the pole. *Cf. JA.* iv, 390, *caṇḍāla-vaŋsa-dhopana-sippa*. Text has a confusion of capital C here.

[4] Lit. 'Frying-pan.' Text has altered here to the masculine form of vocative (Burmese MSS. have it right), but *Comy.* notes that the name is a feminine one.

"Now, my lad, climb the pole and stand on my shoulder!"

"All right, master," replied the pupil to the bamboo acrobat, climbed the pole and stood on his master's shoulder.

Then said the master to his pupil: "Now, Medakathālika, my lad, you watch me and I'll watch you. Thus watched and warded by each other, we'll show our tricks, get a good fee and come down safe from the bamboo pole."[1]

At these words Medakathālika the pupil said to his master:

"No, no! That won't do, master! You look after yourself and I'll look after myself. Thus watched and warded, each by himself, we'll show our tricks, get a good fee and come down safe from the bamboo pole. That's the way to do it!"'

Then said the Exalted One: 'Now, monks, just as Medakathālika the pupil said to his master: "I'll look after myself," so ought ye to observe the station of mindfulness which means "I'll ward myself": likewise that which means "We'll ward another." By warding oneself, monks, one wards another. By warding another one wards himself.

And how, monks, by warding oneself does one ward another?

It is by following after, by cultivating, by making much of him.[2]

And how, monks, by warding another does one ward himself?

It is by forbearance, by harmlessness, by goodwill, by compassion towards him.[3] That, monks, is how he wards himself.

Monks, ye must observe the station of mindfulness which means "I'll ward myself." Ye must observe that which means: "I'll ward another." It is by warding self, monks, that one wards another. It is by warding another that one wards himself.'

---

[1] *Comy.* 'The end of the pole rests on the man's forehead or throat. He must watch the balance of the pole closely, and not attend to the pupil on the end of the pole, who must look after himself.' It is possible, also, that here, as sometimes happens, *both* are balanced on the end of the pole.

[2] *Comy.* His regular systematic life which leads to Arahantship attracts the attention of another, who follows his example and so 'goes to heaven.'

[3] *Anuddayā=anukampā. Comy. anuddayāya sapubba-bhāgāya muditāya.*

(x) *The country-side.*

Thus have I heard: Once the Exalted One was staying among the Sumbhā at Desakā, a township of the Sumbhā. On that occasion the Exalted One addressed the monks, saying:

'Suppose, monks, the multitude flock together, crying: "The fairest lass in all the country-side! The fairest lass in all the country-side!"[1] Then that girl, displaying all her charms,[2] dances for them, sings for them, and a still greater multitude would flock together crying, "The fairest lass in all the country-side is dancing, she is singing!"

Then comes a man, fond of his life, not in love with death, fond of ease, averse from pain, and they say to him: "See here, my man! Here's a bowl brimful of oil. You must carry it round[3] between the crowd and the fairest lass in all the country-side. Behind you in your tracks comes a man with uplifted sword. If you spill a drop, off goes your head!"

Now what think ye, monks? Would that fellow, neglecting that bowl of oil, turn away his attention to outside things[4] and grow slack?'

'Surely not, lord.'

'Well, monks, this is a parable I have made for your understanding. This is the meaning of it. "The bowl brimful of oil," monks, is a term for mindfulness relating to body.[5]

Wherefore, monks, thus must ye train yourselves: "Mindfulness relating to body shall be cultivated by us, shall be made much of, made a vehicle,[6] established, made effective. It shall be increased and well applied."

Thus, monks, must ye train yourselves.'

---

[1] *Janapada-kalyāṇī*. *Cf. D.* i, 193; *K.S.* ii, 159; *JA.* i, 394 (the comment on which our *Comy.* repeats or (?) *vice versa*); vol. i, p. 232, of Lord Chalmers' translation in the Cambridge University series. (For the points of beauty in a woman, *cf.* also *UdA.* 170.)

[2] *Parama-pasāvī.*

[3] Reading *v.l.* of text, *pariharitabbo* (*JA. hāretabbo*).

[4] *Badhiddhā pamādam āhareyya.*

[5] *Kāya-gata-sati.* *Cf. K.S.* iv, 76, etc.

[6] *Cf. K.S.* i, 146.

CHAPTER III.—HABIT AND PERMANENCE

(i) *Habit.*

Thus have I heard: Once the venerable Ananda and the venerable Bhadda were staying at Pāṭaliputra in Cock's Pleasaunce.[1]

Then the venerable Bhadda, rising from his solitude at eventide, went to visit the venerable Ānanda, and on coming to him greeted him courteously and, after the exchange of greetings and courtesies, sat down at one side. So seated the venerable Bhadda said this to the venerable Ānanda:

'Pray, friend Ananda, as to these virtuous habits spoken of by the Exalted One, what is the use of them ?'

'Well said ! well said, friend Bhadda ! Welcome is your penetration,[2] welcome is your ready wit. Goodly is your questioning. You ask this, friend Bhadda, do you not ? As to these virtuous habits spoken of by the Exalted One, what is the use of them ?'

'I do, friend.'

'Well, friend Bhadda, the virtuous habits spoken of by the Exalted One are those which come by the cultivation of four stations of mindfulness. What four ?

Herein, friend, a monk dwells in body contemplating body (as transient), ardent, composed and mindful, by restraining the dejection in the world arising from coveting. He does the same with regard to feelings, mind, and mind-states. These, friend, are the virtuous habits so spoken of by the Exalted One, —those which come by the cultivation of the four stations of mindfulness.'

(ii) *Permanence.*

On the same occasion as the above . . .

Then the venerable Bhadda said to the venerable Ānanda as he sat at one side: 'Pray, friend Ānanda, what is the con-

[1] *Cf. supra*, i, 16, the same couple at the same place.

[2] *Ummaggo*=*paññā*, insight, according to *B.* at *Sn.* 50. Here *Comy.* says it=*paññā-gavesanaŋ*.

dition, what is the cause, why, when the Tathāgata has finally passed away, the good Norm does not last long? What again, friend Ānanda, is the condition, what the cause, why, when the Tathāgata has finally passed away, the good Norm does last long?'

'Well said! Well said, friend Bhadda! Welcome is your penetration. Welcome is your ready wit. You ask this, do you not? What is the condition, what the cause, why, when the Tathāgata has finally passed away, the good Norm does not last long, and likewise why it does last long?'

'I do, friend.'

'Well, friend, it is owing to not cultivating, not making much of four stations of mindfulness. That, friend, is the reason why the good Norm does not last long. Again, it is owing to cultivating and making much of four stations of mindfulness that the good Norm does so last. What are the four? Herein, friend, a monk dwells . . . (*as before*). . . . It is owing to cultivating and making much of . . . and it is owing to not cultivating and making much of these four stations of mindfulness that, when the Tathāgata has finally passed away, the good Norm does last long, and likewise does not last long.'[1]

(iii) *Decay.*

Staying at Pāṭaliputra in Cock's Pleasaunce . . .

(*The same questions and answers, with* decay *and* non-decay of the good Norm *instead of* lasting *and* not lasting.)

(iv) *Puritan.*[2]

Sāvatthī was the occasion . . . The Exalted One said:

'There are these four stations of mindfulness. What four? . . . (*as usual*).'

---

[1] *Comy.* In these first three Suttas people such as Devadatta are referred to.

[2] Text title of section is *Suddhakaŋ* (as in the *uddāna*). The meaning is obscure; but *infra*, text 193, *Suddhikaŋ*, where *Comy.* says 'so called from the disposition of Enlightened Ones' (*bujjhanakānaŋ ajjhāsayena kathitaŋ*). *Cf. K.S.* iii, 126 *n.*, where the same confusion occurs. I take the word 'Puritan' from translation of *S.* i, 165.

(v) *The brahmin.*

Thus have I heard: Once the Exalted One was staying near Sāvatthī, in Jeta Grove at Anāthapiṇḍika's Park. Then a certain brahmin came to see the Exalted One, and on coming to him greeted him courteously and, after the exchange of greetings and courtesies, sat down at one side. So seated that brahmin said this to the Exalted One:

'What is the condition, master Gotama, what is the cause, why, after the final passing away of the Tathāgata, the good Norm does not last long; and again, master Gotama, what is the condition, what the cause, why, after the final passing away of the Tathāgata, the good Norm does last long?'

'It is owing to not cultivating, brahmin, owing to not making much of four stations of mindfulness, that the good Norm does not last long after the final passing away of the Tathāgata . . . (*as before*). . . .'

'Wonderful, master Gotama! . . . Let the worthy Gotama accept me as a disciple, as one who has taken refuge in him, from this day forth so long as my life shall last.'

(vi) *Partial.*

On a certain occasion the venerable Sāriputta and the venerable Moggallāna the Great and the venerable Anuruddha were staying at Sāketa[1] in Cactus Grove.

Now the venerable Sāriputta, together with Moggallāna the Great, rising from their solitude at eventide, went to visit the venerable Anuruddha, and on coming to him greeted him courteously, and, after the exchange of greetings and courtesies, sat down at one side. So seated the venerable Sāriputta said this to the venerable Anuruddha:

'"A pupil! A pupil!" is the saying, friend Anuruddha. Pray, friend Anuruddha, how far is this term applicable?'

---

[1] In Kosala. *Cf. Buddhist India*, p. 40. 'The present city of Ayodhyā stands on a corner of the site of what was once the great city, twenty-four miles in circumference, of Sāketa, about 100 miles N.N.E. of Benares.' For Cactus Grove, *cf. infra* on p. 298 of text.

'By the fact of having partially[1] cultivated the four stations of mindfulness, friend, one is called "a pupil." What are the four?

Herein, friend, a monk dwells contemplating body . . . (*as before*). . . .

It is by the partial cultivation of these four stations of mindfulness, friend, that one is a pupil.'

(vii) *Perfectly.**

The occasion was the same (*and the questioners*) said this to the venerable Anuruddha:

'"An adept! An adept!" is the saying, friend Anuruddha. Pray, friend, how far is this term applicable?'

'By the perfect cultivation, friend, of four stations of mindfulness one is an adept. What four? . . . (*as above*). . . . That is how one is an adept.'

(viii) *The universe.*

The occasion was the same . . . So seated the venerable Sāriputta said this to the venerable Anuruddha:

'By cultivating and making much of how many conditions has the venerable Anuruddha come to great superknowledge?'[2]

'Friend, it is by cultivating and making much of four stations of mindfulness that I have come to great superknowledge. What four?

Herein, friend, a monk dwells in body contemplating body . . .

Moreover, friend, it is by cultivating, by making much of these four stations of mindfulness that I have come to understand the universe with its thousand worlds.'[3]

---

[1] *Padesaŋ*, as opposite to *samattaŋ* below. *Cf. infra* 201, 255-6, 457, *padesa-kāriŋ* (affecting a limited range) opposite to *paripūra-kāriŋ*. *Asl.* 37 = *Expos.* 49. *Comy.* on *S.* iv, 192, *sappadesa* and *nippadesa*. Here it is evidently an adverb like *samattaŋ*,* 'regional (incomplete) knowledge.' *Comy.* MSS. have *paresaŋ* (?), and def. thus: *sekho*, 'one who strives for the three paths and fruits, but has not attained the fourth. Thus anyone on the path, but not Arahant, is *sekho*.

[2] *Cf. K.S.* iv, 263, of the six *abhiññā*.

[3] *Sahassa-loka*. *Comy.* 'The elder used to rise early, and after ablutions sat in his lodging, calling up a thousand *kalpas* of past and

(ix) *Sirivaḍḍha.*[1]

On a certain occasion the venerable Ānanda was staying near Rājagaha, in Bamboo Grove, at the Squirrels' Feeding Ground.

Now at that time the housefather Sirivaḍḍha was sick, afflicted, suffering from a sore disease.

Then the housefather Sirivaḍḍha called to a certain man, saying:

'Come hither, good man! Do you go to the venerable Ānanda, and on coming to him, in my name bowing down at his feet, say this to the venerable Ānanda: "Master, the housefather Sirivaḍḍha is sick, afflicted, suffering from a sore disease. He bows down at the feet of the venerable Ānanda, and says: 'Well for me, master, if the venerable Ānanda would come to the dwelling of the housefather Sirivaḍḍha, out of compassion for him.'"'

'Very well, sir,' said that man, in reply to the housefather Sirivaḍḍha, and went to where the venerable Ānanda was staying. On coming there, he saluted the venerable Ānanda and sat down at one side. As he thus sat that man said this to the venerable Ānanda: 'Master, the housefather Sirivaḍḍha is sick, afflicted, suffering from a sore disease. He bows down at the feet of the venerable Ānanda and begs that he will visit his dwelling, out of compassion for him.'

And the venerable Ānanda assented by silence.

Then the venerable Ānanda, robing himself and taking bowl and outer robe, set off for the dwelling of the housefather Sirivaḍḍha, and on coming there sat down on a seat made ready. Having sat down, he said this to the housefather Sirivaḍḍha:

'Well, housefather! I hope you are bearing up. I hope you

future. Likewise as to present time he contemplated the thousandfold *cakkavāḷa*, and his path therein displayed itself in due order. Thus with clairvoyant eye he knew fully the thousandfold universe. This was his abode (*satta-vihāra*) in the world of sentient beings.

[1] At *M.* ii, 112, a man of this name (Prospero ?) was minister to the rājah Pasenadi. I do not find other mention of him.

are enduring. Do your pains abate and not increase? Are there signs of their abating and not increasing?'[1]

'No, sir, I am not bearing up. I am not enduring. Strong pains come upon me. They do not abate. There is no sign of their abating, but of their increasing.'

'Then, housefather, thus must you train yourself: "I will abide in body contemplating body (as transient), ardent, composed and mindful. . . . So also with regard to feelings . . . mind . . . mind-states." That, housefather, is how you must train yourself.'

'Sir, as to those four stations of mindfulness taught by the Exalted One, they do exist in me,—those conditions. I do live conformably with those conditions.[2] I do abide, lord, in body contemplating body (as transient). . . . I do abide in feelings . . . in mind . . . in mind-states. I am ardent, composed and mindful, by restraining the dejection in the world that arises from coveting.

Moreover, as to those five fetters of the lower sort[3] shown by the Exalted One, I do not see a single one of them in myself that is not abandoned.'

'Good for you, housefather! Well gotten by you, housefather! You have declared the fruits of not returning, housefather!'

(x) *Mānadiṇṇa*.[4]

The occasion was the same . . .

Now at that time the housefather Mānadiṇṇa was sick, afflicted, suffering from a sore disease.

Then the housefather called to a certain man, saying: 'Come hither, my good man! Do you go to the venerable Ānanda . . . (*the same as before down to*) . . . Thus, housefather, must you train yourself.'

---

[1] *Cf. K.S.* iii, 101 (*Vakkali*); iv, 23, etc., for these formulæ.

[2] *Tesu dhammesu sandissāmi.*

[3] *Oram-bhāgiyāni* (the error of belief in a permanent individuality, doubt in the Master and Norm, wrong judgment as to rule and ritual, sensuality and resentment).

[4] Name not found elsewhere.

'Master, even when I am afflicted[1] by such painful feeling as this, I do abide in body contemplating body (as transient), ardent, composed and mindful. . . . So also in feelings . . . mind . . . and mind-states.

Moreover, as to those five fetters of the lower sort, shown by the Exalted One, I do not see a single one of them in myself that is not abandoned.'

'Good for you, housefather! Well gotten by you, housefather! You have declared the fruits of not returning, housefather!'[2]

CHAPTER IV.—UNHEARD BEFORE[3]

(i) *Unheard before.*

Sāvatthī was the occasion . . . The Exalted One said:

'At the thought: The contemplation of body in body, there arose in me, monks, vision of things not taught before:[4] knowledge arose, insight arose, wisdom arose, light arose.

At the thought: Now this contemplation of body in body must be cultivated, there arose in me vision of things not taught before . . .

At the thought: Now this contemplation of body in body has been cultivated, there arose in me vision of things not taught before . . .

Likewise, monks, at the thought: This contemplation of feelings in feelings . . . of mind in mind . . . of mind-states in mind-states . . . At the thought: It ought to be cultivated

---

[1] Text has *puṭṭho* for *phuṭṭho*.

[2] According to *Pāli Dict.* s.v. *anāgāmin*, this, with the case following, are the only instances in the Canon where a man is declared *anāgāmin* (but another is at text 219 and 346). It adds: At *D.* ii, 92, nine others, of whom eight are laymen, are declared after their death to have reached the third stage (*as above*) during life, but they are not called *anāgāmin*. *Comy.* is silent.

[3] Text misprints as Chap. 6.

[4] *Cf. S.* ii, 10; *K.S.* ii, 7, *cakkuṃ*, *ñāṇaṃ* (*paññā*, omitted here), *vijjā*, *āloko udapādi*. Of these Mrs. Rhys Davids remarks *ad loc. cit.*, 'For Gotama's age it was a new gospel.'

. . . it has been cultivated,—on each occasion, monks, there arose in me vision of things not taught before: knowledge arose, insight arose, wisdom arose, light arose.'

(ii) *Dispassion.*

At Sāvatthī . . .

These four stations of mindfulness, monks, if cultivated and made much of, conduce to downright revulsion, to dispassion, to cessation, to calm, to full comprehension, to perfect wisdom, to Nibbāna. What four? . . .

(iii) *Neglected.*[1]

By whomsoever, monks, the four stations of mindfulness are neglected, by them also is neglected the Ariyan way for the utter destruction of Ill.

By whomsoever, monks, the four stations of mindfulness are undertaken, by them also is undertaken the Ariyan way for the utter destruction of Ill.

What are the four?

Herein a monk contemplates body . . .

(iv) *Cultivation.*

At Sāvatthī . . .

Monks, these four stations of mindfulness, if cultivated and made much of, conduce to that state in which no further shore and no hither shore[2] exists. What four? . . .

(v) *Mindful.*

Sāvatthī . . .

Monks, a monk should abide mindful and composed. This is our instruction to you. And how does a monk so abide?

Herein a monk abides, in body contemplating body . . . thus is he mindful.

And how is a monk composed?

---

[1] *Cf. supra*, text 23, *viraddha* as opposite to *āraddha*.

[2] *Cf. supra*, text 24, *a-pāra-apāra*, which text here misprints as *aparâparaŋ* (backwards and forwards), as again Bk. vii, *ad init.*, and above, text 24, 81.

Herein a monk is fully conscious of feelings[1] that arise, fully conscious of feelings that settle in him, fully conscious of feelings that come to an end.[2] He is fully aware of a train of thought that arises, of its settling in him, that it comes to an end.

He is fully aware of perceptions that arise in him, that settle in him, that come to an end. That, monks, is how he is composed.

A monk should abide mindful and composed. This is our instruction to you.

(vi) *One of two.*

At Sāvatthī . . .

Monks, there are these four stations of mindfulness. What four?

Herein a monk abides contemplating body in body . . .

By the cultivating and making much of these four stations of mindfulness, of two fruits one may be expected in this very life, to wit: realization, or, if there be any substrate left, the state of non-return.

(vii) *Desire to do.*[3]

At Sāvatthī . . .

Monks, there are these four stations of mindfulness. What four? . . .

As he dwells in body contemplating body (as transient), ardent, . . . that desire to do, that is in body, is abandoned. By the abandoning of desire to do, the Deathless is realized. So with feelings . . . mind . . . mind-states . . . that desire to do, that is in mind-states, is abandoned. By the abandoning of desire to do, the Deathless is realized.

(viii) *By full understanding.*

There are these four stations of mindfulness. What four? . . .

As he so dwells, body is fully understood. By the fact of

---

[1] *Viditā vedanā*, etc.

[2] *Abbhatthaŋ (abhi+atthaŋ) gacchanti.*

[3] *Chando.* The effacement of project and purpose is to be the aim.

fully understanding body the Deathless is realized. So with regard to feelings . . . mind . . . and mind-states . . . by fully understanding mind-states the Deathless is realized.

(ix) *Cultivation.*

I will teach you, monks, the cultivation of the four stations of mindfulness. Of what sort is the cultivation of them ?

Herein a monk dwells in body contemplating body . . .

This is the way to cultivate the four stations of mindfulness.

(x) *Analysis.*

I will teach you, monks, the four stations of mindfulness, the cultivation thereof and the practice leading to the cultivation of the four stations of mindfulness. Do ye listen to it.

And what, monks, is a station of mindfulness ?

Herein a monk dwells in body contemplating body . . .

And of what sort, monks, is the cultivation of a station of mindfulness ?

Herein a monk dwells contemplating the rise of things[1] in body. He so dwells contemplating the fall of things[2] in body: he dwells contemplating both the rise and the fall of things in body, ardent, composed and mindful. . . .

He dwells in feelings contemplating the rise and fall of things in feelings. . . . So also in mind and mind-states, ardent, composed and mindful. . . . This, monks, is called 'the cultivation of a station of mindfulness.'

And of what sort, monks, is the practice leading to the cultivation of a station of mindfulness ?

It is just this Ariyan eightfold way, to wit: right view . . . and the rest, and right concentration. This, monks, is the practice so leading.

---

[1] *Samudaya-dhammā.*

[2] *Vaya-dhammā. Cf. Dhp.* 113.

CHAPTER V.—THE DEATHLESS

(i) *The Deathless.*

Sāvatthī was the occasion . . .

Monks, do ye dwell with mind well established in the four stations of mindfulness. But let not that be to you the Deathless.[1] In what four ?

Herein a monk dwells contemplating body in body . . .

Monks, do ye dwell with mind well established in the four stations of mindfulness. But let not that be to you the Deathless.

(ii) *Arising.*

Monks, I will teach you both the arising and the ending of the four stations of mindfulness. Do ye listen to it.

And what, monks, is the arising of body ? By the arising of food comes the arising of body. By the ceasing of food comes the ending of body.

By the arising of contact is the arising of feelings. By the ceasing of contact is the ceasing of feelings.

By the arising of name and body[2] comes the arising of mind. By the ceasing of name and body comes the ending of mind.

By the arising of attention comes the arising of mental states. By the ceasing of attention comes the ending of mental states.

(iii) *The Way.*[3]

Sāvatthī (was the occasion) . . .

Then the Exalted One addressed the monks, saying:

'On a certain occasion, monks, I was staying at Uruvela, on the bank of the river Nerañjarā, under the Goatherds' Banyan, after I had just attained enlightenment.

---

[1] *I.e.*, do not confuse the means with the end. *Cf. Pts. of Controversy*, 104 *n.*: 'The Andhakas (and others) held the opinion that the *objects* of mindfulness (namely, the body, etc.) were themselves (the conscious *subject*) mindfulness. (This they deduced from this passage.)'

[2] *Nāma-rūpa*- the individuality ('the fivefold person-pack').

[3] *Cf. supra*, text 167, where a similar Sutta is called *Brahmā*.

Then, monks, as I meditated in solitude, this train of thought arose in my mind: This is the one sole way that leads to the purification of beings, to the utter passing beyond sorrow and grief, to the destruction of woe and lamentation, to the winning of the Method, to the realizing of Nibbāna, to wit: the four stations of mindfulness. What four?

A monk should dwell in body contemplating body (as transient), ardent, composed and mindful. . . . A monk should dwell in feelings contemplating feelings (as transient) . . . in mind contemplating mind . . . in mind-states contemplating mind-states (as transient), ardent, composed and mindful, by restraining the dejection in the world that arises from coveting. This is the one sole way that leads to the purification of beings . . . to wit: the four stations of mindfulness.

Then, monks, Brahmā Sahampati, reading with his mind my mind, just as a strong man might stretch out his bent arm, or draw in his outstretched arm,—even so did Brahmā Sahampati vanish from the Brahma World and appear before me.

Then, monks, Brahmā Sahampati, drawing his outer robe over one shoulder, joined his hands and raised them to me and thus spoke:

"True it is, O Exalted One! True it is, O Happy One! This is the one sole way that leads to the purification of beings. . . . A monk should dwell. . . . This is the one sole way that leads to the purification of beings, to the utter passing beyond sorrow and grief, to the destruction of woe and lamentation, to the winning of the Method, to the realizing of Nibbāna, to wit: the four stations of mindfulness."

Thus spake Brahmā Sahampati. So saying he added this further:

> Beholding this one way for ending birth,
> This way the All-compassionate doth know:
> By this way men ere now have crossed the flood,
> Shall cross and do cross now.'

(iv) *Mindful.*

At Sāvatthī . . .

A monk should dwell mindful. This is our instruction to you, monks.

And how is a monk mindful ?

Herein a monk dwells in body contemplating body . . .

A monk should dwell mindful . . .

(v) *A heap of merit.*[1]

'A heap of merit !' If anyone, monks, should thus name the four stations of mindfulness, rightly would he do so. For indeed, monks, they are one entire heap of merit,—these four stations of mindfulness. What four ?

Herein a monk dwells . . . 'A heap of merit !' . . .

(vi) *Obligation.*[2]

Then a certain monk came to visit the Exalted One. . . . Seated at one side that monk said this to the Exalted One:

'Well for me, lord, if the Exalted One should teach me a teaching in brief, hearing which teaching from the Exalted One I might dwell solitary, remote, earnest, ardent and aspiring.'

'Well then, monk, you ought to purify the rudiments in good states.[3] And what are the rudiments in good states ?

Herein, monk, do you dwell self-controlled according to the self-control of the Obligations,[4] well equipped in your range of practice,[5] seeing danger in minutest faults, and, undertaking the precepts, do you train yourself therein.[6]

Now monk, when you have dwelt self-controlled according to the self-control of the Obligations, in your range of practice

---

[1] *Supra*, text 145.

[2] *Pāṭimokkha*. *Cf*. *D*. iii, 77; *Dialog*. iii, 75.

[3] *Supra*, text 165; *VM*. 4.

[4] *Comy*. 'Here he enjoins the chief of the four *sīlas* (*pāṭimokkha-saŋvaro, indriya-saŋvaro, ājīva-parisuddhi, paccaya-sannissita-sīlā*). *Cf*. *VM*. 16 *ff*.

[5] *Ācāra-gocara*(pasturage)-*sampanno*.

[6] Text has *sikkhasu* for *sikkhāhi*.

well-equipped, seeing danger in minutest faults, and when, undertaking the precepts, you shall have trained yourself therein,—then, monk, leaning on virtue, established in virtue, you should cultivate the four stations of mindfulness. What are the four ?

Herein, monk, do you dwell in body contemplating body (as transient), ardent, composed and mindful . . . so in feelings . . . in mind . . . in mind-states, contemplating mind-states (as transient), ardent, composed and mindful, by restraining the dejection in the world that arises from coveting.

Now, monk, when you, leaning on virtue and established in virtue, shall have thus cultivated the four stations of mindfulness,—then, monk, you may look for that increase in good states which shall come to you, whether by night or by day, and not for decrease in good states.'

Then that monk was delighted with the words of the Exalted One. . . .

And he, living alone, aloof . . . realized . . . 'for me there is no more of being here.'

And that monk was yet another of the Arahants.

(vii) *Wrong conduct.*

Now a certain monk came to see the Exalted One . . . and said:

'Well for me, lord, if the Exalted One should teach me a teaching in brief, hearing which teaching from the Exalted One, I might dwell solitary, remote, earnest, ardent and aspiring.'

'Then, monk, you must purify the rudiments in good states. And what are the rudiments in good states ?

Herein, monk, abandoning wrong conduct in body, do you cultivate right conduct in body. Likewise, abandoning wrong conduct in feelings, you should cultivate right conduct in feelings . . . in mind . . . in mind-states abandoning wrong conduct, you should cultivate right conduct in mind-states.

Then, monk, leaning on virtue, established in virtue, you should cultivate four stations of mindfulness. What four ?

Herein, monk, do you dwell in body contemplating body . . . and the rest.

Now, monk, when you, thus leaning on virtue, established in virtue, shall have thus cultivated these four stations of mindfulness, then, monk, you may look for that increase in good states that shall come to you, whether by night or by day, and not for decrease in them .' . . . (*as above*) . . .

. . . So that monk was yet another of the Arahants.

(viii) *Friends.*

At Sāvatthī . . . The Exalted One said:

'Monks, those for whom you have fellow-feeling, those who may deem you worth listening to, your friends and colleagues, your relatives, your blood relations,—they ought to be roused for, admonished and established in, the cultivation of the four stations of mindfulness. What four?

Herein a monk dwells contemplating body . . .

Monks, those for whom you have fellow-feeling . . . ought to be roused for, admonished and established in, the four stations of mindfulness.'

(ix) *Feelings.*

At Sāvatthī . . . The Exalted One said:

'Monks, there are these three feelings. What three? Feeling that is pleasant, feeling that is painful, feeling that is neither pleasant nor painful. These are the three feelings.

For the full understanding of these three feelings the four stations of mindfulness ought to be cultivated. What four?

Herein a monk dwells . . .'

(x) *Āsavas.*

Monks, there are three āsavas.[1] What three? The āsava which is sensuality, that which is becoming, and the āsava which is nescience. These are the three.

---

[1] It is worth while repeating previous notes on this term, which I leave untranslated. In *Further Dialogues,* Lord Chalmers uses the word 'cankers.' *Cf. Dialog.* iii. 209 *n.*, '*Āsava*, in the sense of surrounding or flowing up to . . . *e.g.*, from the eye (or sight), a flowing, percolating, rolling on into the object . . . *Abhidhamma*, adding *diṭṭhi* (erroneous opinion), gives four. *Comy.* *Cf. Dhs.* §§ 1096-1100.'

For the abandoning of these three āsavas the four stations of mindfulness ought to be cultivated. What four?

Herein a monk dwells . . .

CHAPTER VI.—GANGĀ REPETITION

(*This and the next four chapters, to the end of this Saŋyutta, are abbreviated in text to mere titles, with the exception of* §§ 1-12, *text, Nos.* 51-62. *They are to be developed as in the First Part.*)

(i-xii).

Just as, monks, the river Ganges flows, slides and tends to the east . . . so a monk, by cultivating and making much of the four stations of mindfulness, flows, slides and tends to Nibbāna. And how, monks, does a monk so slide?

Herein a monk dwells in body contemplating body . . . so also in feelings . . . mind . . . and mind-states. . . . Thus does a monk flow, slide and tend to Nibbāna.

CHAPTER SUMMARY[1]

Six on Flowing and sliding to eastward, *and six on* The Ocean.
These two sixes are twelve, and the chapter (*that holds them*) *is thus called.*

(*To be developed by way of* Stations of mindfulness.)

CHAPTER VII.—EARNESTNESS

(i-x).

Tathāgata, Foot, Roof-peak,
Wood, Heart-wood, Jasmine,
Prince, Moon *and* Sun,
With Cloth *makes ten.*

(*To be developed by way of* The Stations of Mindfulness.)

---

[1] Each chapter is summed up in a doggerel stanza (*uddāna*) of titles (often corrupt in text), of which I have attempted to versify only one.

CHAPTER VIII.—DEEDS REQUIRING STRENGTH

(i-xii).

Strength,[1] Seed *and* Snake,
Tree *with* Pot *and* Bearded Wheat,[2]
Sky *and two of* Raincloud,[3]
Ship, For all comers, River.

(*To be developed by way of* The Stations of Mindfulness.)

CHAPTER IX.—LONGING

(i-xiii).

Longing, Conceits, Āsavas, Becoming,
Suffering, Obstruction (*three*),
Stain *and* Pain *and* Feelings,
Craving *and* Thirst *make the chapter.*

(*To be developed by way of* The Stations of Mindfulness.)

CHAPTER X.—THE FLOOD

(i-ix)[4] *as before.*

(x) *Fetters of the higher sort.*[5]

Monks, there are these five fetters of the higher sort. What five? Lust of form, lust of the formless,[6] conceit, excitement and nescience. These are the five.

Now, monks, for the full comprehension, understanding, wearing out, and abandoning of these five fetters of the higher

---

[1] Text misprints *phalaŋ* for *balaŋ*.

[2] Text misprints *sūriyyā* for *sūkiya*.

[3] Text misprints *ākāseṭṭhena vā* for *ākāsa ca dve meghā, nāvā.*

[4] Text has i-xi, and omits *Bhava* and *Tasināya.*

[5] *Cf. D.* iii, 234; *Dialog.* iii, 225.

[6] *I.e.*, of birth in the *rūpa* and *arūpa* worlds.

sort, the four stations of mindfulness must be cultivated. What four?

Herein a monk dwells in body contemplating body (as transient) . . . and the rest . . . . For the full comprehension . . . of these five fetters of the higher sort the four stations of mindfulness must be cultivated.

Chapter Summary

The Flood, The Bond, Grasping, *with* (*bodily*) Ties *and* Tendency, Sense-pleasures, Hindrances, Factors, Fetters of Lower and Higher Sort.

(*As* Kindred Sayings on the Path *were developed, so also* Kindred Sayings on The Four Stations of Mindfulness *must be developed.*)

BOOK IV

KINDRED SAYINGS ON THE FACULTIES

CHAPTER I.—PURITY

(i) *Puritan.*[1]

At Sāvatthī . . . On that occasion the Exalted One said this:

'Monks, there are these five controlling powers.[2] What five?

The controlling power of faith, that of energy, that of mindfulness, that of concentration, and the controlling power of insight. These five.'

(ii) *The stream* (*a*).

'Monks, there are these five controlling powers. What five? . . . (*as before*).

When the Ariyan disciple understands, as they really are, the satisfaction in, the misery of, and the escape from[3] these five controlling powers, such an one, monks, is called "Ariyan disciple who is a stream-winner, not doomed to Purgatory, assured, bound for enlightenment."'

---

[1] *Suddhikaŋ*. *Cf. supra*, text 173 *n*. I borrow the title 'Puritan' from *K.S.* i, 206.

[2] *Indriyāni*. *Cf. K.S.* ii, 114 *ff.* (as sense-faculties or functions), but here to be taken in a moral sense (see *Pāli Dict. s.v.*). They often correspond to the five powers (*balāni*); two, *hiri* and *ottappa*, are added to these five. *Cf. D.* iii, 253. The formula is clear enough when applied as at *K.S.* ii to sense-functions, which have to be abandoned as fetters. *These* powers are the spiritual antitheses of the five bodily senses, and the chief factors of enlightenment.

[3] *Cf. K.S.* iii, 137.

(iii) *The stream* (*b*).

'Monks, there are these five controlling powers. What five? . . . (*as before*).

When the Ariyan disciple understands, as they really are, the arising and the perishing of, the satisfaction in, the misery of, the escape from these five controlling powers, such an one, monks, is called "Ariyan disciple who is a stream-winner, one not doomed to Purgatory, assured, bound for enlightenment."'

(iv) *Arahant* (*a*).

'Monks, there are these five controlling powers. . . .

When a monk, by seeing as they really are, the satisfaction in, the misery of, the escape from these five controlling powers, is freed without grasping,[1]—such an one, monks, is called "Arahant, destroyer of the āsavas, liver of the life, doer of the task, lifter of the burden, winner of his own welfare, one who has worn out the fetters of rebirth, one released by perfect insight."'

(v) *Arahant* (*b*).

(*The same, with the insertion of* By seeing, as they really are, the arising and the perishing . . .)[2]

(vi) *Recluses and brahmins* (*a*).[3]

'There are these five controlling powers. . . .

Monks, whatsoever recluses or brahmins understand not, as they really are, the arising . . . of these five controlling powers, such are not worthy to be accounted recluses among recluses, nor among brahmins as brahmins; nor have those worthies of themselves understood, or even in this life realized, the goal of recluseship or of brahminhood, nor do they dwell in the attainment of it.

But, monks, those recluses or brahmins who have so under-

---

[1] *Anupādā vimutto*. *Cf. Buddh. Psych. Eth.* 197; *D.* iii, 97, etc.

[2] The text is otherwise the same in both §§, but in (*a*) we have 'Ariyan disciple,' in (*b*) 'monk.'

[3] *Cf. K.S.* ii, 15, etc.

stood . . . such are worthy to be accounted among recluses as recluses, and among brahmins as brahmins: and those worthies have of themselves understood and even in this life have realized the goal of recluseship and brahminhood, and they do dwell in the attainment thereof.'

(vii) *Recluses and brahmins* (*b*).

'Monks, whatsoever recluses or brahmins understand not the controlling power of faith, nor understand the arising thereof, nor the ceasing thereof, nor the practice leading to the ceasing thereof . . . Likewise, whatsoever recluses or brahmins understand not the controlling power of energy . . . of mindfulness . . . of concentration . . . of insight, nor understand the arising, the ceasing, the practice leading to the ceasing thereof, such are not worthy to be accounted recluses among recluses, nor brahmins among brahmins, nor have those worthies of themselves understood . . .

But, monks, those . . . who have so understood . . . such are worthy to be accounted . . . and they do dwell in the attainment of it.'

(viii) *Point of view*.

'Monks, there are these five controlling powers. What five? . . .

But from what point of view,[1] monks, should the controlling power of faith be regarded? From that of the four limbs of stream-winning.[2]

And from what point of view, monks, should the controlling power of energy[3] be regarded? From that of the four supreme efforts.[4]

And from what point of view, monks, should the controlling

---

[1] *Kattha.*

[2] *Saddhā.* *Cf. K.S.* ii, 48; *Expos.* i, 191. These are (i) Faith in the Buddha, (ii) in the Doctrine, (iii) in the Order, (iv) Ariyan virtues intact. The first three are included in *saddhindriya* (next §). *Cf. Expos.* i, 157, where faith is likened to the water-purifying gem.

[3] *Viriya. Expos.* 159.

[4] *Do.* 182.

power of mindfulness[1] be regarded? From that of the four stations of mindfulness.

And from what point of view, monks, should the controlling power of concentration[2] be regarded? From that of the four trances.

And from what point of view, monks, should the controlling power of insight[3] be regarded? It should be regarded from the point of view of the four Ariyan truths.

These, monks, are the five controlling powers.'

(ix) *Analysis* (*a*).

'Monks, there are these five controlling powers. . . .

And of what sort, monks, is the controlling power of faith?

Herein, monks, the Ariyan disciple has faith. He has faith in the wisdom of the Tathāgata, thus: He it is, the Exalted One, Arahant, supremely Enlightened One, perfect in knowledge and practice, world-knower, unsurpassed charioteer of men to be tamed, teacher of devas and mankind, a Buddha, an Exalted One.[4] Of such sort, monks, is the controlling power of faith.

And of what sort, monks, is the controlling power of energy?

Herein, monks, the Ariyan disciple dwells resolute in energy, ever striving to abandon bad qualities, to acquire good qualities, strenuously exerting himself,[5] not throwing off the burden in good qualities.[6] This, monks, is called "the controlling power of energy."

And of what sort, monks, is the controlling power of mindfulness?

Herein, monks, the Ariyan disciple is mindful, possessed of supreme discrimination,[7] one who calls to mind and remembers things said and done long ago.

This is called "the controlling power of mindfulness."

---

[1] *Sati. Expos.* 159, 194. [2] *Do.* 161.

[3] *Paññā, do.* 161. [4] *Cf. K.S.* iv, 211.

[5] *Cf. Dhp.* 23: *Te jhāyino sātatikā niccaŋ daḷha-parakkamā.*

[6] *Cf. Dialog.* iii, 246.

[7] *Sati-nepakkena samannāgato. Comy. nipakassa-bhāvo nepakkaŋ. Cf. VM.* 3; *infra*, text 225.

And of what sort, monks, is the controlling power of concentration?

Herein, monks, the Ariyan disciple, making self-surrender the object of his thought, lays hold of concentration, lays hold of one-pointedness. This is called "the controlling power of concentration."

And of what sort, monks, is the controlling power of insight?

Herein, monks, the Ariyan disciple is possessed of insight[1] thus: He has insight for tracing out the rise and fall of things,[2] insight which is Ariyan, penetrating, going on to the utter destruction of Ill. This, monks, is called "the controlling power of insight."

Such, monks, are the five controlling powers.'

(x) *Analysis* (*b*).

'There are these five controlling powers, monks. . . .

And of what sort, monks, is the controlling power of faith?

Herein, monks, the Ariyan disciple has faith. He has faith in the wisdom of the Tathāgata thus: He it is, the Exalted One . . . teacher of devas and mankind, an Enlightened One, an Exalted One. This is called "the controlling power of faith."

And of what sort, monks, is the controlling power of energy?

Herein, monks, the Ariyan disciple dwells resolute in energy, ever striving to abandon bad qualities, to cause the arising of good qualities, strenuously exerting himself, not throwing off the burden in good qualities.

He starts desire,[3] strives, sets going energy, lays hold of thought and exerts effort to prevent the arising of bad qualities not yet arisen. He starts desire, strives, sets going energy, lays hold of thought, and exerts effort to abandon bad qualities

---

[1] *Paññavā.* *Cf. Dialog.* iii, 227.

[2] *Uday' attha-gāminiyā.* [*Comy. udayañ ca atthañ ca gacchantiyā udayabbaya-pariggāhikāya.*]

[3] *Cf. Dhp.* v, 118: *tamhi chandaŋ kayirātha.*

that have arisen. He starts desire . . . for the persistence of good qualities that have arisen, for their non-confusion, for their more-becoming, for their increase and development, for their perfecting.[1] This, monks, is called " the controlling power of energy."

And of what sort, monks, is the controlling power of mindfulness ?

Herein, monks, the Ariyan disciple is mindful, possessed of supreme discrimination, one who calls to mind and remembers things said and done long ago. He dwells in body contemplating body (as transient) . . . in feelings . . . in mind . . . in mind-states, ardent, composed and mindful, by restraining the dejection in the world that arises from coveting. This, monks, is called " the controlling power of mindfulness."

And of what sort, monks, is the controlling power of concentration ?

Herein, monks, the Ariyan disciple, making self-surrender the object of his thought, lays hold of concentration, lays hold of one-pointedness. He, aloof from sensuality, aloof from evil conditions, enters on the first trance, which is accompanied by thought directed and sustained, which is born of solitude, easeful and zestful, and abides therein.

Then, by calming down thought directed and sustained, he enters on (that inward calm, that single-minded purpose, apart from thought directed and sustained, born of mental balance, zestful and full of ease, which is)[2] the second trance, and abides therein. Then (by the fading out of zest he becomes balanced and remains mindful and composed, and experiences with the body that happiness of which the Ariyans aver: The balanced thoughtful man dwells happily; and) he enters on the third trance and abides therein. Then, by rejecting pleasure and pain, by the coming to an end of the joy and sorrow which he had before, he enters on and abides in the fourth trance, which is free of pain and free of pleasure, a state of perfect purity of balance and equanimity. This, monks, is called " the controlling power of concentration."

---

[1] *Cf. D.* iii, 221.

[2] Text abridges parts bracketed.

And of what sort, monks, is the controlling power of insight ?

Herein, monks, the Ariyan disciple has insight thus: He is possessed of insight for tracing out the rise and fall of things, insight that is Ariyan, penetrating, going on to the utter destruction of Ill. He understands, as it really is, "Such is Ill." He understands, as it really is, "Such is the arising of Ill." He understands, as it really is, "This is the practice that goes to the cessation of Ill."

This, monks, is called "the controlling power of insight." These, monks, are the five controlling powers.'

CHAPTER II.—IN A LESS DEGREE[1]

(i) *Laying hold.*

'There are these five controlling powers, monks. What five ? The controlling power of faith . . . and that of insight.

And of what sort, monks, is the controlling power of faith ?

Herein, monks, the Ariyan disciple has faith. He has faith in the Tathāgata's wisdom thus: He it is, the Exalted One, Arahant . . . teacher of devas and mankind, an Enlightened One, an Exalted One. This, monks, is called "the controlling power of faith."

And of what sort, monks, is the controlling power of energy?

It is that energy one lays hold of in practising the four best efforts. This, monks, is called "the controlling power of energy."

And of what sort, monks, is the controlling power of mindfulness ?

It is that mindfulness one lays hold of in practising[2] the four stations of mindfulness. This, monks, is called "the controlling power of mindfulness."

And of what sort, monks, is the controlling power of concentration ?

Herein, monks, the Ariyan disciple, making self-surrender

---

[1] The title of the chapter (*mudutara*) comes from § ii.

[2] *Ārabbha*. *Comy. bhāvento* = 'making more.'

his object of thought, lays hold of concentration, lays hold of one-pointedness of mind. This, monks, is called "the controlling power of concentration."

And of what sort, monks, is the controlling power of insight?

Herein, monks, the Ariyan disciple has insight thus; he is possessed of insight for tracing out the rise and fall of things, insight that is Ariyan, penetrating, going on to the utter destruction of Ill. This, monks, is called "the controlling power of insight."

These, monks, are indeed the five controlling powers.'

(ii) *In brief* (*a*).

Monks, there are these five controlling powers. What five? The controlling power of faith . . . of insight. These are the five.

By the completion and fulfilment, monks, of these five controlling powers one is Arahant. By having them in a less degree,[1] one is a non-returner. Having them in a still less degree, one is a once-returner. By having them in a less degree than that, one is a stream-winner: in a still less degree, a Norm-follower.[2] If one have these five controlling powers in a still less degree than that, he is 'one who walks by faith.'[3]

(iii) *In brief* (*b*).

Monks, there are these five controlling powers. . . .

By the completion and fulfilment of these five controlling powers, monks, one is Arahant . . . by having them in a still less degree than that he is one who walks by faith.

Thus it is, monks, that there is a difference of controlling powers, there is a difference of fruits, of strength, of individuals.[4]

---

[1] *Comy. tehi indriyehi. Cf. Dialog.* iii, 100, for the ascending degrees.

[2] *Saddh' ānusārin*, 'he studies and asks questions and enters later on.' *Dhamm' ānusārin*, 'after one or two hearings of the Truth, he enters the Way.' *Comy. Cf. Pts. of Contr.* 149.

[3] One who has nothing at all of these controlling powers is an outsider, one of the common herd (*puthujjana*). See below, § 8.

[4] *Cf. K.S.* ii, 17; *vemattatā = nānattatā. Comy.*

(iv) *In brief* (*c*).

(*As above, down to*) '. . . one who walks by faith.'

Thus it is, monks, that he who completes his task succeeds completely, while he who does part only succeeds partially.[1]

Thus, monks, these five controlling powers are not barren of results,[2] I declare.

(v) *In detail* (*a*).

Monks, there are these five controlling powers. . . .

By the completion and fulfilment of these five controlling powers, one is Arahant. By having them in a less degree, one obtains release midway.[3] If he have them in a still less degree, he attains release by a reduction of his time.[4] Possessed of them in a still weaker degree, he attains release without much trouble:[5] if in a still weaker degree, with some trouble. If he have them in a less degree than that, he is 'one who goes up stream,' one who goes to the Pure Abodes.[6] If he have them in a still less degree, he is a once-returner: if still less, he is a stream-winner. One who has them in a less degree than that is a Norm-follower, and he who has them in the last degree of all is 'one who walks by faith.'

(vi) *In detail* (*b*).

(*As before, to*) '. . . walks by faith.'

Thus it is, monks, that there is a difference of controlling powers, a difference of fruits, a difference of individuals.

(vii) *In detail* (*c*).

(*As before, to*) '. . . walks by faith.'

So it is, monks, that he who completes his task succeeds completely. He who does part only, succeeds partially.

---

[1] For *padesaŋ cf. supra*, text 174 and § 7. *Comy.* 'He who fulfils the Arahant's path gets the fruits of Arahantship. Others get fruits according to the path they fulfil.'

[2] *Avañjhānitvevâhaŋ*=*avañjhāni iti eva ahaŋ.*

[3] *Antarā-parinibbāyī. Pts. of Contr.* 159; *supra*, text 69.

[4] *Upahacca.* [5] *Asaṅkhāra-p.* [6] He is *anāgāmin.*

Thus, monks, these five controlling powers are not barren of result,[1] I declare.

(viii) *Practising.*

(*As before, to*) '. . . these are the five controlling powers.'

By the completion and fulfilment of these five controlling powers, monks, one is Arahant. If one have them in a less degree, he is practising to realize the fruits of Arahantship. By having them in a still less degree one is a non-returner: in a still less degree, a once-returner: in a still less degree, a stream-winner . . . by faith.

But, monks, he in whom these five controlling powers are in every way, everywhere, wholly and utterly absent, of such an one I say 'he is an outsider, one who stands in the ranks of the many-folk.'[2]

(ix) *Tranquil.*[3]

Now a certain monk came to visit the Exalted One. . . . As he sat at one side that monk said this to the Exalted One:

'"Perfect in faculties! Perfect in faculties!"[4] is the saying, lord. Pray, lord, how far is one perfect in faculties?'

'Herein, monk, a monk cultivates the controlling power of faith, which leads to tranquillity, which leads to the perfect wisdom. He cultivates (the other controlling powers and) the controlling power of insight, which leads to tranquillity, which leads to the perfect wisdom.

Thus far a monk is possessed of perfection in faculties.'

(x) *Destruction of the āsavas.*

Monks, there are these five controlling powers. . . .

By the fact of cultivating and making much of these five controlling powers, by the destruction of the āsavas, a monk in this very life, comprehending it himself, realizes, attains and abides in that liberation of heart, that liberation by insight which is without āsavas.

---

[1] *Cf. A.* i, 235, where the reading is *avajjhāni.*

[2] For these phrases *cf. infra,* text 397.

[3] Text misprints title, which should be *upasamo,* not *upasanno.*

[4] *Indriya-sampanno=paripuṇṇ' indriyo. Comy.*

CHAPTER III.—THE SIX FACULTIES

(i) *No more becoming* or *The knower.*

Monks, there are these five controlling powers. What five? The controlling power of faith, that of energy, that of mindfulness, that of concentration, and the controlling power of insight. These are the five.

Now, monks, so long as I did not fully comprehend, as they really are, the arising and the perishing of, the satisfaction in, the misery of, and the escape from these five controlling powers, just so long, monks, did I not know the meaning of 'being enlightened with supreme enlightenment with regard to the world and its devas, its Māras, its Brahmās, with regard to the host of recluses and brahmins, of devas and mankind.'[1]

But, monks, when I came to know fully, as they really are, the arising and the perishing of, the satisfaction in, the misery of, the escape from these five controlling powers, then, monks, I fully knew the meaning of 'being enlightened with supreme enlightenment . . . as regards these things.' Then arose in me knowledge and insight thus: 'Sure is my heart's release. This is my last birth. Now is there no more becoming.'

(ii) *Vitality.*[2]

Monks, there are these three faculties. What three?

Femininity, masculinity and vitality. These are the three faculties.

(iii) *The Method.*[3]

There are these three controlling faculties. What three?

The consciousness that 'I shall know the unknown,' the consciousness of gnosis, the consciousness of one who has the gnosis.[4] These are the three.

---

[1] *Cf. K.S.* ii, 113 *ff.*

[2] *Jīvita. Cf. Buddh. Psych. Eth.*, p. 19. For femininity, *ibid.*, 190-1. I translate here as 'faculties' better to suit the context.

[3] *Ñāya. Cf. Buddh. Psych.* 121; *D.* iii, 219.

[4] *Buddh. Psych. Eth.* 86; *VM.* 491; *Asl.* 291; *B.* 'The faculty of the *aññātāvin* (the holder of things known), of him who, in the philosophy of the Four Truths, has completed what was to be done.'

(iv) *One-seed-er.*[1]

Monks, there are these five controlling powers. What five? The controlling power of faith, that of energy, that of mindfulness, that of concentration and the controlling power of insight. These are the five.

By the full and perfect completion of these five controlling powers, one is Arahant. By having them in a less degree, one attains release midway. Having them in a still less degree, one attains release by a reduction of his time: having them in a still less degree, he attains release without much trouble: in a less degree than that, he does so with some trouble. If he have them in a still less degree, he is 'one who goes up stream,' and goes to the Pure Abodes. Possessed of them in a less degree than that, he is a once-returner. If in a less degree than that, he is a one-seed-er. Again, possessed of them in a less degree than that, he is reborn in a good family:[2] in a less degree than that, he is one destined to seven more births at most.[3] One who possesses these five controlling powers in a still less degree is a Norm-follower: and if in a less degree, he is 'one who walks by faith.'

---

[1] *Eka-bījī* (*i.e.*, one more life). Text gives an alternative title (not in the *uddāna*), viz., *ekābhiññam*, which is of doubtful authority. *Cf. Pts. of Contr.* 77 *nn.*, 269, and *PuggA.* (*J.P.T.S.*, 1914, p. 195). Our *Comy.* 'Being a stream-winner, he generates just one personality (*attabhāvaŋ* or *mānusakaŋ*), and becomes Arahant'; and refers to *PuggA.*, *i.e.* (by wearing down three fetters, he is stream-winner, no more for Purgatory).

[2] *Kolankolo* (lit. 'from clan to clan,' *kula*). *Cf. PuggA. ad loc.* (*mahābhoga-kulesu nibbattati*). *Comy. So dve vā tīni vā kulāni sandahitvā saŋsaritvā dukkhass' antaŋ karoti: (kulāni=bhavā, v.l. bhagavā).*

[3] *Satta-kkhattu-paramo. Cf. K.S.* ii, 95 *n.*; *A.* i, 233 *ff. Comy.* instances *Anāthapiṇḍika, Visākhā; Culavatha, Mahāratha, Anekavaṇṇa, Nāgadatta* (these four last are *devaputtā*) and *Sakka devarājā*, who after six births in the *deva* (*rūpa*) world, will, on the seventh occasion, be reborn in the Pure Abodes.

(v) *Puritan.*[1]

Monks, there are these six sense-faculties.[2] What six? The sense-faculty of eye, that of ear, of nose, tongue, body and the sense-faculty of mind. These are the six sense faculties.

(vi) *Stream* or *Stream-winner.*

Monks, there are these six sense-faculties. What are the six? (*as before*). When the Ariyan disciple understands, as they really are, the arising and the perishing of, the satisfaction in, the misery of and the escape from these six sense-faculties, such an Ariyan disciple, monks, is called 'Stream-winner, one not doomed to Purgatory, one assured, one bound for enlightenment.'

(vii) *Arahant*[3] or *Enlightened* (*a*).

Monks, there are these six sense-faculties. What six? The sense-faculty of the eye, ear, nose, tongue, body and the sense-faculty of the mind. These are the six.

When a monk,[4] by seeing, as they really are, the arising and the perishing of, the satisfaction in, the misery of and the escape from these six sense-faculties, becomes released without grasping,—such a monk is called 'Arahant, in whom the āsavas are destroyed, one who has lived the life, done the task, lifted the burden, a winner of his own welfare, one who has outworn the fetters of rebirth, one released by perfect insight.'

(viii) *Arahant* or *Enlightened* (*b*).

Monks, there are these six sense-faculties. What six? The sense-faculty of eye and the rest, the sense-faculty of mind.

So long, monks, as I did not fully comprehend, as they really are, the arising and the perishing of, the satisfaction in, the misery of and the escape from these six faculties of

---

[1] *Cf. supra*, text 170, 193.

[2] At *K.S.* iii, 40 *n.*, 130 *ff.* (five, with the mind, as result of them).

[3] Text *arahatā* for *arahā*.

[4] *N.B.* 'monk' not 'Ariyan disciple,' because the life has to be lived by such, in order to attain. (This, of course, is from a monkish point of view.)

sense,—just for so long, monks, did I not know the meaning of 'being enlightened with supreme enlightenment with regard to the world and its devas, its Māras, its Brahmās' . . . but when I came to know fully . . . I fully comprehended the meaning of 'being enlightened with supreme enlightenment as regards' . . . those things. Then arose in me knowledge and sight: 'This is my heart's release. This is my last birth. Now is there no more becoming.'

(ix) *Recluses and Brahmins* (*a*).

Monks, there are these six sense-faculties. What six? . . . Monks, whatsoever recluses or brahmins understand not, as they really are, the arising . . . of these six sense-faculties, such are not worthy to be accounted as recluses among recluses nor as brahmins among brahmins, nor have those worthies understood . . . nor do they dwell in the attainment of it.

But, monks, those recluses and brahmins who . . . have so understood . . . such are worthy to be accounted . . . and those worthies have of themselves understood and even in this very life realized the goal of recluseship and brahminhood, and they do dwell in the attainment thereof.

(x) *Recluses and brahmins* (*b*).

Monks, whatsoever recluses or brahmins understand not the sense-faculty of the eye, and understand not the arising . . . nor understand the practice leading to the ceasing thereof: who understand not the sense-faculty of the ear, nose, tongue, body and mind, nor the arising thereof, nor the practice leading to the ceasing thereof,—such are not worthy to be accounted recluses among recluses, nor as brahmins among brahmins, nor have those worthies realized . . . nor do they dwell in the attainment thereof.

But whatsoever recluses or brahmins do understand the sense-faculty of the eye, ear . . . such are worthy to be accounted as recluses among recluses and as brahmins among brahmins, and those worthies have of themselves understood, and in this very life realized, the goal of recluseship and of brahminhood, and they do dwell in the attainment thereof.

CHAPTER IV.—THE FACULTY OF EASE (OR REFERRING TO THE ABOVE)[1]

(i) *Puritan.*

Monks, there are these five controlling faculties. What five?

The controlling faculty of ease, that of discomfort, that of happiness,[2] that of unhappiness, and the controlling faculty of indifference. These are the five controlling faculties.

(ii) *The stream.*

Monks, there are these five controlling faculties. What five? The controlling faculty of ease . . . the controlling faculty of indifference.

Now, monks, when the Ariyan disciple understands, as they really are, the arising and the perishing of, the satisfaction in, the misery of and the escape from these five controlling faculties, such an Ariyan disciple is called 'Stream-winner not doomed to Purgatory, one assured, one bound for enlightenment.'

(iii) *Arahant.*

Monks, there are these five controlling faculties. . . .

Now when a monk, by understanding, as they really are, the arising and the perishing . . . of these five controlling faculties, such an one is called 'Arahant, one in whom the āsavas are destroyed, one who has lived the life, done his task, lifted the burden, a winner of his own welfare, who has outworn the fetters of rebirth, one who is released by perfect insight.'

(iv) *Recluses and brahmins (a).*

Monks, there are these five controlling faculties. What five? The controlling faculty of ease . . . that of indifference.

---

[1] Text title of this chapter is *Uppaṭi-* for *Uppaṭipātiyā*. *Cf. infra*, § 10. At *Path of Purity* ii, 312, it is trans. 'out of order.'

[2] *Somanassa*. *Cf. D.* ii, 239. It is *sukha*+excitement. *Compend.* 112 *n.*

Whatsoever recluses or brahmins understand not the arising and the perishing of, the satisfaction in, the misery of, and the escape from these five controlling faculties . . . nor do they dwell in the attainment thereof.

But those recluses or brahmins who do understand . . . they do dwell in the attainment thereof.

(v) *Recluses and brahmins* (*b*).

Monks, there are these five controlling faculties. . . .

Whatsoever recluses or brahmins understand not the controlling faculty of ease, nor its arising, who understand not the ceasing thereof, who understand not the practice leading to the ceasing thereof . . . who understand not the controlling faculty of indifference, nor its arising, nor its ceasing, nor the practice leading to the ceasing thereof,—such are not worthy to be accounted . . . nor do they dwell in the attainment thereof.

But they who do so understand . . . they are worthy to be accounted . . . and those worthies do dwell in the attainment thereof.

(vi) *Analysis* (*a*).

Monks, there are these five controlling faculties. What five? . . . (*as before*). . . .

And of what sort, monks, is the controlling faculty of ease?[1]

That ease which is bodily, that agreeableness which is bodily, that ease, that agreeableness which is experienced when it arises from bodily contact,—that, monks, is called 'the controlling faculty of ease.'

And of what sort, monks, is the controlling faculty of discomfort?

That discomfort which is bodily, that disagreeableness which is bodily, that discomfort, that disagreeableness which is experienced when it arises from bodily contact,—that, monks, is called 'the controlling faculty of discomfort.'

And of what sort, monks, is the controlling faculty of happiness?

---

[1] *Cf. Compend.* 112 *n.*

That happiness which is mental, that agreeableness which is mental, that happiness, that agreeableness which is experienced when it arises from mental contact,—that, monks, is called 'the controlling faculty of happiness.'

And of what sort, monks, is the controlling faculty of unhappiness?

That pain which is mental, that disagreeableness which is mental, that pain, that disagreeableness which is experienced when it arises from mental contact,—that, monks, is called 'the controlling faculty of unhappiness.'

And of what sort, monks, is the controlling faculty of indifference?

That bodily or mental feeling experienced, which is neither agreeable nor disagreeable,—that, monks, is called 'the controlling faculty of indifference.'[1]

These indeed, monks, are the five controlling faculties.

(vii) *Analysis* (*b*).

Monks, these are these five controlling faculties. What five? The controlling faculty of ease . . . of indifference.

And of what sort, monks, is the controlling faculty of ease? . . . (*As before down to*) '. . . that, monks, is called the controlling faculty of indifference.'

Now, monks, in these cases, the controlling faculty of ease and the controlling faculty of happiness should be regarded as pleasurable feeling. Likewise the controlling faculty of discomfort and that of unhappiness must be regarded as painful feeling. Likewise the controlling faculty of indifference must be regarded as feeling that is neither pleasant nor painful.

These, monks, are the five controlling faculties.

(viii) *Analysis* (*c*).

(*As in* § vii *down to*) '. . . this, monks, is called the controlling faculty of indifference.'

(*As in* § viii.) Now in these cases, monks, . . . the con-

[1] *Upekkhā* here, it is to be noticed, is the hedonic, not the intellectual (*tatra-majjhatt' upekkhā*) mental balance.

trolling faculty of indifference should be regarded as feeling that is neither pleasant nor painful.

Thus it is, monks, that these five controlling faculties, from being five, become three, and again, from being three, they become five in turn.[1]

(ix) *The fire-stick.*[2]

Monks, there are these five controlling faculties. What five? The controlling faculty of ease, that of discomfort, that of happiness, that of unhappiness, that of indifference.

Now, owing to the contact that is to be experienced as agreeable, monks, arises the controlling faculty of ease. He (who experiences it), being at ease, is fully aware of being so. Also, on the ceasing of that contact to be experienced as agreeable, as to that controlling faculty of ease,—which had arisen owing to that appropriate[3] contact to be experienced as agreeable,—he is aware that it ceases, that it is quieted down.

Again, monks, owing to contact which is to be experienced as disagreeable arises the controlling faculty of discomfort. He (who experiences it), being uncomfortable, is fully aware of being so. Also, on the ceasing of that contact to be experienced as disagreeable, as to that controlling faculty of discomfort,—which had arisen owing to that appropriate contact to be experienced as disagreeable,—he is aware that it ceases, that it is quieted down.

Again, monks, owing to contact which is to be experienced as producing happiness, arises the controlling faculty of happiness. He (who experiences it), being made happy, is fully aware of being so. Also, on the ceasing of that contact to be experienced as producing happiness, as to that controlling faculty of happiness,—which had arisen owing to that appropriate contact to be experienced as producing happiness,—he is aware that it ceases, that it is quieted down.

Again, monks, owing to contact which is to be experienced as producing unhappiness, arises the controlling faculty of

---

1 *Pariyāyena=vicissim.*

2 *Araṇi.* *Cf. K.S.* ii, 67; iv, 145; *Buddh. Psych.* 45; *MP.* 6.

3 *Tajjaŋ=sarūpaŋ.* *Cf. Buddh. Psych. Eth.* 6 *n.*

unhappiness. He (who experiences it), being unhappy, is fully aware of being so. Also, on the ceasing of that contact to be experienced as producing unhappiness,—which had arisen owing to that appropriate contact to be experienced as producing unhappiness,—he is aware that it ceases, that it is quieted down.

(Lastly) monks, owing to the contact which is to be experienced as indifferent arises the controlling faculty of indifference. He (who experiences it), being indifferent, is fully aware of being indifferent. Also, on the ceasing of that contact to be experienced as indifferent, as to that controlling faculty of indifference,—which had arisen owing to that appropriate contact to be experienced as indifferent,—he is aware that it ceases, that it is quieted down.

Just as, monks, from the putting together and rubbing together of two sticks warmth is born, heat is produced; as from the separation and parting of those two sticks the warmth so born ceases and is quenched, just so, monks, owing to contact that is to be experienced as agreeable arises the controlling faculty of ease. He (who experiences it), being at ease, is fully aware of being at ease. Also, on the ceasing . . .

So also, owing to contact that is to be experienced as disagreeable . . . as producing happiness . . . as producing unhappiness . . . as indifferent . . . (in each case) he is aware that it ceases, that it is quieted down.

(x) *Consequent.*[1]

Monks, there are these five controlling faculties. What five? The controlling faculty of discomfort, that of unhappiness, that of ease, that of happiness, and the controlling faculty of indifference.

Now herein, monks, suppose a monk dwells earnest, ardent and aspiring, and there arises in him the controlling faculty

---

[1] Title in text *Uppatika* (?=*uppatita*, 'arisen,' with reference to *uppajjati* in this §). But *Comy.* refers it to Chapter-title: *uppaṭipātikaŋ suttaŋ nāmā ti veditabbaŋ*, *i.e.*, 'with reference to what has gone before' (*yathādhamm' ārammana-vasena paṭipātiyā vuttaŋ*). *Cf. supra*, text 207 *n.*: *supra*, 183 n.

of discomfort. He is aware of it thus: There has arisen in me this controlling faculty of discomfort. Now this is conditioned, has its cause, its constituent parts, its reasons.[1] That the controlling faculty of discomfort should arise without these conditions, causes, constituent parts and reasons, is quite impossible. Thus he comes to know fully both the controlling faculty of discomfort, its arising and its ceasing: and, whence arising, how this controlling faculty of discomfort comes to cease without remainder,[2]—that also he fully knows.

Now, monks, whence does it arise and how does it come to cease without remainder?

Herein a monk, aloof from sense-desires, aloof from evil conditions, enters upon the first trance, which is accompanied by thought directed and sustained, born of seclusion, zestful and easeful, and abides therein. Here the controlling faculty of discomfort, which has arisen, ceases without remainder. This monk is called 'A monk who has understood the ceasing of the controlling faculty of discomfort, one who has collected his mind[3] for the attaining such a condition.'

Now herein again, monks, suppose a monk dwells earnest, ardent and aspiring, and there arises in him the controlling faculty of unhappiness. He is aware of it thus: There has arisen in me this controlling faculty of unhappiness. Now this is conditioned, has its cause, its constituent parts and reasons. That the controlling faculty of unhappiness should arise without these conditions, causes, constituent parts and reasons is quite impossible.

Thus he comes to know fully both the controlling faculty of unhappiness, and its arising and its ceasing. Also he fully knows, whence arising, how this controlling faculty of unhappiness comes to cease without remainder.

---

[1] *Sanimittaŋ, sanidānaŋ, sasaṅkhāraŋ, sappaccayaŋ.*

[2] *Cf. Expos.* i, 235; *VM.* 166; *SnA.* ii, 120; *D.* iii, 222.

[3] Text *upasaŋhāsi*, but Burmese MSS. and *Comy.* *upasaŋharati* ('he pulls himself together'). *Comy.* remarks: *tattha-lābhī samāne uppādan' atthāya cittaŋ upasaŋharati, lābhī samāno samapajjan' atthāya.* For *tathattāya*, 'the state of being such,' *cf. M.* i, 465 *ff.*; *supra*, text 90; *K.S.* iv, 202 *n.* (a synonym in Sanskrit Buddhism for Nibbāna).

Now whence does it arise, and how does it come to cease without remainder?

Herein a monk, by the calming down of thought directed and sustained, attains and abides in the second trance, that inward calming, that single-mindedness of will, apart from thought directed and sustained, that is born of mental balance, zestful and easeful. It is here that the controlling faculty of unhappiness, which has arisen, comes to cease without remainder. Such an one, monks, is called 'A monk who has come to know the ceasing of the controlling faculty of unhappiness, one who has collected his mind for attaining such a condition.'

Now herein again, monks, suppose a monk dwells earnest, ardent and aspiring, and there arises in him the controlling faculty of ease. He is aware of it thus: There has arisen in me this controlling faculty of ease. Now this is conditioned, has its cause, its constituent parts and its reasons. That the controlling faculty of ease should arise without these conditions, causes, constituent parts and reasons, is quite impossible.

Thus he comes to know both the controlling faculty of ease and its arising and its ceasing. Also he fully knows, whence arising, how this controlling faculty of ease comes to cease without remainder.

Now whence does it arise and how does it come to cease without remainder?

Herein a monk, by the fading out of zest, disinterested, mindful and composed, experiences with body that ease of which the Ariyans declare:

'He who is disinterested and alert dwells at ease,'[1] and he so attains and abides in the third trance. It is here that the controlling faculty of ease, which has arisen, comes to cease

---

[1] *Cf. Expos.* 238. (It is to be noticed that the third feeling is neither pain nor pleasure, is opposed to pain and pleasure, is not merely the absence of pain and pleasure: it is called 'hedonic indifference.' The Fourth Jhāna which follows is the purity of mindfulness born of (this) indifference. The Fourth Jhāna, then, is mental emancipation, which is neutral feeling.)

without remainder. Such an one, monks, is called 'A monk who has understood the ceasing of the controlling faculty of ease, one who has collected his mind for attaining such a condition.'

Now herein again, monks, suppose a monk dwells earnest, ardent and aspiring, and there arises in him the controlling faculty of happiness. He is aware of it thus: There has arisen in me this controlling faculty of happiness. Now this is conditioned, has its cause, its constituent parts, its reasons. That the controlling faculty of happiness should arise without these conditions, causes, constituent parts and reasons is quite impossible. Thus he comes to know the controlling faculty of happiness and its arising and its ceasing. Also he fully knows, whence arising, how this controlling faculty of happiness comes to cease without remainder.

Now whence does it arise and how does it come to cease without remainder?

Herein, monks, by abandoning both ease and discomfort, by the ending of both happiness and unhappiness felt before, he attains and abides in the fourth trance, a state of neither ease nor discomfort, an equanimity of utter purity. Herein the controlling faculty of happiness, which had arisen, comes to cease without remainder. Such an one, monks, is called 'A monk who has understood the ceasing of the controlling faculty of happiness, one who has collected his mind for attaining such a condition.'

Now herein again, monks, suppose a monk dwells earnest, ardent and aspiring. Then there arises in him the controlling faculty of indifference. He is aware of it thus: There has arisen in me this controlling faculty of indifference. Now this is conditioned, has its cause, its constituent parts and its reasons. That the controlling faculty of indifference should arise without its conditions, causes, its constituent parts and its reasons, is a thing quite impossible. Thus he comes to know both the controlling faculty of indifference, its arising and its ceasing. Also he fully knows, whence arising, how this controlling faculty of indifference comes to cease without remainder.

Now whence does it arise, and how does it come to cease without remainder?

Herein, monks, passing utterly beyond the feeling of neither perception nor non-perception, he attains and abides in the state of cessation of perception and feeling. Herein the controlling faculty of indifference, which had arisen, comes to cease without remainder.

Such an one, monks, is called 'A monk who has understood the ceasing of the controlling faculty of indifference, one who has collected his mind for attaining such a condition.'

CHAPTER V.—OLD AGE

(i) *Old age.*

Thus have I heard: On a certain occasion the Exalted One was staying near Sāvatthī in East Park, at the terraced house of Migāra's mother.[1]

Now on that occasion the Exalted One, having arisen from his solitude at eventide, was seated warming his back in the westering sunshine.[2]

Then the venerable Ānanda came to see the Exalted One, and on coming to him saluted him and, while chafing his limbs[3] with his hand, said to the Exalted One:

'It is a strange thing, lord! It is a wonder, lord, how the skin of the Exalted One is no longer clear and translucent, and how all his limbs are slack[4] and

---

[1] S. i, 77, iii, 100.

[2] *Comy.* discusses the question as to how the sunshine can pierce through the *Buddha-teja* or *aura*, and concludes that it cannot do so. 'Then what is warmed? The radiance itself is warmed. Just as when one sits under a spreading tree, the sunshine does not touch the body, but the radiance of it spreads all round, and it is like being surrounded by a flame of fire. So we are to understand thus: The Master was sitting warming his aura (?).'

[3] *Comy.* reads 'back.'

[4] *Sithilāni.* *Comy.* 'The flesh, coming away from the bone, attains ooseness and hangs here and there.'

wrinkled,[1] his body bent forward, and a change is to be seen in his sense-faculties of eye, ear, nose, tongue and body!'[2]

'So it is, Ānanda. Old age is by nature inherent in youth, sickness in health, and death in life. Thus it is that my skin is no longer clear and translucent as of yore; my limbs are slack and wrinkled, my body stoops forward and a change is to be noticed in my sense-faculties of eye, ear, nose, tongue and body.'

Thus spake the Exalted One. Having so said, the Happy One as Teacher added this:

Shame on thee,[3] miserable age!
Age that maketh colour fade!
The pleasing image[4] of a man
By age is trampled down.

Tho' one should live a hundred years,
Natheless he is consigned to death.
Death passeth nothing by,
But trampleth everything.

(ii) *Uṇṇābha the brahmin.*

Sāvatthī was the occasion . . .

Now the brahmin Uṇṇābha came to visit the Exalted One, and on coming to him greeted him courteously, and, after the exchange of greetings and courtesies, sat down at one side. So seated, Uṇṇābha the brahmin said this to the Exalted One:

'There are these five sense-faculties, master Gotama, of different scope, of different range. They do not mutually

---

[1] Text *baliya-jātāni*, but Sinh. MSS. and *Comy. vali-jātāni*, which I follow.

[2] *Comy.* 'The sense-faculties are invisible, but as these defects are to be seen it must be owing to decay of the faculties. He speaks inferentially.'

[3] *Dhī taŋ* for *dhītaŋ* of text (*cf. Sn.* v, 440, *dhi-r-atthu jīvitaŋ*). *Comy.* reads *dhikkaŋ* (text *v.l. dhittaŋ*) *jammī jaro* (which is interpreted as *dhikkaŋ tuyhaŋ hotu, vikāyo taŋ phusatu* [?]).

[4] *Bimba* (text, *vimba*)=*attabhāva*. *Comy. Cf. Dhp.* 147: *Passa cittakataŋ bimbaŋ.*

enjoy each other's scope and range. What are the five ? The sense-faculty of eye, that of ear, that of nose, that of tongue, and the sense-faculty of body. Now, master Gotama, as these five sense-faculties are of different scope, of different range, and do not mutually enjoy each other's scope and range, pray, what common ground of resort[1] have they, and who profits by their scope and range ?'

'There are, brahmin, as you say, these five sense-faculties of different scope and different range, and they do not mutually enjoy each other's scope and range. Well, mind is their common ground of resort. It is mind that profits by their scope and range.'

'But, master Gotama, what is the resort of mind ?'

'Mindfulness, brahmin, is the resort of mind.'

'Then, master Gotama, what is the resort of mindfulness ?'

'Release, brahmin, is the resort of mindfulness.'

'What, then, master Gotama, is the resort of release ?'

'Nibbāna, brahmin, is the resort of release.'

'But, master Gotama, what is the resort of Nibbāna ?'

'The question goes too far,[2] brahmin. That question is beyond the compass of an answer. The aim of living the holy life, brahmin, is to plunge[3] into Nibbāna. It has Nibbāna for its goal, Nibbāna for its ending.'

Then the brahmin Uṇṇābha was delighted with the words of the Exalted One and received them gladly. And he rose up from his seat, saluted the Exalted One by the right and went away.

Now not long after the departure of the brahmin Uṇṇābha the Exalted One said to the monks:

---

[1] *Paṭisaraṇaŋ*, 'looking to,' or 'referring to.' At *A.* i, 199, 're-going.' *Cf. Dialog.* i, 122 *n.*; *Pts. of Contr.* 140. At *M.* i, 295, *Mahākoṭṭhita* puts this question to Sāriputta. It is discussed at *Buddh. Psych. Ethics*, where see Mrs. Rhys Davids' extract from *Comy.* on *M.* i *loc. cit.* For 'resort' see next §.

[2] Text *ajjhaparaŋ* (Burmese MSS.), but *M.* i, 304, *accasaraŋ*, *i.e.* it is transcendental. That at *S.* ii, 1898, should be the same, where *Comy. atikkanto.*

[3] *Ogadhaŋ*=*Nibb. abbhantaraŋ, anupaviṭṭhaŋ. Comy.*

'Suppose, monks, in a house with a peaked roof or in a pavilion with a peaked roof, with a window facing east, when the sun is rising and its rays strike through the window, on what do they rest?'[1]

'On the western wall, lord.'

'Just so, monks, the faith of the brahmin Uṇṇābha is bent on, rooted in, rests on the Tathāgata. It is strong, not to be uprooted by any recluse or brahmin or deva or Māra or Brahmā, or by anyone else in the world.

Monks, if at this time the brahmin Uṇṇābha were to make an end, there is no fetter, bound by which, the brahmin Uṇṇābha would come back to this world.'[2]

(iii) *Sāketa.*

Thus have I heard: Once the Exalted One was staying near Sāketa,[3] at Añjana Wood, in Antelope Grove.

On that occasion the Exalted One said this to the monks:

'Monks, is there any method, by reckoning according to which the five controlling faculties are the five powers, and the five powers again are the five controlling faculties?'

'For us, lord, things have the Exalted One as their root, (their guide and their resort.[4] It were well for us if the Exalted One would reveal the meaning of what he has just uttered).'[5]

'Well, monks, there is such a method, by reckoning according to which the five controlling faculties are the five powers, and again the five powers are the five controlling faculties. And of what sort, monks, is that method?

That, monks, which is the controlling faculty of faith is also the power of faith: that which is the power of faith is also the controlling faculty of faith. And it is the same with regard to the controlling faculty of energy, and the rest. . . . That

---

[1] *Cf. K.S.* ii, 71.

[2] He is *anāgāmin*. This instance may be added to the two referred to above on text 178 *n*.

[3] A town in Kosala, formerly the capital (which at this time was *Sāvatthī*); *Buddh. India*, 39. *Cf. M.* i, 149; *A.* ii, 24; iii, 169; iv, 427.

[4] *Paṭisaraṇaṃ*, as above.

[5] *Cf. S.* ii, 24, etc. Here text is abridged.

which is the controlling faculty of insight is again the power of insight, and the power of insight is also the controlling faculty of insight.

Suppose, monks, a river that flows east, slopes east, tends east. In the middle of it is an island. Now, monks, there is a method, by reckoning according to which, the stream of that river is accounted single. Again there is a method, by reckoning according to which, the stream is accounted double.

Now what sort of method is that according to which the stream of that river may be reckoned as single? Thus: The water at the east end and the water at the west end of that island will be reckoned as a single stream. That is the method.

And what sort of method is that according to which the stream of that river may be reckoned as double? Thus: The water on the north side and the water on the south side will be reckoned as a double stream. That is the method according to which the stream may be reckoned as double.

Just in the same way, monks, the controlling faculty of faith is also the power of faith, and the power of faith is also the controlling faculty of faith.

Monks, by the fact of cultivating and making much of the five controlling faculties, a monk, by the destruction of the āsavas, in this very life fully comprehends, realizes for himself and attains intellectual release and release by insight, and abides therein.'

(iv) *Eastern Gatehouse.*[1]

Thus have I heard: Once the Exalted One was staying at Sāvatthī, in Eastern Gatehouse.[2] On that occasion the Exalted One addressed the venerable Sāriputta thus:

'Do you believe, Sāriputta, that the controlling faculty of faith, if cultivated and made much of, plunges into the Deathless, has the Deathless for its goal, the Deathless for its ending?

---

[1] This Sutta is quoted in full at *Nidd.* i, 236, as comment on the text *Sn.* 853, *na saddho na virajjati.*

[2] At *A.* iii, 345, the only place where it seems to be mentioned, the Buddha goes there with Ānanda to bathe. *Koṭṭhaka* is a chamber or storehouse (here, over the gate). By the city gates were public bathing-places.

Do you believe, Sāriputta, that the controlling faculty of energy, if cultivated and made much of, plunges into the Deathless . . . that the controlling faculty of mindfulness . . . of concentration . . . Do you believe, Sāriputta, that the controlling faculty of insight, if cultivated and made much of, plunges into the Deathless, has the Deathless for its goal, the Deathless for its ending ?'

'In this matter, lord, I walk not by faith[1] in the Exalted One, to wit: that the controlling faculty of faith, if cultivated and made much of . . . that the controlling faculty of insight, if cultivated and made much of, plunges into the Deathless, has the Deathless for its goal, the Deathless for its ending.

They, lord, who have not realized, not seen, not understood, not made sure of, not attained this faculty by insight,—such may well walk by faith in others (in believing) that the controlling faculty of faith . . . that of insight, if cultivated and made much of, may so end.

But, lord, they who have realized, seen, understood, made sure of, they who have attained this fact by insight,—such are free from doubt, free from wavering,[2] (in believing) that the controlling faculty of faith, of energy, of mindfulness, of concentration, of insight, if cultivated and made much of . . . will so end.

But I, lord, have realized it, I have seen, understood and made sure of it, I have attained it by insight, I am free from doubt about it,[3] that the controlling faculty of faith . . . of insight, does plunge into the Deathless, has the Deathless for its goal, the Deathless for its ending.'

'Well said ! Well said, Sāriputta ! Indeed they who have not realized, not seen, not understood, who have not made sure of, who have not attained this fact by insight,—such may well walk by faith in others (in believing) that the controlling

---

[1] *Saddhāya gacchāmi.* I take *saddhāya* to be gerund, *saddhahitvā* (as *Comy.* elsewhere).

[2] *Nibbicikicchā* (*ni-vicikicchā*). *Cf. S.* ii, 84.

[3] Here text inserts *paresaŋ* (not in Sinh. MSS.), which makes no sense.

faculty of faith . . . has the Deathless for its goal, for its ending. But indeed, Sāriputta, they who have realized, who have seen, understood, made sure of and attained this fact by insight,—such are indeed free from doubt, free from wavering, (in knowing) that the controlling faculty of faith . . . of insight, if cultivated and made much of, does plunge into the Deathless, has the Deathless for its goal, for its ending.'

(v) *East Park* (*a*).

Thus have I heard: Once the Exalted One was staying near Sāvatthī, in East Park, at the terraced house of Migāra's mother.

On that occasion the Exalted One addressed the monks, saying:

'Monks, by cultivating and making much of what controlling faculties does the monk in whom the āsavas are destroyed declare gnosis, to wit: "I know full well that destroyed is rebirth, lived is the holy life, done is the task, there is no more of being here for me"?'

'For us, lord, things have their root in the Exalted One. . . .'

'Well, monks, by cultivating and making much of a single controlling faculty, a man in whom the āsavas are destroyed may thus declare gnosis . . . And what is that one controlling faculty?

Monks, in the Ariyan disciple who has won insight[1] faith is established as a matter of course,[2] energy is established as a matter of course, mindfulness is established as a matter of course, concentration is established as a matter of course.

It is by cultivating and making much of this single controlling faculty (of insight) that a monk in whom the āsavas are destroyed can declare gnosis, to wit: "I know full well that destroyed is rebirth, lived is the holy life, done is the task, there is no more of being here for me."'

---

[1] *Paññāvato.*

[2] *Tadanvayā* (accordantly)=*taŋ anugacchamānā anuvattamānā*. *Comy.* *Cf.* *S.* iii, 156 (of a bunch of mangoes), *tāni tadanvayāni bhavanti* (go along with it).

(vi) *East Park* (*b*).

The same occasion . . .

'Monks, by cultivating and making much of what controlling faculty does a monk in whom the āsavas are destroyed declare gnosis, to wit: "I know full well that destroyed is rebirth . . . in these conditions"?'

'Lord, for us things have their root in the Exalted One. . . .'

'Well, monks, it is by the cultivation and making much of two controlling faculties that a monk is able to do so. What two?

By Ariyan insight and Ariyan release. That which in him is the Ariyan insight is the controlling faculty of insight, and that which in him is the Ariyan release is the controlling faculty of concentration. It is by cultivating and making much of these two controlling faculties, monks, that a monk in whom the āsavas are destroyed is able to declare gnosis, to wit: "Destroyed is rebirth . . . there is no more of being here for me."'

(vii) *East Park* (*c*).

The same occasion . . .

'Monks, by cultivating and making much of what controlling faculty does a monk in whom the asavas are destroyed declare gnosis, to wit: "I know full well that destroyed is rebirth . . . there is no more of being here for me"?'

'Lord, for us things have their root in the Exalted One. . . .'

'Well, monks, it is by cultivating and making much of four[1] controlling faculties. What four?

The controlling faculty of energy, mindfulness, concentration and insight. These are the four . . .'

(viii) *East Park* (*d*).

The same occasion . . .

'Monks, by cultivating and making much of what controlling faculties does a monk in whom the āsavas are destroyed

---

[1] The section on *three* c.fs. seems omitted.

declare gnosis, to wit: "I know full well that destroyed is rebirth . . . there is no more of being here for me"?'

'Lord, for us things are rooted in the Exalted One. . . .'

'Well, monks, it is by cultivating and making much of five controlling faculties that a monk in whom the āsavas are destroyed is able to do so.

What are the five? The controlling faculties of faith, energy, mindfulness, concentration and insight.

Monks, it is by cultivating and making much of these five controlling faculties that a monk in whom the āsavas are destroyed is able to declare gnosis, to wit: "I know full well that destroyed is rebirth, lived is the holy life, done is the task, there is no more of being here for me."'

(ix) *Scrap-hunter.*

Thus have I heard: On a certain occasion the Exalted One was staying at Kosambī in Ghosita Park.

Now on that occasion the Bhāradvājan, the venerable Scrap-hunter,[1] so called, had declared gnosis, to wit: 'I know full well that destroyed is rebirth, lived is the holy life, done is the task, there is no more of being here for me.'

Then a number of monks[2] came to visit the Exalted One, and on coming to him, saluted him and sat down at one side. So seated, those monks said this to the Exalted One:

'Lord, the Bhāradvājan, the venerable Scrap-hunter, has declared gnosis, to wit: "I know full well that destroyed is rebirth . . . there is no more of being here for me." Pray, lord, in consequence of what observation[3] did the Bhāradvājan, the venerable Scrap-hunter, thus declare gnosis . . . ?'

'Monks, it was in consequence of having cultivated and made much of three controlling faculties that the Bhāra-

---

[1] *Piṇḍola*, of *Bhāradvāja*. There are several of this clan, *e.g.*, at *K.S.* i, 204 ('conjey man') among the *Brahmin Suttas*. At *K.S.* iv, 68 (where see note) he takes refuge with the Master. *Bhāradvāja* is on the river Jumna. *Cf. Buddhist India*, 36.

[2] For *sambahulā* see *n. supra*, text 108.

[3] *Kiŋ atthavasaŋ sampassamānena*, generally equivalent to *kāraṇaŋ* (*causâ*).

dvājan, the venerable Scrap-hunter, thus declared gnosis. What three? The controlling faculty of mindfulness, of concentration, and of insight.[1]

It was in consequence of having cultivated and made much of these three controlling faculties that gnosis was declared by the Bhāradvājan, the venerable Scrap-hunter.

Now these three controlling faculties,—what do they end in?

They end in destruction.

They end in destruction of what?

They end in the destruction of rebirth, old age and death.

Monks, it was because he saw full well that rebirth was destroyed, that old age and death were destroyed, that the Bhāradvājan, the venerable Scrap-hunter, was able to declare gnosis, to wit: "I know full well that destroyed is rebirth, lived is the holy life, done is the task, there is no more of being here for me."'

(x) *Faithful* or *Market.*

Thus have I heard: On a certain occasion the Exalted One was staying among the Angas, at Market[2] so called, a township of the Angas.

Now on that occasion the Exalted One addressed the venerable Sāriputta, saying:

'Tell me, Sāriputta, could an Ariyan disciple who is utterly devoted to,[3] who has perfect faith in the Tathāgata,—could an Ariyan disciple have any doubt or wavering as to the Tathāgata or the Tathāgata's teaching?'

'Lord, an Ariyan disciple who is utterly devoted to the

---

[1] At *UdA.* 252, *Dhammapāla* says, after describing his nickname, his scrap-hunting life, his huge bowl, gradually wasted to a mere sherd, and his subjection to the Master's injunctions: 'on a subsequent occasion, by cultivating controlling-faculty culture, he was established in the topmost fruit of Arahantship.' Our *Comy.* says nothing.

[2] *Āpaṇa* (market). *Cf. Brethren,* 310 *n.* For the Angas *cf. Buddh. India,* p. 23; *Vin.* i, 29, quoted at *SA.* on *S.* i, 1; *KhA.* 115; *M.* ii, 163. 'The Angas dwelt in the country to the east of Magadha, having their capital at Champa, near the modern Bhagalpur.

[3] *Ekanta-gato,* lit. 'downright gone to,' *i.e., saraṇaŋ gato.*

Tathāgata, who has perfect faith in the Tathāgata, could have no doubt, could have no wavering as to the Tathāgata or the Tathāgata's teaching. Of the Ariyan disciple who has faith, lord, this may be expected: he will dwell resolute in energy, ever striving to abandon bad qualities and to acquire good qualities: he will be stout and strong to exert himself, not throwing off the burden in good qualities. His energy, lord, is the controlling faculty of energy.[1]

Of a faithful Ariyan disciple, lord, who is resolute in energy, this may be expected: he will be mindful, possessed of supreme discrimination,[2] one who calls to mind and remembers things said long ago. His mindfulness, lord, is the controlling faculty of mindfulness.

Of a faithful Ariyan disciple, lord, who is resolute in energy, with mindfulness established, this may be expected: he will make self-surrender the object of his thought, he will lay hold of concentration, one-pointedness of mind. His concentration, lord, is the controlling faculty of concentration.

Again, lord, of a faithful Ariyan disciple who is established in mindfulness, whose thought is tranquillized, this may be expected: he will fully understand "A world without end[3] is the round of rebirth. No beginning can be seen of beings hindered by ignorance, bound by craving, who run on, who fare on through the round of rebirth. The utter passionless ceasing of ignorance, of this body of darkness,[4] is this blissful state, this excellent[5] state, to wit:—the calming down of all the activities, the giving up of all bases (for rebirth), the destruction of craving, dispassion, cessation, Nibbāna." His insight, lord, is the controlling faculty of insight.

Lord, that faithful Ariyan disciple, thus striving and striving

---

[1] Text arranges paragraphs here wrongly, *e.g.*, §§ 4, 5, 6, where the first line of each should be joined to the previous §. Also *ti* is omitted after the thoughts expressed in each case.

[2] *Sati-nepakka.* *Cf. supra,* text 197.

[3] For *anamatagga cf. K.S.* ii, 118 *ff.*; iii, 126 (*J.P.T.S.*, 1919, p. 40, for derivation of the word).

[4] *Tame-kāya.* *Cf. Thag.* 128, *tamo-khandha.*

[5] *Paṇītaṃ.* Text has *phaṇītaṃ.*

again, thus recollecting again and again, thus again and again composing his mind, thus clearly discerning again and again, gains utter confidence, when he considers: "As to those things which formerly I had only heard tell of, now I dwell having experienced them in my own person:[1] now by insight have I pierced them through and see them plain." Herein, lord, his faith is the controlling faculty of faith.'

'Well said! Well said, Sāriputta! Indeed, Sāriputta, the Ariyan disciple who is utterly devoted to the Tathāgata, who has perfect faith in the Tathāgata, can have no doubt or wavering in the Tathāgata or the Tathāgata's teaching. Indeed, Sāriputta, of the faithful Ariyan disciple this may be expected':—(*and he repeated all that Sāriputta had said of the controlling faculties of* faith, energy, mindfulness, concentration and insight).

CHAPTER VI[2]

(i) *Sālā.*[3]

Thus have I heard: On a certain occasion the Exalted One was staying among the Kosalans, at Sālā, a brahmin village.

On that occasion the Exalted One addressed the monks, saying:

'Just as, monks, whatsoever brute creatures[4] there be, of them the lion, king of beasts, is reckoned chief, namely in strength, speed and courage,[5] even so, monks, whatsoever

---

[1] *Kāyena phusitvā.* This may stand for *nāma-rūpa* (the individuality, *i.e.*, the bodily substrate+the emotions and mind). *Comy.* says *nāma-kāyena.* On the other hand, it may be a phrase for personal physical (brain)-experience. *Cf. infra,* text 230.

[2] This chapter has no title.

[3] The title of this Sutta is wrong. *Cf. supra,* text 144. In the *uddāna* also the title is wrong and lacks a capital letter in text. *Cf. M.* i, 285.

[4] *Cf. K.S.* iii, 70. *Tiracchāna-gatā pāṇā,* 'animals that go horizontally,' as opposed to upright humans.

[5] *Sūriyena.* So *Comy.* (=*sūra-bhāvena*) and Sinh. MSS. Text has *surena* (Burmese).

principles there be that are on the side of the wisdom,[1] of them the controlling faculty of insight is reckoned chief, namely for attaining the wisdom. And of what sort, monks, are the principles that are on the side of the wisdom ?

Monks, the controlling faculty of wisdom is a principle that is on the side of the wisdom, for it conduces to attaining the wisdom. The controlling faculty of energy . . . that of mindfulness . . . the controlling faculty of concentration . . . the controlling faculty of insight is a principle that is on the side of the wisdom, for it conduces to attaining the wisdom.

Just as, monks, whatsoever brute creatures there be, of them the lion, king of beasts, is reckoned chief, namely in strength, speed and courage,—even so, monks, of the principles that are on the side of the wisdom, the controlling faculty of insight is reckoned chief.'

(ii) *Mallikā.*[2]

Thus have I heard: On a certain occasion the Exalted One was staying among the Mallas at Uruvelakappa, a township of the Mallas.

On that occasion the Exalted One addressed the monks, saying:

'Monks, as long as the Ariyan insight has not uprisen in the Ariyan disciple, just so long is there no stability of the four (other) controlling faculties, there is no abiding steadfastness[3] of the four other controlling faculties. But when the Ariyan insight has arisen in the Ariyan disciple, then, monks, there is stability of the four other controlling faculties, there is abiding steadfastness of the four other controlling faculties.

Just as, monks, so long as the peak of a house[4] with peaked

---

[1] *Bodha-pakkhikā*, translated at *Dialog.* iii, 93, ' wings of wisdom. They are enumerated at *VM.* 678.

[2] Written as *Mallā*, *Mallikā*, *Mallatā*, and *Malatā*. *K.S.* iv, 252; *infra*, text 349 (*cf. A.* iv, 438).

[3] *Ṭhiti, avaṭṭhiti. Cf. Dhs.* § 11 (*Buddh. Psych. Eth.*, p. 13 *n.*), where the three cognate terms *ṭhiti, saṇṭhiti, avaṭṭhiti* (*cittassa*) are translated ' stability, solidity, absorbed steadfastness.'

[4] *Cf. J.P.T.S.*, 1919; *Similes in the Nikāyas* (*do.* 1906-7, pp. 58 *ff.*).

roof be not set up, so long is there no stability of the roof-beams,[1] there is no abiding steadfastness of the roof-beams. But, monks, as soon as the peak of a house with peaked roof is set up, then is there stability and abiding steadfastness of the roof-beams.

In the same way, monks, so long as the Ariyan insight has not uprisen in the Ariyan disciple, so long is there no stability of the other four controlling faculties. But as soon as the Ariyan insight has arisen, then is there stability and abiding steadfastness of the four other controlling faculties. Of what four? Of the controlling faculty of faith, energy, mindfulness and concentration.

Monks, in the Ariyan disciple who has insight faith is established as a matter of course.[2] Energy, mindfulness, concentration are established as a matter of course.'

(iii) *Learner.*

Thus have I heard: On a certain occasion the Exalted One was staying at Kosambi in Ghosita Park. On that occasion the Exalted One addressed the monks, saying:

'Tell me, monks, is there any method by proceeding according to which a monk who is a learner,[3] standing at the level of a learner,[4] can be assured "I am a learner," or a monk who is an adept, standing at the level of an adept, can be assured "I am an adept"?'

'For us, lord, things have their root in the Exalted One, their guide and their resort. It were well for us if the Exalted One would reveal the meaning of what he has just uttered.'

'Well, monks, there is such a method, by proceeding according to which both a monk who is a learner and a monk who is an adept can be so assured. And of what sort is that method, monks?

Herein a monk who is a learner knows full well "This is

---

[1] *Gopānasī* is the curved beam supporting the gable, whose stability depends on pressure from above.

[2] *Tadanvayā.* *Cf. Expos.* 92 ('faith which follows') and *supra* 197 *n.*

[3] For definition see text, *supra* 14.

[4] *Sekha-bhūmiyaŋ ṭhito.*

Ill." He knows full well "This is the arising of Ill." He knows full well "This is the ceasing of Ill. . . . This is the practice leading to the ceasing of Ill." Such, monks, is the method by proceeding according to which a monk who is a learner can be assured "I am a learner."

Again, a monk who is a learner thus ponders: "Is there, I wonder, outside[1] (this Order of monks) anyone, whether recluse or brahmin, who can teach a doctrine that is natural, true and proper,[2] such as the Exalted One teaches?" Then he concludes: "There is no one who can do so." This, monks, is the method, by proceeding according to which a monk who is a learner, standing at the level of a learner, can be assured "I am a learner."

Then again, monks, the monk who is a learner is fully aware of the five controlling faculties, that of faith, that of energy, of mindfulness, of concentration, and the controlling faculty of insight. But as to what is their destiny, what their excellence, what their fruits and final goal, he dwells not in personal experience[3] thereof, nor does he pierce through and through by insight and see them plain. That is the method by proceeding according to which a learner, standing at a learner's level can be assured "I am a learner."

And of what sort, monks, is the method according to which the adept monk standing at the level of an adept can be assured "I am an adept"?

Herein the adept monk fully understands the five controlling faculties, that of faith and the rest and that of insight. Likewise as to what is their destiny, what their excellence, their fruits and final goal, he dwells in personal experience thereof: he pierces them through and through and sees them plain. That, monks, is the method by which an adept monk can be assured that he is an adept.

---

[1] *Ito bahiddhā*. *Cf. M.* i, 56; *D.* ii, 151 (*ito bahiddhā samaṇo pi n' atthi*).

[2] Text *bhūtaŋ, tacchaŋ, tathā* (read *v.l. tathaŋ*). *Cf. D.* i, 190, *api ca Samaṇo Gotamo bhūtaŋ tacchaŋ tathaŋ paṭipadaŋ paññāpeti.*

[3] As above, text p. 226. *Kāyena=nāma-kāyena*. *Comy.* adds *paṭilabhitvā* to *phusitvā* of text.

Then again, a monk who is an adept fully understands the six sense-faculties, to wit: the sense-faculty of eye, ear, nose, tongue, body and mind. He understands: These six sense-faculties must come to cease without remainder, utterly, altogether, in every way and everywhere: nor shall other six sense-faculties arise anywhere or anyhow.[1] He knows that full well.

Such, monks, is the method by proceeding according to which an adept monk can be assured that he is an adept.'

(iv) *In the foot.*

Just as, monks, all the foot-characteristics of such creatures as roam[2] about are joined together in the foot of the elephant, and as the elephant's foot in size is reckoned chief of them, even so, monks, of all the elements[3] whatsoever that conduce to the wisdom the controlling faculty of insight is reckoned chief, that is, for attaining the wisdom.

And of what sort, monks, are those elements that conduce to the wisdom ?

The faculty of faith, monks, conduces to the wisdom: the faculty of energy, of mindfulness, of concentration, the faculty of insight, monks, conduces to the wisdom.

Just as, monks, all the foot-characteristics of creatures that roam about are joined together in the foot of the elephant: as the elephant's foot in size is reckoned chief of them, even so, monks, of all the elements whatsoever that conduce to the wisdom, the controlling faculty of insight is reckoned chief, that is, for attaining the wisdom.

(v) *Heart-wood.*[4]

Just as, monks, of all scented heart-woods whatsoever the red sandalwood is reckoned chief, even so, monks, of all the principles whatsoever that are on the side of the wisdom, the

---

[1] *Kuhiñci kismiñci* are synonyms. *Comy.*

[2] *Cf.* *K.S.* i, 111; *M.* i, 184; *supra,* text 43. Text's *jangalānaŋ* (forest creatures) should read, as above, *jangamānaŋ* (*ambulantium*).

[3] *Padāni=ye keci dhamma-koṭṭhāsā bujjhan' atthāya saŋvattanti. Comy.*

[4] Text-title *sāre* should be *sāraŋ*. *Cf.* text, 43; *S.* iii, 156.

controlling faculty of insight is reckoned chief, that is, for attaining the wisdom.

And of what sort, monks, are the principles that are on the side of the wisdom?

The controlling faculty of faith, monks, is a principle that is on the side of the wisdom. It conduces to attaining the wisdom. The controlling faculty of energy and the rest, the controlling faculty of insight is a principle that is on the side of the wisdom. It conduces to attaining the wisdom.

Just as, monks, of all scented heart-woods the red sandalwood is reckoned chief . . . so also the controlling faculty of insight is reckoned chief, that is, for attaining the wisdom.

(vi) *Established.*

Sāvatthī (was the occasion for this discourse). . . .

Monks, by a monk who is established in one condition the five controlling faculties are cultivated and cultivated well. Established in what condition? In earnestness. And of what sort, monks, is earnestness?

Herein a monk wards his mind amid the āsavas and conditions that go with the āsavas.[1] As he so wards his mind, by cultivating the controlling faculty of faith, he goes to perfection therein . . . by cultivating the controlling faculty of insight he goes to perfection therein.

That, monks, is how in a monk who is established in one condition the five controlling faculties[2] are cultivated and cultivated well.

(vii) *Brahmā.*[3]

Thus have I heard: On a certain occasion the Exalted One was staying at Uruvelā, on the bank of the river Nerañjarā, under the Goatherds' Banyan, just after his attainment of perfect enlightenment.

---

[1] Text *āsavesu ca sâsavesu ca dhammesu,* but *Comy.* only *āsavesu dhammesu* (using the word as adjective), interprets *āsav' uppattiŋ vārento āsavesu ca dhammesu cittaŋ rakkhati.* For *sâsava* see *K.S.* iii, 42. 'Everybody . . . is a co-*āsava* and has to do with grasping.'

[2] Text misprints as *paññindriyāni.*

[3] As in the two passages above, and often elsewhere, the Master's ideas are confirmed by the appearance of Brahmā (*deus ex māchinā*).

Now in the Exalted One, when he had retired to his solitary communing, there arose this mental reflection: There are five controlling faculties which, cultivated and made much of, plunge into the Deathless, have their end and goal in the Deathless. What five? The controlling faculty of faith, energy, mindfulness, concentration and insight. These five, if cultivated and made much of, plunge into the Deathless, have their end and goal in the Deathless.

Then Brahmā Sahampati, reading with his mind the mental reflection of the Exalted One,—just as a strong man might stretch out his bent arm or bend his outstretched arm,—even so did Brahmā Sahampati vanish from the Brahma World and appear before the Exalted One.

Then did Brahmā Sahampati, throwing his outer robe over one shoulder, stretch out his folded palms towards the Exalted One and thus address him:

'Even so, Exalted One! Even so, O Happy One! These five controlling faculties, if cultivated and made much of, do plunge into the Deathless . . . (*and he repeated in full the Exalted One's reflections*). . . .

Once upon a time, sir, when Kassapa was the supremely Enlightened One, I was practising the holy life. Men knew me then as Sahaka the monk.[1] Then it was, sir, that by cultivating and making much of these five controlling faculties,[2] and by restraining[3] sensual lust in things of sense, on the breaking up of body, I was reborn in the Happy World after death, in the Brahma-World. Thereafter men knew me as Brahmā Sahampati, Brahmā Sahampati!

So it is, Exalted One! So it is, O Happy One! I know it! I see it,—that these five controlling faculties, if cultivated and made much of, do plunge into the Deathless, do end and have their goal in the Deathless.'

---

[1] As at *K.S.* i, 172 *n.* (according to *Comy.*).

[2] In like manner Maghavā (Sakka, the Buddhist Indra) reached lordship of the deva-world by cultivating the quality of *appamāda* (of previous section). *Cf. Dhp.* 30.

[3] *Cf. SnA.* 213 (*virājeṭvā=vinetvā*).

(viii) *Boar's Cave.*

Thus have I heard: On a certain occasion the Exalted One was staying near Rājagaha on Vulture's Peak Hill, in the Boar's Cave.[1]

Now on that occasion the Exalted One addressed the venerable Sāriputta saying:

'Tell me, Sāriputta. Seeing what reason therefor[2] does a monk in whom the āsavas are destroyed practise and observe supreme reverence[3] for the Tathāgata or the teachings of the Tathāgata?'

'Lord, it is because he sees therein utter security from the yoke[4] that he practises and observes supreme reverence for the Tathāgata or the Tathāgata's teachings.'

'Well said! Well said, Sāriputta! It is indeed because he sees therein utter security from the yoke . . . But of what sort is that utter security from the yoke which he sees therein, that he observes such reverence?'

'Herein, lord, the monk in whom the āsavas are destroyed

---

[1] *Sūkara-khatā* (lit. 'boar-dug'). *Cf. M.* i, 497 (where Long Nails, the hermit, converses with the Master); *UdA.* 189 (referring to that event) calls it *Sūkara-leṇa*. *Comy.* thus describes it: They say that in Kassapa Buddha's time this cave was found as a hollow in the ground when the earth was yet growing, during the interval between the two Buddhas (*Buddhantara*, like *Manuvantara*, the period between two Manus). One day a boar rooted up (*khaṇi*) the soil in the neighbourhood of the ground concealing the cave. The sky-god rained and washed the soil away, and the mouth of the cave was disclosed. A forest-dweller, on seeing it, exclaimed: 'This must be a resort used by a holy man of olden times. I'll look after it.' So he removed the earth all round, cleaned it out, fenced it in, made it as spick and span as a golden bowl polished with sand, and so turned the cave into a hermit's cell furnished with couch and stool and all, and presented it to the Exalted One for a dwelling-place. The cave was deep, and one had to climb to get there.

At *K.S.* ii, 169 *ff.*, Mahāmoggallāna has clairvoyant sight of things that happened in this neighbourhood in the time of the Buddha Kassapa.

[2] *Atthavasaŋ*. *Cf. supra*, text 224.

[3] *Parama-nipaccâkāra*. *Cf. S.* i, 178; *JA.* i, 232; *A.* v, 66 (where the rājah Pasenadi falls at the Master's feet).

[4] *Yoga-kkhema*. *Cf. K.S.* iv, 51 *n.* (*arahattass' upaṇiso sajeṭṭhako*).

cultivates the controlling faculty of faith, which goes on to the perfect wisdom. He cultivates that of energy, which goes on to the perfect wisdom. He cultivates the controlling faculty of mindfulness, that of concentration, that of insight, which goes on to the perfect wisdom. This, lord, is the utter security from the yoke, seeing which he practises and observes supreme reverence for the Tathāgata or the Tathāgata's teachings.'

'Well said! Well said, Sāriputta! That is indeed the utter security from the yoke which he sees. . . . But of what sort, Sāriputta, is the supreme reverence which such a monk practises and observes towards the Tathāgata or the Tathāgata's teachings?'

'Herein, lord, the monk in whom the āsavas are destroyed dwells reverential and respectful to the Teacher. He dwells reverential and respectful to the Norm, to the training, to the concentration.[1] This, lord, is the supreme reverence which the monk in whom the āsavas are destroyed practises and observes towards the Tathāgata or the teachings of the Tathāgata.'

'Well said! Well said, Sāriputta! It is indeed the supreme reverence which such an one practises and observes towards the Tathāgata or the teachings of the Tathāgata.'

(ix) *Arising* (*a*).

Sāvatthī (was the occasion) . . . The Exalted One said:

'Monks, there are these five controlling faculties which, if cultivated and made much of, if they have not already arisen, do arise: but it is only upon the manifestation of a Tathāgata, Arahant, a fully Enlightened One.

What are the five?

They are the controlling faculty of faith, of energy, of mindfulness, of concentration, and the controlling faculty of insight. These indeed are the five controlling faculties which so arise.'

---

[1] *Samādhi* here in its comprehensive sense of habitual self-restraint and collectedness of mind resulting from the training.

(x) *Arising* (*b*).

Sāvatthī . . .

Monks, there are these five controlling faculties, which, if cultivated and made much of, if they have not already arisen, do arise: but it is only under the discipline of the Happy One. What are the five . . . (*as before*).

CHAPTER VII.—ON THE SIDE OF THE WISDOM[1]

(i) *Fetter.*

Sāvatthī was the occasion . . . Then the Exalted One thus spake.

'Monks, these five controlling faculties, if cultivated and made much of, conduce to the abandoning of the fetters.

(ii) *Tendency.*

These five controlling faculties . . . conduce to the uprooting of tendency.

(iii) *Comprehension* or *The way out.*

These five controlling faculties . . . conduce to comprehension of the way out.

(iv) *Destruction of the āsavas.*

These five controlling faculties, if cultivated and made much of, conduce to the destruction of the āsavas. What five?

The controlling faculty of faith . . . of insight. These five controlling faculties, monks, if cultivated and made much of, conduce to the abandoning of the fetters, to the uprooting of tendency, to the comprehension of the way out and to the destruction of the āsavas.

(v) *Two fruits.*

Monks, there are these five controlling faculties. . . .

By the act of cultivating and making much of these five

---

[1] The following *Suttas* are similar to those at text, 28.

controlling faculties, one of two fruits may be looked for, to wit: realization in this very life, or, if there be any substrate left, at any rate the state of non-return.[1]

(vi) *Seven advantages.*

Monks, there are these five controlling faculties. . . .

By the act of cultivating and making much of these five controlling faculties, seven fruits, seven advantages[2] are to be looked for. What are the seven ?

In this very life, beforehand,[3] one establishes realization. And if not in this very life, beforehand, at any rate one does so at the moment of death.

And if not in this very life, beforehand, or at the moment of death, at any rate, by wearing down the five fetters that bind to the lower world, he is one who wins release midway.

If he do none of these, yet by reduction of his time[4] one wins release, or wins release without much trouble, or again with some trouble: or (if he do none of these) still by having worn down the five fetters that bind to the lower world, he is "one who goes up stream," and he goes to the Pure Abodes.

Monks, it is by the act of cultivating and making much of these five controlling faculties that these seven fruits, these seven advantages are to be looked for.

(vii) *The tree (a).*

Just as, monks, of all trees whatsoever in Rose-apple Land[5] the rose-apple tree is reckoned chief, even so, of all conditions whatsoever which are on the side of the wisdom, the controlling faculty of insight is reckoned chief, that is, for attaining the wisdom.

And of what sort, monks, are the conditions that are on the side of the wisdom ? They are the controlling faculty of faith,

---

[1] *Cf.* text, 129.

[2] As at text, 69; at *D.* ii, 86, there are *five.*

[3] Text *paṭihacca* (warding off). See *n.* to p. 69. *Comy.* reads *paṭigacca* (*paṭikacca*), 'before his time of death.' *Cf. Dialog.* iii, 227.

[4] *Upahacca.*

[5] *Jambudīpa,* a name for India.

of energy, of mindfulness, of concentration and the controlling faculty of insight.

Just as, monks, of all trees whatsoever . . . so of all conditions whatsoever the controlling faculty of insight is reckoned chief, that is, for attaining the wisdom.

(viii) *The tree* (*b*).

Just as, monks, of all trees whatsoever of the Devas of the Thirty-Three the coral tree[1] is reckoned chief, even so, of all conditions whatsoever that are on the side of the wisdom, the controlling faculty of insight is reckoned chief, that is, for attaining the wisdom. And of what sort, monks, are the conditions . . . ?

(ix) *The tree* (*c*).

Just as, monks, of all trees whatsoever of the Asuras the pied trumpet-flower tree[2] is reckoned chief, even so of all conditions whatsoever that are on the side of the wisdom, the controlling faculty of insight is reckoned chief, that is, for attaining the wisdom.

(x) *The tree* (*d*).

Just as, monks, of all trees whatsoever of the Garuda Birds,[3] the silk-cotton tree[4] is reckoned chief, even so, of all conditions that are on the side of the wisdom, the controlling faculty of insight is reckoned chief, that is, for attaining the wisdom.

And of what sort, monks, are the conditions that are on the side of the wisdom ?

The controlling faculty of faith, monks, is a condition that is on the side of the wisdom, likewise that of energy, of mindfulness, of concentration, and the controlling faculty of insight.

---

[1] *Pāricchattako* (umbrella tree) is described in detail at *A.* iv, 117 *ff.*; *JA.* i, 202. According to Childers it is *erythinia indica.*

[2] *JA.* i, 202. According to Childers, *Bignonia suaviolens.*

[3] *Supaṇṇas* or roc-birds. *Cf. K.S.* i, 288 *n.* and *Comy.*

[4] *Kūṭa* (or *koṭa*)-*simbali* (*cf. Shamballa*). According to Childers, *bombax heptaphyllum.* It was supposed to grow on the slopes of Mt. Sineru. For *Simbali-vana, cf. JA. loc. cit.*

Just as, monks, of all trees whatsoever of the Garuda Birds, the silk-cotton tree is reckoned chief, even so, of all conditions that are on the side of the wisdom, the controlling faculty of insight is reckoned chief, that is, for attaining the wisdom.

CHAPTER VIII.—GANGĀ-REPETITION

(i) *Based on seclusion.*[1]

Just as, monks, the river Ganges flows, slides and tends to the east . . . even so a monk, by cultivating and making much of the five controlling faculties, flows, slides and tends to Nibbāna. And how, monks, does a monk so cultivating them . . . tend to Nibbāna ?

Herein a monk cultivates the controlling faculty of faith, which is based on seclusion, on dispassion, on cessation, that ends in self-surrender. So also he cultivates the controlling faculty of energy, of mindfulness, of concentration, and the controlling faculty of insight . . . which ends in self-surrender.

That is how a monk who cultivates . . . tends to Nibbāna.

(ii-xii).

(*As in Kindred Sayings on the Path.*)

SUMMARY[2]

Six on Flowing *and* Sliding to eastward, *and six on* The Ocean.

These two sixes are twelve, and the chapter (that holds them) is so called.

(*All to be developed by way of* The Controlling Faculties.)

---

[1] *Cf. supra*, text, 38 *ff.*; 134 *ff.*; 190 *ff.* As before text abbreviates to mere titles.

[2] These *uddānas* or summaries are generally full of errors, and do not coincide with the subjects of *Suttas*. (Here text says twice six is ten !)

CHAPTER IX.—EARNESTNESS

(i-x) *Based on seclusion.*

Tathāgata, Foot, Roof-peak,
Wood, Heart-wood, Jasmine,
Prince, Moon and Sun,
With Cloth *make ten.*

(*To be developed by way of* The Controlling Faculties.)

CHAPTER X.—DEEDS REQUIRING STRENGTH

(i-xii) *Based on seclusion.*

Strength, Seed *and* Snake,
Tree, *with* Pot *and* Bearded Wheat,
The Sky *and two of* Raincloud,
Ship, For all comers, River.

(*To be developed by way of* The Controlling Faculties.)

CHAPTER XI.—LONGING

(i-xiii) *Based on seclusion.*

Longing, Conceits, Āsava, Becoming,[1]
Suffering, Obstructions (*three*),
Stain *and* Pain *and* Feelings,
Craving *and* Thirst *make the chapter.*[2]

(*To be developed by way of* The Controlling Faculties.)

---

[1] Text misprints as *gavo.*

[2] As before, this line is wrong.

CHAPTER XII.—THE FLOOD

(i-ix) *Based on seclusion.*

(*As before.*)

(x) *Fetters of the higher sort.*[1]

Monks, there are these five fetters of the higher sort. What are the five?

They are: Lust after (rebirth in) the world of form, lust after (rebirth in) the formless world, conceit, excitement and nescience. These are the five fetters of the higher sort.

Monks, for the full comprehension, understanding, wearing out and abandoning these five fetters of the higher sort the five controlling faculties must be cultivated. What are the five?

Herein a monk cultivates the controlling faculty of faith, that is based on seclusion . . . the controlling faculty of energy, that of mindfulness, that of concentration, and the controlling faculty of insight. It is for the full comprehension . . . and abandoning of these five fetters of the higher sort that these five controlling faculties must be cultivated.

SUMMARY

The Flood, The Bond, Grasping, *with* (*bodily*) Ties *and* Tendency,

Sense-pleasures, Hindrance, Factors, Fetters of Lower and Higher Sort.

CHAPTER XIII.—GANGĀ-REPETITION

(i) *Restraint of lust.*

Just as, monks, the river Ganges flows . . .

Herein a monk cultivates the controlling faculty of faith, that ends in the restraint of lust, the restraint of hatred, the restraint of illusion.

---

[1] *Cf. D.* iii, 234; *Dialog.* iii, 225.

He cultivates the controlling faculty of insight . . . even so a monk . . . tends to Nibbāna.

(ii-xii).

SUMMARY

Six on Flowing *and* Sliding to Eastward *and six on* The Ocean.

These two sixes are twelve, and the chapter (that holds them) is so called.

(*All to be developed by way of* Restraint of Lust, *in* Kindred Sayings on the Controlling Faculties.)

CHAPTER XIV.—EARNESTNESS

(i-x) *Restraint of lust.*

CHAPTER XV.—DEEDS REQUIRING STRENGTH

(i-xii) *Restraint of lust.*

CHAPTER XVI.—LONGING

(i-xii) *Restraint of lust.*

CHAPTER XVII.—THE FLOOD

(i-ix) *Restraint of lust.*

(x) *Fetters of the higher sort.*

(*The same as* § x *above, down to*) . . .

What are the five?

Herein a monk cultivates the controlling faculty of faith, that ends in the restraint of lust, the restraint of hatred, the restraint of illusion, and cultivates the controlling faculty of energy, mindfulness, concentration and insight, that end in the restraint of these same. These five controlling faculties must be cultivated for the full comprehension, understanding, wearing out and abandoning of these five fetters of the higher sort.

SUMMARY

(*As at* § x.)

BOOK V

KINDRED SAYINGS ON THE RIGHT EFFORTS

CHAPTER I.—GANGĀ-REPETITION

(i-xii).

SĀVATTHI (was the occasion) . . . The Exalted One said:

'Monks, there are these four right efforts.[1] What are the four?

Herein a monk starts desire for the non-arising of ill, unprofitable states not yet arisen: he makes an effort, sets going energy, he lays hold of and exerts his mind (to this end).

He starts desire for the abandoning of ill, unprofitable states that have arisen, he makes an effort . . .

He starts desire for the arising of profitable states not yet arisen, he makes an effort . . .

He starts desire for the establishing of profitable states that have arisen, for their non-confusion, for their more-becoming, for their increase, cultivation and fulfilment: he makes an effort, sets going energy, he lays hold of and exerts his mind (to this end).

These, monks, are called "the four right efforts."

Just as, monks, the river Ganges flows to the east, slides to the east, tends to the east, even so a monk, by cultivating the four right efforts, making much of the four right efforts, flows, slides and tends to Nibbāna. And how cultivating, how making much of the four right efforts does a monk flow, slide and tend to Nibbāna?

He starts desire for the non-arising of ill, unprofitable states not yet arisen (*all as before*). . . . That is how a monk, by cultivating and making much of the four right efforts, flows, slides and tends to Nibbāna.'

---

[1] *Cf. Dialog.* ii, 344.

CHAPTER II.—EARNESTNESS

(i-x).

Tathāgata, Foot, Roof-peak,
Wood, Heart-wood, Jasmine,
Prince, Moon and Sun,
With Cloth *make ten.*

(*All to be developed as above.*)

CHAPTER III.—DEEDS REQUIRING STRENGTH

(i-xii).[1]

Just as, monks, whatsoever deeds requiring strength are done, all of them are done in dependence on the earth, with the earth for their support, even so a monk, depending on virtue, supported by virtue, cultivates the four right efforts, makes much of the four right efforts.

And how, monks, does a monk, thus depending, thus supported, cultivate and make much of the four right efforts?

Herein a monk starts desire for the non-arising of ill, unprofitable states not yet arisen . . . (*the whole as before*). . . .

SUMMARY

Strength, Seed *and* Snake,
Tree, *with* Pot *and* Bearded Wheat,
The Sky *and two of* Raincloud,
Ship, For all comers, River.

(*To be developed as above.*)

CHAPTER IV.—LONGING[2]

(i-xiii).

Monks, there are these three longings. What three? The longing for sensual delights, the longing for becoming, the longing for the holy life.

---

[1] *Cf. D.* iii, 216; *supra*, text, 45, 135, etc.

[2] *Cf. supra*, text, 54.

It is for the full comprehension of these three longings, monks, for their understanding, for the wearing out and abandoning of them, that the four right efforts must be cultivated. What are the four?

Herein a monk starts desire for the non-arising of ill, unprofitable states not yet arisen . . . (*the whole as before*). . . .

SUMMARY

Longing, Conceits, Āsava, Becoming,
Sufferings, Obstructions (*three*),[1]
Stain *and* Pain *and* Feelings,
Craving *and* Thirst *make the chapter.*

(*All to be developed as above.*)

CHAPTER V.—THE FLOOD

(i-ix) *The Flood.*

(x) *Fetters of the higher sort.*

Monks, there are these five fetters of the higher sort. What five? Lust for (rebirth in) the world of form, lust for (rebirth) in the formless world, conceit, excitement, nescience. These are the five.

Monks, for the full comprehension of these five fetters of the higher sort, for their understanding, for the wearing out and abandoning of them, the four right efforts must be cultivated. What are the four?

Herein a monk starts desire for the non-arising of ill, unprofitable states not yet arisen: he makes an effort, sets going energy, he lays hold of and exerts his mind (to this end).

He starts desire for the abandoning of ill, unprofitable states that have arisen, he makes an effort . . .

He starts desire for the arising of profitable states not yet arisen, he makes an effort . . .

[1] Text of *uddāna* takes *tisso* as a name! thus making the total ten.

He starts desire for the establishing of profitable states that have arisen, for their non-confusion, for their more-becoming, for their increase, cultivation and fulfilment: he makes an effort, sets going energy, he lays hold of and exerts his mind (to this end).

It is for the full comprehension of these five fetters of the higher sort, for the understanding, for the wearing out and abandoning of them, that these four right efforts must be cultivated.

SUMMARY

The Flood, The Bond, Grasping, *with* (*bodily*) Ties *and* Tendency,

Sense-pleasures, Hindrance, Factors, Fetters of Lower and Higher Sort.

(*All to be developed as above.*)

BOOK VI

KINDRED SAYINGS ON THE POWERS

CHAPTER I.—GANGĀ-REPETITION

(i) *Based on seclusion.*

MONKS, there are these five powers. Of what sort are the five?

They are: The power of faith, the power of energy, the power of mindfulness, the power of concentration and the power of insight. These are indeed the five powers, monks.

Just as, monks, the river Ganges flows to the east, slides to the east, tends to the east, even so a monk who cultivates and makes much of these five powers is one who flows to Nibbāna, slides to Nibbāna, tends to Nibbāna.

And how cultivating, how making much of these five powers is a monk one who flows, slides and tends to Nibbāna?

Herein a monk cultivates and makes much of the power of faith, which is based on seclusion, on dispassion, on cessation, which ends in self-surrender.[1] He cultivates and makes much of the power of energy . . . of mindfulness . . . of concentration . . . of insight, which is based on seclusion, on dispassion, on cessation, which ends in self-surrender.

Thus cultivating, thus making much of these five powers, a monk is one who flows, slides and tends to Nibbāna.

(ii-xii).

(*The summaries of this and* Chapters III, IV *are the same as in* Book V *above; all to be developed by way of* The Five Powers.)

[1] Here text inserts by error *vossagga-nissitaŋ* for *v. pariṇāmiŋ.*

CHAPTER V

(i-ix).

(*As in* § x.)

(x) *Fetters of the higher sort.*

Monks, there are these five fetters of the higher sort. What five?

They are: Lust for (the world of) form, lust for the (world of the) formless, conceit, excitement, nescience. These are the five.

It is for the full comprehension, understanding, wearing out and abandoning of these five fetters that the five powers are to be cultivated. What five powers?

Herein a monk cultivates and makes much of the power of faith . . . (*as above*).

(Chapters VI, VII, VIII, IX, X, *on* Ganges, Earnestness, Strength, Longing *and* Flood *are all the same as before.*)

BOOK VII

KINDRED SAYINGS ON THE BASES OF PSYCHIC POWER.[1]

CHAPTER I.—CĀPĀLA[2]

(i) *Neither shore.*[3]

MONKS, these four bases of psychic power,[4] if cultivated and made much of, conduce to going neither to the hither nor to the further shore. What are the four?

Herein a monk cultivates that basis of psychic power of which the features are desire,[5] together with the co-factors of concentration and struggle.

He cultivates that basis of psychic power of which the features are energy, together with the co-factors of concentration and struggle.[6]

He cultivates that basis of psychic power of which the features are thought, together with the co-factors of concentration and struggle.

He cultivates that basis of psychic power of which the

---

[1] (*Chanda-viriya-citta-vīmaŋsa*) each + *samādhi-padhāna* (as *saṅkhāra*).

[2] This chapter is so called after the Cāpāla Shrine of § x below, *q.v.*

[3] Text wrongly *aparâpāraŋ* (' to and fro going,' exactly the opposite of the intended meaning) for *a-pārâpāraŋ* (*a-pāra-apāra*), ' no more of this or that shore,' the state of Arahant, *Nibbāna*. *Cf. supra*, text, 24, 81, 180 *n.*

[4] *Comy.* [*iddhi-pāda=iddhiyā-pādaŋ* or *iddhi-bhūtaŋ pādaŋ*] refers to *Vibh.* 216; *VibhA.* 303; and *VM.* *Cf. Dialog.* ii, 110 *n.*, iii, 214; *S.* i, 116, iii, 96. At *D.* iii, 221, *citta-s.* follows *chanda-s.*

[5] *Chando*, as ' will ' or ' desire to do ' (def. at *Vibh. loc. cit.*, *chandīkatā kattu-kamyatā kusalo dhamma-cchando*). The word ' desire-to-do,' a notable reaching out after such a fit word as our ' will ' had not emerged in the *Nikāyas*.

[6] *Padhāna*. *Cf. Dhs.* 158 *n.*, § 1366; *Buddh. Psych. Eth.*, p. 358, called ' spiritual wrestlings,' or ' efforts ' (as in Bk. V).

features are investigation, together with the co-factors of concentration and struggle.

These four bases of psychic power, monks, if cultivated and made much of, conduce to going neither to the hither nor to the further shore.

(ii) *Neglected.*

By whomsoever, monks, the four bases of psychic power are neglected, by them also is neglected the Ariyan way that goes on to the utter destruction of Ill. By whomsoever, monks, the four bases of psychic power are undertaken, by them also is undertaken the Ariyan way that goes on to the utter destruction of Ill. What are the four ?

Herein a monk cultivates that basis of psychic power of which the features are desire, together with the co-factors of concentration and struggle.

He cultivates that basis of psychic power of which the features are energy, together with the co-factors of concentration and struggle.

He cultivates that basis of psychic power of which the features are thought, together with the co-factors of concentration and struggle.

He cultivates that basis of psychic power of which the features are investigation, together with the co-factors of concentration and struggle.

Monks, by whomsoever these four bases of psychic power are neglected, by them also is neglected the Ariyan way that goes on to the utter destruction of Ill. By whomsoever these four bases of psychic power are undertaken, by them also is undertaken the Ariyan way that goes on to the utter destruction of Ill.

(iii) *Ariyan.*[1]

Monks, these four bases of psychic power, if cultivated and made much of, go hence as the Ariyan hence-goers. For him that acts in accordance therewith they conduce to the utter destruction of Ill. What are the four ?

(*As above.*)

---

[1] As at text 82, for the seven limbs of wisdom.

(iv) *Revulsion.*

Monks, these four bases of psychic power, if cultivated and made much of, conduce to downright revulsion, to dispassion, to cessation, to calm, to full comprehension, to the wisdom, to Nibbāna. What four?

Herein a monk cultivates that basis of psychic power of which the features are desire . . . energy . . . thought . . . investigation, (in each case) together with the co-factors of concentration and struggle.

Monks, these four bases of psychic power, if cultivated and made much of, conduce to downright revulsion . . . to Nibbāna.

(v) *Partial.*[1]

Monks, whosoever in time past, whether recluses or brahmins, have successfully practised[2] psychic power in a partial degree,[3] all such have done so by cultivating and making much of the four bases of psychic power.

Whosoever in future time, whether recluses or brahmins, shall successfully practise psychic power in a partial degree, all such shall do so by cultivating and making much of the four bases of psychic power.

Whosoever in the present time, whether recluses or brahmins, do successfully practise psychic power in a partial degree, all such do so by cultivating and making much of the four bases of psychic power. What four?

Herein a monk cultivates that basis of psychic power of which the features are desire . . . energy . . . thought . . . investigation, (in each case) together with the co-factors of concentration and struggle.

Monks, whosoever, whether recluses or brahmins, in time past, future or present, have practised, shall practise or do now practise successfully psychic power in a partial degree, all such do so by cultivating and making much of just these four bases of psychic power.

---

[1] *Padesaŋ*, as opposite to *samattaŋ* below.

[2] *Abhinipphādesuŋ*, *supra*, text, 156.

[3] Here text has wrongly *iddhi-padesaŋ* for *iddhi-pāde padesaŋ* (as *Comy.*).

(vi) *Perfectly.*

(*Exactly the same, with* perfectly *for* in a partial degree.)

(vii) *Monk.*

Monks, whatsoever monks in time past have, by the destruction of the āsavas, by their own personal knowledge realized in this very life, attained and dwelt in the heart's release, the release by insight that is freed from the āsavas,—all of them have done so by the fact of cultivating and making much of the four bases of psychic power.

Whatsoever monks shall in future time, by the destruction of the āsavas, by their own personal knowledge, realize in this very life, attain and dwell in the heart's release, the release by insight that is freed from the āsavas,—all of them shall do so by the fact of cultivating and making much of the four bases of psychic power.

Whatsoever monks at the present time do, by the destruction of the āsavas, by their own perfect knowledge realize in this very life, attain and dwell in the heart's release, the release by insight, that is freed from the āsavas,—all of them do so by the fact of cultivating and making much of the four bases of psychic power. Of what four?

Herein a monk cultivates that basis of psychic power (*as above*). . . .

(viii) *Enlightened* or *Arahant.*

Monks, there are these four bases of psychic power. What four?

Herein a monk cultivates that basis of psychic power of which the features are desire . . . energy . . . thought . . . investigation, (in each case) together with the co-factors of concentration and struggle. These indeed, monks, are the four bases of psychic power.

It is by the fact of cultivating and making much of these four bases of psychic power, monks, that the Tathāgata is called 'Arahant, a Fully Enlightened One.'[1]

---

[1] *Cf. Dialog.* iii, 210 *n.*, etc.

(ix) *Knowledge.*[1]

At the thought, monks: This is the basis of psychic power which has for its features desire, together with the co-factors of concentration and struggle,—in things unheard of before there arose in me vision, there arose in me knowledge, insight arose, wisdom arose, light arose.

At the thought, monks: This basis of psychic power . . . ought to be cultivated,—in things unheard of before . . . light arose.

At the thought, monks: This basis of psychic power . . . has been cultivated,—in things unheard of before . . . light arose.

At the thought, monks: This is the basis of psychic power which has for its features energy, together with the co-factors of concentration and struggle,—in things unheard of before there arose in me vision . . . light arose.

At the thought, monks: This basis of psychic power . . . ought to be cultivated,—in things unheard of before there arose in me vision . . . light arose.

At the thought, monks: This basis of psychic power . . . has been cultivated,—in things unheard of before there arose in me vision . . . light arose.

At the thought, monks: This is the basis of psychic power which has for its features thought, together with the co-factors of concentration and struggle,—in things unheard of before there arose in me vision . . . light arose.

At the thought, monks: This basis of psychic power . . . ought to be cultivated,—in things unheard of before there arose in me vision . . . light arose.

At the thought: It has been cultivated . . . in things unheard of before . . . light arose.

At the thought, monks: This is the basis of psychic power which has for its features investigation, together with the co-factors of concentration and struggle,—in things unheard of before there arose in me vision . . . light arose.

---

[1] *Cf. K.S.* iv, 158.

At the thought, monks: This basis of psychic power . . . ought to be cultivated,—in things unheard of before there arose in me vision . . . light arose.

At the thought, monks: This basis of psychic power which has for its features investigation, together with the co-factors of concentration and struggle, has been cultivated,—in things unheard of before there arose in me vision, there arose in me knowledge, insight arose, wisdom arose, light arose.

(x) *The shrine.*[1]

Thus have I heard: On a certain occasion the Exalted One was staying near Vesālī in Great Wood, at the House of the Peaked Gable.

Now the Exalted One, robing himself in the forenoon and taking bowl and outer robe, set out for Vesālī to beg for alms. After going his alms-rounds in Vesālī, returning and eating his meal, he called to the venerable Ānanda, saying:

'Ānanda, take a mat.[2] I will go to Cāpāla Shrine for the noonday rest.'

'Very well, lord,' said the venerable Ānanda in reply to the Exalted One, and taking a mat he followed in the footsteps of the Exalted One.

Now when the Exalted One reached Cāpāla Shrine he sat down on the seat made ready. And the venerable Ānanda, saluting the Exalted One, sat down at one side. As he thus sat, the Exalted One said this to the venerable Ānanda:

'Delightful, Ānanda, is Vesālī! Delightful are the shrines of Udena[3] and of Gotama! Delightful is the

---

[1] *Cf. D.* ii, 102, 118; *Dialog.* ii, 110 *n.* Cetiyas: 'Shrines of pre-Buddhist worship'; *Ud.* vi; *UdA.* 322; *A.* iv, 308. *Comy.* here does not notice *Cāpāla*, but *UdA.* has: 'formerly the dwelling-place of the Yakkha Cāpāla.'

[2] Here, says *Comy.*, a skin is meant.

[3] *Udena-C. Comy.* 'A residence at the Yakkha Udena's shrine; so also of Gotama-C.' *Comy.* does not notice the others, and I have not *DA.* at hand. I quote *UdA.* for the others.

Shrine of Seven Mangoes,[1] the Shrine of Many Sons,[2] of Sārandada![3] Delightful is Cāpāla Shrine!

Whosoever, Ānanda, has cultivated and made much of, applied himself to,[4] made a basis of, stood upon, increased[5] and fully undertaken the four bases of psychic power,—such an one, if he so wished, might remain (on earth) for his full span of life,[6] or for what is left of it.

Now, Ānanda, the Tathāgata has cultivated . . . and fully undertaken these four bases of psychic power, and if he chooses he can remain for his full span of life or for what is left of it.'

Now although so broad a hint[7] was thus dropped by the Exalted One, though so broad and clear was his meaning, yet could not the venerable Ānanda penetrate it. Thus he begged not the Exalted One: 'Let my lord the Exalted One remain for the full span of life. Let the Happy One remain for the rest of his span of life, for the profit of many folk, for the happiness of many folk, out of compassion for the world, for the welfare, profit and happiness of devas and mankind,'—so far was his mind misguided by Māra.[8]

---

[1] *Sattamba-C.* 'Seven princesses, daughters of Kiki (*cf. JA.* vi, *Vessantara J.*, 481), rājah of Kāsi (Benares), being strongly stirred, left Rājagaha, and the place where they struggled (for attainment) was called after them "Seven Mangoes Shrine."' According to *JA.* they were reborn in this era as sisters Khemā, Uppalavaṇṇā, Paṭācārā, Gotamā, Dhamadiṇṇā, Mahāmāyā, and Visākhā.

[2] 'A many-branching nigrodha tree. Many men pray for sons to the deva therein dwelling. Hence the name.' *Comy.*

[3] A yakkha of this name. *Cf. Dial.* ii, 80; *A.* iii, 167; iv, 16; *UdA.* 323.

[4] *Yāni-katā. Comy. yutta-yānaŋ viya katā.*

[5] *Paricitā. Comy. samantato citā suvaḍḍhitā.*

[6] Sometimes translated 'the æon' or world-period. But *Comy.* generally takes it as *āyu-kappa* (*tasmiŋ tasmiŋ kāle yaŋ manussānaŋ āyuppamāṇaŋ taŋ paripuṇṇaŋ katvā tiṭṭheyya dhāreyya*), and quotes Mahāsivatthero on the subject.

[7] *Oḷārike nimitte. UdA. thūla-saññ' uppādane.*

[8] *Pariyuṭṭhita-citto. Comy.=ajjhotthata-citto* (*i.e.*, his heart was overspread by illusion). Commentators describe the wiles of Māra. 'He puts his hand into one's mouth and *kneads the heart*, so that it is senseless. . . . He showed the elder a terrifying aspect, so that he could not penetrate the hint dropped by the Master.'

Then a second time the Exalted One said to the venerable Ānanda:

'Delightful is Vesālī, Ānanda . . .'

Then a third time the Exalted One said:

'Delightful is Vesālī, Ānanda . . .' (*repeat in full to*) . . . misguided by Māra.

Thereupon the Exalted One said to the venerable Ānanda:

'Go, Ānanda. Do that for which you deem it the proper time.'[1]

'Very well, lord,' replied the venerable Ānanda to the Exalted One, and rising from his seat he saluted the Exalted One by the right and went and sat down at the root of a tree not far away.

Thereupon Māra, the Evil One, not long after the venerable Ānanda had gone, came to the Exalted One, and on coming to him said this:

'Now let the Exalted One pass away! Now let the Happy One pass away! Now is the time for the passing of my lord the Exalted One! Thus was it spoken[2] by my lord the Exalted One: "O Evil One, I shall not pass away till my monks are disciples trained and disciplined, (who have won the peace from the yoke),[3] of wide knowledge, knowing the Norm by heart, walking according to the ordinances[4] of the Norm, walking dutifully, living in accordance with the Norm,—till they, having of themselves grasped their Master's teaching, be able to proclaim, teach, show forth, establish, open up, analyze and make it plain: till they be able to refute any wrong view arising, which may well be refuted by

[1] A polite formula of dismissal. *UdA.* thinks he sent him away for noonday siesta.

[2] After attaining the wisdom, under the Goatherds' Banyan, on the occasion of the temptation of Māra.

[3] Our text inserts (on the authority of one MS. only) *patta-yoga-kkhemā*, not to be found at *D.*, *Ud.*, or in *Comy.*

[4] *Dhammânudhamma-paṭipannā.* Rhys Davids in *Buddhist Suttas ad loc.*, 'Masters of the lesser corollaries that follow from the larger doctrine.' *Comy.* 'having reached the insight that results from the Ariyan Norm.'

right reasoning,[1] and shall teach the Norm that brings salvation with it."[2]

And now, lord, the Exalted One's monks are indeed disciples trained and disciplined, (who have won peace from the yoke), of wide knowledge, knowing the Norm by heart. They do walk according to the ordinances of the Norm, they do walk dutifully, they do live in accordance with the Norm. They, of themselves grasping their Master's teaching, are able to proclaim, teach, show forth, establish, open up, analyze, and make it plain. They are able to refute any wrong view arising, which may well be refuted by right reasoning: they do teach the Norm that brings salvation with it.

So now let my lord the Exalted One pass away! Let the Happy One pass away! Now is the time for the passing away of my lord the Exalted One! For thus was it spoken by the Exalted One (*and he repeated the Master's words as before, adding* " nuns " *and* " lay-disciples both male and female " *to* " monks," *down to*) . . . Now is the time for the passing away of my lord the Exalted One.

Moreover this was the saying of the Exalted One: " O Evil One, I shall not pass utterly away until this way of holy living (which I teach) be powerful and prosperous, wide-spread and widely known, made popular, proclaimed abroad by devas and mankind."[3]

And now indeed this holy life taught by my lord the Exalted One, this way of holy living, is powerful and prosperous, wide-spread and widely known, made popular, proclaimed abroad by devas and mankind. Therefore let my lord the Exalted One pass utterly away! Let the Happy One pass utterly away! Now is the time for the utter passing away of my lord the Exalted One!'

---

[1] *Saha-dhammena* (*not* 'according to the Norm' or 'by truth'). *Comy.* '*sa-hetukena sa-kāraṇena vacanena.*'

[2] *Sappāṭihāriyaŋ. Comy. yāva-niyyānikaŋ katvā* (making it profitable, salutary). Rhys Davids, 'wonder-working.'

[3] Text *yāva-d-eva manussehi.* Rhys Davids, 'among men.' I follow *Comy.* (as on *S.* ii, 121, etc.). on *Ud.* reading *yāva deva-manussehi,* explained as: *yattaka viññū-jātikā devā c' eva manussā c' atthi; tehi sabbehi suṭṭhu pakāsitaŋ. Cf. K.S.* ii, 75 *n.*

At these words the Exalted One thus spake to Māra the Evil One:

'Trouble not thyself, O Evil One![1] In no long time shall be the utter passing away of the Tathāgata. At the end of three months from now the Tathāgata shall pass utterly away.'

Thereupon the Exalted One, at Cāpāla Shrine, mindful and self-possessed, rejected[2] his life's aggregate.[3] And when the Exalted One had rejected his life's aggregate there was a mighty earthquake and a fearful hair-raising thunder burst from the sky. And seeing the significance thereof[4] the Exalted One uttered on that occasion these solemn words:

> In all its parts, finite[5] and infinite,
> His own life's compound did the Sage reject.
> With inward calm composedly he burst,
> Like shell of armour, the self complex.[6]

---

[1] *Appossukko. Comy. nirālayo* (homeless), as at *DhpA.* iv, 31, but not appropriate in this connexion. *UdA. nirussukko* (indifferent) *vigat' ussāho . . . mā . . . vāyāmaŋ karohi ; nirālayo,* together with a reading *līna-viriyo* (not insistent) for *nirālayo.*

[2] *Comy. ñāṇena paricchinditvā vissaji, pajahi,* 'consciously limiting it, he rejected, abandoned . . . but not like crumbling a clod of earth in one's hand. He made up his mind thus: Just for three months I will reap the fruit of attainment and no longer.' *UdA.* thinks it was 'not because Māra asked or because Ānanda failed to ask, but from lack of any more capable of receiving the Buddha-teaching (*Buddha-veneyyānaŋ abhāvato*).'

[3] *Āyu-saṅkhāraŋ.* At *S.* ii, 266, 'things of physical life.' *Cf. M.* i, 295; *JA.* iv, 215. At *Dialog.* ii, 113, Rhys Davids has: 'He renounced those tendencies, potentialities, which in the ordinary course of things would otherwise have led to the putting together of, the building up of, more life (that is, of course, in this birth. Any more life in a future birth [as *UdA.* notes] he had already renounced, when, under the Wisdom Tree, he attained Nirvāna).'

[4] *Atthaŋ viditvā. Comy.* is silent, but *UdA.* 'the significance of thus rejecting his life's aggregate.'

[5] *Tulaŋ,* 'limited or weighable.' *Comy.* suggests an alternative 'weighing (*tulaŋ=tūlento, tīrento*) Nibbāna (*atulaŋ*) and becoming (*sambhavaŋ.*)'

[6] *Atta-sambhavaŋ. Comy. attani jātaŋ kilesaŋ* and *bhava-gāmi-kammaŋ.* At *D. loc. cit.* the narrative continues with the Buddha's relating all this to Ānanda, and explaining the causes of earthquakes, etc.

CHAPTER II.—THE SHAKING OF THE TERRACED HOUSE[1]

(i) *Formerly* or *Condition*.

Sāvatthī (was the occasion). . . . The Exalted One said:

'Formerly, monks, when I was unenlightened, but just a Bodhisattva, this occurred to me: What, I wonder, is the cause, what is the motive for cultivating the bases of psychic power?

Then, monks, it occurred to me thus:

Herein (monks) one cultivates the basis of psychic power of which the features are desire,[2] together with the co-factors of concentration and struggle, (with this intent): Thus shall not my desire be over-sluggish nor overstrained. It shall not be inwardly cramped nor outwardly diffuse.

So he abides fully conscious of what is behind and what is in front.[3] As (he is conscious of what is) in front, so behind: as behind, so in front: as below, so above: as above, so below: as by day, so by night: as by night, so by day. Thus with wits alert, with wits unhampered, he cultivates his mind to brilliancy.[4]

One cultivates the basis of psychic power of which the features are energy, together with the co-factors of concentration and struggle, (with this intent): Thus shall not my energy be over-sluggish nor yet overstrained. It shall not be inwardly cramped nor outwardly diffuse.

So he abides fully conscious of what is behind and what in front: as (he is conscious of what is) in front, so behind: as behind, so in front: as below, so above: as above, so below:

---

[1] The title comes from § iv of this chapter.

[2] As in Chap. I. *Chanda* + *samādhi-padhāna-saṅkhāra-samannāgata*. For further details see *infra*, text, 277.

[3] Text misprints *paccāpure* for *pacchā-pure*. *Comy.* thinks his exercise is in front of him, but the goal is yet behind him. However, all these terms are defined by the Buddha towards the end of this chapter. *Cf. D.* iii, 223; *A.* i, 236, ii, 45=*Nett.* 16; *Brethren*, 212 (*Thag.* 397), *i.e.*, *yathābhūtaŋ passati*, as at *Sn.* 202.

[4] As at *D.* iii, the aspirant cultivates *āloka-saññaŋ*, 'consciousness of light.'

as by day, so by night: as by night, so by day. Thus with wits alert, with wits unhampered, he cultivates his mind to brilliancy.

One cultivates the basis of psychic power of which the features are thought, together with the co-factors of concentration and struggle, (with this intent): Thus shall not my thought be over-sluggish nor yet overstrained. It shall not be inwardly cramped . . . (*as before*). . . .

One cultivates the basis of psychic power of which the features are investigation, together with the co-factors of concentration and struggle, (with this intent): Thus shall not my investigation be over-sluggish nor yet overstrained. . . . Thus with wits alert, with wits unhampered, he cultivates his mind to brilliancy.

When a monk has thus cultivated and made much of the four bases of psychic power, he enjoys manifold forms of psychic power,[1] thus:—From being one he becomes many, from being many he becomes one: manifest or invisible he goes unhindered through a wall, through a rampart, through a mountain, as if it were through air.[2] He plunges into the earth and shoots up again as if in water. He walks upon the water without parting it, as if on solid ground. He travels sitting cross-legged through the air, like a bird upon the wing. Even this moon and sun, though they be of such mighty power and majesty, he handles and strokes them with his hand. Even as far as the Brahma World he has power with his body.[3]

---

[1] *Cf. D.* i, 78; *S.* ii, 121 (*K.S.* ii, 86); *A.* iii, 280, called *iddhi-pāṭi-hāriyaŋ* and *cha-abhiññā*.

[2] *Āvi-bhāvaŋ, tiro-bhāvaŋ*. *Cf.* Shak. *Mids. Night's Dream*, ii, 1:

> Over hill, over dale,
> Thorough bush, thorough brier,
> Over park, over pale,
> Thorough flood, thorough fire.

[3] Our text (and at *S.* ii, 121) has *kāyena vasaŋ pavatteti*. *A.* i, 170; *D.* i, 78, 218, read *kāyena va saŋvatteti*, where *Dialog.* trans. 'he reaches up to' (but there seems no authority for this meaning of *saŋvatteti*). The former reading seems preferable. *DA.* refers to *VM.* 378 *ff*. Our *Comy.* is silent, having already discussed the passage at *S.* ii, and again refers to *VM.*

When a monk has thus cultivated and made much of these four bases of psychic power, with deva-power of hearing, purified and surpassing that of man, he hears sounds both of devas and of humans, whether far or near.

When a monk has thus cultivated and made much of the four bases of psychic power, he knows the minds of other beings, of other persons, with his own mind grasping them. Of the mind that is lustful he knows it to be so. Of the mind that is free from lust he knows it to be so. Of the mind that is full of hate he knows it to be so. Of the mind that is free from hate he knows it to be so. Of the mind that is deluded he knows it to be deluded. Of the mind that is free from delusion he knows it to be free. Of the mind that is cramped[1] he knows it to be cramped. Of the mind that is diffuse he knows it to be diffuse. He knows the lofty mind as lofty, the mean mind he knows as mean. Of the mind which is inferior he knows it to be so. Of the mind that is superior he knows it to be so. He knows the mind that is uncontrolled to be uncontrolled. He knows the mind that is controlled to be controlled. The mind that is in bondage he knows to be in bondage: the mind that is released he knows to be released.

When a monk has thus cultivated, thus made much of, the four bases of psychic power, he calls to mind his former births in divers ways thus: "One birth, two births, three, four, five, even ten births, twenty, thirty, forty, fifty births; even a hundred births, a thousand, a hundred thousand births." He calls to mind divers æons of involution and evolution.[2] He knows: "Such was I by name, such was I by clan, by caste. Thus was I nourished, thus did I undergo pleasure and pain, such was my span of life." He knows: "Thence I deceased[3] and rose up so and so. There I dwelt, of such and such a name, of such a clan, of such a caste, so nourished; such and such pleasure and pain did I undergo, such my span of life. Thence deceased I rose up in the present life." That is how in fact and detail[4] he calls to mind in divers ways his former births.

---

[1] *Sañkhitta. Cf. supra,* § 1.

[2] *Saŋvatta-vivatta-kappe,* lit. 'uprolling and unrolling.'

[3] *Ento.*

[4] *Sâkāraŋ sa-uddesaŋ.*

When a monk has thus cultivated, thus made much of, the four bases of psychic power, with the deva-sight,[1] purified and surpassing that of man, he beholds beings: as they decease and rise up (elsewhere) he knows them, both mean and exalted, of features fair and foul, gone to weal or gone to woe, according to their deeds, thus: Alas! these good folk,[2] given to the practice of evil deeds, of evil words, of evil thoughts, scoffing at the noble ones,[3] of perverted views and reaping the fruit of their perverted views,—these folk, on the dissolution of body, after death arose again in the Waste, the Downfall and the Constant Round. Ah! and these good folk, given to the practice of good deeds, of good words, of good thoughts, not scoffing at the noble ones, of sound views and reaping the fruits of their sound views,—these beings, on the dissolution of body, after death arose again in the Happy Way, the Heaven World.

Thus with deva-sight, purified and surpassing that of man, does he behold beings as they decease and rise up (elsewhere): he knows them, both mean and exalted, of features fair and foul, gone to weal or gone to woe according to their deeds.

When a monk has thus cultivated, thus made much of the four bases of psychic power, by the destruction of the āsavas, in this very life, by his own unaided powers he attains the heart's release, the release by insight, that is free from the āsavas, realizes it and dwells therein.[4]

(ii) *Of great fruit.*

Monks, these four bases of psychic power, if cultivated and made much of, are of great fruit and great profit. How practised and how made much of are these four of great fruit and great profit?

---

[1] Clairvoyance.

[2] *Ime vata bhonto* (both *voc.* and *nom. plur.* of *bhavant*) *sattā*. Is it (like *ime vata bho*) 'Alas, sirs!' or 'Alas! these good folk'? *Dialog.* iii, *n. ad loc.* trans. 'messieurs ces êtres.'

[3] *Ariyānaŋ.*

[4] At *S.* ii, 121 *ff.* (*K.S.* ii, 86) it is shown that it is possible to 'declare gnosis' (*aññā*) without possessing any of these abnormal powers (*abhiññā*).

Herein a monk cultivates the basis of psychic power the features of which are desire, together with the co-factors of concentration and struggle . . . (*the whole as in previous section*).

(iii) *Desire.*

Monks, if, emphasizing[1] desire, a monk lays hold of concentration, lays hold of one-pointedness of mind, this act is called 'desire-concentration.' He generates desire for the non-arising of ill, unprofitable states that have not yet arisen: he makes an effort, sets going energy, he lays hold of and exerts his mind (to this end). He generates desire for the abandoning of ill, unprofitable states that have arisen: he makes an effort. . . He generates desire for the arising of profitable states not yet arisen: he makes an effort. . . He generates desire for the establishing, for the non-confusion, for the more-becoming, for the increase, cultivation and fulfilment of profitable states that have arisen: he makes an effort, sets going energy, he lays hold of and exerts his mind (to this end).

These, monks, are called "the co-factors of struggling."

Thus, monks, this desire and this desire-concentration and these co-factors of struggle are called (by one name) "the basis of psychic power of which the features are desire, together with the co-factors of concentration and struggle."

Monks, if, by emphasizing energy, a monk lays hold of concentration, lays hold of one-pointedness of mind, this act is called "energy-concentration." He generates desire for the non-arising of ill, unprofitable states. . . He generates desire for the abandoning of ill, unprofitable states. . . He generates desire for the arising of profitable states . . . for the establishing of profitable states that have arisen, for their non-confusion, for their more-becoming, for their increase, cultivation and fulfilment: he makes an effort, he sets going energy, he lays hold of and exerts his mind (to that end).

These are called "the co-factors of struggling."

---

[1] *Nissāya* [*cf. Vibh.* 216, quoted by *Comy.*]=*adhipatiŋ katvā* ; *VM*. ii, 385.

Thus, monks, this energy and this energy-concentration and these co-factors of concentration and struggling are called (in one word) "the basis of psychic power of which the features are energy, together with the co-factors of concentration and struggle."

Now, monks, if by emphasizing thought a monk lays hold of concentration, lays hold of one-pointedness of mind, this act is called "thought-concentration." He generates desire for the non-arising of ill, unprofitable states not yet arisen: he makes an effort, sets going energy, he lays hold of and exerts his mind to this end. He generates desire for the abandoning of ill, unprofitable states that have arisen: he makes an effort . . . He generates desire for the arising of profitable states not yet arisen; he makes an effort. . . He generates desire for the establishing of profitable states that have arisen, for the non-confusion . . . of profitable states that have arisen: he makes an effort. . .

These are called "the co-factors of struggling."

Thus, monks, this (work of) thought and this thought-concentration and these co-factors of concentration and struggling are called (in one word) "the basis of psychic power, the features of which are thought, together with the co-factors of concentration and struggle."

Now, monks, if by emphasizing investigation a monk lays hold of concentration, lays hold of one-pointedness of mind, this act is called "investigation-concentration." He generates desire for the non-arising of ill, unprofitable states not yet arisen: he makes an effort, sets going energy, he lays hold of and exerts his mind to this end. He generates desire for the abandoning of ill, unprofitable states that have arisen: he makes an effort. . . He generates desire for the arising of profitable states not yet arisen: he makes an effort. . . He generates desire for the establishing of profitable states that have arisen, for their non-confusion, for their more-becoming, for their increase, cultivation and fulfilment: he makes an effort, sets going energy, he lays hold of and exerts his mind (to this end). These are called "the co-factors of struggling."

Thus, monks, this (work of) investigation and this investigation-concentration and these co-factors of struggling are called (in one word) " the basis of psychic power of which the features are investigation, together with the co-factors of concentration and struggle." '

(iv) *Moggallāna.*[1]

Thus have I heard: On a certain occasion the Exalted One was staying at Sāvatthī in East Park, at the terraced house of Migāra's mother.

Now on that occasion a number of monks were lodging on the ground-floor of the terraced house of Migāra's mother, and they were frivolous,[2] empty-headed,[3] busybodies,[4] of harsh speech,[5] loose in talk,[6] lacking concentration,[7] unsteady, not composed, of flighty minds, with senses uncontrolled.[8]

So the Exalted One called to the venerable Moggallāna the Great, saying:

' Moggallāna, methinks our fellows in the holy life who are lodging on the ground-floor of this terraced house are frivolous, empty-headed, and so forth. . . . Go you, Moggallāna, and give those monks a good stirring !'

' I will, lord,' replied the venerable Moggallāna to the Exalted One; and he contrived such a feat of magic power[9] that with his great toe he shook and rattled and made the terraced house of Migāra's mother to quake and quake again.

Thereat those monks were panic-stricken. Their hair stood on end. They stood aside exclaiming ' A wonder indeed ! A miracle indeed ! This place is sheltered from the wind.

---

[1] This incident gives the name to the whole chapter, and is told with additional detail at *SnA.* i, 336-9.

[2] For these epithets see *M.* i, 32 (*MA.* 152); *K.S.* i, 84; *PuggA.* 217. *Uddhatā=viphandamāna-cittā. Comy. UdA.* 238, *avūpasanta-cittā.*

[3] *Unnaḷā=uggata-naḷā, tuccha-mānā ; UdA.* ' like a hollow empty reed.'

[4] *Capalā=*' busied with bowl and robe and finery '; *UdA. bahukatā.*

[5] *Mukharā=mukha-kharā ; UdA. pharusa-vācanāya.*

[6] *Vikiṇṇa-vācā=asaŋyata-vacana-palapino ; UdA.* ' given to animal-talk '; *SnA. loc. cit.* gives specimens of their supposed conversation.

[7] *Muṭṭha-ssatino=natthā sati etesaŋ.*

[8] *Asampajānā, asamāhitā, vibbhanta-cittā, pākatindriyā.*

[9] *Comy.* ' by concentrating on the element-of-water-device.'

This terraced house of Migāra's mother stands on deep-set foundations,[1] it is deep-dug, unshakable, unquakable. Yet it shook, it rattled, it quaked and quaked again!'

Then the Exalted One went towards those monks, and when he reached them said: 'What is it, monks? Why are ye panic-stricken, with hair on end? Why do ye stand thus aside?'

'A wonder, lord, indeed! A miracle, lord, indeed! This place is sheltered from the wind. This terraced house of Migāra's mother stands on deep-set foundations. It is deep-dug, unshakable, unquakable. Yet it shook, it rattled, it quaked and quaked again!'

'Yes, monks. It was shaken, it was rattled, it quaked and quaked again. It was done by the monk Moggallāna, with his big toe, because he wished to give you a good stirring. Now, monks, what think ye? By cultivating and making much of what conditions is the monk Moggallāna of such mighty magic power and majesty?'

'For us, lord, things have their root in the Exalted One (they have the Exalted One for their guide and their resort. Well indeed if the meaning of these words should show itself in the Exalted One. Hearing the meaning of them from the Exalted One the monks will bear it in mind).'

'Then do ye listen, monks. It is through cultivating and making much of four bases of psychic power that the monk Moggallāna is of such mighty magic power and majesty. What are the four?

Herein, monks, the monk Moggallāna cultivates the basis of psychic power whose features are desire, together with the co-factors of concentration and struggle. He cultivates that of energy . . . that of thought . . . of investigation (with this intent): Thus shall my investigation not be over-sluggish nor yet overstrained. It shall not be inwardly cramped nor outwardly diffuse. So he abides fully conscious of what is behind and what is in front. As he is conscious of

---

[1] Text *gambhīra-namo*, misprint for *-nemo* (correct in next §), *infra*, text, 444. *Comy.* says *g. āvāto, g. bhūmi.* (*Cf.* Lucretius, i, 77, *atque alte terminus haerens.*)

what is in front, so also of what is behind: as behind, so in front: as below, so above: as above, so below: as by day, so by night: as by night, so by day. Thus with wits alert, with wits unhampered, he cultivates his mind to brilliancy.

Monks, it is by cultivating and making much of these four bases of psychic power that the monk Moggallāna enjoys manifold forms of magic power, thus: From being one, he becomes many . . . (*as above*) . . . even as far as the Brahma World he has power with his body.[1]

Moreover, monks, it is by cultivating and making much of these four bases of psychic power that the monk Moggallāna, by the destruction of the āsavas . . . attains and abides in the heart's release, the release by insight, that is free from the āsavas.'

[The six abnormal powers are to be thus treated.][2]

(v) *The brahmin.*

Thus have I heard: On a certain occasion the venerable Ānanda was staying at Kosambī in Ghosita Park.

Now the brahmin Uṇṇābha[3] came to visit the venerable Ānanda, and on coming to him greeted him courteously, and after the exchange of greetings and courtesies sat down at one side. So seated the brahmin Uṇṇābha said this to the venerable Ānanda:

'What is it, master Ānanda, for which the holy life is lived under Gotama the recluse?'

'For the sake of abandoning desire,[4] brahmin, the holy life is lived under the Exalted One.'

'But is there any way, is there any practice, master Ānanda, for abandoning this desire?'

---

[1] As at § 1 of this chapter. [2] So text. [3] *Cf.* text, 217.

[4] *Chanda*, here in the sense of *taṇhā*, not of 'will,' which occurs alongside of it. *Comy. idha taṇhā-chandassa pahān' atthaŋ.* Mrs. Rhys Davids (*Buddhism*, p. 222-4) discusses it and quotes this passage (*cf. Compendium*, 244 *n.*): 'Desire belongs to our psychology of feeling +will, as a term of *un*moral import, *as such*. Hence it seems to me most important to retain it for *chanda* . . . which is only *im*moral as *kāma-cchanda*, or when substituted for *taṇhā*' (as here).

'There is a way, brahmin, there is a practice for abandoning this desire.'

'Pray, master Ānanda, what is that way and that practice?'

'Herein, brahmin, a monk cultivates the basis of psychic power of which the features are desire, together with the co-factors of concentration and struggle: also that of energy, that of thought, and that of investigation, (in each case) together with the co-factors of concentration and struggle. This, brahmin, is the way, this is the practice for the abandoning of this sensual desire.'

'If that be so, master Ānanda, it were a task without end, not one with an end.[1] That he should get rid of one desire by means of another desire is an impossible thing.'

'Then, brahmin, I will just question you in this matter. Do you answer as you think fit.

Now what think you, brahmin? Was there not previously desire in you (urging you) thus: "I will go to the Park"? When you got to the Park, was not that appropriate[2] desire abated?'

'Yes, indeed it was, master.'

'Was there not previously energy in you (urging you) thus: "I will go to the Park"? When you got there, was not that appropriate energy abated?'

'Yes indeed, master.'

'Was there not previously work of thought in you (urging you) thus: "I will go to the Park"? When you got there, was not that appropriate work of thought abated?'

'Yes indeed, master.'

'Then again, was there not previously in you consideration (which urged you) thus: "I will go to the Park"? When you got to the Park, was not that appropriate consideration abated?'

---

[1] Here *santaka=sa-antaka,* 'con-fined,' limited, opposite to *an-antaka.* I read with Sinh. MSS. *anantakaŋ no santakaŋ* (contrary to the order of the text), for the brahmin changes his views, is 'converted' at the end of the Sutta, where the order of words may stand. *Comy.* is silent here.

[2] *Tajjo.*

'Yes indeed, master.'

'Very well then, brahmin. That monk who is Arahant, one in whom the āsavas are destroyed, who has lived the life, done the task, lifted the burden, who is a winner of his own welfare, who has outworn the fetters of rebirth, one who is released by perfect insight,—that desire which he had previously to attain Arahantship, now that Arahantship is won, that appropriate desire is abated.

That energy which was in him previously for winning Arahantship, now that Arahantship is won, that appropriate energy is abated.

That work of thought for winning Arahantship which he had before, now that Arahantship is won, that appropriate work of thought is abated.

That investigation for winning Arahantship which he had before, that appropriate investigation is abated, now that Arahantship is won.

Now as to that, what think you, brahmin? Since this is so, is it a task that has an end, or is it endless?'

'Sure enough, master Ānanda, since this is so, it is a task that has an end. It is not an endless task.

It is wonderful, master Ānanda. . . . Let the worthy Ānanda accept me as a follower, from this day forth so long as life may last, as one who has gone to him for refuge.'

(vi) *Recluses and brahmins* (*a*) or *Mighty magic power.*

(The Exalted One said:)

'Monks, whatsoever recluses or brahmins in time past were of mighty psychic power and majesty, all of them were so by the fact of cultivating and making much of four bases of psychic power.

Whatsoever recluses or brahmins in future time shall be of mighty psychic power and majesty, all of them will be so by the fact of cultivating . . .

Whatsoever recluses or brahmins are now of mighty psychic power and majesty, all of them are so by the fact of cultivating and making much of four bases of psychic power. What are the four?

Herein a monk cultivates the basis of psychic power of which the features are desire, together with the co-factors of concentration and struggle. He cultivates that of which the features are energy . . . that of which the features are thought . . . that of which the features are investigation, together with the co-factors of concentration and struggle.

Monks, whatsoever recluses or brahmins were in time past, or in future time shall be, or who are now of mighty psychic power and majesty,—all of them have been, shall be, or are now so by the fact of cultivating and making much of these four bases of psychic power.

(vii) *Recluses and brahmins* (*b*) or *Manifold forms.*

Monks, whatsoever recluses or brahmins have in time past enjoyed in divers ways manifold forms of psychic power, thus: From being one, they were many: from being many, they were one: manifest or invisible they went unhindered through a wall, through a rampart, through a mountain, as if it were through the air: they plunged into the earth and shot up again as if in water: they walked upon the water without parting it, as if on solid ground: they travelled sitting cross-legged through the air, like a bird upon the wing: even this moon and sun, though of such mighty magic power and majesty, they handled and stroked with the hand: even as far as the Brahma World they had power with this body:—all of these did so by the fact of cultivating and making much of four bases of psychic power.

Monks, whatsoever recluses or brahmins in future times shall enjoy in divers ways manifold forms of psychic power, such as . . . (*as above*) . . . all of them shall do so by the fact of cultivating and making much of four bases of psychic power.

Monks, whatsoever recluses or brahmins do now enjoy in divers ways manifold forms of psychic power, all of them do so by the fact of cultivating and making much of four bases of psychic power. What four?

Herein a monk cultivates that basis of psychic power whose features are desire, together with the co-factors of concentration and struggle. He cultivates the basis of psychic power of which the features are energy, together with . . . the basis of psychic power of which the features are thought . . . investigation, together with the co-factors of concentration and struggle.

Monks, whatsoever recluses or brahmins have in time past . . . shall in future time . . . do now enjoy in divers ways manifold forms of psychic power,—all of them have done so, shall do so, do now enjoy such by the fact of cultivating and making much of these four bases of psychic power.

(viii) *Monk.*

Monks, it is by cultivating and making much of four bases of psychic power that a monk, by the destruction of the āsavas, realizes even in this very life by his own unaided powers the heart's release, the release by insight which is free from the āsavas, and having won it dwells therein. What are the four?

Herein a monk cultivates the basis of psychic power of which the features are desire . . . energy . . . thought . . . investigation, together with the co-factors of concentration and struggle.

Monks, it is by cultivating and making much of these four bases of psychic power that a monk, by the destruction of the āsavas . . . having won it, dwells therein.

(ix) *Teaching* or *Cultivation.*

Monks, I will teach you both psychic power and the basis of psychic power and the practice that leads to the cultivation of psychic power. Do ye listen to it.

And what, monks, is psychic power?

Herein a monk enjoys in divers ways manifold forms of psychic power, such as: From being one, he becomes many . . . even as far as the Brahma World he has power with his body. This, monks, is called "psychic power."

And what, monks, is the basis of psychic power?[1]

That path, that practice which conduces to the laying hold

---

[1] *Comy. Abhiñña-pādakaŋ catuttha-jjhānaŋ.*

of, to the winning of psychic power,—that, monks, is called "the basis of psychic power."

And of what sort, monks, is the cultivation of psychic power?

Herein a monk cultivates the basis of psychic power of which the features are desire . . . energy . . . thought . . . investigation, together with the co-factors of concentration and struggle. This, monks, is called "the cultivation of the bases of psychic power."

And of what sort, monks, is the practice that leads to the cultivation of psychic power?

It is just this Ariyan eightfold way, to wit: Right view, and the rest . . . right concentration. This, monks, is the practice that leads to the cultivation of the bases of psychic power.

(x) *Analysis.*

I

Monks, these four bases of psychic power, if cultivated and made much of, are of great fruit and great profit. And how cultivated, monks, are they of great fruit and profit?

Herein a monk cultivates the basis of psychic power of which the features are desire, together with the co-factors of concentration and struggle, (with this intent): "Thus shall not my desire be over-sluggish, nor yet overstrained. It shall not be inwardly cramped nor outwardly diffuse." So he abides fully conscious of what is behind and what is in front. . . .[1]

He cultivates the basis of psychic power of which the features are energy, together with the co-factors of concentration and struggle, (with this intent): "Thus shall not my energy be over-sluggish, nor yet overstrained." . . .

He cultivates the basis of psychic power of which the features are thought, together with the co-factors of concentration and struggle. . . .

He cultivates the basis of psychic power of which the features are investigation, together with the co-factors of concentration and struggle, (with this intent): "Thus shall not my

[1] As at text, 277.

investigation be over-sluggish nor yet overstrained. It shall not be inwardly cramped nor outwardly diffuse." So he abides fully conscious of what is behind and what is before him, thus: As in front, so behind: as behind, so in front: as below, so above: as above, so below: as by day, so by night: as by night, so by day. Thus with wits alert, with wits unhampered, he cultivates his mind to brilliancy.

II[1]

And of what sort, monks, is desire that is over-sluggish ?

Desire which is associated with indolence,[2] which is joined with indolence, is called "an over-sluggish desire."

And of what sort, monks, is desire that is overstrained ?

That desire which is associated with excitement,[3] which is joined with excitement, is called "an overstrained desire."

And of what sort, monks, is desire that is inwardly cramped ?

That desire which is associated with sloth and torpor, which is joined with sloth and torpor, is called "an inwardly cramped desire."

And of what sort, monks, is desire that is outwardly diffuse ?

Desire which, outwardly concerned with the five sensual delights, is scattered abroad and dissipated, is called "outwardly diffuse."

And how, monks, does a monk dwell conscious of what is behind and before, thus: As before, so behind: as behind, so before ?

Herein a monk's consciousness of what is behind and what is before is well in hand, well attended to, well considered, well penetrated by insight. That is how a monk dwells conscious of what is behind and before, thus: As before, so behind: as behind, so before.

And how does a monk dwell "as below, so above: as above, so below" ?

Herein a monk surveys this very body[4] upwards from the

---

[1] *Cf.* text, 263. [2] *Kosajja.* [3] *Uddhacca. Cf. Compend.* 18.

[4] *Cf. M.* i, 57; *S.* iv, 111; Warren, *Buddhism in Translations*, 359.

soles of the feet, downwards from the top of the hair of his head, as something enclosed by skin and full of manifold impurities. He thus considers: There are in this body hair of the head, hair of the body, nails, skin, teeth, flesh, nerves, bones, marrow, kidneys, heart, liver, pleura, spleen, lungs, intestines, mesentery, stomach, fæces, bile, phlegm, matter, blood, sweat, lymph, fat, tears, lubricant, saliva, mucus, oil, urine. That, monks, is how a monk dwells "as below, so above: as above, so below."

And how, monks, does a monk dwell "as by day, so by night: as by night, so by day"?

Herein a monk, in cultivating the basis of psychic power of which the features are desire, together with the co-factors of concentration and struggle, employs by day the same signs, characteristics and marks as he does in cultivating this basis by night, and in doing so employs by night the same signs, characteristics and marks as he does by day.

And how, monks, with wits alert, with wits unhampered, does a monk cultivate his mind to brilliancy?

Herein a monk's consciousness of light[1] is well grasped, his consciousness of daylight is well sustained. That is how he cultivates his mind to brilliancy.

III

And of what sort, monks, is energy that is over sluggish? (*The same as above, with* energy *for* desire.)

IV

And of what sort, monks, is thought that is over sluggish? (*The same, with* thought *for* desire.)

---

[1] *Cf. Dialog.* iii, 215, 'acquisition of intuition and insight is when a brother attends to the sensation of light, sustains the perception of daylight, and attends to light no less in the night-time, and thus, with open and unmuffled consciousness, creates a radiant, luminous mind.' *Comy.* 'When in his concentration on a luminous image the reflex is the same to him, whether his eyes are open or shut, by day or by night.'

V

And of what sort, monks, is investigation that is over sluggish ?

(*The same, with* investigation *for* desire, *down to*) . . .

That, monks, is how with wits alert, with wits unhampered, a monk cultivates his mind to brilliancy.

Thus cultivated, monks, thus made much of, the four bases of psychic power are of great fruit, of great profit. It is by means of the four bases of psychic power, thus cultivated and thus made much of, that a monk enjoys in divers ways manifold forms of magic power, thus: Being one, he becomes many. Being many, he becomes one . . . even up to the Brahma World he has power with his body.

Thus, monks, by means of the four bases of psychic power, thus cultivated and thus made much of, by the destruction of the āsavas, a monk by his own unaided power, in this very life, realizes the heart's release, the release by insight, which is free from the āsavas, and having attained it dwells therein.'

(The six psychic powers[1] are to be developed in like manner.)

CHAPTER III

(i) *The way.*

Sāvatthī . . .

Formerly, monks, before my enlightenment with the perfect wisdom, when I was yet a Bodhisattva, this occurred to me: What, I wonder, is the way, what the practice for the cultivation of the bases of psychic power ?

Then, monks, this occurred to me:

That monk[2] cultivates the basis of psychic power of which the features are desire, together with the co-factors of concentration and struggle (with this intent): Thus shall not my desire be over-sluggish nor yet overstrained . . . (*as before*) . . . thus he cultivates his mind to brilliancy.

---

[1] *Chal-abhiññā.* Text thus abbreviates.

[2] As there were then no *bhikkhus* we must take this as framework.

So also with regard to the basis of psychic power of which the features are energy . . . thought . . . investigation (*as before*).

(The six psychic powers are to be thus developed.)

(ii) *The iron ball.*

Sāvatthī . . .

Now the venerable Ānanda went to visit the Exalted One, and on coming to him saluted him and sat down at one side. Thus seated the venerable Ānanda said this to the Exalted One:

'Pray, lord, does the Exalted One understand how to reach[1] by psychic power the Brahma World in his mind-made body?'[2]

'I do so understand, Ānanda.'

'But, lord, does the Exalted One understand how by psychic power to reach the Brahma World in this (physical) body of the four great elements?'

'I do so understand, Ānanda.'

'That the Exalted One, lord, should know[3] how to reach by psychic power the Brahma World both in his mind-made body and in this (physical) body of the four great elements is a wonder and a marvel.'

'Yes, Ānanda. The Tathāgatas are possessed of powers that are wonderful and marvellous.

At such time, Ānanda, as the Tathāgata concentrates body in mind[4] and concentrates mind in body,[5] at such time as he

---

[1] Text should read *upasañkamituŋ* in this and next paragraph and below.

[2] *Cf. VM.* 405.

[3] There is a difficulty of reading here. Text has *yañ ca kho opapāti ha* (?) (Sinh. *v.l. opāti;* Burm. *omāti*), for which *Pāli Dict.* suggests *opapātiyā* (*iddhiyā*). But there is no verb in the sentence, and I would read *pahoti* (*potest*). *Comy.* also seems at a loss. My two Sinh. MSS. of it have *nâpi opātihamā ti, pahoti, taŋ sakkoti.* 'This,' says *Comy.* 'is the pure text of the Buddha's word in Tipiṭaka.' I cannot refer to printed S. ed. of it here.

[4] *Comy. kāyaŋ gahetvā citte āropeti, citta-sannisitaŋ karoti* (makes it dependent on mind), quoting *VM.* ii, 404.

[5] *Comy.* the reverse of the above.

enters on and abides in the consciousness of bliss and buoyancy, then it is, Ānanda, that the Tathāgata's body is more buoyant, softer, more plastic and more radiant.

Just as, Ānanda, an iron ball, if heated all day long,[1] is lighter and softer, more plastic and more radiant, even so at such time as the Tathāgata concentrates body in mind and concentrates mind in body,—at such time as the Tathāgata enters on and abides in the consciousness of bliss and buoyancy, then it is, Ānanda, that the Tathāgata's body is more buoyant, softer, more plastic and more radiant.

Now, Ānanda, whenever the Tathāgata concentrates body in mind and mind in body, and enters on and abides in the consciousness of bliss and buoyancy,—at such time, Ānanda, the Tathāgata's body with but little effort rises up from the ground into the air. He then enjoys in divers ways manifold forms of magic power, thus: From being one he becomes many: from being many he becomes one: . . . even as far as the Brahma World he has power with his body.[2]

Just as, Ānanda, a tuft of cotton seed or a ball of thistle-down, lightly wafted on the wind, with but little effort rises up from the ground into the air,[3] even so at such time as the Tathāgata concentrates body in mind and mind in body and enters on and abides in the consciousness of bliss and buoyancy, —at such time, Ānanda, the Tathāgata's body with but little effort rises up from the ground into the air. He then enjoys in divers ways manifold forms of magic power, thus: From being one he becomes many: from being many he becomes one . . . even as far as the Brahma World he has power with his body.'

(iii) *Monk.*

Monks, there are these four bases of psychic power. What four?

Herein a monk cultivates the basis of psychic power of which

---

[1] For the simile *cf. D.* ii, 335; *Dialog.* ii, 360. This species of magic is called *vikubbanā-iddhi* or *vikubban' iddhi* (power of transformation). *Cf. VM.* 378 [at *VM.* 404, *karajakāyo*]; *Pts.* ii, 205, *e.g.*, the power of adopting the form of a youth or a nāga.

[2] *Cf.* previous chapter. [3] *Cf. Brethren*, ver. 104.

the features are desire . . . energy . . . thought . . . investigation, together with the co-factors of concentration and struggle. These are the four bases of psychic power.

It is by cultivating and making much of these four bases of psychic power that a monk, by destroying the āsavas, even in this very life, realizes by his own unaided power the heart's release, the release by insight, and having attained it dwells therein.

(iv) *Puritan.*[1]

(*The same as in the previous* §.)

(v) *Fruits* (*a*).

Monks, there are these four bases of psychic power . . . (*as before*).

It is by cultivating and making much of these four bases of psychic power that, of two fruits, one may be expected: either realization in this very life, or, if there be any substrate left, at any rate the state of non-return.

(vi) *Fruits* (*b*).

Monks, there are these four bases of psychic power. . . .

It is by cultivating and making much of these four that seven fruits, seven profits may be looked for. What are the seven?

In this very life, previously,[2] one establishes realization: and if not in this very life, previously, at any rate at the moment of death. But if one do not so then, still by having worn down the five fetters of the lower sort, one wins release midway or, failing that, he does so by reduction of his time. Failing that, he passes away without much trouble: failing that, with some trouble: or, striving upstream, he is reborn in the Pure Abodes.

Monks, it is by cultivating and making much of these four bases of psychic power that these seven fruits, these seven profits may be looked for.

---

[1] As before, text has *suddhakaŋ* for *suddhikaŋ*. *Cf.* text, 173, 193 *n.*

[2] Reading *paṭikacca* for text's *paṭihacca*. *Cf.* text, 69, 201, 204, 237, 314, 378 *n.*

(vii) *Ānanda* (*a*).[1]

Sāvatthī was the occasion . . .

Now the venerable Ānanda went to visit the Exalted One . . . and said this:

'Pray, lord, what is psychic power? What is the basis of psychic power? What is the cultivation and practice that leads to the cultivation of psychic power?'

'Herein, Ānanda, a monk enjoys in divers ways manifold forms of psychic power, thus: From being one, he becomes many: from being many, he becomes one . . . even as far as the Brahma World he has power with his body. This, Ānanda, is called "psychic power."

And what, Ānanda, is the basis of psychic power?

It is that way, that practice which conduces to the laying hold of, to the winning of psychic power. This, Ānanda, is called "the basis of psychic power."

And what, Ānanda, is the cultivation of psychic power?

Herein, Ānanda, a monk cultivates the basis of psychic power of which the features are desire . . . energy . . . thought . . . investigation, together with the co-factors of concentration and struggle. This, Ānanda, is called "the cultivation of psychic power."

And what, Ānanda, is the practice that leads to the cultivation of psychic power?

It is just this Ariyan eightfold way, to wit: Right view, and the rest . . . right concentration. This, Ānanda, is called "the practice that leads to the cultivation of psychic power."'

(viii) *Ananda* (*b*).

. . . As he thus sat the Exalted One said this to the venerable Ānanda:

'What, Ānanda, is psychic power . . . what is the practice leading to the cultivation thereof?'

'For us, lord, things have their root in the Exalted One. They have the Exalted One for their guide and their resort. . . .'

---

[1] As at text, 276.

'Herein a monk enjoys in divers ways manifold forms of psychic power . . . (*as above*). . . . This, Ānanda, is called "the practice leading to the cultivation of psychic power."'

(ix) *Monks* (*a*).

Then a number of monks came to see the Exalted One. . . . As they sat at one side those monks said this to the Exalted One:

'Pray, lord, what is psychic power? What is the basis of psychic power? What is the cultivation, what the practice leading to the cultivation of psychic power?'

'Herein, monks, a monk enjoys in divers ways manifold forms of psychic power, thus: From being one . . . even as far as the Brahma World he has power with his body. This, monks, is called "the practice that leads to the cultivation of psychic power."'

(x) *Monks* (*b*).

(*The same as in* § viii, *with* monks *for* Ānanda.)

(xi) *Moggallāna*.

Thereupon the Exalted One addressed the monks, saying:

'What think ye, monks? By cultivating and making much of what conditions is the monk Moggallāna of such mighty magic power and majesty?'

'For us, lord, things have their root in the Exalted One. They have the Exalted One for their guide and their resort. . . .'

'Well, monks, it is by cultivating and making much of four bases of psychic power that the monk Moggallāna is of such mighty magic power and majesty. What four?

Herein the monk Moggallāna cultivates the basis of psychic power of which the features are desire . . . energy . . . thought . . . investigation, together with the co-factors of concentration and struggle (with this intent): Thus shall not my desire be over-sluggish nor overstrained (*as above*, text 277). . . . It shall not be inwardly cramped nor outwardly diffuse. . . . Thus with wits alert, with wits unhampered, he cultivates his mind to brilliancy.

Monks, it is by thus cultivating these four bases . . . that the monk Moggallāna is of such mighty magic power and majesty.

Again, monks, it is by cultivating and making much of these four bases of psychic power that the monk Moggallāna enjoys in divers ways manifold forms of magic power, thus: From being one he becomes many . . . even as far as the Brahma World he has power with his body.

Moreover, monks, it is by cultivating and making much of these four bases of psychic power that the monk Moggallāna, by the destruction of the āsavas, in this very life, of his own unaided power, realizes the heart's release, the release by insight that is free from the āsavas, and having attained it dwells therein.'

(xii) *Tathāgata.*

Then the Exalted One addressed the monks, saying:

'Now what think ye, monks? By cultivating, by making much of what conditions, is the Tathāgata of such mighty magic power and majesty?'

'For us, lord, things have their root in the Exalted One. . . .'

'Well, monks, it is by cultivating, by making much of four bases of psychic power that the Tathāgata is of such mighty magic power and majesty. What are the four?

Herein, monks, the Tathāgata cultivates the basis of psychic power of which the features are desire . . . energy . . . thought . . . investigation, together with the co-factors of concentration and struggle (with this intent): Thus shall not my desire . . . my energy . . . my thought . . . thus shall not my investigation be over sluggish, nor yet overstrained . . . thus with wits alert, with wits unhampered, he cultivates his mind to brilliancy.

Monks, it is by cultivating, by making much of these four bases of psychic power . . .

Moreover, monks, it is by cultivating these four bases of psychic power that the Tathāgata enjoys in divers ways manifold forms of magic power, thus: From being one . . .

Moreover, monks, it is by cultivating . . . that the Tathāgata . . . realizes the heart's release, the release by insight . . . and dwells therein.'

(The six abnormal powers are to be thus developed.)

CHAPTER IV.—GANGĀ-REPETITION.

(i).

Just as, monks, the river Ganges flows to the east, slides to the east, tends to the east, even so, by cultivating the four bases of psychic power a monk flows to Nibbāna, slides to Nibbāna, tends to Nibbāna.

And how cultivating . . . does a monk . . . tend to Nibbāna?

Herein a monk cultivates the bases of psychic power of which the features are desire . . . energy . . . thought . . . investigation, together with the co-factors of concentration and struggle. Thus cultivating . . . a monk . . . tends to Nibbāna.

(ii-xii).

Six on Flowing and Sliding to eastward *and six on* The Ocean.

These two sixes are twelve, and the chapter (that holds them) is so called.

(*All are to be developed by way of* The bases of psychic power.)

CHAPTER V.—EARNESTNESS

(i-x).

Just as, monks, of all beings whatsoever, whether footless or two-footed, or four-footed . . .

> Tathāgata, Foot, Roof-peak,
> Wood, Heart-wood, Jasmine,
> Prince, Moon *and* Sun,
> *With* Cloth *make ten.*

(*All to be developed as above.*)

CHAPTER VI.—DEEDS REQUIRING STRENGTH

(i-xii).

Just as, monks, whatsoever deeds requiring strength are done, all of them are done in dependence on the earth, with the earth for their support, even so a monk, depending on virtue, supported by virtue, cultivates and makes much of the four bases of psychic power. . . .

SUMMARY

Strength, Seed *and* Snake,
Tree *with* Pot *and* Bearded Wheat,
The Sky *and two of* Raincloud,
Ship, For all comers, River.

(*All to be developed as above.*)

CHAPTER VII—LONGING

(i-x).

Monks, there are these three longings. What three? The longing for sensual delight, the longing for becoming, the longing for the holy life. . . . It is for the full comprehension of these three longings, monks, for the understanding of them, for the wearing out and abandoning of them, that the four bases of psychic power are to be cultivated. . . .

SUMMARY

Longing, Conceits, Āsava, Becoming,
Suffering, Obstructions (*three*),
Stain *and* Pain *and* Feelings,
Craving *and* Thirst[1] *make the chapter.*

(*All to be developed as above.*)

---

[1] *Uddāna* here does not agree with that of Bk. I. See *n. ad loc.*

CHAPTER VIII.—THE FLOOD

(i) *The Flood.*

Monks, there are these four floods. What four? The flood of lust, the flood of becoming, the flood of view, the flood of nescience. . . .

(ii-ix).

Fetters of the higher sort.

Monks, there are these five fetters of the higher sort. What five? Lust for [rebirth in the world of] form, lust for [rebirth in] the formless world, conceit, excitement, and nescience. These are the five.

Monks, for the full comprehension of these five fetters of the higher sort, for the understanding of them, for the wearing out and abandoning of them, the four bases of psychic power must be cultivated. What are the four?

Herein a monk cultivates the basis of psychic power of which the features are desire . . . energy . . . thought . . . investigation, together with the co-factors of concentration and struggle. . . .

SUMMARY

The Flood, the Bond, Grasping, *with* [bodily] Ties *and* Tendency,

Sense-pleasures, Hindrance, Factors,[1] Fetters of lower and higher sort.

(*All to be developed by way of the* Four Bases of Psychic Power.)

---

[1] Text misprints as *Gandhā*.

BOOK VIII

KINDRED SAYINGS ABOUT ANURUDDHA

CHAPTER I.—IN SOLITUDE

(i) *In solitude* (*a*).

THUS have I heard: On a certain occasion the venerable Anuruddha was staying near Sāvatthī, at Jeta Grove, in Anāthapiṇḍika's Park.

Now when the venerable Anuruddha was meditating in solitude this train of thought occurred to him:

Whosoever neglect the four arisings of mindfulness, by them also is neglected the Ariyan way that goes on to the utter destruction of Ill. Whosoever undertake the four arisings of mindfulness, by them also is undertaken the Ariyan way that goes on to the utter destruction of Ill.

Now the venerable Moggallāna the Great, reading with his mind the train of thought in the mind of the venerable Anuruddha,—just as a strong man might stretch out his bent arm, or draw in his outstretched arm,—even so did he appear before the venerable Anuruddha . . . and said this to him:

'Friend Anuruddha, to what extent are the four arisings of mindfulness undertaken?'

'Friend, a monk dwells contemplating the rise of things[1] as regards his own personal body, (feelings, mind and mind-states). He dwells contemplating the fall of things as regards his own personal body, being ardent, self-possessed and mindful, by restraining the dejection in the world that arises from coveting.

As regards externals, he dwells contemplating the fall of

[1] *Cf. Pts. of Contr.*, p. 105, 'the cause or genesis of (natal states) cognizable objects, ideas.' *Cf. D.* ii, 290 *ff.* (*Mahāsatipaṭṭhāna Sutta*) and Introd. to *Dialog.* ii, 322 *ff.* (discussion of *paṭṭhāna*).

things in body, (feelings, mind and mind-states). Likewise as regards externals he dwells contemplating the rise of things in body, being ardent, self-possessed and mindful, by restraining . . .

Both as regards his own person and as regards externals, he dwells in body contemplating the rise of things . . . and both the fall and the rise of things in body, being ardent, self-possessed and mindful, by restraining . . .

If he desires: Let me dwell conscious of repulsion in what is not repulsive,—he does so. If he desires: Let me dwell unconscious of repulsion in what is repulsive,—he does so. If he desires: Let me dwell conscious of repulsion in what is both not repulsive and repulsive,—he does so. If he desires: Let me dwell unconscious of repulsion in the repulsive and not repulsive alike,—he does so. If he desires: Avoiding both the not repulsive and the repulsive, let me dwell indifferent, mindful and self-possessed,—he does so.

Inwardly as regards feelings he dwells contemplating the rise of things. Inwardly as regards feelings he dwells contemplating the fall of things. Inwardly as regards feelings he dwells contemplating both the rise and fall of things, ardent, self-possessed and mindful, by restraining[1] the dejection in the world that arises from coveting.

Then, both inwardly and outwardly, as regards feelings he dwells contemplating the rise of things . . . the fall of things . . . both the rise and fall of things, being ardent, self-possessed and mindful, by restraining . . . If he desires: Let me dwell conscious of repulsion in . . . (*as before*). . . .

Inwardly as regards mind he dwells contemplating the rise of things . . . the fall of things . . . both the rise and fall of things.

Outwardly as regards mind . . .

Both inwardly and outwardly as regards mind . . .

If he desires: Let me dwell conscious of repulsion in . . . (*as before*). . . .

Inwardly as regards mind-states he dwells contemplating

[1] Text joins (*vineyyaloke*) as if it were a gerundive.

the rise of things . . . the fall of things . . . both the rise and fall of things. . . .

Outwardly as regards mind-states he dwells contemplating . . .

Both inwardly and outwardly as regards mind-states he dwells contemplating the rise of things . . . the fall of things . . . both the rise and fall of things, ardent, self-possessed and mindful, by restraining the dejection in the world that arises from coveting.

If he desires: Let me dwell conscious of repulsion in what is not repulsive, he so dwells. If he desires: Let me dwell indifferent, avoiding both what is not repulsive and what is repulsive, mindful and self-possessed he so dwells.

Thus far, friend, the four arisings of mindfulness are undertaken by a monk.'

(ii) *In solitude* (*b*).

Sāvatthī was the occasion (for the following). . . .

Now when the venerable Anuruddha was meditating in solitude this train of thought arose in him: By whomsoever the four arisings of mindfulness are neglected, by them also is neglected the Ariyan way that goes on to the utter destruction of Ill. By whomsoever the four arisings of mindfulness are undertaken, by them also is undertaken the Ariyan way that goes on to the utter destruction of Ill.

Then the venerable Moggallāna the Great, reading with his mind the train of thought that was in the mind of the venerable Anuruddha,—just as a strong man might stretch out his bent arm or draw in his outstretched arm,—even so did he appear before the venerable Anuruddha and said this to him:

'Pray, friend Anuruddha, to what extent are the four arisings of mindfulness undertaken by a monk?'

'Herein, friend . . .' (*the whole as in the previous section*).

(iii) *Sutanu.*

On a certain occasion the venerable Anuruddha was staying on the bank of the river Sutanu[1] at Sāvatthī.

---

[1] I have not met this name elsewhere.

Now a number of monks came to visit the venerable Anuruddha, and on coming to him greeted him courteously and, after the exchange of greetings and courtesies, sat down at one side. So seated those monks said this:

'By cultivating and making much of what conditions has the venerable Anuruddha attained great supernormal power?'

'Friends, it is by cultivating and making much of four arisings of mindfulness that I have done so. What four?

Herein, friends, I dwell in body contemplating body (as transient), ardent, self-possessed and mindful, by restraining the dejection in the world that arises from coveting. So also with regard to feelings, mind and mind-states. It is by cultivating and making much of these four arisings of mindfulness, friends, that I have come by great supernormal power.

Moreover, friends, by cultivating . . . these four arisings of mindfulness, I can recognize a mean state as mean, a middling state as middling, and an excellent state as excellent.'[1]

(iv) *Cactus Grove.*

On a certain occasion the venerable Anuruddha, Sāriputta and Moggallāna the Great were staying at Sāketa, in Cactus Grove.[2]

Then the venerable Sāriputta and Moggallāna the Great, rising at eventide from their solitude, went to visit the venerable Anuruddha, and on coming to him greeted him courteously, and after the exchange of greetings and courtesies sat down at one side. As they thus sat the venerable Sāriputta said this to the venerable Anuruddha:

---

[1] *Comy.* 'What states are mean? The twelve unprofitable intentions. . . . What are the middling states? That which is profitable on three grounds: its fruit on three grounds; action that makes no difference (*kiriy' abyākataṃ*) on three grounds; and all body (*rūpa*). What states are excellent? The four paths in full, the four fruits of a recluse's life, and Nibbāna.'

[2] *Kaṇṭakī-vana, supra*, text, 174. *Comy.* (reading *Tikaṇṭakī-*, calls it *mahā karamadda-vana*, which, according to Childers, is *Carissa carandas*, a sort of shrub). *Cf. suvra*, 176, *infra*, 303 of text.

'Friend Anuruddha, what states should be abandoned by a monk who is a pupil, after he has attained them?'

'Friend Sāriputta, the four arisings of mindfulness should be abandoned by a monk who is a pupil, after he has attained them. What four?

Herein, friend, a monk dwells in body contemplating body (as transient), being ardent, self-possessed and mindful, by restraining the dejection in the world that arises from coveting. So also with regard to feelings . . . mind . . . and mind-states.

By a monk who is a pupil, friend Sāriputta, these four arisings of mindfulness should be abandoned after he has attained them.'

(v) *Cactus Grove* (*b*).

At Sāketa was the occasion . . .

As he sat at one side the Venerable Sāriputta said this to the venerable Anuruddha:

'Friend Anuruddha, by a monk who is an adept what states should be abandoned after he has attained them?'

'Friend Sāriputta, by a monk who is an adept the four arisings of mindfulness should be abandoned after he has attained them. What four?

Herein, friend, a monk dwells . . . (*as above*). . . .

These four arisings of mindfulness should be abandoned by a monk who is an adept after he has attained them.'

(vi) *Cactus Grove* (*c*).

Sāketa was the occasion . . . The venerable Sāriputta said this to the venerable Anuruddha:

'Friend Anuruddha, by cultivating and making much of what conditions have you come by such mighty magic power and majesty?'

'Friend, it is by cultivating and making much of four arisings of mindfulness that I have done so. What four?

Herein, friend, I dwell in body contemplating body . . .

Moreover, friend, it is by cultivating and making much of these four arisings of mindfulness that I have come to comprehend the thousandfold world-system.'

(vii) *The destruction of craving.*

Sāvatthī was the occasion . . .

Thereupon the venerable Anuruddha addressed the monks saying:

'Friends, these four arisings of mindfulness, if cultivated and made much of, conduce to the destruction of craving. What four?

Herein a monk dwells in body contemplating body (as transient) . . . feelings . . . mind . . . mind-states, being ardent, self-possessed and mindful. . . .'

(viii) *Sāl-tree Hut.*

On a certain occasion the venerable Anuruddha was staying near Sāvatthī at Sāl-tree Hut.[1] Then the venerable Anuruddha addressed the monks, saying:

'Friends, take the case of the river Ganges which flows to the east, slides to the east, tends to the east. Then there comes a great crowd of folk with pick and basket saying: "We will make this river Ganges flow, slide and tend to the west." Now what think ye, friends? Could that great crowd of folk make the river Ganges flow, slide and tend to the west?'[2]

'Surely not, friend.'

'And why not? It is because, as the river Ganges flows, slides and tends to the east, it were no easy thing to make it flow . . . to the west: insomuch that fatigue and vexation would be the lot of that great crowd of folk.

Just so, friends, in the case of a monk who is cultivating the four arisings of mindfulness and making much of them, suppose the rājah's royal ministers or his friends or boon-companions or kinsmen or blood-relations were to come to

---

[1] *Salaḷâgāre.* *Comy.* 'in a leaf-hut made of a sāl-tree, with a sāl-tree standing at the door. Hence the name.' *Cf.* *JA.* v, 430=***Mil. Panh.*** (trans.) ii, 224, where Rhys Davids says it is Sal or Hal=***Shorea robusta.***

[2] *K.S.* iv, 124; *S.* iv, 191.

that monk and tempt him with the offer of wealth,[1] saying: "Come, good man! Why should these yellow robes torment you? Why parade about with shaven crown and bowl? Come! Return to the lower life, enjoy possessions and do deeds of merit."

But, friends, for that monk, who is cultivating and making much of the four arisings of mindfulness, to reject the training and return to the lower life were a thing impossible. Why so? Because, friends, as that monk's heart has for many a long day been flowing, sliding, tending to seclusion, for him to return to the lower life were a thing impossible.

And how, friends, does a monk cultivate, make much of, the four arisings of mindfulness?

Herein, friends, a monk dwells in body contemplating body (as transient) . . . contemplating feelings in feelings . . . mind in mind . . . mind-states in mind-states (as transient), being ardent, self-possessed and mindful, by restraining the dejection in the world that arises from coveting.

That, friends, is how a monk cultivates, makes much of the four arisings of mindfulness.'

(ix) *The all* or *Ambapālī.*

Once the venerable Anuruddha and Sāriputta were staying at Vesālī, in Ambapālī's Grove.[2]

Now the venerable Sāriputta, rising from his solitude at eventide, went to visit the venerable Anuruddha, and on coming to him . . . sat down at one side. As he thus sat he said this to the venerable Anuruddha:

'Serene, friend Anuruddha, is your air![3] Very clear and shining is your complexion! In what manner of living does the venerable Anuruddha now generally spend his time?'

Friend, my mind is well grounded in four arisings of mindfulness. That is how I generally spend my time. What are the four?

---

[1] Lit. 'should offer by bringing up.' *Abhihaṭṭhuŋ* is ger. of *abhihaŋsati*. *Pāli Dict.* refs. to *Vinaya Texts*, ii, 440 *n.*

[2] *Cf. supra*, text, 142 *n.*

[3] *Indriyāni*, lit. 'sense-faculties.' *Cf. K.S.* ii, 186.

Herein, friend, I dwell in body contemplating body (as transient) . . . in feelings . . . in mind . . . in mind-states, being ardent, self-possessed and mindful, by restraining the dejection in the world that arises from coveting. It is in these four arisings of mindfulness, friend, that my mind is well grounded, and that is how I generally spend my time.

Friend, the monk who is Arahant, who has destroyed the āsavas, who has lived the life, done his task, lifted the burden, won his own welfare, who has worn out the fetters of becoming, who has won full realization and is liberated,—such an one generally spends his time with mind well grounded in these four arisings of mindfulness.'

'A gain for us, friend! Well gotten by us, friend, that face to face with the venerable Anuruddha we have heard him utter his lordly utterance!'[1]

(x) *Grievously afflicted.*[2]

On a certain occasion the venerable Anuruddha was staying near Sāvatthī in Dark Wood, being sick and grievously afflicted.

Now a number of monks came to visit the venerable Anuruddha, and on coming to him . . . said this:

'Pray what is the venerable Anuruddha's life, in that the painful feelings that come upon him make no impression on his mind?'[3]

'Friends, it is because I dwell with my mind well grounded in four arisings of mindfulness. That is why the painful feelings that come upon me make no impression on my mind. What are the four?

Herein, friends, I dwell in body contemplating body, being ardent, self-possessed and mindful. So with regard to feelings . . . mind . . . mind-states. . . .

It is because I thus dwell, friends, that the painful feelings that come upon me make no impression on my mind.'

---

[1] *Āsabhī-vācā* ('bull-like'). *Cf. D.* ii, 15. *Comy.* calls it 'supreme utterance denoting the state of Arahantship.'

[2] Text has an alternative title *Gihīnayo*, which seems a corruption of Sinh. MSS. *Uddāna* has *Bāḷhagilāyanaṃ*.

[3] *Cittaṃ na pariyādāya tiṭṭhanti* ('lay hold of and remain'). *Cf. S.* ii, 235; iii, 101.

CHAPTER II

(i) *Thousandfold.*

On a certain occasion the venerable Anuruddha was staying near Sāvatthī in Jeta Grove, in Anāthapiṇḍika's Park.

Now a number of monks came to visit the venerable Anuruddha, and on coming to him greeted him . . . and sat down at one side. As they thus sat those monks said this to the venerable Anuruddha:

'By cultivating and making much of what conditions has the venerable Anuruddha come by great supernormal power?'

'Friends, it is by cultivating and making much of four arisings of mindfulness that I have come by great supernormal power. What are the four? . . . (*as above*). . . .

Moreover, friends, it is by the fact of cultivating and making much of these four arisings of mindfulness that I have come to comprehend the thousandfold world-system.

(ii) *Psychic power* (*a*).

Moreover, friends, by cultivating . . . these four arisings of mindfulness I enjoy in divers ways manifold forms of magic power, thus: From being one I become many . . . even as far as the Brahma World I have power with my body.

(iii) *Psychic power* (*b*).

Moreover, friends, by cultivating . . . with the deva-power of hearing, purified and surpassing that of man, I hear sounds both of devas and of men, both far and near.

(iv) *Thought-reading.*

Moreover, friends, by cultivating . . . with my mind I read and know the minds of beings, of other persons. I know the lustful mind as lustful, the liberated mind as liberated. . . .

(v) *Causal occasion* (*a*).

Moreover, friends, by cultivating . . . I know as it really is the causal occasion[1] as such, and what is not the causal occasion as such.

(vi) *Causal occasion* (*b*).

Moreover, friends, by cultivating . . . I know in its causal occasion and conditions the fruit of actions[2] done in past, future and present times.

(vii) *Practice.*

Moreover, friends, by cultivating . . . I know, as it really is, all the directions[3] whatsoever of each practice.

(viii) *The world.*

Moreover, friends, by cultivating . . . I know the world as it really is, in its divers shapes and forms.

(ix) *Of divers characters.*

Moreover, friends, by cultivating . . . I know, as they really are, the divers characters of beings.[4]

(x) *Faculty.*

Moreover, friends, by cultivating . . . I know, as they really are, the natures of the minds of other beings, of other persons.[5]

---

[1] *Ṭhānaŋ*. *Cf. Pts. of Contr.*, 139; *A.* iii, 417, where *Comy.* paraphrases as *kāraṇaŋ kāraṇato*. Here *Comy.* says: 'Disciples have this knowledge partially (*ekadesena*), but omniscient Buddhas have it in every particular.' These powers are the attributes [or *dasa-balāni*] of the Tathāgata or of one who utters the bull-like utterance, enumerated at *M.* i, 69 *ff.*

[2] *Kamma-samādāna* (text 266). *Cf. Expositor* ii, 399.

[3] *Sabbattha-gāmini.*

[4] *Nānâdhimuttikaŋ sattānaŋ* (at *M.* i the reading is *-muttikataŋ*).

[5] *Indriya-paro-pariyattiŋ* (at *M.* i, *-yattaŋ*).

(xi) *Trance.*[1]

Moreover, friends, by cultivating . . . I know, as they really are, the corruption, purification[2] and uprising[3] of the attainments in trance, liberation and concentration.

(xii) *Knowledge* (*a*).

Moreover, friends, by cultivating . . . I can remember my divers existences in the past, to wit: One birth, two births and so on . . . thus with all details and characteristics I can remember my divers existences in past time.

(xiii) *Knowledge* (*b*).

Moreover, friends, by cultivating . . . with the deva-sight, purified and surpassing that of men . . . I discern beings going and coming according to their merits.

(xiv) *Knowledge* (*c*).

Moreover, friends, by cultivating and making much of these four arisings of mindfulness, by destroying the āsavas, I realize in this very life, by my own unaided power, I attain and abide in that heart's release, that release by insight which is freed from the āsavas.'

---

1 *Uddāna* has *jānaŋ ;* Sinh. MSS. *jānana.*

2 *Vodāna. Compend.* 68, 'adoption (*gotrabhu*) receives the special name of the moment of purification.'

3 *Cf. Compend.,* 67.

BOOK IX

CHAPTER I.—GANGĀ-REPETITION

(i) *Foremost in purity.*

AT Sāvatthī was the occasion . . . Then the Exalted One said:

'Monks, there are these four trances. What four?

Herein a monk, aloof from sensuality, aloof from evil states, enters on the first trance which is accompanied by thought directed and sustained, born of solitude, zestful and easeful, and abides therein.

Then, by the calming down of thought directed and sustained, he enters on that inward calm, that one-pointedness of mind, apart from thought directed and sustained, that is born of mental balance, zestful and easeful, which is the second trance, and abides therein.

Then, by the fading out of zest, he abides indifferent, mindful and composed, and experiences ease through the body. Having entered on the third trance, which the Ariyans describe in these terms: He who is indifferent and mindful dwells happily,—he abides therein.

Then, by the abandoning of ease, by the abandoning of discomfort, by the ending of the happiness and unhappiness that he had before, entering on that state which is neither pleasant nor painful, that utter purity of mindfulness reached by indifference, which is the fourth trance, he abides therein.

These, monks, are the four trances.

Just as, monks, the river Ganges flows, slides and tends to the east, even so a monk, by cultivating the four trances, by making much of the four trances, flows to Nibbāna, slides to Nibbāna, tends to Nibbāna.

And how cultivating, how making much of the four trances, does a monk . . . tend to Nibbāna?

Herein a monk . . .' (*as before*). . . .

(ii-xii).

SUMMARY

Six on Flowing and sliding to eastward *and six on* The Ocean.
These two sixes are twelve, and the chapter (*that holds them*) *is so called.*

(*All to be developed by way of the* Four Stations of Mindfulness.)

CHAPTER II.—EARNESTNESS

(i-x).

Tathāgata, Foot, Roof-peak,
Wood, Heart-wood, Jasmine,
Prince, Moon *and* Sun,
With Cloth *make ten.*

CHAPTER III.—DEEDS REQUIRING STRENGTH

(i-xii).

Strength, Seed *and* Snake,
Tree *with* Pot *and* Bearded wheat,
The Sky *and two of* Raincloud,
Ship, For all comers, River.

CHAPTER IV.—LONGING

(i-x).

Longing, Conceits, Āsava, Becoming,
Suffering, Obstructions (*three*),
Stain *and* Pain *and* Feelings,
Craving *and* Thirst *make the chapter.*

CHAPTER V.—THE FLOOD

(i-ix) *Flood.*

(x) *Fetters of the higher sort.*

Monks, there are these five fetters of the higher sort. What five?

They are these: Lust after [rebirth in] the world of form, Lust after [rebirth in] the formless world, conceit, excitement and nescience. These are the five.

Monks, for the full comprehension, understanding, wearing out and abandoning of these five fetters of the higher sort, the four trances are to be cultivated. What four?

Herein a monk, aloof from sensuality . . . (*as above*). . .

SUMMARY

The Flood, The Bond, Grasping, *with* (*bodily*) Ties *and* Tendency,
Sense-pleasures, Hindrances, Factors, Fetters of higher and lower sort.

BOOK X

KINDRED SAYINGS ABOUT IN-BREATHING AND OUT-BREATHING

CHAPTER I

(i) *The one condition.*

AT Sāvatthī . . . in the Park. Then the Exalted One said:

'Monks, there is one condition which, if cultivated and made much of, is of great fruit, of great profit. What is that one condition? It is concentration on in-breathing and out-breathing. And how cultivated, monks, how made much of, is concentration on in-breathing and out-breathing of great fruit, of great profit?[1]

Monks, under this rule, a monk who goes to a forest or the foot of a tree or a lonely place, sits down cross-legged, holding the body straight. Setting mindfulness in front of him,[2] he breathes in mindfully and mindfully breathes out. As he draws in a long breath he knows: A long breath I draw in. As he draws in a short breath he knows: A short breath I draw in. As he breathes out a short breath he knows: I breathe out a short breath.

Thus he makes up his mind[3] (repeating): "I shall breathe in, feeling it go through the whole body.[4] Feeling it go through the whole body I shall breathe out. Calming down the bodily aggregate I shall breathe in. Calming down the bodily aggregate I shall breathe out."

---

[1] *Comy.* refers to the section on *ānāpāna-sati* at *VM.* 267 *ff.* *Cf.* *Yogâvacara* (*Manual of a Mystic*) i; *D.* ii, 291=*Dialog.* ii, 317; *M.* i, 56; *MA.* i, 247 *ff.*; *Paṭisambh.* i, 184-6.

[2] Between the eyebrows, where the Hindus place the brow-cakram.

[3] *Sikkhati=ghaṭati, vāyamati.* [*VM. Pāliŋ vatvā.*]

[4] *Paṭisaŋvedi.* [*VM. pākaṭaŋ karonto.*] He visualizes the breath as passing in and through the whole frame and out again.

Thus he makes up his mind (repeating): "Feeling the thrill of zest I shall breathe in. Feeling the thrill of zest I shall breathe out. Feeling the sense of ease[1] I shall breathe in. Feeling the sense of ease I shall breathe out."

He makes up his mind (repeating): "Aware of all mental factors[2] I shall breathe in. Aware of all mental factors I shall breathe out. Calming down the mental factors I shall breathe in. Calming down the mental factors I shall breathe out. Aware of mind I shall breathe in. Aware of mind I shall breathe out."

He makes up his mind (repeating): "Gladdening[3] my mind I shall breathe in. Gladdening my mind I shall breathe out. Composing my mind I shall breathe in. Composing my mind I shall breathe out. Detaching my mind I shall breathe in. Detaching my mind I shall breathe out."

He makes up his mind (repeating): "Contemplating impermanence[4] I shall breathe in. Contemplating impermanence I shall breathe out. Contemplating dispassion I shall breathe in. Contemplating dispassion I shall breathe out. Contemplating cessation I shall breathe in. Contemplating cessation I shall breathe out. Contemplating renunciation I shall breathe in. Contemplating renunciation I shall breathe out."

Thus cultivated, monks, thus made much of, the concentration on in-breathing and out-breathing is of great fruit, of great profit.'[5]

---

[1] '*Sukhaŋ* is bodily and mental.' *VM.*

[2] *Citta-saṅkhārā=vedanâdayo dve khandhā.* *VM.*

[3] *Abhippamodayaŋ=pamodento, hāsento* (by way of concentration and introspection). *VM.*

[4] 'Freeing it from the hindrances by the first *jhāna*; from thought generated and sustained by the second *jhāna*; from zest by the third, from pleasure and pain by the fourth *jhāna*.' *VM.*

[5] He does these repeatedly by calling up (their opposites) permanence, well-being, self, passionate delight, passion, arising (of things), stinginess.' *VM.*

(ii) *Limb of wisdom.*

Sāvatthī . . . in the Park . . . The Exalted One said:

'Monks, concentration on in-breathing and out-breathing, if cultivated and made much of, is of great fruit, of great profit. How cultivated ?

Under this rule, a monk cultivates the limb of wisdom that is mindfulness accompanied by concentration on in-breathing and out-breathing, which tends to seclusion, to dispassion, to cessation, that ends in self-surrender.

He cultivates the limb of wisdom that is Norm-investigation, accompanied by concentration on in-breathing and out-breathing, which tends to seclusion . . .

He cultivates the limb of wisdom that is energy . . . zest . . . tranquillity . . . concentration . . . he cultivates the limb of wisdom that is equanimity, together with concentration on in-breathing and out-breathing, which tends to seclusion, to dispassion, to cessation, which ends in self-surrender.

If thus cultivated and made much of, monks, the concentration on in-breathing and out-breathing is of great fruit, of great profit.'

(iii) *Puritan.*

Sāvatthī . . . in the Park . . . The Exalted One said:

'Monks, if cultivated and made much of, concentration on in-breathing and out-breathing is of great fruit, of great profit. How cultivated ?

Under this rule, a monk who goes to a forest or the foot of a tree, or a lonely place, sits down crosslegged, holding the body erect. Setting mindfulness in front of him he breathes in mindfully and mindfully breathes out.

(*To be developed acc. to* § i, *down to*) . . . "contemplating renunciation I shall breathe out."

Thus cultivated, monk, thus made much of, concentration on in-breathing and out-breathing is of great fruit, of great profit.'

(iv) *Fruits* (*a*).

(*The same as the above with this addition*:)

Monks, if concentration on in-breathing and out-breathing be thus cultivated, thus made much of, one of these two fruits may be looked for: either realization in this very life, or, if there be any substrate left, at any rate the state of non-return.

(v) *Fruits* (*b*).

. . . These seven fruits may be looked for. What seven?

In this very life, previously,[1] one establishes gnosis, and if not in this same life, previously, then one does so at the moment of death.

If not at the moment of death, then, by having worn down the five fetters of the lower sort, he is one who wins release midway.

Failing that, he does so by reduction of his time. Failing that he passes away without much trouble . . . or with some trouble. If he do none of these, he is 'one who goes upstream,' and he is reborn in the Pure Abodes.

These, monks, are the seven fruits, the seven profits to be looked for if concentration on in-breathing and out-breathing be cultivated and made much of.

(vi) *Ariṭṭha*.[2]

Sāvatthī . . . Then the Exalted One addressed the monks, saying:

'Monks, do ye practise concentration on in-breathing and out-breathing?'

At these words the venerable Ariṭṭha said to the Exalted One:

'I, lord, do practise it.'

'But in what way do you practise it, Ariṭṭha?'

'Thus, lord. I abandon sensual desire for lusts that are past. Sensual desire for lusts to come is vanished. Both

---

[1] *Cf. supra*, text, 204.

[2] *Cf. M.* i, 130; *A.* iii, 451; *Vinaya Texts*, ii, 377.

inwardly and outwardly the consciousness of repugnance for things is perfectly disciplined.[1] Mindful I breathe in, mindful I breathe out.[2] That, lord, is how I practise concentration on in-breathing and out-breathing.'

'True, Ariṭṭha. That is concentration on in-breathing and out-breathing. And yet I declare it is not. Now, Ariṭṭha, I will tell you how concentration on in-breathing and out-breathing is done perfectly, in every detail. Do you listen to it. Apply your mind and I will speak.'

'I will, lord,' replied the venerable Ariṭṭha to the Exalted One. The Exalted One said:

'Now, Ariṭṭha, how is concentration on in-breathing and out-breathing done perfectly, in every detail?

In this method, Ariṭṭha, a monk who goes to the forest or the foot of a tree, or a lonely place, sits down cross-legged . . . (*as in* § i) . . . "contemplating renunciation I shall breathe out."

That, Ariṭṭha, is how concentration on in-breathing and out-breathing is done perfectly, in every detail.'

(vii) *Kappina.*

Sāvatthī . . .

Now on that occasion the venerable Kappina the Great[3] was not far off, sitting crosslegged, holding his body erect, with mindfulness set in front of him.

Then the Exalted One saw the venerable Kappina sitting not far off . . . and on seeing him he said to the monks:

'Monks, do ye ever see any wavering or shaking of body in this monk?'

'Lord, so far as we have seen him, whether sitting amid the Order or sitting alone and solitary, we have never observed any wavering or shaking of body in that venerable one.'

---

[1] 'Herein,' says *Comy.* 'he declares the path of non-return.'

[2] 'Here he declares the insight of the path of Arahantship.'

[3] *Cf. K.S.* ii, 194; *Brethren,* 254. He was one of the twelve 'Great' elder brethren of the Order. At *S.* ii, 284, the Master points him out as foremost in preaching, and as 'radiant [*odātaka* (?). This may mean "of light complexion"; for, as he was a monk, it cannot have its usual meaning "dressed in white"], lean and high-nosed.'

'Monks, it is by the fact of cultivating and making much of such concentration that there is no wavering or shaking of body that this monk can attain at will such concentration, can attain it without difficulty, attain it without trouble.

And by cultivating and making much of what sort of concentration is there no wavering and shaking of body? It is by cultivating and making much of the concentration on in-breathing and out-breathing that such is the result. And how cultivated, how made much of does such concentration have such a result?

In this method, monks, a monk who has gone to a forest or the root of a tree, or a lonely place, sits down cross-legged . . . (*as before*).

That, monks, is how, when one cultivates and makes much of the concentration on in-breathing and out-breathing, there is no wavering or shaking of body, no wavering or shaking of mind.'

(viii) *The lamp.*

At Sāvatthī . . . The Exalted One said:

'Monks, intent concentration on in-breathing and out-breathing, if cultivated and made much of, is of great fruit, of great profit. And how cultivated and made much of is it of great fruit and great profit?

In this method, a monk who goes to a forest or the root of a tree, or a lonely place, sits down cross-legged . . . (*as before*). He knows: A long breath I draw in. He knows: A long breath I breathe out. He knows: A short breath I draw in. He knows: A short breath I breathe out. . . . He makes up his mind (repeating): "Contemplating renunciation I shall breathe out."

Thus cultivated, thus made much of, the intent concentration on in-breathing and out-breathing is of great fruit, of great profit.

Formerly, monks, before I myself was enlightened with the perfect wisdom, and was yet a Bodhisattva, I used generally to spend my time in this way of living. As I generally lived in this way, neither my body nor my eyes were fatigued,[1] and my mind was freed from the āsavas.

Wherefore, monks, if a monk should desire: May neither my body nor my eyes be fatigued, and by not clinging may my mind be freed from the āsavas,—he must give strict attention to this same intent concentration on in-breathing and out-breathing.

Wherefore, monks, if a monk should desire: Whatsoever memories and plans I have, attached to the worldly life,[2] may they be abandoned,—he must give strict attention to this same intent concentration. . . .

Wherefore, monks, if a monk should desire: May I dwell conscious of repugnance for what is not repugnant . . . May I dwell unconscious of repugnance for what is repugnant . . . May I dwell conscious of repugnance both for what is not repugnant and for what is . . . Both for what is repugnant and what is not, may I dwell unconscious of repugnance,—he must do likewise.

If he should desire: Rejecting alike what is non-repugnant and what is repugnant, may I dwell indifferent, mindful and composed,—he must do likewise.

If he should desire: Aloof from sensuality, aloof from evil conditions, having entered on the first trance, which is accompanied by thought directed and sustained, that is born of seclusion, zestful and easeful, may I abide therein,—he must do likewise.

If he should desire: By the calming down of thought directed and sustained, entering on that inward calm, that one-pointedness of mind apart from thought directed and sustained, that is born of mental balance, zestful and easeful, which is the second trance, may I abide therein,—he must do likewise.

If he should desire: By the fading out of zest may I dwell

---

[1] *Comy.* 'In some other exercises (*kammaṭṭhānesu*) the body is tired and the eyesight afflicted.' He may here refer to the usual exercises of *haṭha-yoga*, such as, unnatural postures, staring at a bright object or retaining the breath, etc.

[2] *Geha-sita-sara-saṅkappā.* With the refrain: If, etc., *cf.* M. No. 3.

indifferent, mindful and composed: entering on the third trance, which the Ariyans describe thus:—"He who is indifferent and mindful dwells happily,"—he must do likewise.

If he should desire: By the abandoning of ease, by the abandoning of discomfort, by the ending of the happiness and unhappiness which I had before, having entered on that state which is neither pleasant nor painful, that utter purity of mindfulness reached by indifference, the fourth trance, may I abide therein,—he must do likewise.

If he should desire: Passing utterly beyond all consciousness of object, by ending the consciousness of reaction, by disregarding consciousness of diversity, thinking "infinite is space," may I attain and abide in the sphere of infinite space,—he must do likewise.

If he should desire: Passing utterly beyond the sphere of the infinity of space, reaching the sphere of infinite consciousness, thinking "infinite is consciousness," may I abide therein,—he must do likewise.

If he should desire: Passing utterly beyond the sphere of infinite consciousness, thinking "there is nothing at all," reaching the sphere of nothingness may I abide therein,—he must do likewise.

If he should desire: Passing utterly beyond the sphere of nothingness, and reaching the sphere of neither consciousness nor unconsciousness, let me abide therein,—he must give strict attention to this same intent concentration on in-breathing and out-breathing.

Lastly, if a monk should desire: Passing utterly beyond the sphere of neither consciousness nor unconsciousness, reaching the ceasing of consciousness and sensation, let me so abide,—he must give strict attention to this same intent concentration on in-breathing and out-breathing.

Now, monks, if intent concentration of this sort be cultivated and made much of, when he feels a pleasant feeling he understands: That is impermanent. He understands: I do not cling to it. He understands: It has no lure for me.[1]

---

[1] *Cf. K.S.* iv, 143.

If he feels a painful feeling he understands likewise.

So also if he feels a feeling that is neutral.

If he feels a pleasant feeling, he feels it as one released from bondage to it. So also, if he feels a painful feeling and a neutral feeling, he feels them as one released from bondage to them.

If he has a feeling that his bodily endurance has reached its limit, he is aware that he so feels. When he has a feeling that life has reached its limit, he is aware that he feels so. He understands: When body breaks up, after life is used up, all my experiences in this world will lose their lure and grow cold.[1]

Just as, monks, because of oil and because of a wick a lamp keeps burning; but if oil and wick be used up the lamp would go out, because it is not fed,—even so, monks, when one has a feeling that his bodily endurance has reached its limit, that life has reached its limit; when he has a feeling that when body breaks up, after life is used up, all his experiences in this world will lose their lure and grow cold,—then indeed a monk is aware that he so feels.'

(ix) *Vesālī.*

Thus have I heard: On a certain occasion the Exalted One was staying near Vesālī, in Great Wood, at the House with the peaked gable.

Now on that occasion the Exalted One was talking to the monks in divers ways on the subject of the unlovely,[2] was speaking in praise of the unlovely, was speaking in praise of meditation on the unlovely.

After that the Exalted One addressed the monks, saying:

'Monks, I wish to dwell in solitude for the half-month.[3] I am not to be visited by anyone save by the single one who brings my food.'

'So be it, lord,' replied the monks to the Exalted One.

---

[1] *Cf. S.* ii, 83.

[2] As at *Vin.* (*Pārājika* iii); *cf. VinA.* iii, 393, *Asubha-kathā*. *Comy.* refers to *VM.* i, 241 *ff.* (' in this fathom-long body,' etc.).

[3] *Cf. supra*, text, 12.

Thus no one visited the Exalted One save only the single one who brought his food.'

So those monks, saying, 'The Exalted One has in divers ways spoken on the subject of the unlovely, he has spoken in praise of the unlovely, he has spoken in praise of meditation on the unlovely,' spent their time given to meditation on the unlovely in all its varied applications.[1] As to this body, they worried about it, felt shame and loathing for it, and sought for a weapon to slay themselves. Nay, as many as ten monks did so in a single day; even twenty, thirty of them slew themselves in a single day.[2]

Now at the end of that half-month the Exalted One, on returning from his solitary life, said to the venerable Ānanda:

'How is it, Ānanda? The order of monks seems diminished.'

'As to that, lord, the Exalted One spoke to the monks in divers ways on the subject of the unlovely, spoke in praise of the unlovely, spoke in praise of meditation on the unlovely. Then the monks, saying, "The Exalted One has (thus spoken) . . ." spent their time given to meditation on the unlovely in all its varied applications. As to this body, they worried about it, felt shame and loathing for it, and sought for a weapon to slay themselves. Nay, as many as ten monks did so in a single day; even twenty, thirty of them slew themselves in a single day. It were a good thing, lord, if the Exalted One would teach some other method, so that the order of monks might be established in gnosis.'[3]

'Very well then, Ānanda. Summon the monks who dwell in the neighbourhood of Vesālī to the service-hall.'

'Very good, lord,' replied the venerable Ānanda to the Exalted One, and, after summoning all the monks who dwelt in the neighbourhood of Vesālī to the service-hall, he came to the Exalted One and said:

'Lord, the order of monks is assembled. Now let the Exalted One do as he deems fit.'

---

1 *Anekâkāra-vokāraŋ.* 2 *Cf.* the case of Vakkali at *K.S.* iii, 105.

3 *Aññāya saṇṭhaheyya. Comy.=arahatte patiṭṭhaheyya.*

Then the Exalted One went to the service-hall, and on arriving there sat down on a seat made ready. As he thus sat the Exalted One addressed the monks, saying:

'Monks, this intent concentration on in-breathing and out-breathing, if cultivated and made much of,[1] is something peaceful and choice, something perfect in itself,[2] and a pleasant way of living too. Moreover it allays evil, unprofitable states that have arisen[3] and makes them vanish in a moment.[4]

Just as, monks, in the last month of the hot season the dust and dirt fly up,[5] and then out of due season a great rain-cloud lays them and makes them vanish in a moment,—even so intent concentration on in-breathing and out-breathing, if cultivated and made much of, is something peaceful and choice, something perfect in itself, and a pleasant way of living too. Moreover it allays evil, unprofitable states that have arisen, and makes them vanish in a moment.

And how cultivated, monks, how made much of, does intent concentration on in-breathing and out-breathing (have this effect)?

In this method a monk who has gone to the forest or the root of a tree or a lonely place, sits down cross-legged . . . (*as in* § 1) . . . (repeating): "Contemplating renunciation I shall breathe out."

Thus cultivated, monks, thus made much of, intent concentration on in-breathing and out-breathing . . . allays evil, unprofitable states that have arisen, and makes them vanish in a moment.'

---

[1] *Comy. bhāvito=uppādito, vaḍḍhito; bahulīkato=punappunaŋ kato.*

[2] *Asecanako. Comy. nâssa secanan ti* (adulteration, mixing), and defines it as *anāsittako* (unsprinkled), *abbokiṇṇo* (uninterrupted), *pāṭiyekko* (single), *āveṇiko* (unique); and gives another interpretation, viz.: *āsittako, ojavanto, sabhāven' eva madhuro ti* ('the elixir that no infusion needs,' *K.S.* i, 274). This passage is quoted and explained at *VM.* i, 291; *SnA.* ii, 7. *Cf. Thig.* 55; *Mil. Pañh.*, 405.

[3] Text *uppann' uppanno*, but Sinh. MSS. *v.l. uppanne* (as at *Expos.* i, 90).

[4] *Ṭhānaso*, causally, on the spot, at the moment. *Comy. khaṇen' eva.*

[5] *Cf. supra*, text, 50, where reading is *uggataŋ*.

(x) *Kimbilā*.[1]

Thus have I heard: On a certain occasion the Exalted One was staying at Kimbilā, in Bamboo Grove.

Now on that occasion the Exalted One addressed the venerable Kimbila, saying:

'Tell me, Kimbila, how cultivated, how made much of, is the practice of intent concentration on in-breathing and out-breathing of great fruit, of great profit?'

At these words the venerable Kimbila was silent.

Then a second time and a third time the Exalted One addressed the venerable Kimbila (in the same words, and on each occasion the venerable Kimbila was silent).

Thereupon the venerable Ānanda said this to the Exalted One:

'Now is the time for this, Exalted One! Now is the time, O Happy One, for the Exalted One to develop the concentration on in-breathing and out-breathing. Hearing the Exalted One's words the monks will bear them in mind.'

'Very well then, Ānanda. Do you listen. Apply your mind and I will speak.'

'Yes, lord,' replied the venerable Ānanda to the Exalted One, who said:

'How cultivated, Ānanda, how made much of is the intent concentration on in-breathing and out-breathing of great fruit, of great profit?

In this method, Ānanda, a monk who goes to the forest . . . (*as in* § 1). . . .

Thus cultivated, Ānanda, thus made much of, the intent concentration . . . is of great fruit, of great profit.

Now, Ānanda, at such time as a monk, while drawing in a long breath, knows: A long breath I draw in; or, breathing out a long breath, knows: A long breath I breathe out; or, when drawing in a short breath, knows: A short breath I draw in; or, when breathing out a short breath, knows: A short breath I breathe out; or, when he makes up his mind (repeating): "Feeling it go through the whole body I shall

---

[1] For the village, see *S.* iv, 181; for the monk, *Brethren,* 105, 125.

breathe in; feeling it go through the whole body I shall breathe out; calming down[1] the bodily aggregate I shall breathe in; calming down the bodily aggregate I shall breathe out,"—at such time, Ānanda, in body contemplating body (as transient) a monk dwells ardent, self-possessed and mindful, by restraining the dejection in the world that arises from coveting.

Now, Ānanda, I declare that this in-breathing and out-breathing is a certain body.[2] Wherefore, Ānanda, a monk in body contemplating body . . . at such time dwells ardent, self-possessed and mindful. . . .

Again, Ānanda, at such time as a monk makes up his mind (repeating): "Feeling the thrill of zest I shall breathe in: feeling the thrill of zest I shall breathe out: feeling the sense of ease I shall breathe in: feeling the sense of ease I shall breathe out. Aware of the mental factors I shall breathe in: aware of the mental factors I shall breathe out. Calming down the mental factors I shall breathe in: calming down the mental factors I shall breathe out,"—at such time, in feelings contemplating feelings, he dwells ardent, self-possessed, and mindful, by restraining . . .

Now, Ānanda, I declare that this in-breathing and out-breathing, this close attention to it, is a certain feeling.[3] Wherefore, Ānanda, a monk, in feelings contemplating feelings, at such time dwells ardent, self-possessed and mindful. . . .

Again, Ānanda, at such time as a monk makes up his mind (repeating): "Aware of mind I shall breathe in: aware of mind I shall breathe out. Gladdening my mind I shall breathe in: gladdening my mind I shall breathe out. Composing my mind I shall breathe in: composing my mind I shall breathe out. Detaching my mind I shall breathe in: detaching my mind I shall breathe out,"—at such time, in mind

---

[1] Text misprints *passambhayaŋ* as *passam bhayaŋ* here and throughout.

[2] *Kāy' aññataraŋ*. *Comy.* 'one of the earth (extension)-element . . . air (mobile)-element bodies . . . fed on food,' etc. As he contemplates breathing in its bodily process, the exercise is equivalent to a contemplation of body as an aggregate, impermanent, etc.

[3] *Comy.* 'it is *sukha-vedanā*.'

contemplating mind (as transient), a monk dwells ardent, self-possessed and mindful, by restraining the dejection in the world that arises from coveting. What is the cause of that? I declare, Ānanda, that the practice of intent concentration on in-breathing and out-breathing is not a mindfulness that is relaxed or not composed. Wherefore, Ānanda, I say a monk dwells in mind contemplating mind, ardent, self-possessed and mindful. . . .

Again, Ānanda, at such time as a monk makes up his mind (repeating): "Contemplating impermanence I shall breathe in: contemplating impermanence I shall breathe out. Contemplating dispassion I shall breathe in: contemplating dispassion I shall breathe out. Contemplating cessation I shall breathe in: contemplating cessation I shall breathe out. Contemplating renunciation I shall breathe in: contemplating renunciation I shall breathe out,"—at such time, in mind-states contemplating mind-states, a monk dwells ardent, self-possessed and mindful, by restraining . . .

Abandoning whatever dejection arises from coveting, seeing it[1] with the eye of insight, he is completely disinterested.

Wherefore I say, Ānanda, at such a time that monk dwells in mind-states contemplating mind-states, ardent, self-possessed and mindful, by restraining the dejection in the world that arises from coveting.

Suppose, Ānanda, a heap of dust at the place where four high-roads meet, and from the eastern quarter comes a cart or chariot, and that heap of dust is made less. Then from the western quarter . . . from the northern and southern quarters comes a cart or chariot, and that heap of dust is made still less,—just so, Ānanda, by dwelling in body contemplating body . . . by dwelling in feelings contemplating feelings . . . in mind contemplating mind . . . in mind-states contemplating mind-states, evil, unprofitable conditions are made less.'[2]

---

[1] Text misprints *divā* for *disvā* (*sādhukaŋ ajjhupekkhitā*).

[2] *Comy.* 'like the high-road are the sense-spheres. The dust-heap is the impurities therein. The four objects of meditation used in the four stations of mindfulness are like the four carts coming from the four quarters.'

CHAPTER II

(i) *Icchānangala.*

On a certain occasion the Exalted One was staying at Icchānangala,[1] in a jungle thicket of Icchānangala.

On that occasion the Exalted One addressed the monks, saying:

'Monks, I wish to live in solitude for three months. Let no one visit me save the single one who brings my food.'

'Very well, lord,' replied those monks to the Exalted One. Thus no one visited the Exalted One save the single one who brought his food.

Now at the end of those three months the Exalted One, leaving his solitary dwelling, came and addressed the monks, saying:

'Monks, if the wanderers who hold other views should thus question you: "Friends, in what way of life does Gotama the recluse generally spend the rainy season ?" thus questioned, thus should ye make reply to those wanderers holding other views: "Friends, the Exalted One generally spends his time during the rainy season in the intent concentration on in-breathing and out-breathing."

Now, monks, in this method I mindfully breathe in and mindfully breathe out. When I draw a long breath I know: A long breath I draw in. When I breathe out a long breath I know: A long breath I breathe out . . . (*as at* § 1) . . . "contemplating renunciation I breathe out."

Monks, he who would rightly use the words "Ariyan way of life, best of[2] ways, the Tathāgata's way of life" would rightly do so in calling by this name the intent concentration on in-breathing and out-breathing, to wit: "The Ariyan way of life, the best of ways, the Tathāgata's way of life."

---

[1] *Cf. A.* iii, 30, 341; *AA.* iv, 340; *Ud.* ii, 5; *UdA.* 115. A brahmin village of the Kosalans.

[2] *Brahma-vihāra* here to be distinguished from the Four Moods of *supra*, 98 *n.*, for which *cf. Gotama the Man*, Mrs. Rhys Davids, p. 180.

As for those monks who are learners, who have not won their goal,[1] who dwell aspiring for the unsurpassed security from bondage,—for such the intent concentration on in-breathing and out-breathing, if cultivated and made much of, conduces to the destruction of the āsavas.

Moreover, monks, for those monks who are Arahants, in whom the āsavas are destroyed, who have lived the life, done the task, lifted the burden, won their highest good, worn out the fetters of becoming, who by perfect knowledge have become free,—for such also the intent concentration on in-breathing and out-breathing, if cultivated and made much of, conduces both to pleasant living and to[2] mindful composure even in this very life.

Monks, he who would rightly use the words "Ariyan way, best of ways, the Tathāgata's way of life" would rightly do so in calling by this name the intent concentration on in-breathing and out-breathing, to wit: "The Ariyan way of life, the best way of life, the Tathāgata's way of life." '

(ii) *In doubt.*

Once the venerable Lomasavangīsa[3] was living among the Sakyans at Kapilavatthu, in Banyan Park.

Now Mahānāma[4] the Sakyan came to see the venerable Lomasavangīsa, and on coming to him saluted him and sat down at one side. So seated Mahānāma the Sakyan said this to the venerable Lomasavangīsa:

' Sir, is a learner's way of life the same as that of a Tathāgata, or are the two different ?'

' No indeed, friend Mahānāma, a learner's way of life is not that of a Tathāgata. The two are different.

---

[1] *Appattamānasā*. *Cf*. *M*. i, 4; *S*. ii, 229. *Mānaso* seems to mean ' one's aim or intention.'

[2] Here text has a misprint *ceca* for *ca*.

[3] The name would mean ' hairy and skin-diseased,' but the spelling is doubtful. It occurs elsewhere only at *M*. iii, 197, at the same town, where text reads *Lomasakangiyo*. Our text has B. *v.l.* *-kambhiyo*.

[4] Again at text 371, 404, etc., *M*. i, 91, 354. He is called, in the list of great ones at *A*. i, 26, among lay-disciples *paṇīta-dāyaka* (excellent supporter), and became a stream-winner merely on seeing the Master.

Those monks, friend Mahānāma, who are learners, who have not won their goal, who dwell aspiring for the unsurpassed security from bondage,—such dwell having abandoned five hindrances. What five? The hindrances which are sensual desire, resentment, sloth and torpor, excitement and worry, doubt and wavering. Those monks, friend, who are learners . . . have abandoned these hindrances.

But, friend Mahānāma, those monks who are Arahants, in whom the āsavas are destroyed, who have lived the life, done the task, lifted the burden, won their highest good, worn out the fetters of becoming, who by perfect knowledge have become free,—in such these five hindrances are not only abandoned, but cut down at the root, made like a palm-tree stump, made something that has ceased to be, so as not to grow again in future time. What are the five? The hindrances which are sensual desire, resentment, sloth and torpor, excitement and flurry, doubt and wavering, are in them abandoned, cut down at the root . . . (*as before*).

In this way, friend Mahānāma, you are to understand that the learner's way of life is one thing, the Tathāgata's way of life another thing.

Now on a certain occasion, friend Mahānāma, the Exalted One was staying at Icchānangala . . . (*here he repeats the whole of the previous sutta*). . . . So by this method, friend Mahānāma, you are to understand that the learner's way of life is one thing, that of the Tathāgata another thing.'

(iii) *Ānanda (a).*

Sāvatthī . . .

Now the venerable Ānanda came to visit the Exalted One, and on coming to him saluted him and sat down at one side. So seated the venerable Ānanda said this to the Exalted One:

'Pray, lord, is there any one state which, if cultivated and made much of, brings four states to completion? Do four states, if cultivated and made much of, complete seven states? Do seven states, if cultivated and made much of, complete two states?'

'Yes, Ānanda. There is one state which does complete

four. Four states complete seven, and seven complete two. What are they?

Intent concentration on in-breathing and out-breathing, Ānanda, is the one state which, if cultivated and made much of, brings the four arisings of mindfulness to completion. The four arisings of mindfulness, if cultivated and made much of, bring the seven limbs of wisdom to completion. The seven limbs of wisdom, if cultivated and made much of, complete knowledge and release.[1]

I

And how cultivated, how made much of, does intent concentration on in-breathing and out-breathing complete the four arisings of mindfulness?

In this method, Ānanda, a monk who has gone to the forest or the root of a tree, or a lonely place, sits down cross-legged . . . (*as in* § i) . . . and makes up his mind (repeating): "contemplating renunciation I shall·breathe out."

Now, Ānanda, at such time as a monk, in drawing in a long breath, knows:

(*The whole as before to the end of Chap. I, omitting the simile of the dust-heap*). . . .

Thus cultivated, Ānanda, thus made much of, intent concentration on in-breathing and out-breathing completes the four arisings of mindfulness.

II[2]

And how cultivated . . . do the four arisings of mindfulness complete the seven limbs of wisdom?

At such time as a monk dwells, in body contemplating body, with mindfulness established, his mindfulness is not relaxed; at such time as his mindfulness, being established, is not relaxed, the limb of wisdom which is mindfulness is established in that monk. Then it is, Ānanda, that a monk is cultivating the limb of wisdom which is mindfulness. Then it is that the limb of wisdom which is mindfulness by cultivation goes

---

[1] *Cf. VM.* i, 291; *M.* iii, 82.

[2] This section repeats matters at text, 68 *ff.*

to completion in a monk. He, thus dwelling mindful, investigates that state by insight, he examines it, he comes to close scrutiny of it.

At such time, Ānanda, as a monk, thus dwelling mindful, investigates that state by insight,[1] comes to close scrutiny of it, then it is that the limb of wisdom which is Norm-investigation is undertaken by a monk; then it is that a monk cultivates the limb of wisdom which is Norm-investigation. Then it is, Ānanda, that the limb of wisdom which is Norm-investigation goes to completion in a monk. As he investigates that state by insight, as he examines it, as he comes to close scrutiny of it, unwavering energy is established in him.

At such time, Ānanda, as unwavering energy is established in a monk who is investigating that state by insight, examining it, coming to close scrutiny of it, then it is that the limb of wisdom which is energy is established in that monk. Then it is that he cultivates that limb of wisdom: that limb of wisdom goes to completion in that monk owing to cultivation of it; and there arises in him a zest that is not carnal[2] for the energy which he has established.

At such time, Ānanda, as zest that is not carnal arises in a monk whose energy is established, the limb of wisdom which is zest is established in him: then it is that a monk cultivates the limb of wisdom which is zest. At such time the limb of wisdom which is zest goes to completion in that monk owing to cultivation of it. In one who is zestful the body is tranquillized, the mind is tranquillized.

At such time, Ānanda, as the body and mind of a monk who is zestful[3] are tranquillized, the limb of wisdom which is tranquillity is established in him. At such time a monk cultivates this limb of wisdom: it goes to completion in a monk by cultivation. In him whose body is tranquillized, who is happy, the mind is composed.[4]

---

[1] *Comy.* 'by way of impermanence,' etc.

[2] *Nirāmisā pīti=nikkilesā p.* (untainted). *Comy. Cf. K.S.* iv, 147 *n.*, 160 (the zest of the first trance, which is refined in each succeeding stage of trance).

[3] *Pītimanassa.*

[4] *Samādhi-gati,* 'as if in ecstasy (*appanā*).' *Comy.*

When, Ānanda, in a monk whose body is tranquillized, who is happy, the mind is composed, at such time the limb of wisdom which is concentration is established in him: he thus cultivates this limb of wisdom, it goes to completion in him. He is a thoroughly disinterested onlooker[1] of his mind thus composed.

Now, Ānanda, when a monk is a thoroughly disinterested onlooker of his mind thus composed, at such time the limb of wisdom which is equanimity is established in him: it is then that he cultivates this limb of wisdom, it is then that this limb of wisdom goes to completion in him by cultivation of it.

At such time, Ānanda, as a monk dwells in feelings contemplating feelings (as transient), with mindfulness established, at such time his mindfulness is not relaxed. When his mindfulness is established and not relaxed . . . (*all as for* body).[2]

Thus cultivated, Ānanda, thus made much of, the four arisings of mindfulness complete the seven limbs of wisdom.

III

Now, Ānanda, how cultivated, how made much of, do the seven limbs of wisdom complete knowledge and release?

Herein, Ānanda, a monk cultivates the limb of wisdom which is mindfulness, which tends to seclusion, to dispassion, to cessation, to readiness for self-surrender . . . he cultivates the limb of wisdom which is equanimity. . . .

Thus cultivated . . . the seven limbs of wisdom complete knowledge and release.'

(iv) *Ānanda (b).*

Then the venerable Ānanda came to see the Exalted One . . . and the Exalted One said this to him:

(*Here he asks the same question, and Ānanda replies*:)

'For us, lord, things have their root in the Exalted One. . . .'

(*Then the Buddha repeats the whole of the previous Sutta.*)

---

[1] *Ajjhupekkhitā* ('inwardly neutral'). *Cf. n.* on text, 69.

[2] Text does not add the contemplation on mind and mind-states, which should be included here.

(v) *Monks (a).*

(*Here the monks ask the same question, which is replied to exactly as in* § iii.)

(vi) *Monks (b).*

(*Exactly the same as in* § iv, *down to* p. 340 *of text.*)

(vii) *Fetter.*

Monks, intent concentration on in-breathing and out-breathing conduces to the abandoning of the fetters.

(viii) *Tendency.*[1]

. . . It conduces to the utter destruction of tendency.

(ix) *The way.*[2]

. . . It conduces to thorough knowledge of the way.
(*The three above to be developed as in next Sutta.*)

(x) *Destruction of the āsavas.*

Monks, intent concentration on in-breathing and out-breathing conduces to the destruction of the āsavas.

And how cultivated, how made much of, does it conduce to the abandoning of the fetters, to thorough knowledge of the way, to the destruction of the āsavas?

In this method, a monk who goes to the forest . . . (*as in the first Sutta*).

---

[1] *Anusayo. Cf.* text, p. 60. There are seven of these 'inclinations.'
[2] *Addhāna. Cf.* text, 28.

BOOK XI

KINDRED SAYINGS ON STREAM-WINNING

CHAPTER I—VELUDVĀRA[1]

(i) *Rājah.*

SĀVATTHĪ . . . The Exalted One said:

'Monks, although a rājah, a roller of the wheel,[2] holding supreme lordship and dominion over four continents, on the break-up of body is reborn after death in the Happy Lot, in the Heaven World, in the company of the Devas of the Thirty-Three; although he spends his time there in Nandana Grove,[3] attended by a troop of nymphs, supplied and provided with, surrounded by, celestial pleasures of sense, although he is possessed of these four things,[4]—yet is he not released from Purgatory, he is not released from (birth in) the womb of an animal, he is not released from the realm of ghosts, he is not released from Hell, the Way of Woe, the Downfall.

Monks, although an Ariyan disciple lives on gathered scraps,[5] though he be clothed in rags,[6] yet is he possessed of four things;

---

[1] The title of this chapter comes from § vii. It is the name of a brahmin village of the Kosalans.

[2] Universal Ruler. *Cf. DA.* i, 249. The Sutta is quoted at *UdA.* 108 *ff.*

[3] *Cf. K.S.* i, 9 *n.* The Grove in Sakka's Heaven, the lowest of the Devalokas, to which devas went when about to die, 'there to dissolve like snow, or like a wind-blown lamp-flame, and to be reborn.'

[4] Reading *sammannāgato* with $S_{1\text{-}3}$; and *UdA.* Text reads *asamannāgato,* evidently referring to the four dooms following; but the 'four things' are the four continents, as stated below.

[5] *Piṇḍiyālopena.* The name of Piṇḍola (the scrap-gatherer) was bestowed on one of the monks. *Cf.* text, 224.

[6] *Nantakāni. Comy.* 'a cloth of thirteen spans ("hands"), so called from being divided into ten parts (?).'

moreover he is released from Purgatory, he is released from (birth in) the womb of an animal, he is released from the realm of ghosts, he is released from Hell, the Way of Woe, from the Downfall. What are the four things?

Herein, monks, the Ariyan disciple is possessed of unwavering loyalty to the Buddha, thus: (He has faith that) He it is the Exalted One, Arahant, a fully Enlightened One, perfect in knowledge and practice, a Happy One, world-knower, unsurpassed charioteer of men to be tamed,[1] teacher of devas and mankind, a Buddha, an Exalted One.[2]

He is possessed of unwavering loyalty to the Norm, thus: Well proclaimed by the Exalted One is the Norm, seen in this very life, a thing not involving time, inviting one to come and see, leading onward, to be known for themselves by the wise.

He is possessed of unwavering faith in the Order, thus: Walking righteously is the Exalted One's Order, walking uprightly, walking in the right way, walking dutifully is the Exalted One's Order of Disciples: namely, the four pairs of men, the eight sorts of men.[3] That is the Exalted One's Order of Disciples. Worthy of honour are they, worthy of reverence, worthy of offerings, worthy of salutations with clasped hands,—a field of merit unsurpassed for the world.

Then he is possessed of the virtues loved by the Ariyans, virtues unbroken, whole, unspotted, untarnished, giving freedom, praised by the wise: virtues untainted (by craving or delusion), which lead to concentration of the mind.

Such are the four things he is possessed of.

Monks, there is the winning of four continents, and there is the winning of the four things. But to win four continents is not worth a sixteenth part of the winning of the four things.'

---

[1] Text as usual misprints *-damma* as *-dhamma*.

[2] *Cf. K.S.* iv, 187 *nn.* *Comy.* refers to *VM.* i, 221.

[3] Those following the fourfold path to Arahantship in its twofold division.

(ii) *Steeped in.*[1]

'Monks, blessed with four things an Ariyan disciple is a stream-winner, not doomed to the Downfall, one assured, one bound for enlightenment. What four?

Herein, monks, an Ariyan disciple is blessed with unwavering loyalty to the Buddha, thus: He it is, the Exalted One, Arahant . . . teacher of devas and mankind, a Buddha, Exalted One.

He is blessed with unwavering loyalty to the Norm, thus: Well-proclaimed by the Exalted One is the Norm. . . .

He is blessed with unwavering loyalty to the Order, thus: Walking righteously is the Exalted One's Order of Disciples. . . .

He is blessed with the virtues dear to the Ariyans, virtues unbroken . . . which lead to concentration of mind.

Blessed with these four things, monks, the Ariyan disciple is a stream-winner, one not doomed to the Downfall, one assured, one bound for enlightenment.'

Thus spake the Exalted One. Having thus spoken, the Happy One, as teacher, said this:

> Whoso have faith and virtue, loyalty
> And insight of the Norm,—in time[2] they win[3]
> The bliss in which the holy life is steeped.

(iii) *Dīghāvu.*[4]

On a certain occasion the Exalted One was staying at Rājagaha, in Bamboo Grove, at the Squirrels' Feeding-ground.

---

[1] The bliss in which the holy life is steeped, *i.e. Nibbāna.* For *ogadha, cf. jagatogadha, S.* i, 186 ('based on earth'): *amatogadhaŋ* ('plunging into the Deathless'). *Comy.* '*Ogadhitvā ṭhitaŋ, uparimaggattāya sampayuttaŋ sukhaŋ.*' Text has, as alternative title to this Sutta, *Saṭayhaŋ* (as in the *uddāna*), which I cannot translate. Is it for *saṭṭhāyiŋ?*

[2] Text misprints *kālena* as *kāle na (paccanti).*

[3] *Paccanti* of text should be *paccenti=paṭienti*; or *paṭiyanti,* which =*pāpuṇanti. Comy.*

[4] *Dīghâvu=ḍīghâyu* (as a king's title at *J̣A.* v, 120). *Cf. Âvuso* and *āyusmanta.* There are several princes of this name in the *Jātakas.*

Now on that occasion Dīghāvu the lay-disciple was sick afflicted, suffering from a sore disease.

Then Dīghāvu the lay-disciple called to his father Jotika the housefather, saying:

'Come, housefather! Do you go to the Exalted One, and on coming to him, with your head worship at the feet of the Exalted One, and say in my name: "Lord, Dīghāvu the lay-disciple is sick, afflicted, suffering from a sore disease. He worships with his head at the Exalted One's feet." Then say: "It were a good thing, lord, if the Exalted One would come to the house of Dīghāvu the lay-disciple, out of compassion for him."'

'Very good, my lad,' said Jotika the housefather in reply to Dīghāvu the lay-disciple, and went to the Exalted One, and on coming to him saluted him and sat down at one side. So seated, Jotika the housefather said this to the Exalted One:

'Lord, Dīghāvu the lay-disciple is sick, afflicted, suffering from a sore disease. He worships with his head at the feet of the Exalted One and says thus: "It were a good thing, lord, if the Exalted One would come to the house of Dīghāvu the lay-disciple, out of compassion for him."'

And the Exalted One consented by his silence.

Thereupon the Exalted One robed himself, and taking bowl and outer robe set off for the house of Dīghāvu the lay-disciple, and on arriving there sat down on a seat made ready. Having sat down the Exalted One said this to Dīghāvu the lay-disciple:[1]

'Well, Dīghāvu, I hope you are bearing up, I hope you are enduring. Do your pains abate and not increase? Are there signs of their abating and not increasing?'

'No, lord! I am not bearing up. I am not enduring. Strong pains come upon me. They do not abate. There is no sign of their abating but of their increasing.'

'Then, Dīghāvu, thus must you train yourself: "I will be blessed with unwavering loyalty to the Buddha, thus: He it

---

[1] For the stock greetings *cf. S.* iii, 120, etc., *supra*, p. 66.

is the Exalted One, Arahant. . . . Teacher of devas and mankind . . . I will be blessed with unwavering loyalty to the Norm, thus: Well proclaimed by the Exalted One is the Norm . . . I will be blessed with unwavering loyalty to the Order of Disciples, thus: Walking righteously is the Exalted One's Order of Disciples. . . .

Also I will be blessed with the virtues dear to the Ariyans, virtues unbroken . . . which lead to concentration of mind." That, Dīghāvu, is how you must train yourself.'

'As to these four limbs of stream-winning, lord, which have been taught by the Exalted One, all of those conditions are to be found in me, and I do live in accordance with them. Lord, I am indeed blessed with unwavering loyalty to the Buddha . . . to the Norm . . . and to the Order of Disciples. I do possess the virtues dear to the Ariyans . . . which lead to concentration of mind.'

'Therefore, Dīghāvu, resting on these four limbs of stream-winning, you should further practise the six conditions which are constituent parts of knowledge.[1]

Herein, Dīghāvu, do you dwell contemplating impermanence in all the activities,[2] conscious of Ill in impermanence, conscious of there being no self in what is Ill, conscious of abandoning, of dispassion, of cessation. That, Dīghāvu, is how you must train yourself.'

'Lord, as to these same six conditions, which are constituent parts of knowledge, all of them are to be found in me. I do live in accordance with them. I do dwell contemplating impermanence in all the activities, conscious of there being no self in what is Ill, conscious of abandoning, of dispassion, of cessation.

Then, lord, I have this thought: I would not have the housefather Jotika here fall into dejection at my death.'

'Don't you trouble about that, Dīghāvu, my lad! (said his father). Look you, Dīghāvu, my lad! Attend closely to what the Exalted One is saying to you.'

---

[1] *Cha vijjā-bhāgiye dhamme.*

[2] *Comy. sabbesu tebhūmaka-saṅkhāresu.*

So the Exalted One, having thus admonished Dīghāvu the lay-disciple, rose from his seat and went away.

And not long after the Exalted One had gone Dīghāvu the lay-disciple made an end.

Thereupon a number of monks went to see the Exalted One, and on coming to him saluted him and sat down at one side. So seated those monks said this to the Exalted One:

'Lord, that lay-disciple named Dīghāvu, who was admonished in brief by the Exalted One, has made an end. What is his lot? What is his destiny in the life to come?'[1]

'A sage, monks, was Dīghāvu the lay-disciple. He lived according to the Norm.[2] He did not harm me by disputings about the Norm. Dīghāvu, the lay-disciple, monks, by wearing out the five fetters of the lower sort, is reborn by spontaneous birth.[3] His destiny is not to return from that world.'

(iv) *Sāriputta* (*a*).

On a certain occasion the venerable Sāriputta and Ānanda were staying near Sāvatthī, at Jeta Grove, in Anāthapiṇḍika's Park.

Now the venerable Ānanda, rising up from his solitude at eventide, went to see the venerable Sāriputta, and on coming to him . . . said this:

'Tell me, friend Sāriputta, through winning possession[4] of what things are people of this world[5] proclaimed by the Exalted One as stream-winners, not doomed to the Downfall, assured, bound for enlightenment?'

'Friend, it is because of winning four things that people of this world are proclaimed by the Exalted One as stream-winners, not doomed to the Downfall, assured, bound for enlightenment. What are the four things?

---

[1] *Kā gati, ko abhisamparāyo. Cf. D.* ii, 91; *S.* iv, 59, 63 (of Puṇṇa the clansman); also of Suppabuddha the leper at *Ud.* v, 3.

[2] *Dhammassânudhammaŋ pâccapādi* (fr. *paṭipajjati*).

[3] *Opapātika* (without material cause), *i.e.*, in a body of the matter of the super-sphere in which he had 'become.' He is therefore *anāgāmin. Cf. K.S.* iii, 166, iv, 250 *n.* and add this instance to those of (text) 177 *n.*

[4] *Samannāgamana-hetu.*

[5] *Ayam pajā.*

Herein, friend, an Ariyan disciple is blessed with unwavering loyalty to the Buddha . . . the Norm . . . the Order of Disciples, and is blessed with the virtues dear to the Ariyans, virtues unbroken . . . which lead to concentration of mind. These, friend, are the four things. Owing to being blessed with these, people of this world are proclaimed by the Exalted One as stream-winners. . . .'

(v) *Sāriputta* (*b*).

Now the venerable Sāriputta went to see the Exalted One, and on coming to him saluted him and sat down at one side. To the venerable Sāriputta so seated the Exalted One said this:

' " A limb of stream-winning! A limb of stream-winning!" is the saying, Sāriputta. Tell me, Sāriputta, of what sort is a limb of stream-winning?'

'Lord, association with the upright is a limb of stream-winning. Hearing the good Norm is a limb of stream-winning. Applying the mind is a limb of stream-winning. Conforming to the Norm[1] is a limb of stream-winning.'

'Well said, Sāriputta! Well said, Sāriputta! Indeed these are limbs of stream-winning.

Now again, Sāriputta, they say: " The stream! the stream!" Of what sort is the stream, Sāriputta?'

'The stream, lord, is just this Ariyan eightfold way, to wit: Right view . . . and the rest . . . right concentration.'

'Well said, Sāriputta! Well said, Sāriputta! The stream is just this Ariyan eightfold way.

Now again, Sāriputta, they say, " Stream-winner! Stream-winner!" Of what sort is a stream-winner, Sāriputta?'

'Whosoever, lord, is blessed with this Ariyan eightfold way, —such an one of such a name, of such and such a clan, is called " Stream-winner." '

---

[1] *Dhammânudhamma-paṭipatti=pubba-bhāga-paṭipadaŋ. Comy.*

(vi) *The chamberlains.*[1]

Sāvatthī was the occasion (of these events). . . .

Now on that occasion a number of monks were busied with making a robe for the Exalted One, with this idea: When the robe is finished, in three months' time, the Exalted One will go forth on his rounds.

Now at that time Isidatta and Purāṇa, the chamberlains, were staying at Sādhuka[2] on some business or other. Then they heard the news: 'They say that a number of monks are busied with making a robe for the Exalted One with this idea: When the robe is finished, in three months' time, the Exalted One will go forth upon his rounds.'

So Isidatta and Purāṇa, the chamberlains, stationed a man on the high-road (thus instructing him): 'Now, good fellow, as soon as you see that Exalted one, that Arahant, that perfectly Enlightened One coming along, do you come and inform us.'

So after standing there two or three days that man saw the Exalted One coming along, while yet some distance off, and he went to inform the chamberlains, Isidatta and Purāṇa, saying: 'Here comes my lord the Exalted One, that Arahant, that perfectly Enlightened One! Now's the time for you to do what you want!'

So Isidatta and Purāṇa, the chamberlains, went towards the Exalted One, and on coming to him, saluted him, and followed behind the Exalted One step for step.

Then the Exalted One turned aside from the high-road and went to the foot of a certain tree and there sat down on a seat made ready. And Isidatta and Purāṇa, the chamberlains,

---

[1] *Thapatayo,* 'carpenters,' 'carriage-builders,' 'royal attendants.' In Skt. lit. often 'keepers of the women's apartments.' We may call them 'equerries.' It seems that they were in charge of the royal conveyances [see note *infra*]. At *A.* iii, 348, Isidatta is uncle of the woman disciple Migasālā. Her father was Purāṇa. According to *Comy.* here, Isidatta was a 'once returner,' while Purāṇa was a Stream-winner.

[2] Their own property, according to *Comy.*

saluting the Exalted One, also sat down at one side. As they thus sat they said this to the Exalted One:

'Lord, when we heard of the Exalted One that he would go forth on his rounds among the Kosalans, at that time we were disappointed and depressed[1] at the thought: The Exalted One will be far from us. And when, lord, we learned that the Exalted One was starting out from Sāvatthī on his rounds among the Kosalans, again we were disappointed and depressed at the thought: The Exalted One will be far from us.[2]

Again, lord, when we learned that the Exalted One would leave the Kosalans and go on his rounds among the Mallas . . . that he was actually doing so . . . we were disappointed and depressed.

On hearing that the Exalted One would leave the Mallas and go on his rounds among the Vajjī . . . that he was actually doing so . . . that he would leave the Vajjī for Kāsi . . . that he was doing so . . . that he would leave the folk of Kāsi and go on his rounds in Magadha . . . that he was actually doing so . . . again we were disappointed and depressed. . . .[3]

---

[1] *Anattamanatā hoti.*

[2] For the clans here mentioned see Rhys Davids, *Buddhist India*, and map.

[3] To show the loyalty to the Buddha of these two men, I quote and italicize the passage at *M.* ii, 123 (Lord Chalmers' trans.), where the rājah Pasenadi complains to the Buddha that he does not get such loyal service from them. 'Further, there are the carriage-builders, Isidatta and Purāṇa, whom I support, who make my carriages (*mama bhattā, mama yānā*), who owe to me their livelihood and the honours they enjoy. Withal, these men do not serve me as whole-heartedly as they do the Lord. Time was when, being out with my troops on active service, I, to test these two, took up my quarters in a cramped little house, where Isidatta and Purāṇa, after spending the best part of the night in discussing the Doctrine, lay down to rest *with their heads in the direction where they heard the Lord was, and only their feet towards me.* It is wonderful and marvellous, thought I to myself, that these two men, who owe everything in the world to me, yet do not serve me as they serve the Lord. Surely, thought I, it is because these reverend men find in the Lord's teachings a high excellence not elsewhere discovered by them before.'

But, lord, when we heard that the Exalted One would leave the Magadhans for Kāsi and was doing so, then we were delighted and elated at the thought: The Exalted One will be quite near us. And when we heard that he was actually going his rounds in Kāsi among the Magadhans we were likewise delighted and elated.

(*They continue to trace the Master's steps from Kāsi to the Vajjī . . . from the Vajjī to the Mallas . . . from the Mallas to the Kosalans in like terms.*)[1]

But, lord, when we heard that the Exalted One would be going on his rounds from the Kosalans to Sāvatthī, we were delighted and elated at the thought: Now the Exalted One will be quite near us! Then, when we heard: "The Exalted One is staying at Sāvatthī, at Jeta Grove, in Anāthapiṇḍika's Park," then, lord, boundless was our delight and boundless our elation at the thought: The Exalted One is near us!'

'Well then, chamberlains, since living in houses is an oppression, a dust-hole sort of life,[2]—whereas a wanderer's life is a life in the open air, now is the time for you to show some energy.'

'But here too, lord, we have an oppression still more oppressive, indeed it is most oppressive.'

'What is that still greater oppression, chamberlains?'

'Here, lord, when the rājah Pasenadi of Kosala wants to go a-riding in the Park, we have to deck the riding-elephants and set thereon the favourite lovely wives of his majesty, one before and one behind. Now the fragrance of their bodies is so sweet. It's just as if a casket of scent were opened,—these royal ladies are so sweetly scented. Lord, the touch of those ladies is as soft to the hand as[3] a tuft of cotton-wool, so delicately are they nurtured. Well, lord, at such times we have to ward the elephant, and we have to ward the ladies and ward ourselves as well.

In spite of that, lord, we are not conscious of calling up any

---

[1] Text abbreviates here.

[2] *Rajāpatho=rāga-dosa-moha-rajānaŋ patho. Comy.*

[3] Here text should read *va* for *vā*.

evil thought about those ladies. Now, lord, this is (what we mean by) another oppression still more oppressive, nay, most oppressive.'

'Well then, chamberlains, since living in houses is an oppression, a dust-hole sort of life,—whereas the wanderer's life is a life in the open air,—now is the time for you to show some energy.

Now, chamberlains, the Ariyan disciple who is blessed with four things is a stream-winner, he is one not doomed to the Downfall, one assured, one who is bound for enlightenment. What are the four things?

Herein, chamberlains, the Ariyan disciple is blessed with unwavering loyalty to the Buddha, thus: He it is, the Exalted One, Arahant, a perfectly Enlightened One . . . teacher of devas and mankind. He is blessed with unwavering loyalty to the Norm . . . and to the Order of Disciples. He lives at home with heart freed from the taint of stinginess. He is open-handed, pure-handed,[1] delighting in self-surrender, one to ask a favour of,[2] delighting to share charitable gifts. Blessed with these four things, chamberlains, the Ariyan disciple is a stream-winner, one not doomed to the Downfall . . . bound for enlightenment.

Now, chamberlains, you are blessed with[3] unwavering loyalty to the Buddha . . . to the Norm . . . to the Order of Disciples. . . . In your family, whatsoever gifts of charity[4] there be, they are shared fully and impartially[5] by the virtuous and good.

Now what think ye, chamberlains? How many sorts of

---

[1] *Payata-pāṇī, infra*, text, 392. *Cf. Itiv.* 101; *UdA.* 123; *K.S.* i, 294. *Comy. visuddhi-hattha.*

[2] *Yāca-yogo*, not 'given to begging' (as sometimes trans.), but as *Comy. yācitabbaka-yutto.*

[3] The text of this is obscure, viz.: *Tumhe . . . samannāgato hoti* (?). To make sense with what follows it seems we should read: *Tumhe hi samannāgatā hotha*; according to which I translate.

[4] *Deyya-dhammaṃ* includes all the requisites given by laymen to monks.

[5] *Appaṭivibhattaṃ*. *Comy.* 'without saying, "this is for ourselves, that is for the monks."'

men are there among the Kosalans who are like yourselves in this matter of sharing gifts of charity ?'

'A gain for us, lord ! A thing well gotten by us, lord, that the Exalted One should come to know this of us !'

(vii) *Those of Bamboo Gate.*[1]

Thus have I heard: On a certain occasion the Exalted One was going his rounds among the Kosalans, together with a great company of monks, and had reached Bamboo Gate, a brahmin village of the Kosalans.

Now the folk of Bamboo Gate, both brahmins and housefathers, heard the report: 'It is rumoured that[2] master[3] Gotama, the recluse, the Sakyan's son, he who went forth from a Sakyan clan, is on his rounds among the Kosalans together with a great company of monks, and has reached Bamboo Gate. Now there is a goodly rumour gone abroad of Gotama that Exalted One, to this effect: He it is, the Exalted One, Arahant, a fully Enlightened One, perfect in knowledge and practice, a Happy One, world-knower, unsurpassed charioteer of men to be tamed, teacher of devas and mankind, a Buddha, an Exalted One. He makes known this world, together with the world of Devas, Māras and Brahmās, with its host of recluses and brahmins, both of devas and men, having realized it with his own full knowledge. He proclaims the Norm, which is goodly in its beginning, in its middle and its ending, both in its spirit and its letter; he makes clear the holy life in all its fullness and purity. It were well indeed for us to have sight of such Arahants !'

So those brahmins and housefathers of Bamboo Gate went to see the Exalted One, and on coming to him some of them saluted the Exalted One and sat down at one side: some

---

[1] Lit. 'Bamboo-by-the-gate.' I find no other mention of this brahmin village. *Comy.* says: 'So called owing to the tradition of a bamboo-thicket at the entrance of the village.' This chapter is called *Veḷu-dvāra-vagga*. *Comy.* has nothing to say about the earlier part, which occurs at *Ud.* vii, 9 (I give some extracts from *UdA.* 377).

[2] *Khalu* (*anussav' atthe nipāto*, a particle meaning *ut aiunt*).

[3] *Bho,* a term used by brahmins.

conversed with the Exalted One, and, after the exchange of greetings and courtesies, they also sat down at one side. Some stretched out their clasped hands towards the Exalted One and sat down at one side. Some announced their names and families to the Exalted One and sat down at one side: while some others just sat down at one side without saying anything.

As they thus sat the brahmins and housefathers said this to the Exalted One:

'Master Gotama, we are people of such desires, such wishes, such intentions as these: O may we live in a crowded[1] house encumbered with children! May we enjoy the use of Benares sandalwood! May we deck ourselves with garlands and unguents! May we handle gold and silver! When body breaks up, after death may we be reborn in the Happy Lot, the Heaven World! Pray let master Gotama teach us, who have such desires, such wishes and such intentions, a doctrine by which we may so dwell, so enjoy . . . so be reborn in the Heaven World.'

'Then, housefathers, I will teach you a Norm-method which brings profit to oneself. Do ye listen to it. Pay close attention and I will speak.'

'Very well, master,' replied the brahmins and housefathers to the Exalted One. Then the Exalted One said this:

'Now, housefathers, of what sort is the Norm-method which brings profit to self?[2]

In this matter, housefathers, the Ariyan disciple thus reflects: Here am I, fond of my life, not wanting to die, fond of pleasure and averse from pain. Suppose someone should rob me of my life (fond of life as I am and not wanting to die, fond of pleasure and averse from pain), it would not be a thing pleasing or delightful to me. If I, in my turn, should rob of his life one fond of his life, not wanting to die, one fond of pleasure and averse from pain, it would not be a thing pleasing or delightful to him. For a state that is not pleasant or delightful to me

---

[1] Text has *putta-sambādha-sayanaŋ* (as at *UdA.* 331), which would mean, 'a bed crammed with children.' I read with *S.* i, 78 *samayaŋ*, 'a crowd or company.'

[2] *Attūpanāyikaŋ.*

must be so to him also: and a state that is not pleasing or delightful to me,—how could I inflict[1] that upon another ?

As a result of such reflection he himself abstains from taking the life of creatures and he encourages others so to abstain, and speaks in praise of so abstaining. Thus as regards bodily conduct he is utterly pure.[2]

Then again, housefathers, the Ariyan disciple thus reflects: If someone should take with thievish intent what I have not given him, it would not be a thing pleasing or delightful to me. If I, in my turn, should take from another with thievish intent what he has not given me, it would not be a thing pleasing or delightful to him: and a state that is not pleasant, that is not delightful to me, must be so to him also. What does not please me, what does not delight me,—how could I inflict that upon another ?

As a result of this reflection, he himself abstains from taking what is not given, and he encourages others so to abstain, he speaks in praise of so abstaining. Thus as regards bodily conduct he is utterly pure.

Again, housefathers, the Ariyan disciple thus reflects: If someone should have intercourse with my wives, it would not be a thing pleasing or delightful to me. If I, in my turn, should so behave with another's wives, it would not be a thing pleasing or delightful to him: . . . and a state that is unpleasant, not delightful to me,—how could I inflict that upon another ?

As a result of this reflection, he himself abstains from wrong practice in respect of sense desires, and he encourages others to do so, he speaks in praise of such abstinence. Thus as regards personal conduct he is utterly pure.

Again, housefathers, the Ariyan disciple thus reflects: If someone should spoil my fortune[3] by lying speech, it would not be a thing pleasant or delightful to me. If I, in my turn, should spoil another's fortune by lying speech, it would not be a thing pleasant or delightful to him: . . . and a state that

---

[1] *Sanyojeyyaŋ. Cf. D.* ii, 355; lit. 'saddle with.'

[2] *Koṭi-parisuddho* (like *koṭippatto*).

[3] *Atthaŋ bhañjeyya,* as at *S.* iv, 347.

is unpleasant, not delightful to me,—how could I inflict that upon another?

As a result of this reflection he himself abstains from lying speech, he encourages another so to abstain, speaks in praise of abstaining therefrom. Thus as regards conduct in speech he is utterly pure.

Again, housefathers, the Ariyan disciple thus reflects: If someone should estrange me from my friends[1] by slander, it would not be a thing pleasant or delightful to me. If I in my turn should estrange him from his friends, it would not be a thing pleasant or delightful to him: . . . and a state that is not pleasant or delightful to me,—how could I inflict that upon another?

As a result of this reflection, he himself abstains from slander. . . . Thus as regards conduct in speech he is utterly pure.

Again, housefathers, the Ariyan disciple thus reflects: If someone should treat me with harsh speech it would not be a thing pleasant or delightful to me . . . nor to him if I treated him so: . . . and a state that is not pleasant or delightful to me,—how could I inflict that upon another?

As a result of this reflection . . . as regards conduct in speech he is utterly pure.

Again, housefathers, the Ariyan disciple thus reflects: If someone should treat me with pointless,[2] frivolous talk, it would not be a thing pleasant or delightful to me. If I in my turn should so treat him, it would not be pleasant or delightful to him. For a state that is unpleasant, not delightful to me must be so to him also, and a state that is not pleasant, not delightful to me,—how could I inflict that upon another?

As a result of this reflection, he himself abstains from pointless, frivolous talk: he encourages another to do so, he speaks in praise of so doing. Thus as regards conduct in speech he is utterly pure.

---

[1] Text *mittehi bhindeyya; v.l. mitte bh.* For these terms, *cf. DA.* i, 74-6.

[2] Text has *sampabhāsena,* which seems to occur here only. It does not appear in the usual lists of sorts of speech. *Comy.* says it is *samantabhāsena.* I take it to mean 'all round the question, off the point.'

Then he is blessed with unwavering loyalty to the Buddha, thus: He it is, that Exalted One . . . teacher of devas and mankind, a Buddha, an Exalted One.

He is blessed with unwavering loyalty to the Norm, thus: Well proclaimed by the Exalted One is the Norm. . . .

He is blessed with unwavering loyalty to the Order of Disciples, thus: Walking uprightly is the Exalted One's Order of Disciples . . . an unsurpassed field of merit for the world.

He is blessed with the virtues dear to the Ariyans, virtues unbroken . . . that conduce to concentration of mind.

Now, housefathers, since the Ariyan disciple is blessed with these seven good conditions and these four desirable points of vantage,[1] if he so desired, he could himself declare with surety of himself: "Cut off for me is Purgatory, cut off the Way of Woe and the Downfall! Stream-winner am I, not doomed to the Downfall, assured am I, bound for enlightenment"!'[2]

At these words the brahmins and housefathers of Bamboo Gate exclaimed to the Exalted One:

'Excellent, master Gotama! Excellent, master Gotama! Just as if one should raise up what is fallen, or show forth what is hidden, or point the way to him that wanders astray, or hold up a light in the darkness so that they who have eyes may behold objects,—even so in divers ways has the Norm been set forth by the worthy Gotama. We go for refuge to the worthy Gotama, to the Norm and to the Order of monks. Let the worthy Gotama accept us as lay-disciples from this day forth, so long as life may last, who have taken refuge in him!'

(viii) *Brick Hall (a)*.

Thus have I heard: On a certain occasion the Exalted One was staying at Ñātika,[3] in Brick Hall.

Now on that occasion the venerable Ānanda came to see the Exalted One, . . . and on coming to him said this:

---

[1] *Ṭhānehi.*

[2] See next Sutta.

[3] *Cf. Dialog.* ii, 97 *n.*, where it is called *Nādika* (of the Nādikas); *K.S.* ii, 50 *n.*, iv, 55. Text and *Comy.* read *Ñātika* (' the village of two kinsmen,' Cūlapāti and Mahāpīti). Brick Hall was what we should call a ' rest-house,' or ' dâk-bungalow.'

'Lord, the monk named Sāḷha has made an end.[1] What is his lot? What is his destiny in the life to come? Lord, the nun named Nandā has made an end. What is her lot? What is her destiny in the life to come?'

(*He asks the same questions of* Sudatta, the lay-disciple, *and* Sujātā,[2] the lay-woman disciple.)

'The monk Sāḷha, Ānanda, who has made an end, by destroying the āsavas, in this very life, by his own understanding realized the heart's release, the release by insight, and attaining to it dwelt therein.

Nandā the nun, Ānanda, who has made an end, by wearing out the five fetters of the lower sort, has taken birth spontaneously (in the Pure Abodes), there to pass away, destined never to return thence.

Sudatta, the lay-disciple, Ānanda, who has made an end, by destroying three fetters[3] and by weakening those of lust, hatred and delusion, is a once-returner: coming back to this world just once more he will make an end of Ill.

Sujātā, the lay-woman disciple, Ānanda, who has made an end, by destroying three fetters, is a stream-winner, not doomed to the Downfall, assured, bound for enlightenment.

Indeed, Ānanda, it is no wonder that a human being should make an end. But if, when each one dies, you come and ask me about the matter, it is troublesome to the Tathāgata. Wherefore, Ānanda, I will teach you a Norm-teaching called "The Mirror of the Norm,"[4] possessing which the Ariyan disciple may, if he please, himself proclaim of himself thus: "Cut off for me is Purgatory, cut off is rebirth in an animal womb, cut off is the realm of ghosts, the Woeful Way and the Downfall. Stream-winner am I, not doomed to the Downfall, assured, one bound for enlightenment!"

---

[1] For the same events and persons *cf. D.* ii, 91; *Dialog.* ii, 98. The other names of *D.* ii occur in the next Sutta. All three Suttas (viii-x) should here form one as in *D.*, otherwise we must suppose Ānanda to have been very dense or importunate in troubling the Master on two further occasions with the same question. *Cf. Gotama the Man*, p. 167.

[2] *Dialog.* spells *Sugatā.*

[3] *I.e.*, the first three.

[4] *Dhammâdāsaṃ. Comy. dhamma-mayaṃ ādāsaṃ.*

And of what sort, Ānanda, is that Norm-teaching called "Mirror of the Norm," possessed of which the Ariyan disciple can so proclaim of himself?

Herein, Ānanda, the Ariyan disciple is blessed with unwavering loyalty to the Buddha . . . the Norm . . . the Order, and he is blessed with the virtues dear to the Ariyans, virtues unbroken . . . that conduce to concentration of mind.

This, Ānanda, is that Norm-teaching called "Mirror of the Norm," possessed of which the Ariyan disciple may, if he please, himself proclaim of himself, "Cut off for me is Purgatory . . . I am bound for enlightenment!"'

(ix) *Brick Hall* (*b*).

On the same occasion . . . Seated at one side the venerable Ānanda said this to the Exalted One:

'Lord, the monk named Asoka, the nun named Asokī, have made an end. Pray, lord, what is their lot, what is their destiny in the life to come?'

'The monk named Asoka, Ānanda, who has made an end, by the destruction of the āsavas . . . has realized the heart's release. . . . The nun Asokī . . . has been reborn spontaneously . . . (*as above*). . . .

This, Ānanda, is the Norm-teaching called "The Mirror of the Norm," possessed of which the Ariyan disciple may, if he please, himself proclaim of himself: "Cut off for me is Purgatory . . . bound for enlightenment am I!"'

(x) *Brick Hall* (*c*).

On the same occasion . . .

Seated at one side the venerable Ānanda said this to the Exalted One:

'Lord, the lay-disciples named Kakudha,[1] Kāḷinga, Nikata, Kaṭissaha, Tuṭṭha, Santuṭṭha, Bhadda and Subhadda, have made an end at Ñātika. Pray, lord, what is their lot, what their destiny in the life to come?'

'The lay-disciple Kakudha, who has made an end, Ānanda,

[1] So at *D.* ii. Our text has *Kakkaṭo* and *v.l. Kakkuṭo*.

by destroying the five fetters of the lower sort, is reborn spontaneously (in the Pure Abodes), there to pass away, destined not to return thence. The lay-disciples Kāḷinga and the rest who have made an end . . . have done likewise.

More than[1] fifty lay-disciples, Ānanda, who have made an end at Ñātika . . . have done the same. More than[1] ninety lay-disciples, Ānanda, who have made an end at Ñātika, by destroying three fetters, and by weakening those of lust, hatred and delusion, are once-returners. Coming back to this world just once more they will make an end of Ill.

Five hundred and six[2] lay-disciples, Ānanda, who have made an end at Ñātika, by destroying three fetters, are stream-winners, not doomed to the Downfall, assured, bound for enlightenment.

It is no wonder, Ānanda, that a human being should make an end. But if, when each one dies, you come to me and ask about the matter, it is troublesome to the Tathāgata.

Wherefore, Ānanda, I will teach you a Norm-teaching called "The Mirror of the Norm," possessed of which the Ariyan disciple may, if he please, himself proclaim of himself: "Bound for enlightenment am I!"' (*as in* § 1).

CHAPTER II.—THOUSANDFOLD, OR ROYAL PARK

(i) *Thousand.*

On a certain occasion the Exalted One was staying near Sāvatthī in Royal Park.[3]

Now a company of a thousand nuns came to see the Exalted

---

[1] '*Paro-*, *sâdhika-*, =*atireka* (in excess).' *Comy.*

[2] Text *cha atirekāni pañcasatāni*. At *D.* ii *sâtirekāni*. *Comy.* has *cha hi adhikāni* ; S_3 *châdhikāni*. Evidently an unhealthy village, for *Comy.* says that 'owing to snake-wind-sickness (dysentery) 124,000 (?) had died at a single blow in that *village*, among whom were these disciples.'

[3] *Cf. JA.* ii, 15. It was made by the Rājah Pasenadi and the story is told by *Comy.*

One, and on coming to him saluted the Exalted One and stood at one side.[1] As they thus stood, the Exalted One said this to those nuns:

'Nuns, an Ariyan disciple who is blessed with four things is a stream-winner, not doomed to the Downfall, assured, bound for enlightenment. What are the four?

Herein, nuns, the Ariyan disciple is blessed with unwavering loyalty to the Buddha, thus: He it is, the Exalted One, Arahant . . . teacher of devas and men, a Buddha, an Exalted One.

He is blessed with unwavering loyalty to the Norm, thus: Well proclaimed by the Exalted One is the Norm . . .

He is blessed with unwavering loyalty to the Order . . . He is blessed with the virtues dear to the Ariyans, virtues unbroken . . . that lead to concentration of mind.

These, nuns, are the four things blessed with which the Ariyan disciple is a stream-winner. . . .'

(ii) *Brahmins.*

Sāvatthī was the occasion . . . The Exalted One said:

'Monks, the brahmins proclaim this practice which leads to prosperity: they instruct their disciples in it thus:

"Come, good fellow! Rise up betimes and go facing east. Don't avoid a hole,[2] a village pool or cess-pit. You should go to meet your death[3] wherever you may fall. Thus, good fellow, on the break up of body, after death you will be reborn in the Happy Lot, in the Heaven World."

But, monks, this practice of the brahmins is the way of fools, it is the way of infatuation. It conduces not to revulsion, to dispassion, to cessation, to calm, to full comprehension, to the wisdom, it conduces not to Nibbāna.

Now, monks, I too proclaim, in the Ariyan discipline, a practice which leads to prosperity, but it is one which con-

---

[1] It is noticeable that they do not sit down as the men do.

[2] Text has *semhaŋ* (spittle) for *v.l. sombhaŋ*, which evidently should be *sobbhaŋ*.

[3] *Comy.* takes this to mean *maraṇaŋ iccheyyāsi.*

duces to downright revulsion, dispassion, cessation to calm, to full comprehension, to the wisdom, to Nibbāna. And what sort of practice is that which so leads?

Herein, monks, the Ariyan disciple has unwavering loyalty to the Buddha . . . the Norm . . . the Order. He is blessed with the virtues dear to the Ariyans, virtues unbroken . . . which lead to concentration of mind. This, monks, is the practice which leads to downright revulsion . . . to Nibbāna.'

(iii) *Ānanda.*

Once the venerable Ānanda and Sāriputta were staying near Sāvatthī at Jeta Grove, in Anāthapiṇḍika's Park.

Now the venerable Sāriputta, rising from his solitude at eventide, went to visit the venerable Ānanda, and on coming to him greeted him courteously, and after the exchange of greetings and courtesies sat down at one side. As he thus sat the venerable Sāriputta said to the venerable Ānanda:

'Friend Ānanda, by abandoning what things, by winning possession of what things, are people of this world proclaimed by the Exalted One as stream-winners, as not doomed to the Downfall, as assured, as bound for enlightenment?

Friend, it is by abandoning four things, it is by winning possession of four things, that people of this world are thus proclaimed by the Exalted One. What are the four things?

One has no such disloyalty to the Buddha as that possessed by the uneducated manyfolk who, when body breaks up, after death are reborn in Hell, in the Woeful Lot, the Downfall, in Purgatory: but he has such unwavering loyalty to the Buddha as is possessed by the educated Ariyan disciple, who, when the body breaks up, after death is reborn in the Happy Lot, in the Heaven World.

One has no such disloyalty to the Norm . . . to the Order . . . as that possessed by the uneducated manyfolk who . . . are reborn . . . in Purgatory: but he has such unwavering loyalty to them as the Ariyan educated disciple possesses, who . . . is reborn . . . in the Heaven World.

He has no such immorality[1] as that possessed by the uneducated manyfolk who, when body breaks up, after death are reborn . . . in Purgatory: but he is blessed with the virtues dear to the Ariyans, virtues unbroken . . . which lead to concentration of mind . . . such as are possessed by the educated Ariyan disciple, who . . . is reborn . . . in the Heaven World.

Friend, it is by abandoning these four things and by winning possession of these (other) four things that the people of this world are proclaimed by the Exalted One as stream-winners, as not doomed to the Downfall, as assured, as bound for enlightenment.'

(iv) *The Woeful Way* (*a*).

Monks, the Ariyan disciple who is blessed with four things is one who has passed utterly beyond all fear of the Woeful Way.[2] What are the four ?

Herein the Ariyan disciple is blessed with unwavering loyalty to the Buddha . . . the Norm . . . the Order. He is blessed with the virtues dear to the Ariyans. . . . These are the four things . . .

(v) *The Woeful Way* (*b*).

Monks, the Ariyan disciple who is blessed with four things is one who has passed utterly beyond all fear of the Downfall . . . (*as above*).

(vi) *Intimate friends* (*a*).

Monks, those with whom you have sympathy, those who think you should listen to them, whether friends or intimates[3] or kinsmen[4] or blood-relations,—all such should be advised about, grounded in, established in four limbs of stream-winning. What four ?

They should be advised about, grounded in, established in

---

[1] Here text has wrongly *dussīlena hoti* (with *v.l. dussīlyam na*), but is right on text, 382.

[2] *Comy.=manussa-dobhaggaŋ paṭikhittaŋ.*

[3] *Amaccā. Comy.* 'those who take counsel or do business together.' At *DA.* 297, it=*piyasahāyakā*.

[4] *Comy. ñāṭī=sassu*, etc. (mother- and father-in-law).

unwavering loyalty to the Buddha . . . the Norm . . . the Order, and in the virtues dear to the Ariyans, virtues unbroken . . . which conduce to concentration of mind.

Monks, those with whom you have sympathy . . . should be established in these four limbs of stream-winning.

(vii) *Intimate friends* (*b*).

. . . (*As above down to*) . . . they should be established in unwavering loyalty to the Buddha, thus: He it is, the Exalted One . . . There may be change,[1] monks, in the four great elements of earth, water, heat and air, but there can be no change in the Ariyan disciple blessed with unwavering loyalty to the Buddha; by change I mean[2]:—that such an one should be reborn in hell or the womb of an animal or in the realm of ghosts is an utter impossibility.

So of unwavering loyalty to the Norm . . . to the Order. . . .

Then they should be advised about, grounded in, established in the virtues dear to the Ariyans. . . .

There may be change, monks, in the four great elements of earth, water, heat and air, but there can be no change in the Ariyan disciple blessed with the virtues dear to the Ariyans; herein by change I mean this:—that such an one should be reborn in hell, in the womb of an animal or in the realm of ghosts is an utter impossibility.

So, monks, those with whom you have sympathy, those who think you should listen to them, whether friends or intimates or kinsmen or blood-relations,—all such should be advised about, grounded in, established in these four limbs of stream-winning.

(viii) *Visiting the Devas* (*a*).

Sāvatthī was the occasion . . .

Now the venerable Moggallāna the Great, just as a strong man might stretch out his bent arm, or draw in his outstretched

---

[1] *Aññatthattaṃ*, of the elements, 'otherness' of condition or nature, as a result of change of consistency. *Cf. K.S.* iv. 39; *cf. Ang.* i, 152.

[2] 'Here,' says *Comy.*, 'there can be no change of destiny (*gati*) in such.'

arm,—even so did he vanish from Jeta Grove and appear among the Devas of the Thirty-Three.

Then a number of the Devas of the Thirty-Three came to see the venerable Moggallāna the Great, and on coming to him saluted him and stood at one side.[1] As they thus stood the venerable Moggallāna the Great said this to those Devas:

'It is a good thing, friends, to be blessed with unwavering loyalty to the Buddha . . . the Norm . . . the Order. As a result of being blessed with unwavering loyalty to the Buddha . . . the Norm . . . and the Order, some beings here,[2] when body breaks up, after death are reborn in the Happy Lot, in the Heaven World.

A good thing it is, friends, to be blessed with the virtues dear to the Ariyans, virtues unbroken . . . that lead to concentration of mind. As a result of being blessed with these, some beings here are reborn in the Happy Lot, in the Heaven World.'

'It is indeed a good thing, most worthy sir,—this winning of unwavering loyalty to the Buddha, the Norm and the Order . . . and of the virtues dear to the Ariyans. True it is that as a result of this some beings of the world are reborn in the Heaven World.'

(ix) *Visiting the Devas* (*b*).

On a certain occasion the venerable Moggallāna the Great was staying near Sāvatthī, at Jeta Grove, in Anāthapiṇḍika's Park.

Then the venerable Moggallāna the Great, just as a strong man . . . (*as before*). . . .

'It is indeed a good thing, most worthy sir . . . as a result of this, some beings of the world are reborn in the Heaven World.'

(x) *Visiting the Devas* (*c*).

Then the Exalted One, just as a strong man . . . (*as before*). . .

---

[1] Devas apparently do not sit down.

[2] *Idha*, apparently Moggallāna forgets that he is already in the next world; *idha* being generally used of 'this world.'

CHAPTER III.—SARAKĀNI[1]

(i) *Mahānāma* (*a*).

Thus have I heard: On a certain occasion the Exalted One was staying among the Sakyans near Kapilavatthu, in the Banyan Park.

Now Mahānāma[2] the Sakyan came to see the Exalted One, and on coming to him saluted him and sat down at one side. As he thus sat Mahānāma the Sakyan said this to the Exalted One:

'Lord, this town of Kapilavatthu is rich, prosperous, populous, crowded with men,[3] a dense mass of folk.[4] Now, lord, when I enter Kapilavatthu at eventide after waiting upon the Exalted One or the worshipful monks, I meet with elephants, horses, chariots, carts and men, all swaying and rolling along.[5] At such times, lord, my thoughts, which are fixed on the Exalted One, on the Norm and the Order, are simply bewildered. Then it occurs to me: If I were at this very moment to make an end, what would be my lot, what would be my destiny in the life to come?'

'Have no fears, Mahānāma! Have no fears, Mahānāma! Blameless will be your death. You will make a blameless end. For he whose mind, Mahānāma, has for a long time been practised in faith, in virtue, in learning, in giving up and insight,—though this material body of his, of the four elements compounded, from parents sprung, of a nature to be worn away, pounded away, broken and scattered,[6] though this body be devoured by crows and vultures, devoured by

---

[1] Or *Saraṇāni* (text), the name of a Sakyan, gives the title to this chapter and § 4.

[2] For Mahānāma, *cf.* text, 327, 371, etc.

[3] For these phrases, *cf. D.* i, 211; *S.* ii, 106; *Mil. Pañh.*, 130.

[4] *Sambādha-byūhaŋ. Comy. anibbiddha-racchāyo sā paviṭṭha-maggen' eva nigacchati.*

[5] *Bhantena* (fr. *bhamati*); text misprints in each case *bhante na* (as if it were 'lord, not').

[6] *Cf. K.S.* iv, 50 *n.*

kites and dogs,—yet his mind, if longtime practised in faith, virtue, learning, giving up and insight, the mind soars aloft, the mind wins the summit.[1]

Suppose, Mahānāma, a man plunges a jar of butter or a jar of oil into a deep, deep pool of water,[2] and breaks it, and it becomes sherds or fragments, and sinks down to the bottom; but the butter or oil that is in it floats up and reaches the surface,—just so, Mahānāma, if the mind has long been practised in faith . . . though all this material body of his . . . be devoured by all manner of creatures, yet the mind soars up aloft, the mind wins the summit.

Now your mind, Mahānāma, has long been practised in faith, virtue, learning, giving up and insight. Have no fear, Mahānāma! Have no fear, Mahānāma! Blameless will be your death. You will make an end that is blameless.'

(ii) *Mahānāma (b)*.

Thus have I heard: (*as before down to*) . . .

'Have no fear, Mahānāma! You will make a blameless end. For the Ariyan disciple, Mahānāma, who is blessed with four things, bends to Nibbāna, slopes to Nibbāna, tends to Nibbāna. What are the four things?

Herein, Mahānāma, the Ariyan disciple is blessed with unwavering loyalty to the Buddha . . . to the Norm . . . to the Order. He is blessed with the virtues dear to the Ariyans . . . virtues unbroken, which conduce to concentration of mind.

For instance, Mahānāma, if a tree bends to the east, slopes to the east, tends to the east, which way will it fall when its root is cut?'

'It will fall whither it bends, slopes and tends, lord.'

'Just so, Mahānāma, the Ariyan disciple who is blessed with four things bends to Nibbāna, slopes to Nibbāna, tends to Nibbāna.'

---

[1] *Uddhaŋgāmī, visesa-gāmī.*

[2] *Cf.* the same simile at *K.S.* iv, 313.

(iii) *Godha* or *Mahānāma* (*c*).

Kapilavatthu was the occasion . . .

Now Mahānāma the Sakyan came to see Godha[1] the Sakyan, and on coming to him said this:

'Godha, so far as you know, blessed with how many things is a stream-winner (declared) one not doomed to the Downfall, assured, bound for enlightenment?'

'I know, Mahānāma, that he is blessed with three things. What are they?

Herein, Mahānāma, the Ariyan disciple has unwavering loyalty to the Buddha, the Norm and the Order. Blessed with these three things, Mahānāma, the stream-winner is (declared) one not doomed to the Downfall, assured, bound for enlightenment.

But as far as you know, Mahānāma, blessed with how many things is a stream-winner (declared) . . . bound for enlightenment?'

'For my part, Godha, I know[2] that he is blessed with four things . . .

Herein, Godha, the Ariyan disciple is blessed with unwavering loyalty to the Buddha, the Norm and the Order, and he is also blessed with the virtues dear to the Ariyans, virtues unbroken . . . that conduce to concentration of mind. These are the four things, Godha, blessed with which I know that a stream-winner . . . is bound for enlightenment.'

'Wait a bit, Mahānāma! Wait a bit, Mahānāma! The Exalted One will know about this, whether one is blessed with these four things or not. Let us go to see the Exalted One and ask him about it.'

So Mahānāma and Godha the Sakyans went to see the Exalted One . . . and sat down at one side. Then Mahānāma the Sakyan said this to the Exalted One: (*and he repeated the whole of the previous conversation*). . . .

---

[1] The Godhan is not met with elsewhere, but a woman of this family (Sākiyāṇī-G.) appears at text, 396. *Cf. Brethren,* 315 *n.*

[2] Mahānāma, as stated at text, 327, was himself a stream-winner.

'Now suppose, lord, some question of doctrine arises,[1] and on one side is the Exalted One and on the other side is the Order of monks, I myself should be on the side of the Exalted One. Let my lord the Exalted One accept this (as proof of) my loyalty to him.[2]

Again suppose, lord, some question of doctrine arises, and on one side is the Exalted One, and on the other side is the Order of monks, together with the Order of nuns,—I myself should be on the Exalted One's side. So again, lord, if on the one side were the Exalted one, on the other side the Order, both of monks and nuns, together with the male lay-followers, —I myself should side with the Exalted One . . . or if again on the other side were the Order, both of monks and nuns, and the lay-followers, both male and female . . . if added to these were the whole world, with its Devas, its Māras and its Brahmās, its host of recluses and brahmins, both of devas and mankind,—still, lord, I should side with the Exalted One. Let my lord the Exalted One accept this (as proof of) my loyalty to him.'

(Then said the Exalted One, turning to Godha):

'What say you, Godha, in reply to Mahānāma who holds such a view?'

'Lord, of Mahānāma, who holds such a view,[3] I have naught to say save what is lovely and good.'[4]

(iv) *Sarakāni* or *Saraṇāni* (*a*).

Kapilavatthu was the occasion . . .

Now at that time Sarakāni the Sakyan, who had made an end, was proclaimed by the Exalted One a stream-winner, not doomed to the Downfall, assured, one bound for enlightenment.

Thereupon a number of Sakyans, whenever they met

---

1 *Dhamma-samuppādo.* 2 *Pasannaŋ.*

3 Text should read *evamvādim ahaŋ.*

4 *Aññatra kalyāṇā aññatra kusalā.* The phrase occurs at *S.* ii, 118. *Comy.* 'Ignorance is just a bad thing. It is not relieved by what is lovely and good. But all the same he is not to blame.'

together in company, were consumed with indignation, and spoke angrily and scornfully[1] about him thus:

'A strange thing indeed! A wonder indeed! Nowadays anyone may become a stream-winner,[2] inasmuch as Sarakāni the Sakyan, who has died, is proclaimed by the Exalted One a stream-winner . . . one bound for enlightenment. Why! Sarakāni the Sakyan failed in the training and took to drink!'

Now Mahānāma the Sakyan went to see the Exalted One, and on coming to him saluted him and sat down at one side. As he thus sat Mahānāma the Sakyan said this to the Exalted One:

'Here, lord, Sarakāni the Sakyan, who has died, was proclaimed a stream-winner . . . by the Exalted One. Thereupon a number of Sakyans, whenever they meet together in company, are consumed with indignation: they speak angrily and scornfully about him, thus: "A strange thing indeed! . . . Why Sarakāni the Sakyan failed in the training and took to drink!"'

'Mahānāma, a lay-disciple who has for a long time taken refuge in the Buddha, the Norm and the Order,—how could such an one go to the Downfall? He who would rightly apply the words "A lay-disciple who has gone for refuge to the Buddha, the Norm and the Order" might rightly apply them to Sarakāni the Sakyan. Mahānāma, Sarakāni the Sakyan is one who did so. How could such an one go to the Downfall?

Now herein, Mahānāma, take the case of a man who is blessed with unwavering loyalty to the Buddha, thus: He it is, the Exalted One . . . teacher of devas and mankind . . . He is blessed with unwavering loyalty to the Norm . . . and to the Order. Moreover he is one who is joyous and swift in wisdom,[3] one who has won release. Now by the destruction

---

1 *Ujjhāyanti, khīyanti, vipācenti. Ujjhāyantī ti=avajjhāyanti, lāmakato cintenti; khīyantī ti=kathenti, pakāsenti* ('point at'; not in *Pāli Dict.* in this meaning). See examples in Childers and *S.* i, 232, on which I quote *Comy. Vipācentī ti=tattha tattha kathenti, vitthārenti.*

2 *Ettha dāni ko na bhavissati.*

3 For *hāsupañña* and *javana-pañña, cf. K.S.* i, 88 *n.*; *M.* iii, 25; *JA.* iv, 136; *infra*, text, 412.

of the āsavas, in this very life, by his own understanding he has realized the heart's release, the release by insight, and having attained it dwells therein. Such an one, Mahānāma, is fully released from hell, from rebirth in the womb of an animal's womb, from the realm of ghosts, he is fully released from the Waste, the Woeful Way, from the Downfall.

But suppose again in this connexion, Mahānāma, a certain one who is blessed with unwavering loyalty to the Buddha, to the Norm and to the Order. He is joyous and swift in wisdom, but he has not won release. Yet by destroying the five fetters of the lower sort he is spontaneously born (in the Pure Abodes), destined there to pass away, not to return hither from thence. This one too, Mahānāma, is fully released from . . . the Downfall.

Again in this connexion, Mahānāma, suppose one who is blessed with unwavering loyalty to the Buddha, to the Norm and to the Order, but he is not joyous and swift in wisdom, he has not won release. Yet by destroying three fetters and weakening lust, hatred and delusion he is a Once-returner. Once more he comes back to this world and makes an end of Ill. He too, Mahānāma, is fully released from the Waste . . . from the Downfall.

Again, Mahānāma, suppose a certain man blessed with unwavering loyalty to the Buddha, to the Norm and to the Order: but he is neither joyous and swift in wisdom, nor has he won release: but by destroying three fetters he is a Stream-winner, he is not doomed to the Downfall, he is assured, bound for enlightenment. This man, Mahānāma, is fully released from Hell, from rebirth in an animal's womb, from the Waste, from the Woeful Way, from the Downfall.

Again, Mahānāma, suppose a certain one who is not even blessed with unwavering loyalty to the Buddha, to the Norm and to the Order. He is not joyous and swift in wisdom, he has not won release. But maybe he has these things,—the controlling factor of faith, that of energy, mindfulness, concentration and the controlling faculty of insight: and the things proclaimed by the Tathāgata are moderately approved[1] by him by insight. Even this man, Mahānāma, is one who goes not to Hell, goes not to the womb of an animal, goes not to the realm of ghosts, he goes not to the Waste, the Woeful Way, to the Downfall.

Once more in this matter, Mahānāma, suppose a certain one who has (none of the first named possessions, but he has) just these things,—the controlling faculty of faith . . . and that of insight: yet if he have merely faith, merely affection for the Tathāgata,[2] he is one who goes not to Hell . . . goes not to the Downfall.

Why, Mahānāma, if these great sāl trees here[3] could know what is spoken well and what is spoken ill, I would proclaim even these great trees to be Stream-winners . . . bound for enlightenment. Much more then[4] do I proclaim Sarakāni the Sakyan to be one. Mahānāma, Sarakāni the Sakyan fulfilled the (threefold) training at his death.'[5]

(v) *Sarakāni* or *Saraṇāni* (*b*).

Kapilavatthu was the occasion . . .

Now on that occasion Sarakāni the Sakyan, who had made an end, was proclaimed a Stream-winner . . . bound for enlightenment.

Thereupon a number of Sakyans, whenever they met together in company, were consumed with indignation, and spoke angrily and scornfully about him saying: 'A strange thing indeed! A wonder indeed! Nowadays anyone may become a Stream-winner, inasmuch as Sarakāni the Sakyan . . . is so proclaimed by the Exalted One. Why, Sarakāni was one who failed to complete the training!'

---

[1] *Mattaso nijjhānaŋ khamanti. Cf. K.S.* iii, 177 *n.*, where *Comy.* says *pamānaso olokanaŋ khamanti;* but here says, *pamānena ca ol. kh. Iminā dhammânusārī-maggattha-puggalaŋ dasseti. Mattaso,* abl. of *mattā.*

[2] *Cf.* Majjhima i, 142.

[3] 'Here he pointed to four great sāl trees standing near.' *Comy.*

[4] *Kimanga pana. Cf. S.* iii, 268; *MP.* 27.

[5] *Sikkhaŋ samādiyī=tīsu sikkhāsu paripūrakārī ahosi. Comy.* (The three are *adhisīla, adhicitta, adhipaññā,* 'the higher morals, mind and wisdom'; *cf. K.S.* iii, 69: A. i. 231 *ff.*)

Now Mahānāma the Sakyan went to see the Exalted One . . . and said this:

'Here, lord, Sarakāni the Sakyan, who has made an end, was proclaimed a Stream-winner by the Exalted One . . .' (*and he repeated the abuse of the others as in previous Sutta*). . . .

'Mahānāma, a lay-disciple who has for long taken refuge in the Buddha, the Norm and the Order,—how could such an one go to the Downfall?

He who would rightly use the words "a lay-disciple who has for long gone to refuge in the Buddha, the Norm and the Order" would rightly apply them to Sarakāni the Sakyan. Mahānāma, Sarakāni the Sakyan is one who did so. How could such an one go to the Downfall?

Now herein, Mahānāma, take the case of a certain one who has reached absolute loyalty to the Buddha . . . the Norm . . . the Order. Such an one is fully released from the Waste, the Woeful Way, from the Downfall.

Again, Mahānāma, take the case of a certain one who has reached absolute loyalty to the Buddha, the Norm and the Order. He is joyous and swift in wisdom and has won release. By destroying the five fetters of the lower sort he wins release midway[1] or by reduction of his time, or else with little trouble, or else with some trouble, or he is one who goes up stream and goes to the Pure Abodes. Such an one, Mahānāma, is fully released from the Waste, the Woeful Way, from the Downfall.

Again, Mahānāma, in this connexion take the case of a certain one who has reached absolute loyalty to the Buddha, the Norm and the Order: but he is not joyous and swift in wisdom, he has not won release. Yet by destroying three fetters and by weakening lust, hatred and delusion he is a Once-returner. He comes back once more to this world and makes an end of Ill. This one also, Mahānāma, is fully released from the Waste, the Woeful Way, the Downfall.

Again in this connexion, Mahānāma, a certain one has reached absolute loyalty to the Buddha, the Norm and the Order: but he is neither joyous and swift in wisdom, nor has he

---

[1] Text, 285, etc.

won release. Yet by destroying three fetters he is a Stream-winner . . . bound for enlightenment. This one also, Mahānāma, is fully released . . . from the Downfall.

Herein again, Mahānāma, take the case of one who has not reached absolute loyalty to the Buddha, the Norm and the Order. He is neither joyous and swift in wisdom, nor has he won release: but he is blessed with the controlling faculty of faith, energy, mindfulness, concentration and insight. Also the things proclaimed by the Tathāgata are moderately approved by him with insight. Even this one, Mahānāma, is one who goes not . . . to the Downfall.

Once again, Mahānāma, take the case of a certain one who has neither reached absolute loyalty to the Buddha, the Norm and the Order, nor is joyous and swift in wisdom, nor has won release: but he has just these conditions, the faculty of faith . . . and insight: moreover he has merely faith in, merely affection for the Tathāgata. He also, Mahānāma, is one who goes not to the Downfall.

Suppose now, Mahānāma, a bad field,[1] a bad piece of land, not yet stubbed, and the seeds (to be sown) are broken, rotten, spoiled[2] by wind and heat; incapable of sprouting,[3] badly planted,[4] and the sky-god supplies no suitable rain.[5] Would those seeds come to growth, increase, abundance ?'

'Surely not, lord.'

'Just so, Mahānāma, in this connexion, when the Norm is wrongly preached, ill expounded, leads to no profit, does not conduce to tranquillity, and is not expounded by a Fully Enlightened One, I declare it like unto a bad field. The disciple who lives according to that Norm and walks in accordance therewith, who walks obedient thereto, who practises its precepts,—such I declare to be like that bad seed.

But suppose, Mahānāma, a good field, a good piece of land,

---

[1] *Cf.* the simile at *S.* iii, 54 (*K.S.* iii, 46).

[2] Text has *-hatam* for *hatāni.*

[3] I read *sāradāni* for text's *sārāni,* according to Sinh. MSS. [as at *S.* ii, *loc. cit.*, where see note].

[4] *Comy.* 'ill and irregularly set and wrongly cultivated.'

[5] *Sammādhāraŋ,* not as in *Dict.*, a 'heavy' shower.

well stubbed, and the seeds sown therein are unbroken, not rotten, unspoiled by wind and heat, capable of sprouting, happily planted, and the sky-god supplies a constant rain,—would those seeds come to growth, increase, abundance ?'

'Surely they would, lord.'

'Well, just so, Mahānāma, here the Norm is rightly preached, well expounded, it leads to profit, it conduces to tranquillity, it is expounded by a Fully Enlightened One. I declare it to be like unto a good field. The disciple who lives according to this Norm, who walks in accordance therewith, who walks obedient thereto, who practises its precepts,—such I declare to be the good seed. Much more then do I declare that Sarakāni the Sakyan is such an one. Mahānāma, Sarakāni the Sakyan at the time of his death was one who fulfilled the training to perfection.'

(vi) *Immoral* or *Anāthapiṇḍika* (*a*).

Sāvatthī was the occasion . . .

Now at that time the housefather Anāthapiṇḍika was sick, afflicted, suffering from a sore disease.

Then the housefather Anāthapiṇḍika called to a certain man, saying: 'Come hither, good fellow! Go you to the venerable Sāriputta, and on coming to him worship in my name with your head at the feet of the venerable Sāriputta and say: "Sir, the housefather Anāthapiṇḍika is sick, afflicted, suffering from a sore disease." Then say: "It were well, sir, if the venerable Sāriputta would come to the house of the housefather Anāthapiṇḍika, out of compassion for him."'

'Very well, master,' replied that man (*and did as he was bidden*). . . . Seated at one side he said this to the venerable Sāriputta:

'Sir, the housefather Anāthapiṇḍika is sick . . . he says it were well if the venerable Sāriputta would come to his house, out of compassion for him.'

And the venerable Sāriputta consented by silence.

So the venerable Sāriputta, robing himself in the forenoon and taking bowl and outer robe, set off for the dwelling of the housefather Anāthapiṇḍika, with the venerable Ānanda following behind, and on reaching it sat down on a seat made ready. Having sat down he said this to the housefather Anāthapiṇḍika:

'Well, housefather! Are you bearing up? Are you enduring? Do your pains abate and not increase? Is there any sign of their abating and not increasing?'

'No, sir, I am not enduring. I am not bearing up. Strong pains come upon me. They do not abate. There is no sign of their abating but of their increasing.'

'Well, housefather! You have no such disloyalty to the Buddha as the uneducated manyfolk possess, who on the break up of body, after death are reborn in the Waste, the Woeful Way, the Downfall, in Hell, but you have unwavering loyalty to the Buddha, thus: He it is, the Exalted One, Arahant . . . Teacher of Devas and mankind, a Buddha, an Exalted One. If you were to bethink you of your unwavering loyalty to the Buddha, in a moment[1] your pains would be allayed.

Housefather, you have no such disloyalty to the Norm as the uneducated manyfolk possess, who . . . after death . . . are reborn . . . in Hell. But you have unwavering loyalty to the Norm, thus: Well proclaimed by the Exalted One is the Norm . . . to be understood by the wise, each for himself. If you were to bethink you of your unwavering loyalty to the Norm, in a moment your pains would be allayed.

Housefather, you have no such disloyalty to the Order as the uneducated manyfolk possess, who after death . . . are reborn . . . in Hell. But you have unwavering loyalty to the Order, thus: Walking uprightly is the Exalted One's Order of Disciples . . . a field of merit unsurpassed for the world. If you were to bethink you of your unwavering loyalty to the Order, in a moment your pains would be allayed.

You, housefather, are not possessed of immorality such as the uneducated manyfolk possess, who . . . after death are reborn . . . in Hell. But in you are the virtues dear to the Ariyans, virtues unbroken . . . which conduce to concentration of mind. If you were to bethink you of those virtues which are in you, in a moment your pains would be allayed.

---

[1] *Ṭhānaso=khaṇen' eva. Comy.*

You, housefather, have not wrong view . . . wrong aim . . . wrong speech . . . wrong action . . . wrong way of living . . . wrong effort . . . wrong mindfulness . . . wrong concentration, such as are possessed by the uneducated manyfolk, who after death when body breaks up are reborn in Hell: but you have right view . . . right concentration, housefather. If you were to bethink you of your right view. . . your right concentration, in a moment your pains would be allayed.

Housefather, you have not wrong knowledge, wrong release, such as are possessed by the uneducated manyfolk, who are . . . reborn in Hell: but you have right knowledge, right release. If you were to bethink you of your right knowledge, your right release, in a moment your pains would be allayed.'

Thereat in a moment the pains of the housefather Anāthapiṇḍika were allayed.

So the housefather Anāthapiṇḍika served the venerable Sāriputta and Ānanda [with a meal] from his own cooking-pot.

And when the venerable Sāriputta had eaten his fill and withdrawn his hand from his bowl, the housefather Anāthapiṇḍika went to him, took a low seat and sat down at one side. As he thus sat, the venerable Sāriputta thanked the housefather Anāthapiṇḍika with these verses:[1]

> Whoso hath faith in the Tathāgata
> Unwavering and fixed, whose life is good,
> Praised by the Ariyans and dear to them;
> Whoso is likewise loyal to the Order,
> And looks straight forth—' he is not poor ' they say,
> ' Not lived in vain the life of such a man.'
> Wherefore the wise should cultivate (these three)
> Faith, virtue and clear-seeing of the Norm,
> Bearing the Buddha's message in his mind.

Now when the venerable Sāriputta had thanked the housefather Anāthapiṇḍika with these verses, he rose up from his seat and went away.

Then the venerable Ānanda went to see the Exalted One,

[1] The verses occur at *S*. i, 232; *A*. ii, 57, iii, 54; *infra*, text, 405.

and on coming to him saluted him and sat down at one side. So seated, the Exalted One said this to the venerable Ānanda:

'Why, Ānanda, how is it that you come here at this hour?'[1]

'Lord, the venerable Sāriputta has been admonishing the housefather Anāthapiṇḍika (*and he related the incident*)[2] in such and such a way: . . .'

'Sāriputta is a sage, Ānanda. Sāriputta is of great wisdom, Ānanda, as indeed he must be who can divide up the four limbs of stream-winning in ten ways.'[3]

(vii) *Immoral* or *Anāthapiṇḍika* (*b*).

Sāvatthī was the occasion . . .

(*The same as before with Ānanda as admonisher, down to*): '. . . There is no sign of their abating.'

'Housefather, terror and trembling and fear of death, as to what may be hereafter,—these come upon the uneducated manyfolk who have four qualities. What four?

Herein, housefather, the uneducated manyfolk have disloyalty. When they bethink them of their disloyalty to the Buddha, terror and trembling and fear of death, as to what may be hereafter, come upon them.

Again, housefather, the uneducated manyfolk have disloyalty to the Norm . . . to the Order. They have immorality, and when they bethink them of these things, terror and trembling and fear of death, as to what may be hereafter, come upon them. These, housefather, are the four things, possessed of which, terror and trembling . . . come upon the uneducated manyfolk.

But, housefather, the educated Ariyan disciple, possessing four qualities, has no such terror and trembling and fear of death, as to what may be hereafter.

---

[1] *Divādivassa.* It would now be about midday. But visits were to be made in the afternoon. *Cf.* however Jāt. No. 151.

[2] Presumably, for text omits to repeat them in full, which is rare.

[3] *Das' ākārehi.* Here the four limbs are supported by the ten points (the eightfold way, with knowledge and release).

Herein, housefather, the educated Ariyan disciple is blessed with unwavering loyalty to the Buddha . . . to the Norm and to the Order. He is blessed with the virtues dear to the Ariyans, virtues unbroken . . . which conduce to concentration of mind. When he bethinks him of these virtues dear to the Ariyans which he is blessed with, no terror, no trembling, no fear of death, as to what may be hereafter, comes upon him. These are his four possessions, housefather.'

'I am not afraid, master Ānanda! How could I be afraid? I have unwavering loyalty to the Buddha, the Norm and the Order. Moreover, master Ānanda, as to those obligations binding on a housefather,[1] pointed out by the Exalted One, I see not a single one of them which is broken in me.'

'Well for you, housefather! Well gotten by you! You have declared the fruits of stream-winning, housefather.'

(viii) *Guilty dread* or *Anāthapiṇḍika* (*c*).

Sāvatthī was the occasion . . .

Then the housefather Anāthapiṇḍika went to see the Exalted One, and on coming to him saluted him and sat down at one side. As he thus sat, the Exalted One said this to the housefather Anāthapiṇḍika:

'Housefather, when the fivefold guilty dread[2] is allayed in the Ariyan disciple and he is possessed of the four limbs of stream-winning, and has well seen and well penetrated the Ariyan Method[3] by insight, he, if he so desire, may himself proclaim thus of himself: "I am one who has cut off the doom of Hell, of rebirth in an animal's womb, in the Realm of Ghosts; cut off is the Waste, the Woeful Way, the Downfall; a Stream-winner am I, one not doomed to the Downfall, assured, bound for enlightenment!" Now, housefather, what is the fivefold guilty dread that is allayed in him?

It is that guilty dread, housefather, which he who kills begets in this very life, as a result of his killing: it is that guilty dread

---

[1] *Gihi-sāmīcikāni* (*sikkhāpadāni*)=*gihi-anucchavikāni*. *Comy.*

[2] *Cf. S.* ii, 68; iv, 343; *Vibh.* 378.

[3] *Ñāya*. *Cf. Dialog.* ii, 327 *n.*

about the future life, which he who kills begets: that feeling of painful dejection felt by him, that guilty dread, is allayed in him who abstains from killing.

That same guilty dread, housefather, both as a result of stealing, of wrong practice in sensual lust, of falsehood,—that same guilty dread begotten in this very life by one who is addicted to the negligence caused by liquor and intoxicants and resulting from such practice,—that guilty dread about the future life, that feeling of painful dejection felt by him,—that guilty dread is allayed in him who abstains from the negligence caused by liquor and intoxicants.

This, housefather, is the guilty dread that is allayed in him.

And with what four limbs of stream-winning is he blessed?

Herein, housefather, the Ariyan disciple is blessed with unwavering loyalty to the Buddha, the Norm and the Order, and he has the virtues dear to the Ariyans, virtues unbroken . . . which conduce to concentration of mind. These are the four limbs of stream-winning with which he is blessed.

And what, housefather, is the Ariyan Method which he has well seen and well penetrated by insight?

Herein, housefather, the Ariyan disciple well and thoroughly attends to the arising-by-way-of-cause, thus: This being, that is. By the arising of this, that arises. This not being, that is not. By the ceasing of this, that ceases. Thus conditioned by ignorance, activities come to pass.[1] (Conditioned by the activities, consciousness: conditioned by consciousness, name-and-shape: conditioned by name-and-shape, sense: conditioned by sense, contact: conditioned by contact, feeling: conditioned by feeling, craving: conditioned by craving, grasping: conditioned by grasping, becoming: conditioned by becoming, birth: conditioned by birth, old age and death, grief, lamentation, suffering, sorrow and despair come to pass.) Such is the arising of this whole mass of Ill.

But from the utter fading and ceasing of ignorance comes the ceasing of activities: (from ceasing of activities, ceasing of consciousness: from ceasing of consciousness, ceasing of name-

[1] *Cf. K.S.* ii, 2 *ff.*

and-shape: from ceasing of name-and-shape, ceasing of sense: from ceasing of sense, ceasing of contact: from ceasing of contact, ceasing of feeling: from ceasing of feeling, ceasing of craving: from ceasing of craving, ceasing of grasping: from ceasing of grasping, ceasing of becoming: from ceasing of becoming, ceasing of birth: from ceasing of birth, ceasing of old age and death, grief, lamentation, suffering, sorrow and despair cease). Such is the ceasing of this whole mass of Ill.

This is the Ariyan Method which he has well seen and well penetrated.

Now, housefather, since in the Ariyan disciple this fivefold guilty dread is allayed, since he is blessed with these four limbs of stream-winning, and has well seen and well penetrated this Ariyan Method, he, if he so desire, may himself proclaim of himself thus: " I am one who has cut off the doom of Hell, of rebirth in the womb of an animal, in the Realm of Ghosts, the Waste, the Woeful Way, the Downfall. Stream-winner am I, not doomed to the Downfall, assured, bound for enlightenment!" '

(ix) *Fear* or *The Monk.*

Sāvatthī was the occasion . . .

Then a number of monks came to see the Exalted One, and on coming to him saluted him and sat down at one side. So seated the Exalted one said this to those monks:

(*The whole as before.*)

(x) *Licchavī* or *Nandaka.*

On a certain occasion the Exalted One was staying at Vesālī, in Great Grove, at the House of the Peaked Gable.

Then Nandaka, minister of the Licchavī, came to see the Exalted One, and on coming to him saluted him and sat down at one side. As he thus sat, the Exalted One said this to Nandaka:

' Nandaka, possessed of four things the Ariyan disciple is a Stream-winner, not doomed to the Downfall, assured, bound for enlightenment. What are the four?

Herein, Nandaka, the Ariyan disciple is blessed with unwavernig loyalty to the Buddha, the Norm and the Order, and with the virtues dear to the Ariyans, virtues unbroken . . . which conduce to concentration of mind.

Blessed with these four things the Ariyan disciple is also blessed with long life, both heavenly and human, blessed with beauty, blessed with happiness, blessed with good name, and blessed with sovereignty, both heavenly and human.[1] This, Nandaka, I know, not from hearsay of any recluse or brahmin, but I have ascertained it for myself, seen it for myself, understood it for myself, and so do I tell it you.'

Just then someone came up to Nandaka, the minister of the Licchavī, and said to him:

'It is time for your bath, my lord.'

'Enough of that, good fellow!' said Nandaka. 'Enough of this outward washing! This inner washing shall be enough for me, to wit: this loyalty to the Exalted One.'

CHAPTER IV.—FLOOD OF MERIT

(i) *Flood*[2] (*a*).

Sāvatthī was the occasion . . . The Exalted One said:

'Monks, there are these four floods of merit, floods of good things, that bring happiness. What are the four?

Herein, monks, the Ariyan disciple has unwavering loyalty to the Buddha . . . This is the first flood of merit, of good things, bringing happiness.

Again, monks, he has unwavering loyalty to the Norm. . . . This is the second flood of merit, of good things, bringing happiness.

Again, monks, he has unwavering loyalty to the Order. . . . This is the third.

Lastly, monks, the Ariyan disciple possesses the virtues dear to the Ariyans, virtues unbroken . . . which conduce to concentration of mind. This is the fourth flood.

---

[1] *Cf. Dhp.* 109 (*ayu, vaṇṇa, sukhaŋ, balaŋ*). Here and at *S.* iv, 275, we should read *ādhipateyya* for *adhi-*.

[2] *Abhisanda. Cf. A.* ii, 54. *Comy. puñña-nadiyo.*

These, monks, are the four floods of merit, floods of good things, that bring happiness.

(ii) *Flood* (*b*).

Monks, there are these four floods of merit . . . (*as before for the three*).

Then again, monks, the Ariyan disciple lives at home with heart free from the taint of stinginess.[1] He is open-handed, pure-handed, delighting in self-surrender, one to ask a favour of, delighting to share charitable gifts. This, monks, is the fourth flood of merit. . . . These are the four floods of merit . . . that bring happiness.

(iii) *Flood* (*c*).

Monks, there are these four floods of merit . . . (*as before for the three*).

Then again he is a sage, possessed of insight into the rise and fall of things, insight which is Ariyan, penetrating, going on to the utter destruction of Ill.[2] This is the fourth flood of merit . . . and these are the four floods of merit, floods of good things, that bring happiness.'

(iv) *The path to the Devas* (*a*).

Sāvatthī was the occasion . . . The Exalted One said:

'Monks, there are these four deva-paths to the Devas,[3] for the purification of impure beings, for the cleansing of foul beings. What four?

Herein the Ariyan disciple has unwavering loyalty to the Buddha. . . . That is the first path.

Then he has unwavering loyalty to the Norm. . . . That is the second path. Also he has unwavering loyalty to the Order. That is the third path. Moreover he is blessed with

---

[1] *Cf.* te..t, 351.

[2] *Cf.* text, 197.

[3] *Devapadaŋ* (explained in next Sutta), either 'path to heaven' or 'path trodden by heaven-farers.' Here *Comy. devānaŋ ñāṇena, deve vā ñāṇena akkantapadāni,* adding 'persons who have these four fruits are reborn as *devatā*.'

the virtues dear to the Ariyans . . . that is the fourth deva-path to the Devas, for the purification of impure beings, for the cleansing of foul beings.

(v) *The path to the Devas* (*b*).

(*As before.*) . . . He has unwavering loyalty to the Buddha. . . .

(vi) *Joined the company.*[1]

Monks, the devas are glad to talk to one who is blessed with four things. What four?

Herein, monks, the Ariyan disciple is blessed with unwavering loyalty to the Buddha . . . the Norm . . . the Order. Now those devas[2] who, being likewise blessed with unwavering loyalty, have deceased here and risen up there, think thus: The Ariyan disciple is blessed with just the same unwavering loyalty to the Buddha as ourselves, who deceased there and rose up here. So they say to him: " Come hither into the company of the devas."

And it is the same with regard to unwavering loyalty to the Norm and to the Order.

Then one is blessed with the virtues dear to the Ariyans, virtues unbroken . . . that conduce to concentration of mind. Those devas who also are so blessed, who have deceased here and risen up there, think thus: The Ariyan disciple is blessed with the same virtues dear to the Ariyans as ourselves, who have deceased there and risen up here. And they say to him: " Come hither into the company of the devas."

'Monks, the devas are glad to talk to one who is blessed with these four things.'

(vii) *Mahānāma.*

On a certain occasion the Exalted One was staying near Kapilavatthu in Banyan Park.

Now Mahānāma the Sakyan went to see the Exalted One . . . and said this:

'Pray, lord, how far is one a disciple?'

---

[1] *Sabhāgataŋ* (like *parisa*-gato, and *explebo numerum* of Virgil, *Aen.* vi, 545; and *deva-nagaraŋ* or *deva-puraŋ* or *sagga-padaŋ puresi*).

[2] *Devatā,* here one who has died and gone to *Devaloka.*

'By going for refuge to the Buddha, Mahānāma, to the Norm and to the Order, one is a disciple.'

'But, lord, how far is a disciple virtuous?'

'From the time when a disciple abstains from killing, from stealing, from wrong conduct in sensual lusts, from falsehood and from addiction to the neglect caused by intoxicants,—thus far, Mahānāma, a disciple is virtuous.'

'But, lord, how far is a disciple a believer?'

'Herein, Mahānāma, a disciple believes in the wisdom of the Tathāgata, thus: He it is, the Exalted One . . . teacher of Devas and mankind, a Buddha, an Exalted One. Thus far, Mahānāma, a disciple is a believer.'

'But, lord, how far is a disciple given to generosity?'

'Herein, Mahānāma, a disciple dwells at home with a heart freed from the taint of stinginess. He is open-handed, pure-handed, delighting in self-surrender, one to ask a favour of, one who rejoices in the dispensing of charitable gifts. Thus far, Mahānāma, a disciple is given to generosity.'

'Pray, lord, how far is a disciple blessed with insight?'

'Herein, Mahānāma, a disciple is a sage, blessed with insight into the rise and fall of things, insight which is Ariyan, penetrating, going on to the utter destruction of Ill. Thus far, Mahānāma, a disciple is possessed of insight.'

(viii) *Raining.*

Just as, monks, when on the mountain-top the sky-god rains down big drops, that water flows down and in its course floods the mountain-gullies, clefts and spurs, and, flooding these, fills up the little pools: then the big pools, filling, flood the great lakes: the great lakes, filling, flood the rivulets: the rivulets, filling, flood the great rivers: the great rivers, being flooded, fill up the mighty ocean,—even so in the Ariyan disciple who has unwavering loyalty to the Buddha, the Norm and the Order, and has the virtues dear to the Ariyans, these conditions flow onwards and reach the further shore and lead to the destruction of the āsavas.[1]

---

[1] *Comy.* points out that here the order of words is deceptive. They conduce to the destruction of the āsavas *on their way* to *Nibbāna* (*pāraṃ*).

(ix) *Kāḷi.*

On a certain occasion the Exalted One was staying near Kapilavatthu, in Banyan Park.

Now the Exalted One, robing himself in the forenoon and taking bowl and outer robe, started off to the house of Kāḷigodhā,[1] the Sakyan lady, and on arriving sat down on a seat made ready. Then Kāḷigodhā, the Sakyan lady, came to the Exalted One and saluting him sat down at one side. As she thus sat the Exalted One said this to her:

'Godhā, the Ariyan woman disciple who is blessed with four things is a Stream-winner, one not doomed to the Downfall, one assured, one bound for enlightenment. What are the four?

Herein, Godhā, the Ariyan woman disciple has unwavering loyalty to the Buddha, the Norm and the Order. She dwells at home with heart free from the taint of stinginess. She is open-handed, pure-handed, delighting in self-surrender, one to ask a favour of, one who delights in dispensing charitable gifts. Blessed with these four things, Godhā, the Ariyan woman disciple is a Stream-winner.'

'Lord, as to these four limbs of stream-winning declared by the Exalted One, all of them are to be seen in me, and I do live according to those things. I do have unwavering loyalty to the Buddha, to the Norm and to the Order. Moreover, whatsoever gifts of charity are to be made in the family, they are shared fully and impartially by the virtuous and good.'

'That is a gain for you, Godhā! It is a thing well gotten for you, Godhā! You have declared the fruits of stream-winning, Godhā!'

(x) *Nandiya.*

On a certain occasion the Exalted One was staying near Kapilavatthu, in Banyan Park.

Then Nandiya the Sakyan went to see the Exalted One, and on coming to him . . . said this:

'Pray, lord, if an Ariyan disciple is in every way, altogether,

---

[1] For this family, *cf.* text, 371; *Brethren*, p. 315 *n.*

in every respect and utterly, without the four limbs of stream-winning, can he in such case be called "An Ariyan disciple who lives remiss"?'

'Of such an one, Nandiya, who . . . utterly lacks the four limbs of stream-winning, I declare him to be one who stands without, in the ranks of the manyfolk.

Moreover, Nandiya, I will tell you how the Ariyan disciple is one who lives remiss and one who lives in earnest. Do you listen. Apply your mind and I will speak.'

'I will, lord,' replied Nandiya the Sakyan to the Exalted One. The Exalted One said:

'And how, Nandiya, is the Ariyan disciple one who dwells remiss?

Herein, Nandiya, the Ariyan disciple is blessed with unwavering loyalty to the Buddha. He is content with that unwavering loyalty to the Buddha, but he makes no further effort, either to get seclusion by day or meditation by night. As he thus dwells remiss he has no delight. Without delight in a thing there is no zest. Zest lacking, there is no calm. Without calm one dwells in discomfort. In him who dwells in discomfort the mind is not tranquillized. In the mind that is not tranquillized the teachings do not show clear.[1] Owing to the teachings being obscure to him he is reckoned one who dwells remiss.

Again, Nandiya, suppose the Ariyan disciple is blessed with unwavering loyalty to the Norm . . . to the Order . . . and is blessed with the virtues dear to the Ariyans, virtues unbroken . . . which conduce to concentration of mind. He is quite content with those virtues dear to the Ariyans, but makes no further effort, either for seclusion by day or meditation by night. As he thus dwells remiss he has no delight. Delight lacking, there is no zest. No zest, no calm. If there be no calm, one lives in discomfort. In him who so lives, the mind is not tranquillized. To the mind not tranquillized the teachings do not show clear. Owing to the teachings being obscure he is one who dwells remiss.

---

[1] *Comy.* 'by way of *vipassanā*.'

And how, Nandiya, does the Ariyan disciple dwell in earnest?

Herein, Nandiya, the Ariyan disciple is blessed with unwavering loyalty to the Buddha, the Norm and the Order; but he is not content with that unwavering loyalty: he makes a further effort to get seclusion by day and meditation by night. As he thus dwells in earnest, delight springs up. In him that is delighted, zest is born. The body of the zestful man is tranquillized. One whose body is tranquil lives at ease. In him who lives at ease the mind is concentrated. To the concentrated mind the teachings show clear. Owing to the teachings being clear he is reckoned one who dwells in earnest.

Moreover, Nandiya, the Ariyan disciple who is blessed with . . . the virtues dear to the Ariyans . . . is not content with those virtues, but makes a further effort to get seclusion by day and meditation by night. As he thus dwells in earnest, delight springs up in him . . . because the teachings are clear to him he is reckoned one who dwells in earnest.'

CHAPTER V.—FLOOD OF MERIT, WITH VERSES

(i) *Flood* or *Capacious*[1] (*a*).

'Monks, there are these four floods of merit, floods of good things, that bring happiness. What are the four?

Herein, monks, the Ariyan disciple is blessed with unwavering loyalty to the Buddha. That is the first flood of merit.

Then he is blessed with unwavering loyalty to the Norm . . . to the Order. These are the second and third floods of merit.

Then he is blessed with the virtues dear to the Ariyans. . . . That is the fourth flood of merit, of good things, that brings happiness. These are the four floods.

---

[1] *Sayhaka* (sub-title of this Sutta, but not in *uddāna*) seems to mean *capax*. *Sayha* is gerund of *sahati*. See stanzas below and text, 391.

Now it is no easy thing to reckon up the measure of merit that accrues to the Ariyan disciple who is blessed with these four floods of merit, these four floods of good things, that bring happiness. One cannot say they are thus and thus in quantity. Nay, they are only to be described in terms like "incalculable, boundless."

Just as, monks, it is no easy thing to reckon the water in the mighty ocean thus: There are so many gallons of water, so many hundred, so many thousand, so many hundreds of thousand gallons of water in it. Nay, one can only say of it: "It is a mighty mass of water, incalculable and boundless." Just so, monks, it is no easy thing to reckon up the measure of merit that accrues to the Ariyan disciple who is blessed with these four floods of merit, these four floods of good things, that bring happiness. One cannot say they are thus and thus. Nay, they are only to be described in terms like "incalculable, boundless."' Thus spake the Exalted One:

> The mighty sea, unmeasured mighty lake,
> The fearsome home of multitudes of pearls,—
> As rivers, serving countless hosts of men,
> Flow widely forth and to that ocean come:
> Just so on him that giveth food, drink, clothes,
> Who bed and seat and coverlet provides,
> Torrents of merit flood that mortal wise,
> As rivers, bearing water, reach the Main.[1]

(ii) *Flood* or *Capacious* (*b*).

'Monks, there are these four floods of merit . . . (*as before*). . . .

Herein the Ariyan disciple is blessed with unwavering loyalty to the Buddha, to the Norm and to the Order.

He dwells at home with a heart free from the taint of stinginess: he is open-handed, pure-handed, delighting in self-surrender, one to ask a favour of, one who delights in dispensing charitable gifts. This is the fourth flood of merit, flood of good things, that bring happiness.

---

[1] *Cf. K.S.* iv, 267.

Now it is no easy thing to reckon up the measure of merit . . . (*as above*) . . . they can only be described in terms like "incalculable, boundless."

Just as, monks, where[1] these great rivers flow together, meet together, to wit: Ganges, Yamunā, Aciravatī, Sarabhū and Mahī, it is no easy task to reckon the quantity of water there, thus: so many gallons of water, so many hundred gallons and so forth . . . it is only to be described in terms like "incalculable, boundless." '

Thus spake the Exalted One. Then as Teacher he added this:

The mighty sea, unmeasured mighty lake (*as above*). . . .

(iii) *Flood* or *Capacious* (*c*).

'Monks, there are these four floods of merit . . .

Herein, monks, the Ariyan disciple is blessed with unwavering loyalty to the Buddha, the Norm and the Order.

Moreover he is a sage, blessed with insight into the rise and fall of things, insight that is Ariyan, penetrating, going on to the utter destruction of Ill. This is the fourth flood of merit, of good things, that bring happiness. Such, monks, are the four floods of merit . . .

Now it is no easy thing to sum up the measure of merit . . . (*as before*) . . . that great mass of merit is incalculable, boundless.'

Thus spake the Exalted One:

> Desiring merit, in the good set firm,
> Who cultivates the way to reach the Deathless,
> He, winning to the essence of the Norm,[2]
> Rejoicing in destruction of the taints,[3]
> Quakes not to think: The Lord of Death will come.

---

[1] *Comy.* reads *yatthavā* with *v.l.* of text.

[2] *Dhamma-sārâdhigamo.* *Comy.* 'The Ariyan Norm is called *sāra*; *dh. sār.* is to reach the fruits of it.'

[3] *Khaye rato*=*kilesa-kkhaye rato.* *Comy.*

(iv) *Very rich* or *Wealthy* (*a*).

Monks, the Ariyan disciple who is blessed with four things is called 'Rich, very rich, of great possessions,[1] of great fame.' What four things?

Herein the Ariyan disciple is blessed with unwavering loyalty to the Buddha, the Norm and the Order, and is blessed with the virtues dear to the Ariyans. . . . These are the four things.

(v) *Very rich* (*b*).

(*Exactly the same as the above.*)

(vi) *Monks*, or *Puritan.*[2]

Blessed with four things the Ariyan disciple is a Stream-winner, one not doomed to the Downfall, assured, bound for enlightenment. What four?

Herein the Ariyan disciple is blessed with unwavering loyalty . . .

(vii) *Nandiya.*

Kapilavatthu was the occasion . . .

As he thus sat at one side, the Exalted One said this to Nandiya the Sakyan:

'Nandiya, the Ariyan disciple who is blessed with four things . . . is bound for enlightenment . . .'

(viii) *Bhaddiya.*

(*The same.*) . . .

(ix) *Mahānāma.*

(*The same.*) . . .

(x) *Limb.*

Monks, there are these four limbs of stream-winning. What four?

Consorting with the good, hearing the Good Norm, thorough mindful attention and practice in accordance with the Norm.

These are the four limbs of stream-winning.

---

[1] *Comy.* 'The Ariyan wealth (of *saddhā, sīla, hiri, ottappa, suta, cāga, paññā*).'

[2] Text has *Suddaka* for ? *suddhika.*

CHAPTER VI.—DISCREET[1]

(i) *With verses.*

Monks, blessed with four things the Ariyan disciple is a Stream-winner. . . . What four?

Herein the Ariyan disciple is blessed with unwavering loyalty to the Buddha, the Norm and the Order, and the virtues dear to the Ariyans . . .

The Exalted One said this:

> Whoso hath faith in the Tathāgata
> Unwavering and fixed, whose life is good,
> Praised by the Ariyans and dear to them;
> Whoso is likewise loyal to the Order
> And looks straight forth—' He is not poor,' they say,
> ' Not lived in vain the life of such a man.'
> Wherefore the wise should cultivate (these three)
> Faith, virtue and clear-seeing of the Norm,
> Bearing the Buddha's message in his mind.[2]

(ii) *Spending the rainy season.*

On a certain occasion the Exalted One was staying near Sāvatthī, in Jeta Grove, at Anāthapiṇḍika's Park.

On that occasion a certain monk who had just spent the rainy season near Sāvatthī, had come to Kapilavatthu on some business or other.

Now the Sakyans of Kapilavatthu heard it said that a certain monk who had spent the rainy season at Sāvatthī was come to Kapilavatthu.

Then the Sakyans of Kapilavatthu went to visit that monk, and on coming to him saluted him and sat down at one side. So seated the Sakyans said this to that monk:

' Pray, sir, is the Exalted One well and strong?'

' He is, friends.'

' Pray, sir, are Sāriputta and Moggallāna well and strong?'

' They are, friends.'

' Pray, sir, is the Order of Monks well and strong?'

---

[1] The title comes from § 4.   [2] As at text, 384.

'They are, friends.'

'Sir, during this retreat of the rainy season, have you heard anything face to face with the Exalted One? Have you learned anything from him?'

'Yes, friends. I have heard and learned this face to face with the Exalted One: "Monks, few indeed are those monks, who, by destroying the āsavas, have of themselves in this very life by their own knowledge realized the heart's release, the release by insight, and abide therein. More numerous are those monks who, by destroying the five fetters of the lower sort, are reborn spontaneously (in the higher worlds), there to pass utterly away, destined not to return from that world."

Moreover, friends, I heard this face to face with the Exalted One:

"Monks, few indeed are those monks who, by destroying the five fetters of the lower sort, are reborn spontaneously (in the higher worlds), there to pass utterly away, not destined to return from that world. More numerous are those monks who, by destroying three fetters and wearing down lust, hatred and delusion, are Once-returners. Coming back once more to this world they will make an end of Ill."

Further, friends, I learned this face to face with the Exalted One:

"Monks, few are those monks who, by destroying three fetters and wearing down lust, hatred and delusion, are Once-returners, who, coming back once more to this world, shall make an end of Ill. More numerous are those monks who, by destroying three fetters, are Stream-winners, not doomed to the Downfall, assured, bound for enlightenment."'

(iii) *Dhammadinna.*

On a certain occasion the Exalted One was staying near Benares, at Isipatana in the Deer Park.

Then Dhammadinna[1] the lay-disciple came with five hundred

---

[1] *Comy.* He was one of the seven laymen who had followings of 500. The others were Visākhā the woman lay-disciple, Ugga the housefather, Citta the housefather, Hatthaka Ālavaka, Cūḷa and Anāthapiṇḍika the housefathers.

lay-disciples to see the Exalted One, and on coming to him saluted him and sat down at one side. As they thus sat, Dhammadinna the lay-disciple said this to the Exalted One:

'Let my lord the Exalted One admonish us! Let my lord the Exalted One admonish us, that it may be for our profit and welfare for many a long day.'

'Then, Dhammadinna, thus must ye train yourselves: As to those discourses[1] uttered by the Tathāgata, deep, deep in meaning, transcendental[2] and concerned with the Void,[3] from time to time we will spend our days learning them. That is how you must train yourselves, Dhammadinna.'

'Lord, it is no easy thing for us, living as we do in crowded houses,[4] encumbered with children, enjoying the use of Benares sandal-wood, decking ourselves with garlands and unguents, handling gold and silver,—it is no easy thing for us from time to time to spend our days learning those discourses uttered by the Tathāgata. . . . Let my lord the Exalted One teach us some other teaching, to us who stand firm in the five precepts.'

'Then, Dhammadinna, ye must train yourselves in this way: We shall be blessed with unwavering loyalty to the Buddha, to the Norm and to the Order. We shall be blessed with the virtues dear to the Ariyans, virtues unbroken . . . which conduce to concentration of mind. That is how you must train yourselves, Dhammadinna.'

'Lord, as to these four limbs of stream-winning taught by the Exalted One, those conditions are seen to exist in us already. We do live according to them. Lord, we do possess unwavering loyalty to the Buddha, to the Norm and the Order. We do possess the virtues dear to the Ariyans, virtues unbroken, whole, unspotted, untarnished, giving freedom, praised by the wise; virtues untainted (by craving or delusion) which conduce to concentration of mind.'[5]

---

1 *Suttantā*. *Cf*. *S*. ii, 267; *K.S*. ii, 179.

2 *Comy*. 'Such as the *Asankhata-saŋyutta*,' etc. (*S*. iv, 360 *ff*.).

3 *Suññā*=*Nibbāna*. *Cf*. *VM*. 513. *Comy*. refers to *Khajjanika-sutta*, etc. (*S*. iii, 81).

4 Text, 353.

5 Text, 343.

'Well for you, Dhammadinna! Well gotten by you, Dhammadinna! You have declared the fruits of stream-winning, Dhammadinna!'

(iv) *Visiting the sick.*

On a certain occasion the Exalted One was staying among the Sakyans at Kapilavatthu, in Banyan Park.

Now on that occasion a number of monks were busied making robes for the Exalted One, 'for,' said they, 'when the rains are over, the Exalted One will go forth on his rounds.'

Now Mahānāma the Sakyan heard it said: 'A number of monks are busied making robes for the Exalted One, and so forth . . .' and he went to the Exalted One, saluted him and sat down at one side. So seated Mahānāma the Sakyan said this to the Exalted One:

'I hear it said, lord, that a number of monks are busied making robes for the Exalted One with the idea that, when the rains are over, the Exalted One will set forth on his rounds. Now, lord, we have never heard[1] from the Exalted One's own lips how a discreet[2] lay-disciple who is sick, afflicted, suffering from a sore disease, should be admonished by another discreet lay-disciple.'

'A discreet lay-disciple, Mahānāma, who is sick . . . should be admonished by another discreet lay-disciple with the four comfortable assurances, thus: "Take comfort, dear sir, in your unwavering loyalty to the Buddha, saying: He it is the Exalted One, Arahant, fully enlightened One . . . Teacher of Devas and mankind, a Buddha, an Exalted One. Take comfort, dear sir, in your unwavering loyalty to the Norm, thus: Well proclaimed is the Norm. . . . Take comfort, dear sir, in your unwavering loyalty to the Order. Take comfort, dear sir, in your possession of the virtues dear to the Ariyans,[3] virtues unbroken . . . which conduce to concentration of mind." A discreet lay-disciple, Mahānāma, who is sick . . . should be

[1] Text, *na kho te etaŋ . . . sutaŋ;* but *Comy. na kho pan' etaŋ=na kho amhehi eva.*

[2] *Sappañño=sotâpanno. Comy.*

[3] Text has *ariyakantāni sīlāni,* etc., which I think should be *ariyakantehi sīlehi,* etc.

admonished by another discreet lay-disciple with these four comfortable assurances.

Then, supposing he has longing for his parents, he should thus be spoken to:

If he say: "I have longing for my parents," the other should reply: "But, my dear sir, you are subject to death. Whether you feel longing for your parents or not, you will have to die. 'Twere just as well for you to abandon the longing you have for your parents."

If he should say: "That longing for my parents is now abandoned," the other should reply: "Yet, my dear sir, you still have longing for your children. As you must die in any case, 'twere just as well for you to abandon that longing for your children."

If he should say: "That longing for my children is now abandoned," the other should reply: "Yet my dear sir, you still have longing for the five human pleasures of sense."

Then, if he say, "That longing for the five human pleasures of sense is now abandoned," the other should reply: "My friend, the heavenly delights are more excellent than the five human pleasures of sense. 'Twere well for you, worthy sir, to remove your thoughts from them and fix them on the Four Deva Kings."

Suppose the sick man say, "My thoughts are removed from human pleasures of sense and fixed upon the Four Deva Kings," then let the other say: "More excellent than the Four Deva Kings and more choice are the Suite of the Thirty-three . . . (*and so on in order*) . . . the Yama Devas, the Devas of Delight, the Creative Devas, the Devas who rejoice in the work of other Devas . . . the latter are more excellent and choice than the former . . . so 'twere better for you to fix your thoughts on the Brahmā World."

Then if the sick man's thoughts are so fixed, let the other say: "My friend, even the Brahmā World is impermanent, not lasting, prisoned in a person.[1] Well for you, friend, if

[1] *Sakkāya pariyāpannā* (subject to individuality), as at *S.* iii, 85; *K.S.* iii, 71.

you raise your mind above the Brahmā World and fix it on cessation from the person-pack."

And if the sick man say he has done so, then, Mahānāma, I declare that there is no difference between the lay-disciple who thus avers and the monk whose heart is freed from the āsavas, that is, between the release of the one and the release of the other.'[1]

(v) *Four Fruits* (*a*).

Monks, these four conditions, if cultivated and made much of, conduce to realizing the fruits of stream-winning. What four?[2]

Following after the good, hearing the Good Norm, systematic attention to it and living in accordance with the precepts of the Norm.

These four conditions, if cultivated and made much of, conduce to realizing the fruits of stream-winning.

(vi-viii) *Four Fruits* (*b*).

These four conditions, if cultivated and made much of, conduce to realizing the fruits of (*a*) once-returning, (*b*) not-returning, (*c*) Arahantship.

(ix-xi) *Acquiring*, *growth* and *increase*.

The same four conduce to acquiring insight, the growth of insight, the increase of insight.

CHAPTER VII.—GREAT INSIGHT

(i-xiii).

(*The same four conditions as above*) if cultivated and made much of, conduce to comprehensive, manifold, extensive, profound, unbounded,[3] abundant, many-sided, swift, buoyant,[4] joyous, instant, sharp and fastidious insight.

---

[1] *Nānākaraṇaŋ yadidaŋ vimuttiyā vimuttin ti.* *Comy.* 'in the matter of path-and-fruit penetration.'

[2] *Comy.* refers to *Paṭisambhidā*, ii, 189 *ff.* (quoted in full at *SA.* on *S.* i, 63=*K.S.* i, 87). The qualities are all attributed to Sāriputta.

[3] *Pts.* has wrong reading *assāmanta* (?) for *appamatta* (Sinh. MSS. *asamatta*).

[4] *Lahu* at *Pts.* Text has *bahula-*.

BOOK XII

KINDRED SAYINGS ABOUT THE TRUTHS

CHAPTER I.—CONCENTRATION

(i) *Concentration.*

SĀVATTHĪ was the occasion . . . The Exalted One said:

'Monks, do ye practise concentration. The monk who is concentrated knows a thing as it really is. And what does he know as it really is ?

In this connexion he knows as it really is, This is Ill. This is the arising of Ill. This is the ceasing of Ill. This is the practice that leads to the ceasing of Ill.

Do ye practise concentration, monks. The monk who is concentrated knows a thing as it really is. Wherefore, monks, an effort must be made to realize: This is Ill. . . . This is the practice that leads to the ceasing of Ill.

(ii) *Meditation.*

Monks, do ye apply yourselves to meditation. The monk who is meditative knows a thing as it really is. And what does he know as it really is ?

In this connexion he knows as it really is: This is Ill. . . . This is the practice that leads to the ceasing of Ill.

Monks, do ye apply yourselves to meditation. . . . Wherefore an effort must be made to realize: This is Ill. . . . This is the practice . . .

(iii) *Clansman* (*a*).

Monks, whatsoever clansmen have in time past rightly gone forth from the home to the homeless life,—all of them have done so to get full comprehension of the four Ariyan truths, as they really are.

Monks, whatsoever clansmen shall in future time . . . whatsoever clansmen do now rightly go forth from the home to the homeless life,—all of them do so to get full comprehension of the four Ariyan truths. Of what four ?

The Ariyan truth of Ill, the Ariyan truth of the arising of Ill, the Ariyan truth of the ceasing of Ill, the Ariyan truth of the practice that leads to the ceasing of Ill.

Monks, whatsoever clansmen . . . Wherefore an effort must be made to realize: This is Ill. . . . This is the practice . . .

(iv) *Clansman* (*b*).

Monks, whatsoever clansmen in past time have rightly gone forth . . . in future time . . . in present time . . . all of them have fully comprehended, as they really are, the four Ariyan truths. . . .

Wherefore, monks, an effort must be made to realize . . .

(v) *Recluses and brahmins* (*a*).

Monks, whatsoever recluses or brahmins in time past have gained the highest wisdom in its reality, all of them have done so[1] by penetrating, as they really are, the four Ariyan truths. Whatsoever recluses in future time shall do so . . . whatsoever recluses and brahmins in the present time do gain the highest wisdom in its reality, all of them do so by penetrating, as they really are, the four Ariyan truths. What are the four ?

The Ariyan truth of Ill . . . the Ariyan truth of the practice that leads to the ceasing of Ill.

Whatsoever recluses or brahmins . . .

Wherefore, monks, an effort must be made to realize: This is Ill. . . .

(vi) *Recluses and brahmins* (*b*).

Monks, whatsoever recluses or brahmins in time past have declared that they have in very truth gained the highest wisdom, all of them have declared that they have penetrated in very truth the four Ariyan truths. . . . Whatsoever recluses or brahmins in future time . . . in the present time do declare . . . Wherefore, monks, an effort must be made to realize . . .

---

[1] Text should read *abhisambujjhiŋsu*.

(vii) *Thoughts.*

Monks, think not evil, unprofitable thoughts, such as: thoughts of lust, thoughts of hatred, thoughts of delusion.[1] Why do I say so?

Because, monks, these thoughts are not concerned with profit, they are not the rudiments of the holy life, they conduce not to revulsion, to dispassion, to cessation, to tranquillity, to full understanding, to the perfect wisdom, they conduce not to Nibbāna.

When ye do think, monks, ye should think thus: This is Ill. This is the arising of Ill. This is the ceasing of Ill. This is the practice that leads to the ceasing of Ill. Why do I say this?

Because, monks, these thoughts are concerned with profit, they are rudiments of the holy life . . . they conduce to Nibbāna. Wherefore an effort must be made to realize: This is Ill. . . .

(viii) *Reasoning.*

Monks, reason not ill, unprofitable reasonings,[2] such as: Eternal is the world or Not eternal is the world: Finite is the world or Infinite is the world: Life is the same as body, or Life and body are different: The Tathāgata exists after death or The Tathāgata exists not after death, or He both exists and exists not after death, or The Tathāgata neither exists nor not-exists after death. Why do I say this?

Because, monks, these reasonings are not concerned with profit . . . they conduce not to Nibbāna.

When ye reason, monks, reason thus: This is Ill. . . . This is the practice that leads to the ceasing of Ill. Why so?

Because, monks, these reasonings are concerned with profit . . . they conduce to Nibbāna. Wherefore an effort must be made to realize: This is Ill. . . .

---

[1] Quoted at *Mil. Pañh.*, 379.

[2] *Mā akusalaŋ cittaŋ cinteyyātha.* In the previous section we have *mā akus. vitakke vitakkeyyātha.* The contrast seems to be between 'discursive thought' and 'directed thought.' *Cf.* text, 446; *K.S.* iv, **276.**

(ix) *Wordy warfare.*

Monks, wage not wordy warfare,[1] thus: "You know not about this Norm-discipline. I do know about this Norm-discipline. How could you know about it? You have fallen on wrong views. I have come by right views. You spoke last what should come first, and first what should come last. I am speaking to the point, you are not. What you have thought out so long[2] is quite upset. Your view is confuted. Go, explain yourself. You are shown up. Clear yourself if you can!" Why do I say this?

Because, monks, such talk is not concerned with profit . . . it does not conduce to Nibbāna.

When ye talk, monks, talk about: "This is Ill. This is the arising of Ill. This is the ceasing of Ill. This is the practice that leads to the ceasing of Ill." Why do I say that? Because, monks, such talk is concerned with profit . . . it conduces to Nibbāna.

Wherefore, monks, an effort must be made to realize: This is Ill. . . .

(x) *Talk.*

Monks, talk ye not childish[3] talk of divers kinds, such as: talk about rājahs, robbers, great ministers: talk of armies, panic and battle:[4] talk of food and drink and clothes, beds, flowers, garlands and perfumes: talk of relatives, vehicles, villages, suburbs, towns and districts: talk about women[5] and champions:[6] talk about streets[7] and gossip at the well: ghost-

---

[1] *Cf. D.* iii, 117; *K.S.* iii, 13 *n.*; *DA.* i, 91.

[2] Reading (as at *S.* ii, 12) *adhiciṇṇaŋ*, text's *v.l.* for *āciṇṇaŋ*.

[3] *Cf. Dialog.* iii, 33 *n.*; *DA.* i, 89 (repeated here by *Comy.*). Here *tiracchānakathā* ('animal talk') is paraphr. by *Comy.* as 'not conducive to the path to heaven or to release.'

[4] Text should read *yuddhaka.*

[5] Text adds *purisa-* [of B. MSS.]. See *Dialog. n. ad loc.*

[6] *Sūra-k.* Our *Comy.* adds to *DA.* saying 'there is a reading *sūra-k.* ("about drunkards").'

[7] Not in the sense of 'street-gossip,' but as *Comy.* 'Talk of this or that street, as well or badly built, or inhabited by so and so.'

stories, desultory talk and fabulous[1] talk about (the origin of) land and sea: talk of being and not-being. Why do I say this?

Because, monks, such talk is not concerned with profit, it is not the rudiments of the holy life . . . it does not conduce to Nibbāna.

Monks, when ye talk, talk about: "This is Ill. This is the arising of Ill. This is the ceasing of Ill. This is the practice that leads to the ceasing of Ill." Why do I say this?

Because, monks, this talk is concerned with profit, it is the rudiments of the holy life; because it conduces to revulsion, to dispassion, to cessation, to tranquillity, to full understanding, to the wisdom: because it conduces to Nibbāna.

Wherefore, monks, an effort must be made to realize: This is Ill. This is the arising of Ill. This is the ceasing of Ill. This is the practice that leads to the ceasing of Ill.'

CHAPTER II.—THE FOUNDATION OF THE KINGDOM OF THE NORM[2]

(i) *Spoken by the Tathāgata* (*a*).

Thus have I heard: Once the Exalted One was dwelling near Benares, at Isipatana, in the Deer-Park.

Then the Exalted One thus spake unto the company of five monks:[3]

'Monks, these two extremes should not be followed by one who has gone forth as a wanderer. What two?

Devotion to the pleasures of sense,[4] a low practice of

---

[1] *Akkhāyika*, 'fabulous narratives.'

[2] Sometimes translated as 'The setting rolling of the wheel of the Norm.' *Cf. Vin.* i, 10. [In his *Introd.* to *Buddhist Suttas*, Prof. R. D. erroneously ascribes this Sutta to *Anguttara N.*] Preached originally on the full-moon day of Āsāḷha (July-August), a festival still kept up in Ceylon.

[3] The five co-wanderers were Kondañña, Vappa, Bhaddiya, Mahānāma, and Assaji.

[4] Text has several misprints: *kāmesu kāmesu khallika-*, which should be *kāmesu kāma-sukh. . . . puthujjaniko* . . . and further on, *anupagamma*.

villagers,[1] a practice unworthy, unprofitable, the way of the world (on the one hand); and (on the other) devotion to self-mortification, which is painful, unworthy and unprofitable.

By avoiding these two extremes the Tathāgata has gained knowledge of that middle path which giveth vision, which giveth knowledge, which causeth calm, special knowledge,[2] enlightenment, Nibbāna.

And what, monks, is that middle path which giveth vision . . . Nibbāna?

Verily it is this Ariyan eightfold way, to wit: Right view, right aim, right speech, right action, right living, right effort, right mindfulness, right concentration. This, monks, is that middle path which giveth vision, which giveth knowledge, which causeth calm, special knowledge, enlightenment, Nibbāna.

Now this, monks, is the Ariyan truth about Ill:

Birth is Ill, decay is Ill, sickness is Ill, death is Ill: likewise sorrow and grief, woe, lamentation and despair.[3] To be conjoined with things which we dislike: to be separated from things which we like,—that also is Ill. Not to get what one wants,—that also is Ill. In a word, this body, this fivefold mass which is based on grasping,—that is Ill.

Now this, monks, is the Ariyan truth about the arising of Ill:

It is that craving that leads back to birth, along with the lure and the lust that lingers longingly now here, now there: namely, the craving for sensual pleasure, the craving to be born again, the craving for existence to end. Such, monks, is the Ariyan truth about the arising of Ill.

And this, monks, is the Ariyan truth about the ceasing of Ill:

Verily it is the utter passionless cessation of, the giving up, the forsaking, the release from, the absence of longing for this craving.

---

1 *Gammo=gāma-vasīnaŋ santako. Comy.*

2 *Comy.* 'of the four truths.'

3 These last omitted by the Vinaya version.

Now this, monks, is the Ariyan truth about the practice that leads to the ceasing of Ill:

Verily it is this Ariyan eightfold way, to wit: Right view, right aim, right speech, right action, right living, right effort, right mindfulness, right concentration.

Monks, at the thought of this Ariyan truth of Ill, concerning things unlearnt before, there arose in me vision, insight, understanding: there arose in me wisdom, there arose in me light.

Monks, at the thought: This Ariyan truth about Ill is to be understood,—concerning things unlearnt before, there arose in me vision, insight, understanding: there arose in me wisdom, there arose in me light.

Monks, at the thought: This Ariyan truth about Ill has been understood (by me),—concerning things unlearnt before, there arose in me vision, insight, understanding: there arose in me wisdom, there arose in me light.

Again, monks, at the thought of this Ariyan truth about the arising of Ill, concerning things unlearnt before, there arose in me vision, insight, understanding: there arose in me wisdom, there arose in me light.

At the thought: This arising of Ill[1] is to be put away,—concerning things unlearnt before . . . there arose in me light.

At the thought: This arising of Ill[1] has been put away,—concerning things unlearnt before . . . there arose in me light.

Again, monks, at the thought of this Ariyan truth about the ceasing of Ill, concerning things unlearnt before . . . there arose in me light.

At the thought: This ceasing of Ill must be realized,—concerning things unlearnt before . . . there arose in me light.

At the thought: This Ariyan truth about the ceasing of Ill has been realized,—concerning things unlearnt before . . . there arose in me light.

Again, monks, at the thought of this Ariyan truth about the

---

[1] Here Burmese MSS. (*v.l.* of text) omit *Ariya-*. But we must omit *ariya-saccaŋ*; otherwise the text would mean 'the Ariyan truth about the arising of Ill is to be put away. *Craving* has to be put away.' The frame has obscured the picture here.

practice leading to the ceasing of Ill, concerning things unlearnt before . . . there arose in me light.

At the thought: This Ariyan truth about the practice leading to the ceasing of Ill must be cultivated,—concerning things unlearnt before . . . there arose in me light.

At the thought: This Ariyan truth about the practice leading to the ceasing of Ill has been cultivated,—concerning things unlearnt before there arose in me vision, insight, understanding: there arose in me wisdom, there arose in me light.

Now, monks, so long as my knowledge and insight of these thrice revolved twelvefold Ariyan truths, in their essential nature, was not quite purified,—so long was I not sure that in this world, together with its Devas, its Māras, its Brahmās, among the hosts of recluses and brahmins, of Devas and mankind, there was one enlightened with supreme enlightenment.

But, monks, so soon as my knowledge and insight of these thrice revolved twelvefold Ariyan truths, in their essential nature, was quite purified,—then, monks, was I assured what it is to be enlightened with supreme enlightenment with regard to the world and its Devas, its Māras, its Brahmās, and with regard to the hosts of recluses and brahmins, of Devas and mankind. Now knowledge and insight have arisen in me so that I know: Sure is my heart's release. This is my last birth. There is no more becoming for me.'

Thus spake the Exalted One, and the company of five monks were glad and rejoiced at the words of the Exalted One.

Now when this sermon had been spoken, there arose in the venerable Kondañña the pure and stainless eye to see the Norm, to wit: Whatsoever is of a nature to arise is likewise of a nature to cease.

Moreover, when the foundation of the kingdom of the Norm had been thus established by the Exalted One, the Devas of the earth raised the cry: 'At Benares, at Isipatana, in the Deer-Park, hath been established by the Exalted One this kingdom of the Norm unsurpassed, this kingdom not to be overset by any recluse or brahmin, any Deva or Māra or Brahmā, or by anyone whatsoever in the world.'

When the Devas of the Four Kings heard the cry of the

Devas of the earth, they also raised the cry: 'At Benares . . . hath been established . . .'

When the Devas of the Thirty-Three, the Yama Devas, the Devas of Delight, the Creative Devas, the Devas who rejoice in the works of other Devas, and the Devas of the company of Brahmā, heard the cry of the Devas of the Four Kings, they also raised the cry: 'At Benares, at Isipatana, in the Deer-Park, hath been established by the Exalted One this kingdom of the Norm unsurpassed, this kingdom not to be overset by any recluse or brahmin, any Deva or Māra or Brahmā, or by anyone whatsoever in the world.'

Thus at that very hour, at that very moment, in an instant of time the cry reached even to the Brahma World, and this thousandfold world-system quaked and quaked again: it was shaken to and fro, and an immeasurable mighty radiance shone forth, surpassing even the magic power of the Devas.

Thereupon the Exalted One uttered this solemn saying:

'Kondañña indeed has understood! Kondañña indeed has understood!'

Thus it was that the venerable Kondañña won his name of 'Kondañña-who-hath-understood.'[1]

(ii) *Spoken by the Tathāgata* (*b*).[2]

Monks, at the thought: This is the Ariyan truth about Ill,—there arose in me, concerning things unlearned before by Tathāgatas, vision, insight, understanding and wisdom, there arose in me light.

Monks, at the thought: This Ariyan truth about Ill is to be understood . . . At the thought: This Ariyan truth about Ill has been understood (by me),—there arose in me, con-

---

[1] *Aññāta-Kondañña.* 'Hereupon,' says the Vinaya account, 'Kondañña asked for ordination, and it was given in these words: "Come, monk! Well proclaimed is the Norm. Live the holy life for the utter destruction of Ill." This was full ordination (*upasampadā*) for that venerable one.' Then Vappa and Bhaddiya gained insight, and a little later Mahānāma and Assaji. Thus there were six in the Order.

[2] In this Sutta the only difference from the previous one is the inclusion of the word *Tathāgatas.*

cerning things unlearned before by Tathāgatas, vision, insight, understanding and wisdom, there arose in me light.

Monks, at the thought: This is the Ariyan truth about the arising of Ill . . . there arose in me light.

Monks, at the thought: This arising of Ill (according to the Ariyan truth) must be put away . . . has been put away, . . . there arose in me light.

Monks, at the thought: This is the Ariyan truth about the ceasing of Ill . . . there arose in me light.

At the thought: This Ariyan truth about the ceasing of Ill must be realized . . . has been realized . . . there arose in me light.

Monks, at the thought: This is the Ariyan truth about the practice that leads to the ceasing of Ill . . . there arose in me light.

At the thought: This Ariyan truth about the practice that leads to the ceasing of Ill must be cultivated . . . has been cultivated,—concerning things unheard before by Tathāgatas there arose in me vision, insight, understanding and wisdom, there arose in me light.

(iii) *Factors.*

Monks, there are these four Ariyan truths. What four? The Ariyan truth about Ill, that about the arising of Ill, that about the ceasing of Ill, and the Ariyan truth about the practice that leads to the ceasing of Ill.

And what, monks, is the Ariyan truth about Ill?

Ill, it should be said, is the fivefold factor of grasping: the grasping of body, of feeling, of perception, of the activities, of consciousness. This, monks, is called 'the Ariyan truth about Ill.'

And what, monks, is the Ariyan truth about the arising of Ill?

It is that craving that leads back to rebirth, along with the lure and the lust that linger longingly now here, now there: namely, the craving for sensual delight, the craving to be born again, the craving for existence to end. This is the Ariyan truth about the arising of Ill.

And what, monks, is the Ariyan truth about the ceasing of Ill?

Verily it is the utter passionless cessation of, the giving up, the forsaking, the release from, the absence of longing for this craving. This is the Ariyan truth about the ceasing of Ill.

And what, monks, is the Ariyan truth about the practice that leads to the ceasing of Ill?

Verily it is this Ariyan eightfold way, to wit: Right view, right aim, right speech, right action, right living, right effort, right mindfulness, right concentration. This is the Ariyan truth about the practice that leads to the ceasing of Ill.

These, monks, are the four Ariyan truths. Wherefore an effort must be made to realize: This is Ill. This is the arising of Ill. This is the ceasing of Ill. This is the practice that leads to the ceasing of Ill.

(iv) *Sphere of sense.*

Monks, there are these four Ariyan truths. What four? (*as above*). . . . And what, monks, is the Ariyan truth about Ill?

Ill, it should be said, is the six personal spheres of sense. What six?

The sense-sphere of the eye, of the ear, the nose, the tongue, the body, the mind. This, monks, is called 'the Ariyan truth about Ill.'

And what, monks, is the Ariyan truth about the arising of Ill?

It is that craving that leads back to rebirth (*as above*). . . . This is called 'the Ariyan truth about the arising of Ill.'

And what, monks, is the Ariyan truth about the ceasing of Ill?

(*The rest as above.*) . . .

Wherefore, monks, an effort must be made to realize: This is Ill. . . .

(v) *Bearing in mind* (*a*).

'Monks, do ye bear in mind the four Ariyan truths taught by me?'

At these words a certain monk said:

'I, lord, do bear in mind the Ariyan truths taught by the Exalted One.'

'And how, monk, do you bear them in mind?'

'Thus, lord: I bear in mind that Ill is the first Ariyan truth taught by the Exalted One. The arising of Ill is the second. The ceasing of Ill is the third. The practice that leads to the ceasing of Ill is the fourth Ariyan truth taught by the Exalted One. That, lord, is how I bear them in mind.'

'Well done, monk! Well done, monk! You rightly remember them. Ill was indeed taught by me as the first Ariyan truth. The arising of Ill was the second. The ceasing of Ill was the third. The practice that leads to the ceasing of Ill was the fourth Ariyan truth taught by me.

Thus, monk, do you bear in mind the four Ariyan truths taught by me.

Wherefore, monk, an effort must be made to realize: This is Ill. . . .'

(vi) *Bearing in mind* (*b*).

'Monks, do ye bear in mind the four Ariyan truths taught by me?'

At these words a certain monk said:

'I, lord, do bear them in mind.'

'And how, monk, do you bear them in mind?'

'Thus, lord. I bear in mind that Ill is the first Ariyan truth taught by the Exalted One. Whatsoever recluse or brahmin should say: "This Ill is not the first Ariyan truth taught by Gotama the recluse. Rejecting this Ill as first Ariyan truth, I will proclaim another Ill," he could not do so.

The arising of Ill is the second Ariyan truth taught by the Exalted One . . . the ceasing of Ill is the third . . . the practice that leads to the ceasing of Ill is the fourth. Whatsoever recluse or brahmin should say: "This practice that leads to the ceasing of Ill is not the fourth Ariyan truth taught by Gotama the recluse. Rejecting this practice, I will proclaim some other practice that leads to the ceasing of Ill as fourth Ariyan truth," he could not do so.

That, lord, is how I bear in mind the four Ariyan truths taught by the Exalted One.'

'Well done, monk! Well done, monk! Ill is indeed the first Ariyan truth taught by me. Whatsoever recluse or brahmin should say . . . he could not do so . . . (*as before*). . . .

Thus, monk, do you bear in mind . . . Wherefore, monk, an effort must be made to realize: This is Ill . . . this is the practice that leads to the ceasing of Ill.'

(vii) *Ignorance.*

Now a certain monk came to see the Exalted One . . . and sat down at one side. As he thus sat that monk said this to the Exalted One:

'"Ignorance! Ignorance," is the saying, lord. Pray, lord, what is ignorance, and how far is one the victim of ignorance?'

'Monk, being ignorant about Ill, its arising, its ceasing and about the practice that leads to its ceasing is called "ignorance," and one who is thus ignorant is a victim of ignorance.

Wherefore, monk, you must make an effort to realize: This is Ill. . . .'

(viii) *Knowledge.*

Then a certain monk came to see the Exalted One. . . . So seated he said this:

'"Knowledge! Knowledge," is the saying, lord. Pray, lord, what is knowledge, and how far is one possessed of knowledge?'

'Knowing about Ill, its arising, its ceasing and the practice that leads to its ceasing is called "knowledge," monk: and he who has this knowledge is one possessed of knowledge.

Wherefore, monk, an effort must be made to realize: This is Ill. . . .'

(ix) *Illustration.*[1]

Monks, the Ariyan truth of This is Ill has been pointed out by me. Therein are numberless shades and variations of meaning.[2] Numberless are the ways of illustrating this Ariyan truth of This is Ill.

The Ariyan truth of This is the arising of Ill . . . This

---

[1] *Saṅkāsanā.* Other synonyms are *pakāsanā, vivaraṇā, vibhājan' uttānī-karaṇa, paññatti.* *UdA.* 9; *Netti* 5, etc.

[2] *Vaṇṇā byañjanā:* 'like a cook's flavourings and sauces.' *Comy.*

is the practice that leads to the ceasing of Ill has been pointed out by me. Therein are numberless shades and variations of meaning. Numberless are the ways of illustrating this Ariyan truth of This is the practice . . .

Wherefore, monks, an effort must be made to realize: This is Ill. . . .

(x) *True.*[1]

Monks, these four things are true, not false,[2] not alterable.[3] What four?

The fact of Ill, monks, is true, not false, not changeable. The fact of the arising of Ill . . . the fact of the ceasing of Ill . . . the fact of the practice that leads to the ceasing of Ill is true, not false, not changeable. These are the four things that are true, not false, not changeable. Wherefore, monks, ye must make an effort to realize: This is Ill . . . this is the practice that leads to the ceasing of Ill.

CHAPTER III.—KOṬIGĀMA

(i) *Knowledge* (*a*).

Thus have I heard: On a certain occasion the Exalted One was staying among the Vajjians at Koṭigāma.[4] Then the Exalted One addressed the monks saying:

'Monks, it is through not understanding, not penetrating four Ariyan truths that we have run on, wandered on, this long long road, both you and I. What are the four?

Through not understanding, not penetrating the Ariyan truth of Ill . . . we have run on, wandered on, this long long road, both you and I.

But now, monks, the Ariyan truth of Ill is understood, is penetrated, likewise the Ariyan truth of the arising, the ceasing of Ill . . . is penetrated. Uprooted is the craving

---

[1] The adj. *tatha=saccaŋ*. *Cf. tatha-bhāvo,* the eternally, constantly true. *Cf. S.* ii, 26; *VM.* ii, 494 *ff.*; *MA.* i, 49; quoted at *Kathāvatthu,* ii, 325; *Pts. of Contr.*, 189.

[2] *A-vi-tathaŋ.* [3] *An-aññathaŋ.* Text misprints in § 3.

[4] Not found elsewhere except at Dīgha, ii, 90 and *JA*, ii, 232, 'a village of the Vajjians, on the Ganges.'

to exist, destroyed is the channel[1] to becoming, there is no more coming to be.'

Thus spake the Exalted One. Then as Teacher he added this:

Who have not really seen the fourfold Ariyan truth
A long long road must wander on thro' many births.
Clean gone is that which leads to birth when these are seen;
Torn up the root of Ill. There is no more becoming.[2]

(ii) *Knowledge* (*b*).[3]

'Monks, whatsoever recluses or brahmins understand not, as it really is, This is Ill: this is the arising of Ill: this is the ceasing of Ill: this is the practice that leads to the ceasing of Ill,—such are not reckoned as recluses among recluses nor as brahmins among brahmins, nor have those worthies, in this very life, of themselves realized by their own knowledge the reality of recluseship or of brahminhood.

But whatsoever recluses or brahmins have understood, as it really is, the meaning of: This is Ill . . . those worthies have indeed of themselves, in this very life, realized by their own knowledge the reality of recluseship and brahminhood.'

Thus spake the Exalted One. Having thus spoken the Happy One added this as Teacher:

Who understand not Ill, and how Ill comes to be,
And how Ill ceases utterly without remains,
Nor know the Way that leads on to Ill's ending,
Such lack the heart's release, they lack release by insight.
Helpless to make an end, to birth and eld they go.

But understanding Ill and how Ill comes to be,
And where Ill ceases utterly without remains,
Knowing the Way that leads on to Ill's ending,
Blessed with the heart's release, blessed with release by insight,
They, able to end all, go not to birth and eld.

---

[1] *Bhava-netti* (lit. 'conduit').

[2] *Cf. D.* ii, 91; *Vin.* i, 231.

[3] This Sutta occurs at *Itivutt.* 105-6, and in a different setting at *Sn.* v, 725: *cf. SnA.* 504. Our *Comy.* passes it by.

(iii) *Fully enlightened.*

Sāvatthī (was the occasion). . . . The Exalted One said:

'Monks, there are these four Ariyan truths. What four? The Ariyan truth of Ill . . . These are the four.

Monks, by the fact of understanding, as they really are, these four Ariyan truths, a Tathāgata is called "Arahant, a Fully Enlightened One."

Wherefore, monks, ye must make an effort to realize: This is Ill. . . .'

(iv) *Arahants.*

Sāvatthī . . . The Exalted One said:

'Monks, whatsoever Arahants, fully enlightened ones, in past time had full understanding (of things) as they really are, all of them had full understanding of the four Ariyan truths as they really are.

Whatsoever Arahants, fully enlightened ones, shall in future time have full understanding of things as they really are, all of them will have full understanding of the four Ariyan truths as they really are.

Whatsoever Arahants, fully enlightened ones, do now fully understand things as they really are, all of them have full understanding of the four Ariyan truths as they really are. What are the four?

The Ariyan truth of Ill . . .

Wherefore, monks, an effort must be made to realize: This is Ill . . . this is the practice that leads to the ceasing of Ill.'

(v) *Destruction of the āsavas.*[1]

Monks, in him who knows, in him who sees, do I declare the āsavas to be destroyed: not in him who knows not, who sees not. And what, monks, is the destruction of the āsavas in him who knows, who sees?

In him who knows, who sees: This is Ill . . . there is destruction of the āsavas.

[1] *Cf. S.* ii, 29; *Pts. of Contr.*, 116.

Wherefore, monks, an effort must be made to realize: This is Ill. . . .

(vi) *Friends.*[1]

Monks, those for whom ye have fellow-feeling, those who may deem you worth listening to, your friends and colleagues, your kinsmen and blood-relations,—they ought to be roused to, admonished and established in, the comprehension of the four Ariyan truths as they really are. What four?

The Ariyan truth of Ill . . .

Wherefore, monks, an effort must be made to realize: This is Ill. . . .

(vii) *True.*

Monks, there are these four Ariyan truths. What four?

The Ariyan truth of Ill . . . the Ariyan truth of the practice that leads to the ceasing of Ill.

Now, monks, these four Ariyan truths are true, not false, not alterable. That is why they are called Ariyan truths.

Wherefore, monks, an effort must be made . . .

(viii) *The world.*

Monks, there are these four Ariyan truths . . .

In the world with its Devas, its Māras, its Brahmās, its host of recluses and brahmins, of Devas and mankind, the Tathāgata is an Ariyan. Therefore are they called 'Ariyan truths.'[2]

Wherefore, monks, an effort must be made . . .

(ix) *To be fully understood* or *Comprehended.*

Monks, there are these four Ariyan truths . . .

Of these four Ariyan truths, one is to be fully understood, one is to be abandoned, one is to be realized, one is to be cultivated.

Which Ariyan truth is to be fully understood?

---

[1] Text, 189.

[2] *Comy.* 'They are called "truths of the Ariyans," not "Ariyan truths," but are penetrated by way of the Ariyan truth.'

Ill, as an Ariyan truth, is to be fully understood. The arising of Ill, as an Ariyan truth, is to be abandoned. The ceasing of Ill, as an Ariyan truth, is to be realized. The practice that leads to its ceasing is to be cultivated. Wherefore, monks, an effort must be made . . .

(x) *Gavampati.*[1]

On a certain occasion a number of monks were staying among the Cetīs[2] at Sahajātā.[3]

Now on that occasion a number of elder monks, after going their rounds and eating their meal, were sitting in the pavilion. As they sat there in company their talk chanced to fall on this subject:

'Friends, he who sees Ill also sees the arising of Ill, he also sees the ceasing of Ill and the practice that leads to the ceasing of Ill.'

At these words the venerable Gavampati said this to the elder monks:

'Friends, I have heard this, I have learned this from the very lips of the Exalted One: "Monks, whoso seeth Ill sees also the arising, the ceasing of Ill and the practice that leads to the ceasing thereof. Whoso seeth the arising of Ill sees also Ill, its ceasing and the practice that leads thereto. Whoso seeth the ceasing of Ill sees also Ill, its arising and the practice that leads to the ceasing thereof. Whoso seeth the practice that leads to the ceasing of Ill, he also sees Ill, the arising of Ill and the ceasing of Ill." '

---

[1] Lit. 'bull' (lord of cows). A son of a Benares merchant; ordained by the Master in the very early days. *Cf. Vin.* i, 19; *Brethren*, p. 42; *Dialog.* ii, 373; *Pts. of Contr.*, 133.

[2] The Cetīs (*cf. Buddhist India*, 28, 29), probably of Nepal. Text reads *Cetesu.*

[3] Sinh. MSS. *Sahajāniyaŋ (-nāyaŋ)*. *Comy. Sahajātāyaŋ*; text (B), *Sahañcanike* (?). *Cf. Vin.* ii, 300; *A.* iii, 355 (*Sahajātiyaŋ*).

CHAPTER IV.—SIŊSAPĀ GROVE

(i) *Siŋsapā.*[1]

Once the Exalted One was staying at Kosambī in Siŋsapā Grove.

Then the Exalted One, gathering up a few siŋsapā leaves in his hand, said to the monks:

'What think ye, monks? Which are the more numerous, just this mere handful of siŋsapā leaves I have here, or those in the grove overhead?'

'Very few in number, lord, are the leaves in the handful gathered up by the Exalted One: much more in number are those in the grove overhead.'

'Just so, monks, much more in number are those things I have found out, but not revealed; very few are the things I have revealed. And why, monks, have I not revealed them?

Because they are not concerned with profit, they are not rudiments of the holy life, they conduce not to revulsion, to dispassion, to cessation, to tranquillity, to full comprehension, to the perfect wisdom, to Nibbāna. That is why I have not revealed them.[2]

And what is it, monks, that I have revealed?

Just that This is Ill. This is the arising of Ill. This is the ceasing of Ill. This is the practice that leads to the ceasing of Ill. And why so?

Because, monks, this is concerned with profit. It is the rudiments of the holy life. It does conduce to revulsion, to dispassion, to cessation, to tranquillity, to full comprehension, to the perfect wisdom. It does conduce to Nibbāna. Therefore have I revealed it.

Wherefore, monks, an effort must be made to realize: This is Ill . . . this is the practice that leads to the ceasing of Ill.'

---

[1] Of the tree *Dalbergia Sisu* or the Asoka tree. *Cf. A.* i, 136; *D.* ii, 316; *M.P.* 413.

[2] *Cf. D.* ii, 100.

(ii) *The acacia tree.*

Monks, if anyone should say: 'Without penetrating, as it really is, the Ariyan truth of Ill, without penetrating, as it really is, the Ariyan truth of the ceasing of Ill, without penetrating, as it really is, the Ariyan truth of the practice that leads to the ceasing of Ill, I will make an utter end of Ill,' it would be an impossibility for him to do so.

Just as, if anyone should say: 'I will make a leaf-basket[1] of acacia leaves or of Judas-tree leaves or of myrobalan leaves, and fetch water in it, or use them for a fan,'[2] it would be impossible for him to do so,—even so for him to make an utter end of Ill without[3] penetrating these four Ariyan truths would be an impossibility.

But, monks, if anyone should say: 'I will make a leaf-basket of lotus-leaves or pulāsa[4] leaves or creeper leaves, or make a fan of them,' it could be done. So also if one were to say: 'I will make an utter end of Ill by penetrating these four Ariyan truths,' it could be done.

Wherefore, monks, an effort must be made to realize: This is Ill. . . .

(iii) *The stick.*[5]

Monks, just as a stick, when thrown up into the air, falls, now on its butt, now on its middle, now on its tip, even so beings, hindered by ignorance, fettered by craving, run on, wander on, pass on from this world to the next and thence come back again to this world. What is the cause of it?

---

[1] *Puṭaŋ.* Palm fronds of different sorts are used for baskets in the tropics, and a plantain-leaf is used to make a cup. The leaves here mentioned would be too small for such purposes.

[2] *Tālapatta*, the bread leaves of the palmyra or of the talipat are used for fans and writing on. Lit. 'I will fetch water or a palm-leaf.'

[3] Text should read *anabhisamecca.*

[4] *Palāsa* (used above as the name of a small leaf) cannot stand here. I read *pulāsa* (*cf. JA.* iii, 478) with Sinh. MSS. It is a jungle tree with large leaves.

[5] *Cf. S.* ii, 185.

Through the fact of not seeing four Ariyan truths. What four? The Ariyan truth of Ill . . .

Wherefore, monks, an effort must be made to realize: This is Ill. . . .

(iv) *Turban.*[1]

'Monks, when one's turban or head is ablaze, what is to be done?'

'Lord, when one's turban or head is ablaze, for the extinguishing thereof one must put forth extra desire, effort, endeavour, exertion, impulse,[2] mindfulness and attention.'

'Well, monks, letting alone,[3] paying no heed to, the blazing turban or head, for the comprehension, as they really are, of the four not penetrated Ariyan truths, one must put forth extra desire, effort, endeavour, exertion, impulse, mindfulness and attention. What are the four?

The Ariyan truth of Ill . . . Wherefore, monks, an effort must be made to realize: This is Ill. . . .'

(v) *A hundred years.*

Suppose, monks, a man whose span of life is a hundred years.[4] Then they say to that man who lives a hundred years: 'See here, good fellow! At early dawn they will torture you with a hundred spears, again at midday and again at eventide. Now look you, friend, thus tortured day by day with three hundred spears, you will live on to a hundred, reach a hundred years of age. At the end of a hundred years you shall comprehend four Ariyan truths hitherto not comprehended.'

Well, monks, a clansman who had any sense might well undertake it.[5] Why?

Because, monks, incalculable[6] is the beginning of this faring

---

[1] *Cf. S.* i, 108, iii, 143 *n.* (ref. at *VM.* ii, 645); *A.* ii, 93.

[2] *Appaṭivāni* ('unfettered actions').

[3] *Ajjhupekkhitvā;* this word curiously has two opposite meanings: to attend to and to neglect (look with complacency on). Hence some MSS. read *anajjkh.* (The simile is ref. to at *PvA.* 149, in a similar sense.) *Cf. supra,* 69 *n.* [4] Text should read *vassa-sata-jīvin tam enaŋ.*

[5] *Alaŋ upagantuŋ* (the torture).

[6] *Anamatagga* ('un-thought of-beginning'). *Cf. K.S.* ii, cap. xv *ff.*

on. The earliest point is not revealed (of the pain) of blows from spears, swords and axes. Even if this were to befall one, monks, I would not deem the full comprehension of four Ariyan truths to be won with sorrow and woe, but with joy and gladness. What are the four ?[1]

The Ariyan truth of Ill . . . Wherefore, monks, an effort must be made to realize: This is Ill. . . .

(vi) *Living creatures.*

Suppose, monks, a man should cut up all the grass, sticks, branches and stalks in this Jambudīpa[2] and gather them together in a heap; were to bind them together and make a stake thereof. Then, having made a stake of them, suppose he spitted all the mighty creatures in the mighty ocean on mighty stakes; likewise all the creatures of middle size on stakes of middle size; likewise all the creatures of minute size on stakes of minute size.

All the bulky creatures in the mighty ocean might thus be used up: but, though he should use up and consume all the grass, sticks, branches and stalks in this Jambudīpa, yet would there still remain in the mighty ocean a majority of the minute animals which could not be impaled on stakes. Why so ? Because of the minuteness of their bodies.

Even thus widespread is the ruin of things. Yet from such widespread ruin he is saved who has the gift of sight to see, who understands, as it really is, This is Ill . . . who understands, as it really is, This is the practice that leads to the ceasing of Ill.

Wherefore, monks, an effort must be made to realize: This is Ill. . . .

(vii) *The parable of the sun* (*a*).

Monks, just as the dawn is the forerunner, the harbinger, of the arising of the sun, even so is right view the forerunner, the harbinger, of fully comprehending the four Ariyan truths.

---

[1] Text misprints *vadāmi,* l. 7, *pharasu* (l. 4), and at l. 8 omits *abhisamayaŋ.*

[2] India.

Of a monk who has right view it may be expected that he will understand: This is Ill, as it really is . . . that he will understand, as it really is, This is the practice that leads to the ceasing of Ill.

Wherefore, monks, an effort must be made to realize: This is Ill. . . .

(viii) *The parable of the sun* (*b*).

So long, monks, as moon and sun arise not in the world, so long is there no shining forth of great light, of great radiance. Then is there gloom and darkness, a murk of gloom and darkness, no telling whether it is night or day, no telling of months or half-months, no telling of the seasons of the year.

But, monks, when moon and sun shine in the world, then is there a shining forth of great light, of great radiance. Then is there no more gloom and darkness, no more murk of gloom and darkness, but one can tell whether it is night or day, one can tell the months and the half-months and the seasons of the year.

Just so, monks, so long as a Tathāgata arises not in the world, even so long is there no shining forth of the light, of great radiance. Then is there gloom and darkness, a murk of gloom and darkness, then is there no proclamation of the four Ariyan truths, no teaching, no setting forth, no establishing, opening up, analyzing or making of them plain.

But, monks, as soon as a Tathāgata arises in the world, then is there a shining forth of great light, of great radiance. Then is there no more gloom and darkness, no more murk of gloom and darkness; then is there proclamation of the four Ariyan truths, then is there teaching, setting forth, establishing, opening up, analyzing and making of them plain. Of what four Ariyan truths ?

The Ariyan truth of Ill . . . Wherefore, monks, an effort must be made to realize: This is Ill. . . .

(ix) *Foundation stone.*

Monks, whatsoever recluses or brahmins understand not, as it really is, the meaning of: This is Ill . . . such maybe scan the face of[1] some recluse or brahmin and conclude: Surely this worthy is one who knowing knows and seeing sees!

Just as, monks, a tuft of cotton-wool or a ball of thistle-down, lightly wafted on the wind, is cast down on level ground, and the east wind whirls it west, and the west wind whirls it east, the north wind whirls it south and the south wind whirls it north. What is the cause of that? Monks, it is the lightness of the ball of thistledown.

Just so, monks, whatsoever recluses or brahmins understand not, as it really is, the meaning of: This is Ill . . . such maybe scan the face of some recluse or brahmin and conclude: Surely this worthy is one who knowing knows and seeing sees! What is the cause of that? It is through not seeing clearly the four Ariyan truths.

But whatsoever recluses or brahmins do understand, as it really is, the meaning of: This is Ill . . . such scan not the face of some recluse or brahmin and conclude: Surely this worthy is one who knowing knows and seeing sees!

Again, monks, just as an iron pillar or threshold of a door[2] or some deep-set pedestal is unshakable, unquakable: if there came from the eastern quarter a violent blast of wind and rain, it could not shake it, could not make it quake and quake again. If likewise from the west and north and south there came a violent blast of wind and rain, yet it could not shake it, could not make it quake and quake again. Why not? Because, monks, that threshold is deep set, that pedestal is deep set.

Even so, monks, whatsoever recluses or brahmins understand not, as it really is, the meaning of: This is Ill . . . such need not to scan the face of some recluse or brahmin and

---

[1] *Mukhaŋ ullokenti=ajjhāsayaŋ* (disposition). *Comy.*

[2] *Cf.* text, 270; *Dhp.* 18, 298; *Sn.* 229 (*SnA.* 185).

conclude: Surely this worthy is one who knowing knows and seeing sees! Why so? Because of seeing clear the four Ariyan truths. What four? The Ariyan truth of: This is Ill. . . .

Wherefore, monks, an effort must be made to realize: This is Ill. . . .

(x) *Dogmatists* (*vādino*).

Monks, whatsoever monk understands, as it really is, the meaning of: This is Ill . . . suppose from the east there comes a recluse or brahmin looking for dogma, searching for dogma, in hopes of refuting such dogma, it would be impossible for such recluse or brahmin to shake that monk in his belief, standing as he does on truth:[1] it would be impossible to make him quake or waver. Likewise if there came from west or north or south a recluse or brahmin looking for dogma, searching for dogma, in hopes of refuting such, it would be impossible for such recluse or brahmin to shake that monk in his belief, impossible to make him quake or waver.

Suppose, monks, a stone column sixteen cubits long, and eight cubits of it are sunk in the ground below the pedestal, while eight cubits are above the pedestal. Then from the east and west and north and south there comes a blast of wind and rain,—it could not shake it, could not make it quake or waver. What is the cause of that? Because, monks, the pedestal is deep set, the stone column is deep dug.

Just in the same way, monks, whatsoever monk understands, as it really is: This is Ill . . . suppose from east and west and north and south there comes a recluse or brahmin looking for dogma, searching for dogma, in hopes of refuting such dogma, it would be impossible for such recluse or brahmin to shake that monk in his belief, standing as he does on truth, impossible to make him quake or quaver. Why so? It is because he clearly sees four Ariyan truths. What four? The Ariyan truth of: This is Ill. . . .

Wherefore, monks, an effort must be made to realize: This is Ill. . . .

---

[1] *Saha-dhammena*=*dhammena*. It might mean 'by fair means.'

CHAPTER V.—THE PRECIPICE

(i) *Reasoning.*

On a certain occasion the Exalted One was staying near Rājagaha, in Bamboo Grove, at the Squirrels' Feeding Ground.

Now on that occasion the Exalted One addressed the monks, saying:

'Once upon a time, monks, a certain man left Rājagaha with this intention: " I will speculate about the world "; and he came to Sumāgavā[1] Lotus Pond. On reaching it he sat down on the bank of the lotus pond and fell to speculating about the world.[2]

Now, monks, that man saw an army with its four divisions (of elephants and horses, chariots and infantry) entering a lotus stalk. On seeing it he thought: I must be mad! I must be out of my mind,[3] for I have seen what does not exist in the world!

Well, monks, that man went into the town and told a great crowd of folk: " Sirs, I must be mad! I must be out of my mind, for I have seen what does not exist in the world!"

" How's that, good fellow? How are you mad? How are you out of your mind? What have you seen that's not in the world?"

" Why, sirs, it's like this. I left Rājagaha with this intention: 'I will speculate about the world'; and I came to Sumāgavā Lotus Pond. When I got there I sat down on the bank of the pond and fell to speculating about the world. Then, sirs, I saw an army with its four divisions entering a lotus stalk.[4] That, sirs, is how I must be mad, must be out of my mind, for I saw what does not exist in the world."

---

[1] Text has *Sumāgadhā*, but Sinh. MSS. and *Comy.*, which I follow, *Sumāgavā* (a tank near Rājagaha).

[2] *Loka-cintā. Comy.* 'Such as: Who made the moon and sun? Who made the earth, the ocean, beings, mountains, mangoes, coconuts, etc.?'

[3] *Viceto=vikhitta-citta. Comy.*

[4] Here the Asuras would seem to be fairies or nature-spirits.

" Indeed, good fellow, you are mad, you are out of your mind! What you saw does not exist in the world!"

Now, monks, what that man saw was real, not unreal.

Once upon a time, monks, the hosts of the Devas and the Asuras were arrayed for battle, and in that battle the Devas won the day, the Asuras were defeated; and the Asuras, defeated and panic-stricken, entered Asura Town by way of a lotus-stalk, in terror of the Devas.[1]

Wherefore, monks, reason not about the world[2] thus: "Eternal is the world or Not eternal is the world. Finite is the world or Infinite is the world. Life is the same as body or Life and body are different. The Tathāgata exists after death or The Tathāgata exists not; or He both exists and exists not; or The Tathāgata neither exists nor not-exists after death." Why do I say this?

Because, monks, it is not concerned with profit, it is not the rudiments of the holy life: because it conduces not to revulsion, to dispassion, to cessation, to tranquillity, to comprehension, to the perfect wisdom, because it conduces not to Nibbāna.

When ye reason, monks, reason thus: This is Ill. This is the arising of Ill. This is the ceasing of Ill. This is the practice that leads to the ceasing of Ill. Why do I say so?

Because, monks, such reasonings are concerned with profit . . . they conduce to Nibbāna.

Wherefore, monks, an effort must be made to realize: This is Ill. . . .'

(ii) *The precipice.*

On a certain occasion the Exalted One was staying near Rājagaha, on the hill Vulture's Peak. Then the Exalted One addressed the monks, saying: ' Monks, let us go to Splendid Spur[3] for the noonday rest.'

' So be it, lord,' replied those monks to the Exalted One.

So the Exalted One with a number of monks came to

---

[1] Text *bhāyamānā*, but *v.ll.* and *Comy. mohayamānā*, expl. as *devānaŋ cittaŋ mohattā*.

[2] Text, 418.

[3] *Paṭibhāna-kūṭo* (? *prati-bhā-*, 'splendour'). Not mentioned elsewhere. *Comy.* 'a great mountain-like perforated rock.'

Splendid Spur. Now a certain monk saw the great precipice and on seeing it said to the Exalted One:

'Lord, this is indeed a great precipice! This is indeed a fearsome precipice, lord! Pray, lord, is there anywhere a precipice greater and more frightful?'

'Yes, monk. There is indeed a precipice greater and more frightful. And what is that?

Monks, whatsoever recluses or brahmins understand not, as it really is, the meaning of This is Ill . . . such delight in activities that lead to rebirth, that lead to old age, to death, sorrow, grief, woe, lamentation and despair. Thus taking delight, they compose a compound[1] of activities that conduce to rebirth . . . lamentation and despair. Thus composing a compound of activities that lead (to such ends), they fall down the precipice of rebirth, of old age, of death . . . they fall down the precipice of lamentation and despair. Such are not released from rebirth . . . lamentation and despair. They are not released from Ill, I declare.

But, monks, those recluses or brahmins who do understand, as it really is, the meaning of This is Ill . . . such take not delight in activities that conduce to rebirth . . . lamentation and despair. Not taking delight therein they compose not a compound of activities that conduce to rebirth . . . lamentation and despair. Not composing a compound of activities that so lead, they fall not down the precipice of rebirth, old age, death . . . lamentation and despair. They are utterly released from rebirth . . . they are released from Ill, I declare.

Wherefore, monks, an effort must be made to realize: This is Ill . . . this is the practice that leads to the ceasing of Ill.'

(iii) *Distress.*

'Monks, there is a Hell called "The Great Distress." Therein, whatsoever object one sees with the eye, one sees it as repulsive, not attractive: as repellent, not as charming: one sees it as unpleasant, not as pleasant.

---

[1] *Saṅkhāre abhisaṅkharonti.* *Cf. S.* iii, 87; *K.S.* iii, 73.

Whatsoever sound one hears with the ear, one hears it as repulsive . . . whatsoever taste . . . whatsoever smell . . . whatsoever tangible one contacts with body, one contacts it as repulsive . . . whatsoever mental states one is conscious of with mind, one is conscious of them as repulsive, not attractive: as repellent, not as charming: as unpleasant, not as pleasant.'

At these words a certain monk exclaimed to the Exalted One:

'Lord, that is indeed a great distress! A great distress indeed, lord! Pray, lord, is there any other distress greater or more fearsome?'

'There is indeed, monks, a distress greater and more fearsome. And what is that?

Whatsoever recluses or brahmins understand not, as it really is, the meaning of: This is Ill . . .' (*the whole as in previous Sutta to the end*).

(iv) *The peaked house.*

'If anyone, monks, should say: "Without comprehending as it really is, the Ariyan truth of Ill . . . I will make an utter end of Ill," it would be impossible for him to do so.

Suppose, monks, one should say: "Without building the lower part of a house, I will fix the upper part," he could not do it. Just so, monks, if one should say: "Without fully comprehending, as it really is, the meaning of: This is Ill . . . I will make an utter end of Ill," he could not do it.

But if one should say: "By fully comprehending, as it really is, the meaning of the Ariyan truth of This is Ill . . . I will make an utter end of Ill," he could do so.

Suppose, monks, someone should say: "After building the lower part of a house I will fix the upper part," he could do so. Just so, if one should say: "By fully comprehending, as it really is, the meaning of the Ariyan truth of This is Ill . . . I will make an utter end of Ill," he could do so.

Wherefore, monks, an effort must be made to realize: This is Ill. . . .'

(v) *The keyhole.*[1]

On a certain occasion the Exalted One was staying at Vesālī in Great Grove, at the Hall of the Peaked Gable.

Now the venerable Ānanda, robing himself in the forenoon and taking bowl and outer robe, went into Vesālī to beg.

Then the venerable Ānanda saw a number of Licchavi youths in the gymnasium,[2] making practice at archery,[3] shooting even at a distance through a very small keyhole, and splitting an arrow,[4] shot after shot, without ever a miss.

Now when the venerable Ānanda saw it he exclaimed to himself: 'Practised shots are these Licchavi youths! Well practised shots indeed are these Licchavi youths, to be able to shoot like this even at a distance!'

So when the venerable Ānanda had gone his rounds in Vesālī, had returned and eaten his meal, he went to see the Exalted One, and on coming to him saluted him and sat down at one side. So seated the venerable Ānanda said this to the Exalted One:

'Here, lord, robing myself in the forenoon and taking bowl and outer robe I set out for Vesālī on my begging rounds. Then, lord, I saw a number of Licchavi youths in the gymnasium making practice at archery, shooting even from a distance through a very small keyhole, and splitting an arrow, shot after shot, with never a miss. And I said to myself, lord: "Practised shots are these Licchavi youths! Well practised shots indeed are these Licchavi youths, to be able even at a distance to splinter an arrow through a very small keyhole, shot after shot, with never a miss!"'

'Now what think you, Ānanda? Which is the harder, which is the harder task to compass: To shoot like that or

---

[1] *Chiggaḷa.* In next Sutta it has a different meaning.

[2] *Santhâgāre. Comy. sippa-gaṇhana-sālāyaŋ.*

[3] *Upāsanaŋ karonte.* For amazing feats of archery see *JA.* v, 130 *ff.*, referred to below.

[4] *Asanaŋ atipātente=kaṇḍaŋ atikkamente*: 'getting the better of a shaft' *Comr.* (who explains that the arrow following split the one before it).

to pierce one strand of a hair, a hundred times divided, with another strand?'[1]

'Why, lord, of course to split a hair in such a way is the harder, much the harder task.'

'Just so, Ānanda, they who penetrate the meaning of: This is Ill . . . pierce through something much harder to pierce.

Wherefore, Ānanda, you must make an effort to realize: This is Ill . . .'

(vi) *Gross darkness.*

The Exalted One said . . .

'Monks, there is a darkness of interstellar space;[2] impenetrable gloom, such a murk of darkness as cannot enjoy the splendour of this moon and sun, though they be of such mighty magic power and majesty.'

At these words a certain monk said to the Exalted One:

'Lord, that must be a mighty darkness, a mighty darkness indeed! Pray, lord, is there any other darkness greater and more fearsome than that?'

'There is indeed, monk, another darkness, greater and more fearsome. And what is that other darkness?

Monk, whatsoever recluses or brahmins understand not, as it really is, the meaning of: This is Ill . . . such take delight in the activities which conduce to rebirth.[3] Thus taking delight they compose a compound of activities which conduce to rebirth. Thus composing a compound of activities they fall down into the darkness of rebirth, into the darkness of old age and death, of sorrow, grief, woe, lamentation and despair. They are not released from birth and death . . . and despair. They are not released from Ill, I declare.

---

[1] *Comy.* (referring to the feats of Jotipāla at *JA.* v, 130), if I understand it aright, says: 'Splitting a hair into a hundred strands he takes one (? strand) and binds an egg-plant (*vātingaṇa*, misinterpreted at *JA.* trans. in the *Cambridge Series*) on its middle, and binds another strand to the tip of his arrow. Then standing at the distance of one *usabha* (? 140 cubits) he pierces, with the end tied on his arrow, that which is tied to the egg-plant.' *Cf. DhpA.* i, 288.

[2] *Lokantarikā aghā.*

[3] Text, 449.

But, monk, those recluses or brahmins who do understand, as it really is, the meaning of: This is Ill . . . such take not delight in the activities which conduce to rebirth. Thus not taking delight they compose not a compound of such activities. Thus not compounding . . . they fall not down into the darkness of rebirth . . . old age . . . sorrow . . . and despair. They are released therefrom. They are released from Ill, I declare.

Wherefore, monk, an effort must be made to realize: This is Ill. . . .'

(vii) *Yoke-hole (a).*[1]

'Suppose, monks, a man should throw into the mighty ocean a yoke with a single hole, and there were a blind turtle to pop up to the surface once in every hundred years.

Now what think ye, monks? Would that blind turtle push his neck through that yoke with one hole whenever he popped up to the surface, once at the end of every hundred years?'

'It might be so, lord, now and again, after the lapse of a long time.'

'Well, monks, sooner I declare would that blind turtle push his neck through that yoke with one hole, popping up to the surface once in a hundred years, than would a fool who has gone to the Downfall become a man again.[2]

What is the reason for that?

Because, monks, here prevails no practice of the holy life, no righteous living, no doing of good deeds, no working of merit, but just cannibalism and preying on weaker creatures. Why so?

It is through not seeing the four Ariyan truths, to wit: The Ariyan truth of Ill, the Ariyan truth of the arising of Ill,

---

[1] *Chiggaḷa*. *Cf.* above and *M.* iii, 169; *Expos.* i, 80; *Sisters*, 173; *Brethren*, 30; *Mil. Pañh.*, 204.

[2] At *M.* iii, 169, he may become a man again, but only in a low caste, in miserable conditions. Apparently those who fail to reach the state of Stream-winning by the end of the *kalpa* are 'thrown down' and have to begin again an elementary condition when the next *kalpa* starts.

the Ariyan truth of the ceasing of Ill, the Ariyan truth of the practice that leads to the ceasing of Ill.

Wherefore, monks, an effort must be made to realize: This is Ill. . . .'

(viii) *Yoke-hole (b).*[1]

'Suppose, monks, this mighty earth were one mass of water, and a man were to throw down thereon a yoke with one hole. Then comes a wind from the east and wafts it west, and a wind from the west wafts it east: a north wind wafts it south and a south wind wafts it north. Then once at the end of a hundred years a blind turtle pops up to the surface. Now what think ye, monks? Would that blind turtle push his neck through that yoke with one hole whenever he popped up to the surface at the end of a hundred years?'

'It is unlikely,[2] lord, that the blind turtle would do that.'

'It is just as unlikely, monks, that one will get birth in human form; just as unlikely that a Tathāgata should arise in the world, an Arahant, a fully Enlightened One; just as unlikely, monks, that the Norm and Discipline proclaimed by a Tathāgata should be shown in the world.

But now indeed, monks, this state of human birth is won, and a Tathāgata has arisen in the world, and the Norm and Discipline proclaimed by the Tathāgata is shown in the world.

Wherefore, monks, ye must make an effort to realize: This is Ill. . . .'

(ix) *Sineru (a).*

'Suppose, monks, a man should lay down on Sineru, lord of mountains, seven grains of gravel as large as beans.[3]

Now what think ye, monks? Which is the more, those seven grains of gravel as large as beans laid there, or Sineru, lord of mountains?'

---

[1] This Sutta introduces the passages (from *M.* iii) omitted in the previous one.

[2] *A-dhiccaŋ*. *Comy. idaŋ adhicc' uppatikaŋ* (viz. provided that the yoke did not rot away, or the sea dry up, or the turtle die), and suggests the meaning as *yad' icchā-vasena* ('at pleasure')!

[3] *Cf. S.* ii, 134-7; *K.S.* ii, 95 *ff.*

'Why, lord, this is greater, this Sineru, lord of mountains. Very small are the seven grains of gravel laid down as large as beans. They cannot be reckoned, cannot be compared with it: they do not come to the merest fraction of a part when compared with Sineru, lord of mountains.'

'Even so, monks, for the Ariyan disciple who is blessed with vision, for a person of understanding, far greater is this Ill which he has destroyed, which he has used up, and infinitely small is that Ill which remains. It cannot be reckoned, cannot be compared therewith. It does not come to the merest fraction of a part of it, when set beside that Ill which he has destroyed, which he has used up,—that is, it is just a period of seven lives at most,[1] for the man who understands, as it really is, the meaning of: This is Ill. . . .

Wherefore, monks, an effort must be made to realize: This is Ill. . . .'

(x) *Sineru (b).*

'Suppose, monks, Sineru, lord of mountains, should come to[2] extinction, should come to an end, all save seven grains of gravel as large as beans. Now what think ye, monks? Which is the more, that part of Sineru, lord of mountains, which has come to extinction, come to an end, or those seven grains of gravel as large as beans?'

'Why, lord, that part of Sineru, lord of mountains, is the more. Very small are seven grains of gravel as large as beans. They cannot be reckoned, they cannot be compared with it: they do not come to the merest fraction of a part when set beside all that part of Sineru which is extinguished, which has come to an end.'

'Just so, monks, for the Ariyan disciple who is blessed with vision, for a person of understanding, far greater is this Ill which he has destroyed, which he has used up . . .' (*as above*).

---

[1] *Sattakkhattuŋ paramatā*. *Cf. n.* to *K.S.* ii, 95. *Comy.* 'a measure of seven existences (rebirths)'; *i.e.*, such a man is a Stream-winner.

[2] *Cf. S.* ii, 138. Text inserts *yam* here, omitted by Sinh. MSS., but required in next §.

CHAPTER VI.—COMPREHENSION[1]

(i) *Tip of the nail.*

Then the Exalted One, taking up a little dust on the tip of his finger-nail, said to the monks:

'Now what think ye, monks? Which is the greater, this little dust I have taken up on the tip of my finger-nail, or this mighty earth?'

'Greater, lord, is this mighty earth. Exceeding small[2] is this little dust taken up on the tip of the Exalted One's finger-nail: it cannot be reckoned, it cannot be compared therewith. It does not come to the merest fraction of a part of it when set beside the mighty earth,[3]—this little dust taken up on the tip of the Exalted One's finger-nail.'

'Well, just so, monks, for the Ariyan disciple who is blessed with vision, for the person who has understanding, far greater is this Ill which he has destroyed, which he has used up, and infinitely small is that Ill which remains. It cannot be reckoned, cannot be compared therewith. It does not come to the merest fraction of a part of it when set beside that Ill which he has destroyed, which he has used up,—that is, it is just a period of seven lives at most for the man who understands, as it really is: This is Ill. . . . This is the practice that leads to the ceasing of Ill.

Wherefore, monks, ye must make an effort to realize: This is Ill. . . .'

(ii) *The tank.*

'Suppose, monks, there were a tank of fifty yojanas in length, fifty yojanas in width, fifty in depth, full of water, brimful, so that a crow could drink therefrom; and thence a man draws water on the tip of a blade of grass.

Now what think ye, monks? Which is the more, the water

---

[1] All the similes of this chapter are nearly the same as those at *S.* ii, 133.

[2] Text should read *appamattak' āyaŋ* B.

[3] Text should read *-pathaviŋ*; and *dukkhan ti* (p. 460, l. 3).

drawn up on the tip of a blade of grass or the water that is in the tank?'

'This, lord, is the more, the water in the tank. Very little is the water drawn up on the tip of a blade of grass: it cannot be reckoned, cannot be compared therewith. It does not come to the merest fraction of a part of it when set beside the water in the tank,[1]—that water drawn up on the tip of a blade of grass.'

'Just so, monks, for the Ariyan disciple . . .' (*as above*).

(iii) *Confluence* (*a*).

'Suppose, monks, that where these great rivers, to wit: Ganges, Yamunā, Aciravatī, Sarabhū and Mahī flow together, meet together, a man draws two or three drops of water.

Now what think ye, monks? Which is the more: those two or three drops of water thus drawn up or the water at the confluence?'

'Why, lord, this is the more, the water at the confluence. Exceeding small are the two or three drops of water drawn up: they cannot be reckoned, they cannot be compared therewith. They do not amount to the merest fraction of a part of the water at the confluence,—these two or three drops of water thus drawn up.'

'Just so, monks, to the Ariyan disciple . . .' (*as above*).

(iv) *Confluence* (*b*).

'Suppose, monks, that where those great rivers the Ganges, Yamunā, Aciravatī, Sarabhū and Mahī flow together, meet together, the water wastes away and comes to an end, except two or three drops.

Now what think ye, monks? Which is the greater: the water at the confluence, which has wasted away and come to an end, or those two or three drops that remain?'

'Why, lord, this water at the confluence, that has wasted away, come to an end, is the greater. Exceeding small are those two or three drops that remain: they cannot be reckoned,

---

[1] Text should read *pokkharaṇiyā*.

cannot be compared therewith. They do not amount to the merest fraction of a part of the water at the confluence, which has wasted away, come to an end,—these two or three drops that remain.'

'Just so, monks, to the Ariyan disciple . . .' (*as before*).

(v) *The earth* (*a*).

'Suppose, monks, that a man lays together on the mighty earth seven balls of clay as big as kola-stones.[1]

Now what think ye, monks? Which is the greater: those balls of clay as big as kola-stones, thus laid together, or this mighty earth?'

'Why, lord, this mighty earth is the greater. Exceeding small are the balls of clay as big as kola-stones: they cannot be reckoned, they cannot be compared therewith. They do not amount to the merest fraction of a part of this mighty earth,—those balls of clay as big as kola-stones.'

'Just so, monks, to the Ariyan disciple . . .' (*as before*).

(vi) *The earth* (*b*).

'Suppose, monks, the mighty earth should waste away, come to an end, all except just seven balls of clay as big as kola-stones.

Now what think ye, monks? Which is the greater: that part of the mighty earth which has wasted away, come to an end, or those seven balls of clay, as big as kola-stones, that remain?'

'Why, lord, greater is that part of the mighty earth which has wasted away, come to an end. Exceeding small are the seven balls of clay as big as kola-stones that remain: they cannot be reckoned, cannot be compared therewith. They do not amount to the merest fraction of a part of the mighty earth that has wasted away, come to an end,—those seven balls of clay as big as kola-stones.'

'Just so, monks, to the Ariyan disciple . . .' (*as above*).

---

[1] The fruit of the jujube tree.

(vii) *The ocean* (*a*).

'Suppose, monks, the water in the mighty ocean should waste away, be used up, all except two or three drops of water.

Now what think ye, monks? Which is the more: that water of the mighty ocean which has wasted away, been used up, or those two or three drops of water that remain?'

'Why, lord, greater is the water of the mighty ocean . . . exceeding small are those two or three drops of water that remain. . . .'

'Just so, monks, to the Ariyan disciple . . .' (*as above*).

(viii) *The ocean* (*b*).

'Suppose, monks, the water in the mighty ocean should waste away, be used up, all except two or three drops of water.

Now what think ye, monks? Which is the more: that water of the mighty ocean which has wasted away, been used up, or those two or three drops of water that remain?'

'Why, lord, greater is the water of the mighty ocean . . . exceeding small are those two or three drops that remain. . . .'

'Just so, monks, to the Ariyan disciple . . .'

(ix) *Simile of the mountain* (*a*).

'Suppose, monks, a man should lay down together on Himâlaya, lord of mountains, seven grains of gravel as large as mustard seeds.

Now what think ye, monks? Which is the greater: those seven grains of gravel as large as mustard seeds, or this Himâlaya, lord of mountains?'

'Why, lord, greater is this Himâlaya, lord of mountains. Exceeding small are the seven grains of gravel as large as mustard seeds thus laid together. They cannot be compared . . .'

'Just so, monks, to the Ariyan disciple . . .'

(x) *Simile of the mountain* (*b*).

'Suppose, monks, that Himâlaya, lord of mountains, should waste away, come to an end, except for seven grains of gravel as large as mustard seeds.

Now what think ye, monks? Which is the greater: that part of Himâlaya, lord of mountains, that has wasted away, come to an end, or those seven grains of gravel as large as mustard seeds?'

'Why, lord, this is the greater, Himâlaya, lord of mountains. Exceeding small are the seven grains of gravel as large as mustard seeds. They cannot be reckoned, cannot be compared therewith: they do not amount to the merest fraction of a part when laid beside that part of Himâlaya that has wasted away, come to an end,—those seven grains of gravel as large as mustard seeds.'

'Well, monks, it is just so to the Ariyan disciple who is blessed with wisdom, to the person who has understanding. Far greater is this Ill he has destroyed, used up, and infinitely small is the Ill that remains. It cannot be reckoned, cannot be compared therewith. It does not amount to the merest fraction of a part when laid beside that Ill he has destroyed, used up,—that is, it is just a period of seven lives at most, for the man who understands, as it really is, the meaning of: This is Ill. This is the arising of Ill. This is the ceasing of Ill. This is the practice that leads to the ceasing of Ill.

Wherefore, monks, an effort must be made to realize: This is Ill . . .'[1]

CHAPTER VII.—CYCLIC-REPETITION

(i) *Other than.*

Then the Exalted One, taking up a little dust on the tip of his finger-nail, addressed the monks, saying:

'Now what think ye, monks? Which is the greater: this little dust I have taken up on the tip of my finger-nail, or this mighty earth?'

'Why, lord, this is the greater, this mighty earth . . .' (*as before*). . . .

---

[1] Here the third simile of *S.* ii, 139 (of Sineru and beans) is omitted.

'Just so, monks, few are those beings that are reborn among men: more numerous are these beings that are reborn other than men. What is the cause of that?

It is through not seeing[1] four Ariyan truths. What four? The Ariyan truth of Ill, the Ariyan truth of the arising of Ill, the Ariyan truth of the ceasing of Ill, the Ariyan truth of the practice that leads to the ceasing of Ill.

Wherefore, monks, an effort must be made to realize: This is Ill. . . .'

(ii) *Outlying.*

Then the Exalted One, taking up a little dust . . . (*as before*). . . .

Just so, monks, few are those beings that are reborn in the middle districts: more numerous are they that are reborn in the outlying districts, among the unreasoning barbarians.[2]

Wherefore, monks, an effort must be made . . .

(iii) *Insight.*

. . . (*As before.*) . . .

Just so, monks, few are those beings that are blessed with the Ariyan eye of insight: more numerous are these beings that are sunk in ignorance and bewilderment.

(iv) *Intoxicating liquor.*

. . . Just so, monks, few are those beings that are abstainers from intoxicants, fermented[3] or distilled, producing indolence: more numerous are they who are non-abstainers therefrom.

---

[1] Text should read *adiṭṭhattā*.

[2] *Aviññātaresu milakkhesu* (Skt. *mleccha*) in the sense of the Greek *barbaroi*. *Cf. DA.* i, 177; *SnA.* ii, 397=*SA.* on *S.* i, 188. 'Such as Damiḷā (Tamils), Kirātā, Yavanā (Milakkhā),' Dravidians of S. India, etc. *Comy.*

[3] *Comy.* *surā=piṭṭha-surā* (barley-ferment), *odaniya-surā* (rice-ferment), *pūva-surā* (sweetmeats ?), *kiṇṇa-pakkhittā* (yeast-mixture), *sambhāra-saŋyuttā* (a concoction of *kañji*), which are called 'the fivefold secretion (*āsava*) of flowers'; but does not mention any sort of toddy, though I think *pūva* (? jaggery) which is made from fermented kitul-palm juice, would include such.

(v) *Water-born.*

. . . Just so, monks, few are those beings that are born on land: more numerous are they that are born in water. What is the cause of that ?

(Through not seeing the four Ariyan truths.)[1] . . .

(vi) *Reverent to mothers.*

. . . Just so, monks, few are those beings[2] that reverence[3] their mothers: more numerous are they that reverence not their mothers. . . .

(vii) *Reverent to fathers.*

. . . Just so, monks, few are those beings that reverence their fathers: more numerous are they that reverence not their fathers. . . .

(viii) *Reverent to recluses.*[4]

. . . Just so, monks, few are those beings that reverence recluses: more numerous are they that reverence not recluses. . . .

(ix) *Reverent to brahmins.*[5]

. . . Just so, monks, few are those beings that reverence brahmins: more numerous are they that reverence not brahmins. . . .

(x) *Respect to elders.*[6]

. . . Just so, monks, few are those beings that pay respect to the elders of the clan: more numerous are they that pay not respect to[7] the elders of the clan. . . .

---

[1] Text thus far. Presumably § 1 is referred to.

[2] Text should read *sattā*.

[3] These terms (vi-ix) occur at *Pv.* ii, 7; *PvA.* 104.

[4] *Sāmaññā=samana-pūjakā*, def. at text, 25.

[5] Here in the derived meaning of *bāhita-pāpa-pūjakā*. *Comy.* 'a synonym for those who have attained perfection.'

[6] Text follows *uddāna* in wrongly printing *Pacāyika*, which should read *apacāyika*.

[7] Text again wrong in reading *jeṭṭhâpacāyino* (taking it as negative of *pacāyika*) in the second instance. It should be *jeṭṭhânapacāyino*.

CHAPTER VIII.—FEW ABSTAIN[1]

(i) *Life.*

(*As in previous Suttas.*) . . .

Just so, monks, few are those beings that abstain from taking the life of creatures: more numerous are these beings who do not so abstain. What is the cause of that?

It is through not seeing four Ariyan truths.

(ii) *Not given.*

. . . Just so, monks, few are those beings that abstain from taking what is not given. . . .

(iii) *Sensual lust.*

. . . Just so, monks, few are those beings[2] that abstain from wrong practice in sensual lust. . . .

(iv) *Falsehood.*

. . . Just so, monks, few are those beings[2] that abstain from falsehood. . . .

(v) *Slander.*

. . . that abstain from slander. . . .

(vi) *Harsh speech.*

. . . that abstain from harsh speech. . . .

(vii) *Idle chatter.*

. . . that abstain from idle chatter. . . .

---

[1] For this chapter see *D.* i, 5 *ff.* (*Brahmajāla-sutta*); *Dialog.* i, 5 (where the Buddha is represented as saying: 'These are the trifles of mere morality which the unconverted man, when praising the *Tathāgata*, would speak in praise of'). These are the practices deemed unfit for a monk.

[2] Text should read *sattā*.

(viii) *Seed.*

. . . that abstain from spoiling[1] the different sorts of crops[2] and vegetation.[3] . . .

(ix) *Unseasonable.*

. . . that abstain from eating at unseasonable hours.[4] . . .

(x) *Scents and unguents.*

. . . that abstain from the use of flowers, scents, unguents as adornments and finery: more numerous are these beings that do not abstain from such use.

CHAPTER IX.—UNCOOKED-GRAIN REPETITION[5]

(i) *Nautch.*

. . . just so, monks, few are those beings that abstain from going to see exhibitions[6] of nautch-dancing and singing: more numerous are they that do not so abstain. . . .

(ii) *Bed.*

. . . from high and broad beds. . . .

(iii) *Silver.*

. . . from accepting gold[7] and silver. . . .

---

1 *Cf. A.* ii, 197; *DA.* 77, 81. *Comy. bīja-gāma=mūla-, khandha-, agga-, phalu-, bīja-bījaŋ.*

2 *Bhūta-gāma=nīla-tiṇa-rukkhâdi* (*DA.* reads *alla-tiṇa*).

3 *Samārambha,* 'uprooting or cutting down.'

4 *I.e.,* after midday.

5 As at *D.* i, 5. This chapter is merely a continuation of the previous list from which *Comy.* does not separate it.

6 *Visūka-dassanā. Comy.* (as at *DA.* i, 77) explains as *patāni-bhūtā* (? exhibited) and includes peacock-dancing.

7 *Jātarūpa* is uncoined gold.

(iv) *Uncooked grain.*

. . . from accepting gifts of uncooked grain. . . .

(v) *Uncooked flesh.*

. . . from accepting gifts of uncooked flesh. . . .

(vi) *Girls.*

. . . from accepting women or girls. . . .

(vii) *Female and male slaves.*

. . . from accepting female and male slaves. . . .

(viii) *Goats and sheep.*

. . . from accepting goats and sheep. . . .

(ix) *Fowls and swine.*

. . . from accepting fowls and swine. . . .

(x) *Elephants.*

. . . from accepting elephants, cattle, horses and mares. . . .

CHAPTER X.—MORE NUMEROUS

(i) *Fields.*

. . . Just so, monks, few are those beings that abstain from accepting fields, whether cultivated or waste: more numerous are they who do not so abstain.

(ii) *Buying and selling.*

. . . from buying and selling. . . .

(iii) *Errands.*

. . . from sending messengers or going as such. . . .

(iv) *Giving false measure.*

. . . from cheating with scales, copper vessels or measures.[1]

(v) *Perverting justice.*

. . . from taking bribes to pervert justice, cheating and crooked ways.[2] . . .

(vi) *Flogging, plundering and violence.*

. . . Just so, monks, few are those beings that abstain from cutting, flogging, binding, highway robbery, plundering and violent deeds: more numerous are these beings that do not so abstain. What is the cause?

It is through not seeing four Ariyan truths. What four? The Ariyan truth of This is Ill. . . . This is the practice that leads to the ceasing of Ill.

Wherefore, monks, an effort must be made to realize: This is Ill. . . .

CHAPTER XI.—THE FIVE DESTINIES

(i) *The five destinies* (the same title for all).

Then the Exalted One, taking up a little dust on the tip of his finger-nail, addressed the monks, saying:

'Now what think ye, monks? Which is the greater: this little dust I have taken up on the tip of my finger-nail, or this mighty earth?'

'Why, lord, this mighty earth is the greater. Exceeding small is this little dust taken up on the Exalted One's finger-nail. It cannot be reckoned, cannot be compared therewith.

---

[1] *Tūla-, kaŋsa-, māna-kūṭā.* *Comy.* takes *kaŋsa-k.* [as at *DA.*] as 'passing off bronze vessels as gold ones'; *Dialog.* i, 6, 'bronzes,' perhaps copper coins. I think the context requires the meaning to be 'pots for measuring,' *e.g.*, liquor.

[2] *Ukkotaṇa-vañcana; nikati-sāci-yogā.* *Cf. PuggA.* 240. The first is taken to mean 'taking bribes in giving a verdict about landownership, etc.' Text misprints *sāvi-y.*

It does not amount to the merest fraction of a part when laid beside this mighty earth,--this little dust taken up on the Exalted One's finger-nail.'

'Just so, monks, few indeed are those beings that, deceasing as human beings, are reborn among human beings: more numerous are these beings that, deceasing as human beings, are reborn in Purgatory. . . .

(ii).

. . . more numerous are these beings that, deceasing as human beings, are reborn in the womb of an animal.

(iii).

. . . that are reborn in the Realm of Ghosts. . . .

(iv-vi).

. . . few are those beings that, deceasing as human beings, are reborn among the Devas: more numerous are these beings that, deceasing as human beings, are reborn in purgatory . . . in the womb of an animal . . . in the Realm of Ghosts. . . .

(vii-ix).

. . . few are those beings that, deceasing as Devas, are reborn among the Devas: more numerous are these beings that, deceasing as Devas, are reborn in Purgatory . . . in the womb of an animal . . . in the Realm of Ghosts. . . .

(x-xii).

. . . that, deceasing as Devas, are reborn among men: more numerous are these beings that, deceasing as Devas, are reborn in Purgatory . . . the Realm of Ghosts. . . .

(xiii-xv).

. . . that, deceasing from Purgatory, are reborn among human beings: more numerous are these beings that, deceasing from Purgatory, are reborn in Purgatory . . . the Realm of Ghosts. . . .

(xvi-xviii).

. . . that, deceasing from Purgatory, are reborn among the Devas: more numerous are these beings that, deceasing as Devas, are reborn in Purgatory . . . the Realm of Ghosts. . . .

(xix-xxi).

. . . that, deceasing from life as animals, are reborn among human beings: more numerous are these beings that, deceasing as animals, are reborn in Purgatory . . . the Realm of Ghosts. . . .

(xxii-xxiv).

. . . that, deceasing as animals, are reborn among the Devas, more numerous are these beings that, deceasing as animals, are reborn in Purgatory . . .

(xxv-xxvii).

. . . that, deceasing from the Realm of Ghosts, are reborn among human beings: more numerous are these beings that, deceasing from the Realm of Ghosts, are reborn in Purgatory . . . in the womb of an animal . . . in the Realm of Ghosts. . . .

(xxviii).

. . . that, deceasing from the Realm of Ghosts, are reborn among the Devas: more numerous are these beings that, deceasing from the Realm of Ghosts, are reborn in Purgatory.

(xxix).

. . . that, deceasing from the Realm of Ghosts, are reborn among the Devas: more numerous are these beings that, deceasing from the Realm of Ghosts, are reborn in the womb of an animal.

(xxx).

. . . Just so, monks, few indeed are those beings that, deceasing from the Realm of Ghosts, are reborn among the Devas: more numerous are these beings that, deceasing from the Realm of Ghosts, are reborn in the Realm of Ghosts. What is the cause of that ?

It is through not seeing four Ariyan truths. What four? The Ariyan truth of Ill: the Ariyan truth of the arising of Ill: the Ariyan truth of the practice that leads to the ceasing of Ill.

Wherefore, monks, an effort must be made to realize: This is Ill. This is the arising of Ill. This is the ceasing of Ill. This is the practice that leads to the ceasing of Ill.'

Thus spake the Exalted One. And those monks were pleased with what was said by the Exalted One and took delight therein.

THE GREAT CHAPTER OF KINDRED SAYINGS IS ENDED

HERE ENDS SAṆYUTTA-NIKĀYA

or

THE BOOK OF THE KINDRED SAYINGS

INDEX

I.—GENERAL.

ABANDONING, 44, 113
Abhaya, Prince: questions the B. on condition and cause, 107
Abstinence from faults, 393 *ff.*
Aciravatī, river, 32, 344, 387
Adept (defined), 154, 204 *ff.*, 265
Aloofness, 55
Ambapālī's Grove, 119 *ff.*
Analysis, 184, 248 *ff.*
Anāthapiṇḍika: sickness and cure of, 329 *ff.*; taught about fear, 333; Park of, 1, 58, 121, 140, 153, 269, 301, 319, 346
Angas, the, 200
Añjana Grove (*or* Park), 60, 194
Antelope (Deer) Park, 60, 194
Anuruddha: at Sāketa, 153; at Jeta Grove, 261, 269; at Cactus Grove, 264; at Sāl-tree Hut, 266; at Ambapālī's Grove, 267; in Dark Wood (sick), 268
Arahant, 170, 176, 181, 183, 367
Arising, 64
Arisings (*see* Stations) of Mindfulness, 119-68
Aritṭha (monk), 278
Ariyan: Eightfold Way, 1-50; disciple, 170, 200, 298, 308, 317, 334; woman, 340; profitable things, 69, 226; straight ways, 146; insight, 173, 198; release, 198; method, 334; truths, 353 *ff.*
As before, above, after, below, 249
Asoka (monk), 313
Asokī (nun), 313
Assaji, 360 *n.*
Associated, 19
Asuras, 213, 377-8
Attention, 71, 78, 87, 161
Ayodhyā, 153 *n.*
Ānanda: sees Jānussoṇi, 4; instructs Bhadda, 14: with the B. at Vesālī, 130 *ff.*, 151; instructs nuns, 134; with Cunda, 141; comforts Sirivaḍḍha, 155; taught about old age by the B., 230; teaches Uṇṇābha at Kosambī, 243; questions the B. about his psychic powers, 252-5; at Great Wood, 284; taught breathing exercises, 286; mindfulness, 291 *ff.*; with Sāriputta, 301, 316, 330; questions the B. at Brick Hall, 312; taught the Mirror of the Norm, 313; with the Licchavī, 381
Āsavas, 45, 165, 367

Bamboo acrobat, 148
Bamboo Gate (village), 307
Bamboo Grove, 66 *ff.*, 155, 377
Banyan Park, 290, 320, 338, 340, 349
Bases of psychic power, 225-60
Bāhiya (Bāhika), monk, 145
Beat (native), 125
Becoming, 45 *and reps.*
Before . . . behind, etc., 249
Beluva, village, 130
Benares: sandalwood, 308; First Sermon at, 359
Bhadda, lay-disciple, 313; monk, with Ānanda, 14, 151
Bhaddiya, 360 *n.*
Bhāradvāja, 199 *ff.*
Birth, spontaneous, 301
Boar's cave, 209
Body: arising of, 161; discomfort of, 184; decay of, 192; powers of, 236, 257; constituents of, 250; physical and mind-made, 252; weakness of, 277, 281 *n.*; of contemplation, 287
Bondage, 119, 114
Bonds (*see* Fetters), 48
Bo-tree, 80
Brahma-vihāras, 98 *n.*, 289 *n.*

Brahma-world, 208, 236, 252, 257, 350
Brahmā Sahampati, appears to the B. at Uruvelā, 207
Brahmin practice, 315
Breathing, 275-95
Brick Hall, 211
Buddha, loyalty to the, 304 *n.*
Buoyancy, 253

Cactus Grove, 265
Calm, 5
Cāpāla Shrine, 225, 230, 234
Carnal taint, 56
Causal occasion, 270
Cause and condition, 107 *ff.*
Cessation, 73, 113
Cetī, the, 369
Chamberlains, 303
Chants, 106
Checks, 79
Clairvoyance (deva-sight), 238, *etc.*
Clansmen, 352
Clothsellers' Grove, 138
Cock's Pleasaunce, village, 14, 151
Co-factors, 235, 239 *ff.*
Compassion, 99, 112
Composure, 158
Comprehension, 44, 368
Conceits, 44, 81
Concentration, 9, 19, 94, 123 *n.*, 275 *ff.*, 342
Conduct, 21
Confluence, 387
Conscience, 5
Consciousness, 102, 159
Contemplation, 157, 160, 275 *ff.*
Control, 61.
Controlling Faculties, 169-222
Corruptions, 78
Cravings, 46
Creatures, 65
Crossing over, 22
Cultivation, 158, 160
Cunda: the Great, sickness and cure of, 68; novice, 141

Darkness, body of, 201; of space, 302
Dark Wood, 268
Death, 112; fear of, 332
Deathless, the, 7, 44, 50, 160, 195, 208
Deeds, 36 *ff.*
Deer (Antelope) Park, 347; First Sermon at, 359
Demerit, 124
Desaka district, 70, 148, 150
Desire (*chanda*), 11 *ff.*, 28, 159; as basis of psychic power, 225 *n.*; classified, 239, 249; sensual, 70, 81, 243
Destinies (the five), 396
Destruction: of fetters, 25; of āsavas, 26, 367; of craving, 72
Detachment, 5
Devas, classes of, 350, 378; paths to the, 337
Dhammadiṇṇa, lay-disciple, 347
Differences, 177
Direction of mind, 136
Disciple (Ariyan), defined, 338 *ff.*; woman-, 340; discreet, 349; two great, 144
Discoloured (corpse), 111
Discomfort, 184
Dispassion, 113, 158
Distaste, 113
Distress, the Great (Hell), 379
Dīghāvu, layman; sickness and death of, 299
Doctrine in brief, 121; doctrines, 131, 142
Dogmatists, 376
Doubt, 93, 106, 124
Downfall, the, 327, *etc.*
Dread, fivefold, 333
Drowsiness, 52
Drugged, 131, 141
Dust-hole life, 305

Earnestness, 29, 115, 341
Earth, 388
Eastern Gatehouse, 195
East Park, 191, 197, 241
Eastward, 32, *etc.*
Effort, right, 8, 173
Eightfold Way, the, 1-50; (First Sermon), 357
Elation of mind, 97
Elements: five sensual, 20; four great (essentials), 318
Elephant (treasure), 82
Endurance, 5
Energy, 5; as limb of wisdom, 51-118; 173, 255 *ff.*
Enlightened, 228
Equanimity (as limb of wisdom), 51-118

Equipped, 19
Errands, 395
Excitement (hindrance), 81, 93, 134
Experience, 11, 12
External, 92, 122, 261
Eye, 193

Factor (*anga*), 84; factors (5), 41, 49, 75; co-, 229, 239; mental, 276; of grasping, 361
Faculties, sense-, 61, 181; controlling, 169-222; of sex, 179; of gnosis, 179; of knowledge, 270
Failure in training, 324
Faith, 5, 138, 175, 196; -cure, 330
Falcon, 125
Falsehood, 393
Fear (*see* Dread), 322
Feature, alluring, 52; repulsive, 88
Feelings (3), 19, 46, 165, 268
Fetters, 25, 49, 117, 167, 221-4, 295, 347
Fields, good and bad, 328, 395
Fire, 96
Fist of teacher, 132
Flogging, 396
Floods (4), 47, 116, 221, 336, 342
Flurry, 81, 93, 124
Food, 85 *ff.*
Foot, 34, 206
Former births, 237
Fortune, 309
Foul, 111 *n.*, 112
Foundation, 375
Friends, 318, 368
Friendship with the lovely, 2, 27, 29 *ff.*
Fruits: of recluseship, 23; of liberation, 79; two, 110, 211; of non-return, 157; seven, 278; four, 351
Full understanding, 159, 368

Ganges, 32 *ff.*, 42, 114, 143, 214 *ff.*, 223, 272, 387
Garuda birds, 213
Gavampati, monk, 369
Generosity, 339
Ghosita Park, 63, 199, 204, 243
Gloom, 133
Gnosis, 57 *n.*, 197 *ff.*, 238 *n.*, 284, 311
Goatherds' Banyan, 147, 161, 207
Godha the Sakyan, 322; Godhā, 340
Good, the, 76; states, 122, 145, 164
Goodwill, 5, 88, 98, 112
Gotama Shrine, 230
Grasping, 26; factors of, 41, (4), 48
Gravel, 384
Great benefit, etc., 110, 114
Great Wood (Grove), 283, 335, 381

Habits, 62
Haliddavasana, town, 98
Happiness and unhappiness, 188 *ff.*
Happy One, 13, 65, 297
Harbinger, 27, *etc.*
Harmlessness, 5
Heap (of merit), 124, 163; of dust, 288
Heart-wood, 35, 206
Heedfulness, 5
Heir Apparent (treasure), 82
Hell, 379, *etc.*
Higher Fetters, 49, 221
Himâlaya, 37, 51, 127, 389
Hindrances (5), 49, 52, 76 *ff.*, 81, 91 *ff.*, 98, 108, 140
Hither shore, 226
Holy life (righteous), the, 2 *ff.*, 6 *ff.*; highest, 24, 25 *ff.*, 43 *n.*, 190
Horse (treasure), 82
House, peaked, 63, 194, 203, 308; (name), 230, 235, 283, 381
Housefather (treasure), 82
Householder, 17
Hundred years (life of), 372
Hunter of monkeys, 127

Icchānangala, village, 289, 291
Ignorance, 1, 364
Ill, 6, 69, 205, 347, 352 *ff.*, 361 *ff.*
Illustration, 364
Impermanence, 113
Increase, 79
Indolence, 249
Insight, 28, 198, 339, 350, 391
Instruction, 70
Intelligent, 83
Intoxicants, 391
Investigation (of Norm), 226 *ff.*
Isidatta, chamberlain, 303
Isipatana, 347, 359

Jambudīpa, 373
Jasmine, 35
Jānussoni, brahmin, 4
Jeta Grove, 1, 58, 121, 153, 261, 269, 301, 305, 316, 319, 346
Jewel (treasure), 82
Jotika, housefather, 299
Judas tree, 371

Kakudha, layman, 313
Kapilavatthu, 290, 320 *ff.*, 338, 340, 345, 349
Kappina, the Great, 279
Kassapa, Buddha, 208
Kassapa, the Great, 66
Katissaha, layman, 313
Kāḷigodhā, Sakyan lady, 340
Kālinga, layman, 313
Kāsi, 305
Kimbila, monk; Kimbilā, village, 286
Knowing, 26, 70; knowledge, 271, 364, 366
Koliyans, 98
Kondañña, 360
Kosalans, 122, 202, 304 *ff.*
Kosambī, 63, 199, 204, 243, 370
Koṭigāma, village, 365
Kuṇḍaliya, wanderer, 60

Lay-disciple, decease of, 312 *ff.*; sick, 349
Laying hold, 175
Learner (*see* Pupil), 13, 150, 204, 289, 290
Licchavī, the, 334, 381
Life (*see* Holy)
Limbs: of wisdom, 51-118, 277; of stream-winning (*anga*), 302, 345
Lion, 292
Liquor, 391
Living, right, 8
Lomasavangīsa, monk, 290
Longings, 43, 115, 350
Looker-on, 56, 294
Lovely, the, 2, 27, 29 *ff.*
Lower (fetters), 49, 157, 347
Lust, 52, 92, 393, *etc.*

Magadha, 304
Magadhese, 141
Maghavā, 208
Magic power, 241
Mahānāma, Sakyan, 290; asks the B. about his death, 320 *ff.*; about Sarakāni, 323 *ff.*; about disciples, 338; about comforting sick, 349
Mahī, river, 32, *etc.*, 387
Malevolence, 52, 81, 108
Mallas, the, 203, 304
Manyfolk, 178
Many Sons Shrine, 231
Market, town, 200
Material food, 53
Mānadinna, housefather, 156
Māra, 83, 126, 179, 230
Meditation, 352
Merit, 124, 163, 342 *ff.*
Method, the Ariyan, 90, 119, 147, 162, 179, 334
Middle Way, the, 1-50, 356 *ff.*
Midway release, 177
Migāra's mother, 197, 241
Mind, 5; elated, 97; non-direction of, 136; -made body, 252; -reading, 236, *etc.*
Mindfulness, 113; arisings (stations) of, 119-169; of body, 150, 158 *ff.*, 163; resort of, 193; established, 201; in concentration, 275
Mirror of the Norm, 312, 314
Modes, four best, of life, 98 *n.*
Moggallāna the Great, 67, 144, 153; miracle of, 241; 256, 264; visits devas, 319
Monkey-trap, 127
Monks, 1 *n.*
Mountain, 51, *etc.*

Name and body, 151
Nandaka, Licchavī, 335
Nandana Grove, 296
Nandiya, Sakyan, 340, 345; Wanderer, 10
Native beat, 125 *ff.*
Nāḷagāmaka (of Magadha), 141
Nālandā, 138
Neglected, 158, 226
Neither shore, 225
Nerañjarā, river, 147, 207
Nibbāna, 7, 10, 34; resort of, 193
Nikata, lay-disciple, 313
No food (for hindrances), 88
No more (birth), 68
No return, 110; fruits of, 157
Norm, the, 17, 142 *ff.*; duration of, 152; foundation of, 356; investigation of, 51-118; car of, 4; -follower, 177

Novices, 123
Nuns, lodging of the, 134; taught by Ānanda, 134 *ff.*

Ñātika, 311

Obligations, the, 163
Obstructions, 45
Ocean, 33, 389, *etc.*
Old age, 191
Once-returner, 180, 347
One-seed-er, 180
Order of monks, director of the, 132; virtues of, 297
Otherness, 143
Outlying districts, 391
Outsider, 178
Outwardly, 249
Oversluggish (desire), 249
Overstrained (desire), 249

Pains, 46
Pair of disciples, 144
Park, Anāthapiṇḍika's, 275 *ff.*
Partially, 177, 227
Pasenadi, rājah, 2 *n.* 1, 209 *n.* 3, 305, 314 *n.* 3
Passion, 29 *ff.*
Pāṭaliputta, 14, 15, 151
Peace, 5; from bondage, 110
Peaked house, 63, 203, 283, 380
Penetration, 73, 151
Pepper Tree Grotto, 66
Perfection, 178, 221
Permanence, 151
Perversion, 16
Piṇḍola, 199 *n.* 1, 296 *n.* 5
Pleasantness of life, 114
Pleasures, 48
Point of view, 171
Practice, 16, 255
Prince, 35
Profitable things (Ariyan), 69, 226
Psychic powers, 225, 236, 246, 251, 256, 269
Pupil (*see* Learner), 265
Purāṇa, chamberlain, 303
Pure Abodes, 58, 177, 180, 254
Puritan, 169, 183, 277
Pūraṇa Kassapa, views of, 107

Rain-cloud, 40
Range, 163
Rājagaha, 66 *ff.*, 107, 155, 209
Rājah, 59, 296
Realization, 110
Reasonings, 354
Recluses, 23, 170, 184, (and brahmins), *passim*
Refuge, 143
Regret, 52
Release, 26, 60, 198
Relics (of Sāriputta), 141 *ff.*
Remiss, 341
Remorseful, 137
Repugnant, 101, 279, 281
Repulsive feature, 88
Repulsiveness, 112
Resort, 193
Restraint, 30 *ff.*, 79
Reverence and respect, 392
Revulsion, 69
Right View, etc., 150
Righteousness, 5
Rise and fall, 75, 173, 175, 263, 337
Roller of the Wheel, 81 *ff.*, 296
Roof-peak, 35
Royal Park, 314
Rudiments, 121, 145, 163

Sahajāta, village, 369
Sahaka, monk, 208
Sahampati, Brahmā, 147, 162, 208
Sakka, heaven of, 293 *n.* 3
Sakkara, 2
Sakyans, 2, 290, 320, 346, 349
Saṅgārava, brahmin (on chants), 102
Santuṭṭha, lay-disciple, 312
Sarabhū, river, 32, 387
Sarakāni, Sakyan, 323-9
Sādhuka, town, 303
Sāketa, village, 60, 153, 264
Sālā, village, 122, 202
Sāl Tree Hut, 266
Sāḷha, monk, 312
Sārandada Shrine, 231
Sāriputta, 3, (on seven limbs of wisdom), 58; visits Upavāṇa, 62; questions the B. about superman, 137; declares faith in the B., 138; death of, 141; with Moggallāna and Anuruddha, 153; on the Deathless, 195; on gnosis, 197; on faith, 200; on reverence for the B., 209; questions Anuruddha, 265 *ff.*; teaches Ānanda, 301; on stream-winning, 302, 316; visits sick man, 329

Sāvatthī, 1-58, 81-112, 121-200, 207-224, 235-280, 301-6, 314-35, 352, 367
Scrap-gatherer, 199, 296
Season, right and wrong, 95 *ff.*
Seclusion, 31-3
Security from yoke, 209
Seed, 37; seed-er, one-, 180
Seeing, 108
Self, the, 122, 143, 145; warding of the, 149; -possession, 29
Sense: elements, 20; -faculties (6), 61, 181, 193; -spheres, 362; -delights, 43, 47-8; -desire, 79, 92, 102
Shame, 2
Shrines, 230
Sick man, 66, 68, 155, 299, 329, (exhorted), 349
Sickness of the B., 131
Siŋsapa Grove, 370
Similes: bearded wheat, 9, 39; pot, 19, 38; sunrise, 27, 65, 84; rivers, 32; foot, 34; roof-peak, wood, heart-wood, jasmine, prince, moon, sun, cloth, 35-6; seed, snake, 37, 50; tree, 38; sky, 39; rain-cloud, ship, 40; guest-house, 41; Ganges and course, 42; rājah's wardrobe, 59; postures of animals, 65; faults of gold, 77; parasitic trees, 80; kindling and quenching fire, 96-7; bowl of water, mixed with dye, heated, overspread, ruffled by wind, set in dark (and the reverse), 103-6; falcon and quail, 125; hunter, monkey and pitch-trap, 127; cook and sauces, 129; cart and helps, 132; border town and warden, 139; bamboo-acrobat and self-warding, 149; fire-stick, 187; peaked house, 194; elephant's foot, 206; heart- and sandal-wood, 206; cotton-seed, iron ball heated, 253; lamp and wick, 283; rain in drought, 285; dust at crossways, 288; raising fallen, showing light, etc., 311; jar of butter and pool, 321; falling tree, 321; rain-flood, 339; water in ocean, 343; leaves of trees, 371; stick thrown up, 371; turban ablaze, 372; hundred years of torture, 372; grass, etc. in Jambudīpa, 373; sun scatters gloom, 374; tuft of cotton and wind, 375; iron pillar, 375; stone column, 376; gravel, etc. on Sineru, 385 *ff.*; dust on nail, water in tank, 386-91; confluence of rivers, 387; clay balls, 388; water in ocean, 389; gravel on Himâlaya, 389
Sineru, Mt., 384
Sirivaḍḍha, housefather, 155
Skeleton, study of, 109-11
Sloth and torpor, 52, 88, *etc.*, 124
Sluggishness, 249
Snake, 37, 50
Sole way, 119
Solitude, 11, 261
Span of life, 231
Speculations, 378
Speech (*see* Talk), 393
Splendid Spur, 378
Spontaneous birth, 301
Squirrels' Feeding-ground, 67, 298, 377
States, good, 122, 145; various, 292
Stations (arisings) of mindfulness, 39, 60, 119-68
Stream-winner, 167, 171, 177, 181, 296-351, 302, 316, 346
Strength, 36, *etc.*
Struggling, co-factors of, 239
Subhadda, lay-disciple, 312
Substrate, 113
Sudatta, lay-disciple, 312
Sujāta, lay-disciple, 312
Sumāgadha Lotus Pond, 377
Sumbhā, the, 74, 148, 150
Superman, 137
Suppabuddha, 301 *n.*
Suppression, 12
Sutanu, river, 263
Sympathy (in the Four Moods), 99, 112
Systematic, 28, 54, 64, 71, 77-8, 87

Taint, 56
Talk: frivolous, 310; childish (divers), 355; harsh, false, slanderous, 393
Tathāgata: chief of beings, 33; released by knowledge, 60; his body kept going, 132; passing of, 153; powers of, 252 *ff.*, 257; way of life of, 289; faith in, 331

Teacher's fist, 132
Teaching in brief, 145, 163-4
Tendency, 26, 48, 295
Thirsts (3), 47
Thirty-three, Devas, 213, 350
Thought, systematic, 28, 29; -process, 136; unprofitable, 354
Torpor, of mind and body, 52, 81, 92-3, 108, 124
Trances, 9, 174, 271-2, 276 *n.*, 281 *ff.*
Tranquillity (limb of wisdom), 50 *ff.*; of body and mind, 94, 178
Tree, falls as it bends, 38, 321; various trees, 86; coral, trumpet, silk-cotton, 213
Turban, 372
Turtle, blind, 383

Udāyi (*or* -in), monk, 72 *ff.*
Udena Shrine, 230
Ukkāvela, town, 143
Unheard of, things, 157
Unlovely, the, 283
Uṇṇābha, brahmin, 192, 243
Unprofitable, states, 16
Unseasonable, 394
Unsystematic, attention, 52, 71, 78
Unworthy, 18
Upavāṇa, monk, 63
Uprising, 13
Uruvelā, 147, 161, 207
Uruvelakappa, town of Mallas, 203
Uttiya, monk, 20, 146

Vajjī, the, 304, 365
Veludvāra, 307 *n.*
Vesālī, 119, 120, 130 *ff.*, 230 *ff.*, 283, 335, 381
View, right and wrong, 1-50; point of, 171
Virtue, 27, 55, 61, 65
Virtuous, 339
Vitality, 179
Vultures' Peak, hill, 67, 107, 209, 378

Wanderers, of other views, 6, 25, 26, 91 *n.*, 95, 289; Park of, 90, 98
Warding self and others, 149
Wardrobe, rājah's, 59
Washing, outward, 336
Waste, the, 330, *etc.*
Wavering, 81, 93, 106, 108; of body, 279
Way: the Eightfold, 1-50, 357 *ff.*; sole, 119; of life, Ariyan, 289; out, 26; of the B., 12; of woe, 296
Wealth, Ariyan, 345 *n.*
Wearing out, 44
Well-to-do, 83
Wheel (treasure), 82
Wisdom, 5; on the side of, 211; limbs of, 51-118
Witless, 83
Woeful Lot, the (*see* Way of woe), 316-7, *etc.*
Woman (treasure), 82
Woods, various sorts of, 35
Wordy war, 355
World: heaven, 316, 319, *etc.*; -system, 256; without end, 201
Worm-eaten (corpse), 111
Wretched, 83
Wrong: view, etc. (*see* Eightfold Way), 1-50; season, 95, 97; practice, 17

Yama Devas, 350, 360
Yamunā (Jumna), river, 32 *ff.*, 344
Yojanas, 386
Yoke: of Norm-car, 5; security from the, 209, 232; -hole, 383 *ff.*

Zest, 87, 90, 135, 293
Zestful, 9, 188 (*see* Trances)

II.—SOME PALI WORDS IN THE NOTES.

Akkhāyika, 356
Accasaraŋ, 193
Ajjhattika, 84
Ajjhaparaŋ, 193
Ajjhārūha, 80
Ajjhupekkhitā, 56, 294, 3'
Aññā, 57, 238
Aññāta-Kondañña, 360
Aṭṭhikatvā, 79
Aṭṭa-sambhava, 234
Adhicca, 384
Adhippāya, 91
Anamatagga, 201, 372
Anāgāmin, 157, 194
Anuggāhaka, 142
Anuddayā, 149
Anupabbajjaŋ, 55
Anupāda, 26
Antarā-parinibbāyī, 57
Apatthaddhā, 125
Apārâpāra, 158
Appaṭivāni, 372
Appossukka, 234
Abhisameta, 75
Araṇi, 186
Avaḍḍhamānā, 125
Asubha, 111
Asecanaka, 285
Āgantuka, 41
Āgamma, 3
Ācāra-gocara, 163
Ānāpāṇa-sati, 275
Āpaṇa, 200
Āyu-saṅkhārā, 234
Ārambha-dhātu, 54, 87
Āloka-saññī, 235
Āvibhāva, 236
Āsabhī, 138, 268

Iti-vāda, 60
Iddhi-pāda, 225
Indriyāni, 169

Ukkoṭana-vañcana, 396
Ujjhāyanti, 324
Uddhata, 241
Uddhambhāgiya, 49
Uddhumātaka, 111
Unnaḷa, 241
Upakkilesa, 77
Upahacca, 57, 177
Upāsana, 381
Upekkhā, 185

Uppatika, 187
Ummagga, 14, 151

Ekodī-bhūta, 123
Ela-mūga, 83

Ogadha, 193
Opapātika, 301
Orambhāgiya, 49, 156
Oḷārika, 231

Kaṇha-dhamma, 22
Kathā-pābhataŋ, 141
Kammaṭṭhāna, 281
Kalyāṇa, 2
Kāyika, 94
Kussubbha, 37
Kūṭa, 213
Koṭṭhaka, 195
Khalu, 307
Khilā, 45, 77

Gamma, 357
Gotrabhū, 271

Caṇḍāla, 148
Capala, 241
Citta-saṅkhārā, 276
Cetasika, 94
Cetiya, 230
Chanda, 28, 159, 225, 235, 243
Chiggaḷa, 383

Janapada-kalyāṇī, 150
Jhāna, 276

Ñāya, 17, 118, 179

Ṭhānaso, 40, 285
Tatha, 365
Tathatta, 76
Tadanvaya, 198
Tamatagga, 133
Tālapatta, 371
Tiracchāna-kathā, 355
Tūla, 396
Thapati, 303

Dīpa, 133
Dukkhatā, 45
Deyya-dhamma, 306
Deva-manussā, 233
Deva-padaŋ, 337

Deva-samuppāda, 323
Dhamma, 17; kaṇha-, 22; -sannāha, 5
Dhamm' anvaya, 139
Dhamma, 131, 142
Dhammânudhamma, 232

Nantakāni, 296
Nāma-rūpa, 161
Nikkama, 54, 87
Nighā, 46
Nidāna, 4
Nibbāna-dhātu, 7
Nibbedha, 73
Nimitta, 52
Nirāmisa, 293
Nissaraṇa, 103
Nissāya, 239
Nīvaraṇa, 49

Pakkhika, 176
Pañc' oḍḍita, 127
Paṭikkula, 100
Paṭigacc' eva, 142
Paṭigha, 52
Paṭipadā, 16
Paṭibhāti, 68
Paṭibhāna, 378
Paṭisaŋvedi, 275
Paṭisaŋharāmi, 135
Paṭisaraṇaŋ, 193
Paṭihacca, 57, 212
Padesena, 11, 12, 154, 177, 227
Padhāna, 225
Pabbhāra, 38
Pamokkha, 60
Payata-pānī, 306
Parakkama-dhātu, 87
Parinibbāyī, 57
Paryādāya, 40
Pariyuṭṭhita-citta, 231
Parivicaya, 93
Parisâvacara, 60
Pāṭimokkha, 163
Pābhataŋ, 141
Pāricchattaka, 213
Pubba-nimitta, 27
Pubbenâparaŋ, 134
Pettika, 126

Balāni, 169
Bahiddhā, 205
Bāhira, 85
Bimba, 192
Buddha-teja, 191
Bodha-pakkhika, 203

Bhattu, 128
Bhaddaka, 14
Bhava-netti, 366
Bhūta-gāma, 37, 394
Bhecchati, 9
Bho, 307
Bhonto, 238
Brahma, 4
Brahmacariya, 2, 24, 43
Brahmacārin, 15

Mañku, 60
Mattaso, 326
Madhuraka-jāta, 131
Mahāpurisa, 137
Milakkha, 391
Mukkara, 241
Muṭṭha-ssati, 241

Yāca-yoga, 306
Yoga-kkhema, 209

Rajāpatha, 305

Līna, 95
Lepa, 127
Loka-cinta, 377

Vikubbanā-iddhi, 253
Vineyya, 119
Vibhava, 46
Viraddha, 21
Vega-missaka, 132
Vodāna, 271

Sa-upanisa, 19
Saŋvatta-kappa, 237
Sattakkhattuŋ, 385
Sattamba-cetiya, 231
Santaka (sa-antaka), 244
Saddh' ānusārin, 176
Sappāṭihāriya, 233
Sabbatthika, 98
Sabhā-gata, 338
Samatta, 227
Samatha, 54
Samādhi-gati, 293
Sampabhāsa, 310
Sahagata, 109
Sikkhati, 275
Sikkhā, 326
Simbali, 213
Suddhika (suddhaka), 152, 169
Subha-nimitta, 52
Sūkara-khata, 209
Sekha, 123
Somanassa, 183

Hāsu-paññā, 324

ERRATA AND ADDITIONS TO 'KINDRED SAYINGS,' VOLS. I-IV.

(*Including those already listed.*)

VOL. I.

Preface, p. viii, l. 22: read *Sārattha-*, and next page, l. 6.

P. 21, n. 2: for *vibhajetvā* read *vibhajitvā*.

P. 26 n., l. 2: for *five* read *seven*.

P. 30, n. 5: for 266 read 269.

P. 35, l. 7: after 'as in a knot,' next line:—

> 'In whom is no fault found, nor may there be
> Forsaking o't, there'd be no wrath t'appease:
> How then in such a case were one (proved) good ?'

P. 51, n. 4: *Comy.* has 'In time of trouble, though he be dirty, yet does she reckon him . . .'

P. 53, n. 1: 462 refers to text. *Comy.* has *nipphatti*.

P. 61, l. 10: after *stain* add *the*.

P. 63, n. 1: for 355 read 335.

P. 65, n. 1: for '*from* (the hip)' read *on*.

P. 65, n. 2, l. 5: for 224 read 244.

P. 67, n. 2: for 175 read 174.

Pp. 67, 69, 71, 73: headlines should read Māgha, Kāmada, Tāyana, Suriya.

P. 69, last line: Sinh. texts read *abuddhā*.

P. 92, n. 3: *Sangharāja*. *Comy.* has *sanjhārāga*, 'the flush of the evening sky.'

P. 94, l. 3: Belaṭṭhi's son. Mrs. R. D. prefers 'of the Belaṭṭhis,' but *Comy.* has *Belaṭṭha* and paraphrases *Belaṭṭhassa-putto*.

P. 94, l. 10: cf. *Manu*, iv, 135 *f.*, which omits 'fire,' and has 'brahmin' for 'bhikkhu.'

P. 95, l. 22: for *good-will* read *good well*.

Pp. 97, 99, 101, 103: headlines should read 'The King; Self-guarded; At the Seat of Judgment; Sacrifice.'

P. 105, n. 1: for 'in case he should . . . life' read 'that they might act as informers to him.'

P. 116, n. 1, l. 4: for *appatti* read *uppatti*.

P. 118, n. 4, last line: for *chaḍḍhaka* read *chaḍḍaka*.

P. 119, last line: read As opposed . . . 'the colour . . . stake.'—*Comy.*

P. 127 n., l. 11: read *gens d'armes*.

P. 129, n. 2: *dhammani* (P. text), Sinh. t. *vammani*. In my edition of *Comy.*, p. 169, I read *ghammani-*, 'in time of drought.'

P. 135, n. 2: for *fooling* read *footing*.

P. 138, n. 6: for *kaveyya* read *kāveyya*, and see *SA.* i, 176 for emended reading.
P. 151, n. 5: *dele* line under *khandha*.
P. 155, l. 20: read *departed*.
P. 156, l. 14: after 'said to him' read 'O recluse, we would be thy devoted slaves.'
P. 157, l. 13: read *daughters*.
P. 160, n. 3, last line: for *atthikinī* read *atthinī*.
P. 162 n., l. 1: for *cuts* read *spins*.
P. 165, l. 7: ('twixt eyebrows') should be 'eyelashes,'—*i.e.*, in your very presence.
P. 166, n. 5: for *Yāma* read *Yama*.
P. 172, l. 6: *dele* only.
P. 177, n. 2: ref. *S.* vi, p. vii (B) is to Index Volume.
P. 181: n. 1 refers to l. 6.
P. 185, l. 4: after *like* read *as*.
P. 186, n. 1, l. 5: for *vūpa's* read *rūpa's*.
P. 190, n. 2: for *informal* read *infernal*.
P. 207, n. 6: for *gandhe* read *ganthe*. After the stanzas of para. 7 add: 'When he had thus spoken, Puritan the Bhāradvāja said: . . .' Continue as at end of next section, § 8.
P. 212, n. 8: read *khāribhāro*.
P. 217: transpose * to 'I weed.'
P. 219, n. 1: read *Sn. v.*
P. 236, n. 4: *arato*. At *SA.* i, 269 I read *araṇo*.
P. 236, n. 2: *atha saṭṭhi-*, etc. . . . At *SA.* i, 270 I read *atha cha-nissitā*.
P. 237, n. 1: read *paṭighe*.
P. 245, n. 1: 'thought the Master' apply only to the words 'I must show . . .'
P. 250, n. 4: read *Comy. sarāyāmase*. Text has *sārāyāmase*, 'we remind.'
P. 253, n. 1: for *finger* read *thumb* (*anguṭṭhaka*).
P. 256, n. 5: read *vissamana-*.
P. 257, n. 5: tr. comma to after *adornments*.
P. 258: tr. ref. 2 to after *Holy*.
P. 258: n. 1, l. 3: read 277.
P. 266, l. 1: read 'who know this.'
P. 290, l. 13: 'our tasks . . .' should be repeated in last stanza.
P. 292, n. 1: for *gold* read *silver*.
P. 297, n. 1: *Comy.* defines *cetyā* as *cittī-kat' atthena* (in sense of 'reverence').
P. 303, l. 4: self-armed. *Attadaṇḍa* = 'stick-taken' (*atta* from *ādadāti*).
P. 303 n., l. 3: read *paṭikkhipanti*.
P. 305, l. 13: add 'with the Asuras.'
P. 315, l. 5: for 9 read 91.

P. 317 (Pāli) *Attha,* l. 9: read *ubhinnam.*

P. 319: *Paccagū,* see *SA.* i, 171: *papaŋ*; read -dāna-.

P. 320: *Yamataŋ,* see *SA.* i, 52.

VOL. II.

Title-page: for F. H. read F. L. Woodward.

Errata: read *p.* 109.

P. 7, l. 5: read 'before, vision arose.'

P. 13, n. 1: read '*Comy.* reads *kinti attā me ti*?'

P. 38, n. 1: his name, Kaḷāra, acc. to *Comy.*, means 'tusker.'

P. 39, l. 2: for *and* read *that.*

P. 40, l. 24: read 'By self-deliverance.'

P. 40, n. 2: read 'from within.'

P. 55, title to 6: 'Tree' (*rukkha* of text should read *dukkha,* 'Ill').

P. 91, l. 24: *dele* 'in a tumbril.'

P. 91, l. 27: read *prince's.*

P. 109, n. 4: read 'are much-heard.'

P. 192, n. 3: read *-makkha-.*

P. 194: correct page number.

P. 197: read '*Devadatta* 108, 163 *f.*'

VOL. III.

P. 31, n. 3 (*upasamo*): refers to n. 2. *Dele* 3 after 'not yours.'

P. 88, l. 17: for 'that question,' etc., read 'Ye have been trained by me in discussion [by question and answer] of those things thus and thus.'

P. 112, n. *re* Channa: *Comy.* on *S.* iv says the latter was 'another Channa.'

P. 118, l. 26: read *Ayojjhā* and add to Index, p. 211.

P. 127, ll. 1, 3, 4, 14: read 'self.'

P. 131, n. 2: add 'and revised at *K.S.* v, 40.'

P. 212: read *Devadaha.*

P. 213: [Makkhali]: read (Gosāla for ghosāla).

VOL. IV.

P. 9, n. 1: read 304 for 364.

P. 41, n. 1, ll. 3, 4: read ḍ for d (in *daŋseti*).

P. 68, n. 1, l. 6: for *shred* read *sherd.*

P. 123, n. 4: read *M.* ii.

P. 130, n. 7, l. 3: read '*evaŋkārī,* the . . .'

P. 200, l. 8: read 'He that cometh.'

P. 220, l. 12: read *sherds.* Omit note, and *cf. S.* v, 70.

P. 229, l. 6: for 'white with men's bones' read 'afflicted with mildew,' and *cf. A.* i, 160. So at l. 26.

P. 262, n. 2: *dele* comma after *which.*

P. 262, n. 4: read *Seṭṭha.*

P. 289: insert *Rādha,* 25 after *Raft.*

P. 290, l. 3: read 128. After *Suṇāparanta* read 35 for 55.